VOLATILE BODIES

9 - instrumentalism

20 - if the body is a point where one rethinks the opposition between inside and outside, then it is also a prime location for the rhetorical, performative determination and creation of the ideas of selves and others in a historically and culturally shifting field. The rhetoric about essentialism and the performance of essentialism put us of the determinative and creative process. The body, and its essentic practice, becomes location to rethink and reconfigure the binary opposition between self and other in a specific cultural and historical setting.

THEORIES OF REPRESENTATION AND DIFFERENCE

General Editor, Teresa de Lauretis

VOLATILE BODIES

Toward a Corporeal Feminism

Elizabeth Grosz

Indiana University Press

Bloomington and Indianapolis

This book is a publication of

Indiana University Press
601 North Morton Street
Bloomington, IN 47404-3797 USA

http://iupress.indiana.edu

Telephone orders 800-842-6796
Fax orders 812-855-7931
Orders by e-mail iuporder@indiana.edu

The paper used in this publication meets the minimum requirements
of American National Standard for Information Sciences—Permanence
of Paper for Printed Library Materials, ANSI Z39.48-1984.

Manufactured in the United States of America

Library of Congress Cataloging-in-Publication Data

Grosz, E. A. (Elizabeth A.)
        Volatile bodies : toward a corporeal feminism / Elizabeth Grosz.
        p.   cm.—(Theories of representation and difference)
        Includes bibliographical references and index.
        ISBN 0-253-32686-9 (alk. paper).—ISBN 0-253-20862-9
(pbk. : alk. paper)
        1. Feminist theory. 2. Body, Human—Social aspects.
3. Gender identity. I. Title. II. Series.
    HQ1190.G76   1994
    305.42'01—dc20   93-28611

6 7 8 9 10 06 05 04 03 02 01

Contents

Introduction and Acknowledgments

This book is a kind of experiment in inversion. It is based on a wager: that subjectivity can be thought, in its richness and diversity, in terms quite other than those implied by various dualisms. Dualism is the belief that there are two mutually exclusive types of "thing," physical and mental, body and mind, that compose the universe in general and subjectivity in particular. Dualism underlies the current preoccupations not only of many philosophers but also of feminist theorists. Feminists, like philosophers, have tended to ignore the body or to place it in the position of being somehow subordinate to and dependent for all that is interesting about it on animating intentions, some sort of psychical or social significance. Feminist theory, with its commonly close relation to psychoanalytic theory and to various forms of phenomenology, has tended, with some notable exceptions, to remain uninterested in or unconvinced about the relevance of refocusing on bodies in accounts of subjectivity.

The objective of the inversion attempted here is to displace the centrality of mind, the psyche, interior, or consciousness (and even the unconscious) in conceptions of the subject through a reconfiguration of the body. If subjectivity is no longer conceived in binarized or dualist terms, either as the combination of mental or conceptual with material or physical elements or as the harmonious, unified cohesion of mind and body, then perhaps other ways of understanding corporeality, sexuality, and the differences between the sexes may be developed and explored which enable us to conceive of subjectivity in different terms than those provided by traditional philosophical and feminist understandings.

The wager is that all the effects of subjectivity, all the significant facets and complexities of subjects, can be as adequately explained using the subject's corporeality as a framework as it would be using consciousness or the unconscious. All the effects of depth and interiority can be explained in terms of the inscriptions and transformations of the subject's corporeal surface. Bodies have all the explanatory power of minds. Indeed, for feminist purposes the focus on bodies, bodies in their concrete specificities, has the added bonus of inevitably raising the question of sexual difference in a way that mind does not. Questions of sexual specificity, questions about which kinds of bodies, what their differences are, and what their products and consequences might be, can be directly raised in ways that may more readily demonstrate, problematize, and transform women's social subordination to men.

This project does not involve the abandonment of the terms associated with the subject's psyche or interior. It is not part of a reductionist endeavor. It does not claim that notions such as agency, reflection, consciousness—indeed, all the categories of interiority—are unnecessary, useless, or wrong or that these terms are capable of ready transcription into other terms. Rather, they can be remapped, refigured, in terms of models and paradigms which conceive of subjectivity in terms of the primacy of corporeality, which regard subjectivity on the model not of latency or depth but of surface. It is for this reason that I have sought out models and conceptions of corporeality that, while nondualist as well as nonreductionist, remain committed to both a broad, nonphysicalist materialism and an acknowledgment of sexual difference.

This book is thus "about" something which it does not explicitly discuss. It is a book "on" sexuality, with all the rich resonances of this slippery and ambiguous term. There are at least four different senses of this term which may be relevant to help specify the concerns dealt with in what follows. First, sexuality can be understood as a drive, an impulse or form of propulsion, directing a subject toward an object. Psychoanalysis is uncontestably the great science of sexuality as drive. Second, sexuality can also be understood in terms of an act, a series of practices and behaviors involving bodies, organs, and pleasures, usually but not always involving orgasm. Third, sexuality can also be understood in terms of an identity. The sex of bodies, now commonly described by the term *gender*, designates at least two different forms, usually understood by means of the binary opposition of male and female. And fourth, sexuality commonly refers to a set of orientations, positions, and desires, which implies that there are particular ways in which the desires, differences, and bodies of subjects can seek their pleasure.

As a concept, sexuality is incapable of ready containment: it refuses to stay within its predesignated regions, for it seeps across boundaries into areas that are apparently not its own. As drive, it infests all sorts of other areas in the structures of desire. It renders even the desire not to desire, or the desire for celibacy, as sexual; it leaks into apparently nondrive-related activities through what Freud described as sublimation, making any activity a mode of its own seeking of satisfaction. As a set of activities and practices, it refuses to accept the containment of the bedroom or to restrict itself to only those activities which prepare for orgasmic pleasure. It is excessive, redundant, and superfluous in its languid and fervent overachieving. It always seeks more than it needs, performs excessive actions, and can draw any object, any fantasy, any number of subjects and combinations of their organs, into its circuits of pleasure. As a determinate type of body, as sexually specific, it infects all the activities of the sexes, underlying our understandings of the world well beyond the domain of sexual relations or the concrete relations constituting sexual difference. Our conceptions of reality, knowledge, truth, politics, ethics, and aesthetics are all effects of sexually specific—and thus far in our history, usually male—bodies, and are all thus implicated in the power structures which feminists have described as patriarchal, the structures which govern relations between the sexes.

Sexual difference is thus a mobile, indeed volatile, concept, able to insinuate itself into regions where it should have no place, to make itself, if not invisible, then at least unrecognizable in its influences and effects. It becomes a pivotal term in negotiating the intersections of feminism and modern European philosophy and in locating the body as a central term in this negotiation. I seek here some of the common assumptions regarding the body shared by both feminist theory and mainstream philosophy and some of the ways in which these assumptions may be problematized or even bypassed using the work of a disparate group of theorists—Freud, Lacan, Schilder, Goldstein, Luria, Merleau-Ponty, Nietzsche, Foucault, Lingis, and Deleuze and Guattari, among others. All provide crucial ingredients for an understanding of sexuality and sexual difference, though it is significant that none of them has explicitly devoted himself to developing a theory of the body. At most, conceptions of corporeality are presumed by them, or they refer to the body without making it the center of focus. The readings of their diverse writings I have undertaken here involves producing or extracting their sometimes implicit conceptions of the body and the role the body plays in social, cultural, and psychical life and, more critically, confronting these male theorists with the question of sexual difference as it arises in the work of a number of feminist theorists, including Luce Irigaray, Julia Kristeva, Mary Douglas, Iris Marion Young, and Judith Butler, who have all in their disparate ways provided accounts of female embodiment which question many presumptions in these male texts.

This book is a refiguring of the body so that it moves from the periphery to the center of analysis, so that it can now be understood as the very "stuff" of subjectivity. The subject, recognized as corporeal being, can no longer readily succumb to the neutralization and neutering of its specificity which has occurred to women as a consequence of women's submersion under male definition. The body is the ally of sexual difference, a key term in questioning the centrality of a number of apparently benign but nonetheless phallocentric presumptions which have hidden the cultural and intellectual effacement of women: it helps to problematize the universalist and universalizing assumptions of humanism, through which women's—and all other groups'—specificities, positions, and histories are rendered irrelevant or redundant; it resists the tendency to attribute a human nature to the subject's interior; and it resists tendencies to dualism, which splits subjectivity into two mutually exclusive domains. But, of course, it is not without problems of its own, major risks and dangers with which it must negotiate and deal.

The body has thus far remained colonized through the discursive practices of the natural sciences, particularly the discourses of biology and medicine. It has generally remained mired in presumptions regarding its naturalness, its fundamentally biological and precultural status, its immunity to cultural, social, and historical factors, its brute status as given, unchangeable, inert, and passive, manipulable under scientifically regulated conditions. The ways in which bodies, men's and women's bodies, are understood by the natural sciences is, however, no more accurate than the ways the social sciences and humanities understand them: in all cases, how bodies are conceived seems to be based largely on prevailing social conceptions of the relations between the sexes. It is not the case that the objective accounts provided by the sciences feed into and find support from popular conceptions. Rather, bodies provide a neuralgic locus for the projection and living out of unreflective presumptions regarding the sexes and their different social, sexual, and biological roles. The sciences themselves are not immune to—indeed, they depend for the very mode of their formulations and operations on—everyday assumptions and beliefs of scientists and others regarding knowledge, power, desire, and bodies. Rethinking the body implies major epistemological upheavals not only for the humanities, which have tended toward idealism, but equally for the natural and social sciences, which have at least aspired to materialism. Both broad "types" of knowledge are implicated in and in part are responsible for prevailing understandings of bodies and are thus vulnerable to transformation and upheaval in challenges to these prevailing models.

It is hardly surprising, given these attributions, that feminists have tended to remain wary of any attempts to link women's subjectivities and social positions to the specificities of their bodies. One of my purposes in this book has been to rescue the body from this status, to demonstrate that although these may represent dominant models for understanding corporeality, they are not incontestable. They may be challenged and superseded by other conceptions. I hope to show that the body, or rather, bodies, cannot be adequately understood as ahistorical, precultural, or natural objects in any simple way; they are not only inscribed, marked, engraved, by social pressures external to them but are the products, the direct effects, of the very social constitution of nature itself. It is not simply that the body is represented in a variety of ways according to historical, social, and cultural exigencies while it remains basically the same; these factors actively produce the body as a body of a determinate type.

I will deny that there is the "real," material body on one hand and its various cultural and historical representations on the other. It is my claim throughout this book that these representations and cultural inscriptions quite literally constitute bodies and help to produce them as such. The bodies in which I am interested are culturally, sexually, racially specific bodies, the mobile and change-able terms of cultural production. As an essential internal condition of human bodies, a consequence of perhaps their organic openness to cultural completion, bodies must take the social order as their productive nucleus. Part of their own "nature" is an organic or ontological "incompleteness" or lack of finality, an amenability to social completion, social ordering and organization.

The body is a most peculiar "thing," for it is never quite reducible to being merely a thing; nor does it ever quite manage to rise above the status of thing. Thus it is both a thing and a nonthing, an object, but an object which somehow contains or coexists with an interiority, an object able to take itself and others as subjects, a unique kind of object not reducible to other objects. Human bod-ies, indeed all animate bodies, stretch and extend the notion of physicality that dominates the physical sciences, for animate bodies are objects necessarily differ-ent from other objects; they are materialities that are uncontainable in physicalist terms alone. If bodies are objects or things, they are like no others, for they are the centers of perspective, insight, reflection, desire, agency. They require quite different intellectual models than those that have been used thus far to represent and understand them. I am not suggesting that medical, biological, even chemical analyses of bodies are "wrong" or "inappropriate"; my claim is the simpler one that the guiding assumptions and prevailing methods used by these disciplines (indeed, by any disciplines) have tangible effects on the bodies studied. Bodies are not inert; they function interactively and productively. They act and react. They generate what is new, surprising, unpredictable.

It is this ability of bodies to always extend the frameworks which attempt to contain them, to seep beyond their domains of control, which fascinates me and occupies much of this book. This signals the permeability of the question of sexual difference, its uncontainability within any particular sphere or domain, its refusal to respect the boundaries separating private and public, inside and out-side, knowledge and pleasure, power and desire. As Irigaray has asserted, the question of sexual difference is *the* question of our epoch. It infects the most objective and "disinterested" knowledges, the most benign and well-intended so-cial and political policies, the very infrastructural organization of institutions, group practices, and interpersonal relations. All knowledges and social practices have thus far represented the energies and interests of one sex alone. I am not suggesting that women have had no input into cultural production—quite the contrary. Women's contributions have never been acknowledged or represented in the term chosen by women themselves. In other words, there are other ways of undertaking cultural activity and intellectual endeavor than those developed thus far. A completely different set of perspectives—this time based on women's specificities, experiences, positions, rather than on those of men, who hide them-selves and their specificities under the banner of some universal humanity—is possible and needs to be explored. This book does not undertake this exploration but, I hope, may help provide some raw materials which may be useful in undertaking such exploration and innovation.

In seeking to invert the primacy of a psychical interiority by demonstrating its necessary dependence on a corporeal exteriority, I have tried to avoid many of the common metaphors that have been used to describe the interactions of mind and body, metaphors of embodiment, of containment, machine metaphors, two-sided coins, hydraulic models—models which remain committed to dualism. I do not believe, for reasons I will make explicit in the first chapter, that monist models, which rely on a singular substance with the qualities and attributes of both mind and body, provide satisfactory representations of both the articulation and the disarticulation of mind and body, the resonances and dissonances that characterize subjectivity. I have taken a model that I came across in reading the work of Lacan, where he likens the subject to a Möbius strip, the inverted three-dimensional figure eight. Lacan uses it in a different context and for different purposes, but it seems quite suitable for a way of rethinking the relations between body and mind. Bodies and minds are not two distinct substances or two kinds of attributes of a single substance but somewhere in between these two alternatives. The Möbius strip has the advantage of showing the inflection of mind into body and body into mind, the ways in which, through a kind of twisting or inversion, one side becomes another. This model also provides a way of problematizing and rethinking the relations between the inside and the outside of the subject, its psychical interior and its corporeal exterior, by showing not their fundamental identity or reducibility but the torsion of the one into the other, the passage, vector, or uncontrollable drift of the inside into the outside and the outside into the inside.

The model of the Möbius strip provides not only a guiding framework for the chapters that follow but also a way of organizing its content. The book is divided into eight chapters unevenly distributed over four parts. The first chapter (part I) is an attempt to explain the relevance and impact of rethinking bodies for the ways in which both philosophical and feminist thought conceive of themselves. The remaining three sections are regulated by the Möbius model. Part II, "The Inside Out," focuses on the ways in which the subject's corporeal exterior is psychically represented and lived by the subject. Chapters 2, 3, and 4 respectively discuss the psychoanalytic, neurological, and phenomenological accounts of the lived body or body image, the ways in which the body must be psychically constituted in order for the subject to acquire a sense of its place in the world and in connection with others. One chapter is thus devoted to Freudian and Lacanian accounts of the genesis of the body image or imaginary anatomy, another to Merleau-Ponty and the phenomenological understanding of the body image, and a third to various neurophysiological and neuropsychological accounts of impairment of the body image. Instead of simply focusing on typical cases of psychical, neurological, and phenomenological development, in these chapters I seek out anomalous cases, cases of psychical and neurological breakdown, in order to make clear that we do not have a body the same way that we have other objects. Being a body is something that we must come to accommodate psychically, something that we must live.

Part III, "The Outside In," explores a further inflection of the Möbius strip, this time from the corporeal to the psychical, from surface to depth. In chapters 5, 6, and 7, I explore the work of theorists of corporeal inscription, primarily Nietzsche, Foucault, and Deleuze and Guattari, respectively. Each explores the position of the body as the site of the subject's social production, as the site of the proliferation of the will to power (in Nietzsche), of docility and resistance (in Foucault), of becoming and transformation (in Deleuze and Guattari). Each of these philosophers seeks to undermine the pretensions of consciousness to know itself, to exert a guiding direction, to be the site of rationality. Each instead emphasizes the productivity of the body, the ways in which the social inscriptions of bodies produce the effects of depth.

These two parts explore and analyze the various accounts of corporeality which may prove useful in rethinking sexual difference in corporeal terms. But it is significant that none of the male theorists discussed here is very enlightened about or illuminating on the question of sexual specificity. None seems prepared to admit that his researches, if they make sense of the body, do so with reference to the male body. None seems aware that the specificities of the female body remain unexplained. The question of sexual difference—in this case, the specificity of flows in and through the sexed body—becomes the object of investigation of the fourth and final part, "Sexual Difference." Chapter 8 thus focuses on the elision of fluids in the male body and the derogation of the female body in terms of the various forms of uncontrollable flow. What it makes clear, though, is that the metaphorics of flow is simply one among a number of ways in which sexual difference may be thought. If bodies are inscribed in particular ways, if these inscriptions have thus far served to constitute women's bodies as a lack relative to men's fullness, a mode of incapacity in terms of men's skills and abilities, a mode of women's naturalness and immanence compared with men's transcendence, then these kinds of inscription are capable of reinscription, of transformation, are capable of being lived and represented in quite different terms, terms that may grant women the capacity for independence and autonomy, which thus far have been attributed only to men.

This book is the result of a protracted project, ten years in conception, three years in writing. It is a literal patchwork, written in pieces, many of which do not fit together easily, in many locations and over different times. It was deflected and put off by many other projects and commitments and by my own anxieties and uncertainties regarding its political and social commitments. The product of passion and intense fascination, it has also been fueled by the energy of profound theoretical insecurity and the full awareness that I have skated along the brink of a theoretical precipice overhanging extreme political isolation. In clinging to this border, the border of that dangerous foreign territory that I name phallocentric theory or male philosophy, I have refused to simply abandon that ground to the men who first claimed it (and their male intellectual heirs); and I have refused to labor on it, to look after it, to tend it with respect and reverence, as women are usually expected to do. I have, however, tried to use this terrain to bear products that its proprietors may not be happy with and that may threaten to reshape that land in terms which contest this proprietary relation.

I have risked alarming some feminists, with whom I feel political and conceptual alignments, who worry about the perilous closeness of the material covered in this book—theories of bodies—to those facets of patriarchal thought that have in the past served to oppress women, most notably the patriarchal rationalization of male domination in terms of the fragility, unreliability, or biological closeness to nature attributed to the female body and the subordinate character attributed to women on account of the close connections between female psychology and biology. Women have been objectified and alienated as social subjects partly through the denigration and containment of the female body. This project hovers close to many patriarchal conceptions of the body that have served to establish an identity for women in essentialist, ahistorical, or universalist terms. But I believe that it does so in order to contest these terms, to wrest a concept of the body away from these perils. Whether this has been successful remains for the reader to judge.

Working on a terrain somewhere between traditional philosophy and post-modern feminism, I must undertake a set of delicate negotiations between these two sets of terms, two traditions or terrains, using various key philosophical texts—written by men—to challenge prevailing philosophical beliefs about bodies, to develop accounts which might serve feminist purposes, and to place these accounts in the context of women's corporeal experiences and intellectual reflections which may serve as a measure of the validity and applicability of these various male accounts of what they claim are broad universals to women.

Some of this book was written with strong, unwavering support from my colleagues and students; other parts were written in utter isolation and solitude. Written across two continents, over a number of years, in an area as changeable and indeterminate, as dangerous, as this one, the text I have produced is neither a clear-cut, singularly focused monograph nor a collection of disparate, randomly related essays. Somewhere between a book and an anthology, this text presents a series of disparate, indeed kaleidoscopic and possibly contradictory, thoughts, theories, perspectives, interacting, maybe clashing or maybe coalescing, always in uneasy tension, straining against each other and against any overall unity and homogeneity. This text does not have a single point or moral but is about the creating of shifting frameworks and models of understanding, about the opening up of thought to what is new, different, and hitherto unthought.

These negotiations would not have been possible without wide-ranging support at both a personal and a theoretical level. I began thinking about and writing on this project for the Women and Philosophy Conference held in Adelaide, Australia, in 1981. It underwent a long period of gestation and interrogation during my years of teaching in the Department of General Philosophy, University of Sydney. There Moira Gatens and I taught an undergraduate course on the philosophy of the body which made it clear to me that this was an important project that required at least a book-length approach. I remain increasingly grateful to her insights and ideas, her rigorous and critical approach, and to our continuing conversations on, and sometimes arguments about, the body that have ensued over the past ten years. This project would no doubt have been much broader, more critical, more incisive, if it had been undertaken together.

The project was deepened and developed as a result of the time I spent at the Humanities Research Centre at the Australian National University in 1986, where, for the first time, I had the luxury of undertaking research with no teaching commitments. Many of the key insights and the framework of the book were conceived there. But a large percentage of this book was written in the peace, inspiration, and energy provided by the faculty and students at the History of Consciousness program at the University of California, Santa Cruz. I am particularly grateful for the support and encouragement provided by Teresa de Lauretis, who urged me to commit myself to writing this book, as well as to Victor Burgin, James Clifford, Donna Haraway, Francette Pacteau, and Hayden White, whose friendship stabilized my fifteen months there. Parts of this book were written in Manhattan, dynamized by its energy and unhinged by its chaos. Without Dion Farquhar's urbane humor, not to mention her spare room, some of what I think are the best parts of this book would not have been written. The final chapters of the book were written at the Institute for Critical and Cultural Studies at Monash University, where I have found a most conducive setup for solid research and teaching. I would like to thank Robert Pargetter for the opportunity of taking up one of the most exciting teaching positions in the arts in Australia and Gail Ward for her level-headed support and wit in the short time I have been at Monash. Throughout the protracted writing, Barbara Allen has provided me with the most tangible emotional and intellectual support, as well as the space to think and to write; she found herself enlisted as an audience to listen to and read my wayward thoughts whenever they occurred and has done so with grace and great patience. I will always be deeply grateful for her calm and sensible approach to my various neuroses and anxieties, my insecurities and moments of manic bravado.

I am especially grateful to Linda Alcoff, Teresa Brennan, Sneja Gunew, Philipa Rothfield, and Elizabeth Wilson for agreeing to read the manuscript and for their insights, criticisms, comments, and suggestions for improvement. I have particular respect for and gratitude to Pheng Cheah and Vicki Kirby for their detailed and incisive comments, and at times for the disagreements I have had with them over the notions of corporeality, inscription, and the problematic of deconstruction (which, while not dealt with explicitly here, underlies the ways in which this project was conceived and developed). They have pushed me further and further along the pathway of the problematic of inscription before which I have hestitated. Dianne Chisholm, Andrea Goldsmith, Cathryn Vasseleu, and Cathryn Waldby must also be thanked for their feedback and comments on particular chapters. I would like to thank all of these kind and generous readers for their critical insights and their various recommendations for changes. Although I can only list them, I cannot indicate how much I owe, both intellectually and personally, to the following people, without whose encouragement and support this book would not have been possible. I hope all of you know how much you have meant to me, how much you have helped me to go on when every impulse within me was urging me to give up. My special thanks then to Judith Allen, Geoffrey Batchen, Barbara Caine, Joan Catapano, Joanne Finkelstein, Anna Gibbs, Sneja Gunew, Meaghan Morris, Rosemary Pringle, Gayatri Spivak, Barbara Sullivan, Terry Threadgold, and Sophie Watson. It would not have been possible without you. And finally, I happily acknowledge the affirming security I have been given by a family whose opinion and support I have never needed to question, who have always been there, and who would have loved me even if this book had never been, perhaps foolishly, contemplated. This book is dedicated to you: to Eva and Imre Gross, Tom Gross, Irit Rosen, Tahli Fischer, Daniel and Mia Gross.

Melbourne
April 1993

PART I

Introduction

1 | Refiguring Bodies

T HE BODY HAS remained a conceptual blind spot in both mainstream Western philosophical thought and contemporary feminist theory. Feminism has uncritically adopted many philosophical assumptions regarding the role of the body in social, political, cultural, psychical, and sexual life and, in this sense at least, can be regarded as complicit in the misogyny that characterizes Western reason. Feminists and philosophers seem to share a common view of the human subject as a being made up of two dichotomously opposed characteristics: mind and body, thought and extension, reason and passion, psychology and biology. This bifurcation of being is not simply a neutral division of an otherwise all-encompassing descriptive field. Dichotomous thinking necessarily hierarchizes and ranks the two polarized terms so that one becomes the privileged term and the other its suppressed, subordinated, negative counterpart.[1] The subordinated term is merely the negation or denial, the absence or privation of the primary term, its fall from grace; the primary term defines itself by expelling its other and in this process establishes its own boundaries and borders to create an identity for itself. Body is thus what is not mind, what is distinct from and other than the privileged term. It is what the mind must expel in order to retain its "integrity." It is implicitly defined as unruly, disruptive, in need of direction and judgment, merely incidental to the defining characteristics of mind, reason, or personal identity through its opposition to consciousness, to the psyche and other privileged terms within philosophical thought.

More insidiously, the mind/body opposition has always been correlated with a number of other oppositional pairs. Lateral associations link the mind/body opposition to a whole series of other oppositional (or binarized) terms, enabling them to function interchangeably, at least in certain contexts. The mind/body relation is frequently correlated with the distinctions between reason and passion, sense and sensibility, outside and inside, self and other, depth and surface, reality and appearance, mechanism and vitalism, transcendence and immanence, temporality and spatiality, psychology and physiology, form and matter, and so on. These lateral associations provide whatever "positive" characteristics the body may be accorded in systems where it is the subordinated counterpart of mind. These terms function implicitly to define the body in nonhistorical, naturalistic, organicist, passive, inert terms, seeing it as an intrusion on or interference with the operation of mind, a brute givenness which requires overcoming, a connection with animality and nature that needs transcendence. Through these associations, the body is coded in terms that are themselves traditionally devalued.

Most relevant here is the correlation and association of the mind/body opposition with the opposition between male and female, where man and mind, woman and body, become representationally aligned. Such a correlation is not contingent or accidental but is central to the ways in which philosophy has historically developed and still sees itself even today.[2] Philosophy has always considered itself a discipline concerned primarily or exclusively with ideas, concepts, reason, judgment—that is, with terms clearly framed by the concept of mind, terms which marginalize or exclude considerations of the body. As soon as knowledge is seen as purely conceptual, its relation to bodies, the corporeality of both knowers and texts, and the ways these materialities interact, must become obscure. As a discipline, philosophy has surreptitiously excluded femininity, and ultimately women, from its practices through its usually implicit coding of femininity with the unreason associated with the body.[3] It could be argued that philosophy as we know it has established itself as a form of knowing, a form of rationality, only through the disavowal of the body, specifically the male body, and the corresponding elevation of mind as a disembodied term.[4]

Philosophy and the feminist theories which implicitly rely on its concepts and methods refuse to recognize but at the same time must rely on modes of corporeality for their form, structure, and status, for framing key questions and providing criteria for the validity and truth of their modes of explanation. Philosophy seems to adopt an ambiguous fascination with the functioning and status of the body. On one hand, there is a recognition of the role of the body, in the sense that virtually all the major figures in the history of philosophy discuss its role in either the advancement or, more usually, the hindrance of the production of knowledge. On the other hand, there is also a refusal to recognize, which is evidenced by the fact that when the body is discussed, it is conceptualized in narrow and problematic, dichotomized terms. It is understood in terms that attempt to minimize or ignore altogether its formative role in the production of philosophical values—truth, knowledge, justice, etc. Above all, the sexual specificity of the body and the ways sexual difference produces or effects truth, knowledge, justice, etc. has never been thought. The role of the specific male body as the body productive of a certain kind of knowledge (objective, verifiable, causal, quantifiable) has never been theorized.

Given the coupling of mind with maleness and the body with femaleness and given philosophy's own self-understanding as a conceptual enterprise, it follows that women and femininity are problematized as knowing philosophical subjects and as knowable epistemic objects. Woman (upper case and in the singular) remains philosophy's eternal enigma, its mysterious and inscrutable object—this may be a product of the rather mysterious and highly restrained and contained status of the body in general, and of women's bodies in particular, in the construction of philosophy as a mode of knowledge.[5]

Philosophy and the Body

Since the inception of philosophy as a separate and self-contained discipline in ancient Greece,[6] philosophy has established itself on the foundations of a profound somatophobia. While I cannot here present an adequate or detailed discussion of the role of the body in the history of philosophy, I can at least indicate in a brief sketch some of the key features of the received history that we have inherited in our current conceptions of bodies. The body has been regarded as a source of interference in, and a danger to, the operations of reason. In the *Cratylus,* Plato claims that the word *body* (*soma*) was introduced by Orphic priests, who believed that man was a spiritual or noncorporeal being trapped in the body as in a dungeon (*sēma*). In his doctrine of the Forms, Plato sees matter itself as a denigrated and imperfect version of the Idea. The body is a betrayal of and a prison for the soul, reason, or mind. For Plato, it was evident that reason should rule over the body and over the irrational or appetitive functions of the soul. A kind of natural hierarchy, a self-evident ruler–ruled relation, alone makes possible a harmony within the state, the family, and the individual. Here we have one of the earliest representations of the body politic.[7] Aristotle, in continuing a tradition possibly initiated by Plato in his account of *chora* in *Timaeus* where maternity is regarded as a mere housing, receptacle, or nurse of being rather than a coproducer, distinguished matter or body from form, and in the case of reproduction, he believed that the mother provided the formless, passive, shapeless matter which, through the father, was given form, shape, and contour, specific features and attributes it otherwise lacked. The binarization of the sexes, the dichotomization of the world and of knowledge has been effected already at the threshold of Western reason.

The matter/form distinction is refigured in terms of the distinction between substance and accident and between a God-given soul and a mortal, lustful, sinful carnality. Within the Christian tradition, the separation of mind and body was correlated with the distinction between what is immortal and what is mortal. As long as the subject is alive, mind and soul form an indissoluble unity, which is perhaps best exemplified in the figure of Christ himself. Christ was a man whose soul, whose immortality, is derived from God but whose body and mortality is human. The living soul is, in fact, a part of the world, and above all, a part of nature. Within Christian doctrine, it is as an experiencing, suffering, passionate being that generic man exists. This is why moral characteristics were given to various physiological disorders and why punishments and rewards for one's soul are administered through corporeal pleasures and punishments. For example, in the Middle Ages, leprosy was regarded as the diseased consequence of lechery and covetousness, a corporeal signifier of sin.[8]

What Descartes accomplished was not really the separation of mind from body (a separation which had already been long anticipated in Greek philosophy since the time of Plato) but the separation of soul from nature. Descartes distinguished two kinds of substances: a thinking substance (*res cogitans*, mind) from an extended substance (*res extensa*, body); only the latter, he believed, could be considered part of nature, governed by its physical laws and ontological exigencies. The body is a self-moving machine, a mechanical device, functioning according to causal laws and the laws of nature. The mind, the thinking substance, the soul, or consciousness, has no place in the natural world. This exclusion of the soul from nature, this evacuation of consciousness from the world, is the prerequisite for founding a knowledge, or better, a science, of the governing principles of nature, a science which excludes and is indifferent to considerations of the subject. Indeed, the impingements of subjectivity will, from Decartes's time on, mitigate the status and value of scientific formulations. Scientific discourse aspires to impersonality, which it takes to be equivalent to objectivity. The correlation of our ideas with the world or the reality they represent is a secondary function, independent of the existence of consciousness, the primary, indubitable self-certainty of the soul. Reality can be attained by the subject only indirectly, by inference, deduction, or projection. Descartes, in short, succeeded in linking the mind/body opposition to the foundations of knowledge itself, a link which places the mind in a position of hierarchical superiority over and above nature, including the nature of the body.[9] From that time until the present, subject or consciousness is separated from and can reflect on the world of the body, objects, qualities.

Dualism

Descartes instituted a dualism which three centuries of philosophical thought have attempted to overcome or reconcile. Dualism is the assumption that there are two distinct, mutually exclusive and mutually exhaustive substances, mind and body, each of which inhabits its own self-contained sphere. Taken together the two have incompatible characteristics. The major problem facing dualism and all those positions aimed at overcoming dualism has been to explain the interactions of these two apparently incompossible substances, given that, within experience and everyday life, there seems to be a manifest connection between the two in willful behavior and responsive psychical reactions. How can something that inhabits space affect or be affected by something that is nonspatial? How can consciousness ensure the body's movements, its receptivity to conceptual demands and requirements? How can the body inform the mind of its needs and wishes? How is bilateral communication possible? Dualism not only poses irresolvable philosophical problems; it is also at least indirectly responsible for the historical separation of the natural sciences from the social sciences and humanities, the separation of physiology from psychology, of quantitative analysis from qualitative analysis, and the privileging of mathematics and physics as ideal models of the goals and aspirations of knowledges of all types. Dualism, in short, is responsible for the modern forms of elevation of consciousness (a specifically modern version of the notion of soul, introduced by Descartes) above corporeality.

This separation, of course, has its costs. Since the time of Descartes, not only is consciousness positioned outside of the world, outside its body, outside of nature; it is also removed from direct contact with other minds and a sociocultural community. At its extreme, all that consciousness can be sure about is its own self-certain existence. The existence of other minds must be inferred from the apparent existence of other bodies. If minds are private, subjective, invisible, amenable only to first-person knowledge, we can have no guarantee that our inferences about other minds are in fact justified. Other bodies may simply be complex automata, androids or even illusions, with no psychical interior, no affective states or consciousness. Consciousness becomes, in effect, an island unto itself. Its relations to others, to the world, and its own body are the consequences of mediated judgments, inferences, and are no longer understood as direct and unmediated.

Cartesian dualism establishes an unbridgeable gulf between mind and matter, a gulf most easily disavowed, however problematically, by reductionism. To reduce either the mind to the body or the body to the mind is to leave their interaction unexplained, explained away, impossible. Reductionism denies any interaction between mind and body, for it focuses on the actions of either one of the binary terms at the expense of the other. Rationalism and idealism are the results of the attempt to explain the body and matter in terms of mind, ideas, or reason; empiricism and materialism are the results of attempts to explain the mind in terms of bodily experiences or matter (today most commonly the mind is equated with the brain or central nervous system).[10] Both forms of reductionism assert that either one or the other of the binary terms is "really" its opposite and can be explained by or translated into the terms of its other.

There are not only good philosophical but also good physiological reasons for rejecting reductionism as a solution to the dualist dilemma. As soon as the terms are defined in mutually exclusive ways, there is no way of reconciling them, no way of understanding their mutual influences or explaining their apparent parallelism. Moreover, attempts to correlate ideas or mental processes with neurological functions have thus far failed, and the project itself seems doomed.[11]

Cartesianism

There are at least three lines of investigation of the body in contemporary thought which may be regarded as the heirs of Cartesianism. They indicate, even if negatively, the kinds of conceptions that feminist theory needs to move beyond in order to challenge its own investments in the history of philosophy.

① In the first line of investigation, the body is primarily regarded as an object for the natural sciences, particularly for the life sciences, biology and medicine; and conversely, the body is amenable to the humanities and social sciences, particularly psychology (when, for example, the discipline deals with "emotions," "sensations," "experiences," and "attitudes"), philosophy (when, for example, it deals with the body's ontological and epistemological status and implications), and ethnography (where, for example, the body's cultural variability, its various social transformations, are analyzed). The body either is understood in terms of organic and instrumental functioning in the natural sciences or is posited as *merely* extended, *merely* physical, an object like any other in the humanities and social sciences. Both, in different ways, ignore the specificity of bodies in their researches. The more medicalized biologistic view implies a fundamental continuity between man and animals, such that bodies are seen to have a particularly complex form of physiological organization, but one that basically differs from organic matter by degree rather than kind. In a sense, this position is heir to the Christian concept of the human body being part of a natural or mundane order. As an organism, the body is merely a more complex version of other kinds of organic ensembles. It cannot be qualitatively distinguished from other organisms: its physiology poses general questions similar to those raised by animal physiology.[12] The body's sensations, activities, and processes become "lower-order" natural or animal phenomena, part of an interconnected chain of organic forms (whether understood in cosmological or ecological terms). The natural sciences tend to treat the body as an organic system of interrelated parts, which are themselves framed by a larger ecosystemic order. The humanities reduce the body to a fundamental continuity with brute, inorganic matter. Despite their apparent dissimilarity, they share a common refusal to acknowledge the distinctive complexities of organic bodies, the fact that bodies construct and in turn are constructed by an interior, a psychical and a signifying view-point, a consciousness or perspective;

② The second line of investigation commonly regards the body in terms of metaphors that construe it as an instrument, a tool, or a machine at the disposal of consciousness, a vessel occupied by an animating, willful subjectivity. For Locke and the liberal political tradition more generally, the body is seen as a possession, a property of a subject, who is thereby dissociated from carnality and makes decisions and choices about how to dispose of the body and its powers (in, for

instrumentalism as a residual Cartesianism which treats the body as an instrument for the mind, desires, will etc.

example, the labor market). Some models, including Descartes's, construe the body as a self-moving automaton, much like a clock, car, or ship (these are pervasive but by no means exclusive images), according to the prevailing modes of technology. This understanding of the body is not unique to patriarchal philosophies but underlies some versions of feminist theory which see patriarchy as the system of universal male right to the appropriation of women's bodies (MacKinnon, Dworkin, Daly, and Pateman), a position that has been strongly criticized by other feminists (e.g., Butler and Cornell). In many feminist political struggles (those, for example, which utilize the old slogan "get your laws off my body") which are openly and self-consciously about women's bodies and their control by women (e.g., campaigns around such issues as sexual harassment and molestation, rape, the control of fertility, etc.), the body is typically regarded as passive and reproductive but largely unproductive, an object over which struggles between its "inhabitant" and others/exploiters may be possible. Whatever agency or will it has is the direct consequence of animating, psychical intentions. Its inertia means that it is capable of being acted on, coerced, or constrained by external forces. (This is not of course to deny that there are real, and frequent, forms of abuse and coercive mistreatment of women's bodies under the jealous and mutilating hostility of some men, but rather to suggest that frameworks within which women's bodies must be acknowledged as active, viable, and autonomous must be devised so that these practices can no longer be neatly rationalized or willfully reproduced.) As an instrument or tool, it requires careful discipline and training, and as a passive object it requires subduing and occupation. Such a view also lies behind the models of "conditioning" and "social construction" that are popular in some feminist circles, especially in psychology and sociology (Gilligan, Chodorow).

In the third line of investigation, the body is commonly considered a signifying medium, a vehicle of expression, a mode of rendering public and communicable what is essentially private (ideas, thoughts, beliefs, feelings, affects). As such, it is a two-way conduit: on one hand, it is a circuit for the transmission of information from outside the organism, conveyed through the sensory apparatus; on the other hand, it is a vehicle for the expression of an otherwise sealed and self-contained, incommunicable psyche. It is through the body that the subject can express his or her interiority, and it is through the body that he or she can receive, code, and translate the inputs of the "external" world. Underlying this view too is a belief in the fundamental passivity and transparency of the body. Insofar as it is seen as a medium, a carrier or bearer of information that comes from elsewhere (either "deep" in the subject's incorporeal interior or from the "exterior" world), the specificity and concreteness of the body must be neutralized, tamed, made to serve other purposes. If the subject is to gain knowledge about the external world, have any chance of making itself understood by others, or be effective in the world on such a model, the body must be seen as an unresistant pliability which minimally distorts information, or at least distorts it in a systematic and comprehensible fashion, so that its effects can be taken into account and information can be correctly retrieved. Its corporeality must be reduced to a predictable, knowable transparency; its constitutive role in forming thoughts, feelings, emotions, and psychic representations must be ignored, as must its role as threshold between the social and the natural.

These seem to be some of the pervasive, unspoken assumptions regarding the body in the history of modern philosophy and in conceptions of knowledge considered more generally. Insofar as feminist theory uncritically takes over these common assumptions, it participates in the social devaluing of the body that goes hand in hand with the oppression of women.

Spinoza's Monism

The Cartesian tradition has been more influential than any other tradition in establishing the agenda for philosophical reflection and in defining the terrain, either negatively or positively, for later concepts of subjectivity and knowledge. Yet there have been a handful of what could be called anomalous philosophers, such as Spinoza, Nietzsche, and Vico, who have self-consciously questioned the terms within which Cartesian dualism and all its offshoots are framed. Spinoza's work represents a highly influential position that rejects Cartesian dualism; it has provided inspiration for a number of the theorists who will be examined here.[13]

Gatens (1988) claims that Spinoza's work may provide a way to bypass the dualisms which dominate traditional philosophy while providing the basis for an understanding of difference (i.e., a nonoppositional notion of difference), that is useful, perhaps necessary, to reformulate male and female relations.

> Spinoza's writings offer the possibility of resolving some of the current difficulties in the much-debated relation between feminist theory and dominant theory. This "resolution" is not so much concerned with "answers" to these difficulties as with providing a framework in which it is possible to pose problems in quite "different" theoretical terms. (Gatens 1988: 68)

Spinoza's most fundamental assumption is the notion of an absolute and infinite substance, singular in both kind and number. If substance is infinite and nondivisible, it cannot be identified with or reduced to finite substances or things. Finite things are not substances but are modifications or affections of the one substance, modes or specifications of substance. An individual entity (human or otherwise) is not self-subsistent but is a passing or provisional determination of the self-subsistent. Substance has potentially infinite attributes to express its nature. Each attribute adequately expresses substance insofar as it is infinite (the infinity of space, for example, expresses the attribute of extension), yet each attribute is also inadequate or incomplete insofar as it expresses substance only in one form. Extension and thought—body and mind—are two such attributes. Thus, whereas Descartes claims two irreducibly different and incompatible substances, for Spinoza these attributes are merely different aspects of one and the same substance, inseparable from each other. Infinite substance—God—is as readily expressed in extension as in thought and is as corporeal as it is mental. There is no question of interaction, for they are like two sides of a coin. The dilemma of Cartesian dualism—how the will (which is not extended) can move the body (which is extended) and how body informs the will of its needs—is displaced. An act of will and the movements of the body are a single event appearing under different aspects; they are two expressions of one and the same thing. To every mode of extension there exists a mode of thought. Their interrelations or complementarity is based on the common ground of which both are equally dependent aspects.

Not only does Spinoza displace the dualism Descartes posits; he also frees notions of the body from the dominant mechanistic models and metaphors with which the Cartesian tradition surrounded it.[14] The machine metaphor is, in any case, only appropriate for the bodies of animals and not of plants, relying as it does on a model of a system or connected structure of moving parts whose energy is provided by some outside power source (the tension of the clock spring, the heat of the steam engine, the combustion of fuel). Metabolism is not simply the efficient fueling of a pregiven machine, for it must provide for the genesis, growth, and continual replacement of the parts comprising the machine. On a Spinozist understanding, metabolism is the very becoming of the machine, its mode of performance or existence, not simply the impetus or input for a preexistent entity or compound. In other words, metabolism is not simply a system of energy inputs provided from outside the machine-body but is a continuous process in the self-constitution of the organism. One theorist suggests the metaphor not of the machine or of two sides of the one coin (a metaphor which implies a structural homology, a one-to-one correlation) but of a flame:

> As in a burning candle, the permanence of the flame is a permanence, not of substance but of process in which at each moment the "body" with its "structure" of inner and outer layers is reconstituted of materials different from the previous and following ones so the living organism exists as a constant exchange of its own constituents and has its permanence and identity in the continuity of this process. (Jonas, in Spicker 1970: 55)

With nothing individual about it, substance cannot provide this kind of identity: the individuality of the body, of things, is the consequence of their specific modalities, their concrete determinations, and their interactions with the determinations of other things. The forms of determinateness, temporal and historical continuity, and the relations a thing has with coexisting things provide the entity with its identity. Its unity is not a function of its machinic operations as a closed system (i.e., its functional integration) but arises from a sustained sequence of states in a unified plurality (i.e., it has formal rather than substantive integrity). As Gatens notes,

> The Spinozist account of the body is of a productive and creative body which cannot be definitively "known" since it is not identical with itself across time. The body does not have a "truth" or a "true nature" since it is a process and its meaning and capacities will vary according to its context. We do not know the limits of this body or the powers that it is capable of attaining. These limits and capacities can only be revealed in the ongoing interactions of the body and its environment. (Gatens 1988: 68–69)

Spinoza bypasses Cartesian dualism and the problem of other minds. His work may arguably provide the grounds for the emergence of an antihumanism that has flourished since the 1960s. Since the soul is the correlate idea of an actually existing body, the degree of sophistication, differentiation, and clarity of the idea is exactly proportionate to the state of the body. This implies that soul is not only an attribute of human bodies but that it is an expression of the organization of a specific type of body. "Soul" is granted to animals, plants, and even inorganic matter, although of course the type of "soul" will vary according to the type and complexity of the body. There are as many types and degrees of soul or mind as there are types and degrees of matter. Spinoza thus introduces the idea of an infinite gradation of "animateness" or soul in accordance with the type of physical organization of the body. The mind is the idea of the body to the exact degree that the body is an extension of the mind.

In a theme that will be echoed in the neurophysiology we will later explore, Spinoza claims that the total state of the body at a particular moment is a function of the body's own formal pattern and inner constitution on one hand and, on the other, the influence of "external" factors, such as other bodies. There are no essential attributes, no inherent "nature" for the organism. In displacing the mind/body dualism, Spinoza is also upsetting the prevailing oppositions between nature and culture, between essence and social construction. In short, bodies, individualities, are historical, social, cultural weavings of biology. The organism or entity strives to affirm, to maximize its potentialities, its powers, its possibilities. This impetus is not simply an effect of its inner constitution but can only be gauged, actualized, in terms of the concrete options its situation affords it. Not being self-identical, the body must be seen as a series of processes of becoming, rather than as a fixed state of being. The body is both active and productive, although not originary: its specificity is a function of its degrees and modes of organization, which are in turn the results or consequences of its ability to be affected by other bodies. In opposition to the Cartesian model, then, subjectivity or the psyche is no more certain and incapable of doubt than the body: there is no single founding principle, such as the immediacy of self-consciousness, to guarantee knowledge or to construct knowledge in the form of a science.

As Spinoza's model of the body is fundamentally nonmechanistic, nondualistic and antiessentialist, it is not surprising that Spinoza's work has wide resonances not only with contemporary French thought (the impact of Spinozism on French theory from Althusser through Foucault to Deleuze, Derrida, and Irigaray is often noted but rarely elaborated [but see Norris 1991] but also with the radical accounts of the organism in the work of a number of neurophysiologists (who will be discussed in chapter 3). Yet, although Spinoza's monism represents a significant departure from Cartesian dualism, it has its own associated problems and limitations. In this context, I will only elaborate two. First, although Spinoza is a monist rather than a dualist, he is committed to a psychophysical parallelism which cannot explain the causal or other interactions of mind and body: "The body cannot determine the mind to thought, neither can the mind determine the body to motion nor rest, nor to anything else, if there be anything else" (Spinoza, *Ethics*, 111, Prop. 2). Insofar as they may be understood as necessarily interlocked, there can be no question of their interaction. Second, Spinoza is committed to a notion of the body (and indeed the subject) as total and holistic, a completed and integrated system (albeit one that grows and transforms itself). Organic bodies are the result of composite minor totalities brought together to form higher-level integrations and unifications through various processes of stratification, a cumulative complexity in which the uppermost level is the beneficiary of all its subordinated members—a position not dissimilar to the contemporary obsession with the notion of ecosystem as a higher-order unity of various subsystems, themselves composed of microsystems, integrated to form totalities which are in turn totalized.

Both these assumptions seem to me to avoid the two conditions necessary for a feminist reconfiguration of the notion of the body: that human bodies have irreducible neurophysiological and psychological dimensions whose relations remain unknown and that human bodies have the wonderful ability, while striving for integration and cohesion, organic and psychic wholeness, to also provide for and indeed produce fragmentations, fracturings, dislocations that orient bodies and body parts toward other bodies and body parts.

If Cartesianism today indicates a problematic site for feminist theory and for theories of subjectivity, perhaps the kinds of non-Cartesian accounts initiated by Spinoza and developed by Foucault, Deleuze, and others may prove more fruitful and useful for feminist purposes. That is the path this book sets out to explore.

Feminism and the Body

Misogynist thought has commonly found a convenient self-justification for women's secondary social positions by containing them within bodies that are represented, even constructed, as frail, imperfect, unruly, and unreliable, subject to various intrusions which are not under conscious control. Female sexuality and women's powers of reproduction are the defining (cultural) characteristics of women, and, at the same time, these very functions render women vulnerable, in need of protection or special treatment, as variously prescribed by patriarchy. The male/female opposition has been closely allied with the mind/body opposition. Typically, femininity is represented (either explicitly or implicitly) in one of two ways in this cross-pairing of oppositions: either mind is rendered equivalent to the masculine and body equivalent to the feminine (thus ruling out women a priori as possible subjects of knowledge, or philosophers) or each sex is attributed its own form of corporeality. However, instead of granting women an autonomous and active form of corporeal specificity, at best women's bodies are judged in terms of a "natural inequality," as if there were a standard or measure for the value of bodies independent of sex. In other words, women's corporeal specificity is used to explain and justify the different (read: unequal) social positions and cognitive abilities of the two sexes. By implication, women's bodies are presumed to be incapable of men's achievements, being weaker, more prone to (hormonal) irregularities, intrusions, and unpredictabilities.

Patriarchal oppression, in other words, justifies itself, at least in part, by connecting women much more closely than men to the body and, through this identification, restricting women's social and economic roles to (pseudo) biological terms. Relying on essentialism, naturalism and biologism,[15] misogynist thought confines women to the biological requirements of reproduction on the assumption that because of particular biological, physiological, and endocrinological transformations, women are somehow *more* biological, *more* corporeal, and *more* natural than men. The coding of femininity with corporeality in effect leaves men free to inhabit what they (falsely) believe is a purely conceptual order while at the same time enabling them to satisfy their (sometimes disavowed) need for corporeal contact through their access to women's bodies and services.

Where patriarchs have used a fixed concept of the body to contain women, it is understandable that feminists would resist such conceptions and attempt to define themselves in non- or extracorporeal terms, seeking an equality on intellectual and conceptual grounds or in terms of an abstract universalism or humanism. The hostility that misogynist thought directs toward women and femininity has been commonly rationalized through the deprecation and derision of women's bodies. That to a large extent explains the initial feminist suspicion of or hostility to reexploring, reexamining, notions of female corporeality, retrieving and representing women's bodies from points of view and interests relevant to women themselves.[16] In recent reevaluations of corporeality, feminists have found unexpected allies in the writings of a number of those wayward male philosophers who have proposed alternative or critical frameworks from which to help formulate an understanding of the sexual (and racial) specificity of bodies and subjectivities.

Feminists have exhibited a wide range of attitudes and reactions to conceptions of the body and attempts to position it at the center of political action and theoretical production. It may be worthwhile providing a brief overview of a distinct number of abstract or possible positions within feminist theory to show what potential there is for reconsidering and retheorizing the body outside patriarchal and racist categories and conceptual frameworks. These positions are by no means hard and fast; there are certainly a number of theorists who either fit more than one category or are not adequately described by any category. Yet I believe these categories do make clear both an historical development and a number of differing, perhaps even opposed, views of the body.

Egalitarian Feminism

The first category includes, figures as diverse as Simone de Beauvoir, Shulamith Firestone, Mary Wollstonecraft, and other liberal, conservative, and humanist feminists, even ecofeminists. Here, the specificities of the female body, its particular nature and bodily cycles—menstruation, pregnancy, maternity, lactation, etc.—are in one case regarded as a limitation on women's access to the rights and privileges patriarchal culture accords to men; in the other, in more positive and uncritical terms not uncommon to some feminist epistemologists and ecofeminists, the body is seen as a unique means of access to knowledge and ways of living. On the negative view, women's bodies are regarded as an inherent limitation on women's capacity for equality, while on the positive side, women's bodies and experiences are seen to provide women with a special insight, something that men lack. Both sides seem to have accepted patriarchal and misogynist assumptions about the female body as somehow more natural, less detached, more engaged with and directly related to its "objects" than male bodies.

As a consequence, in the negative view, feminists have sought to move beyond the constraints of the body. The female body limits women's capacity for equality and transcendence; it is a hindrance to be overcome, an obstacle to be surmounted if equality is to be attained. Many feminists within this category see a conflict between the role of mother and that of political or civic being.[17] Insofar as woman adopts the role of mother, her access to the public, social sphere is made difficult if not impossible, and the equalization of the roles of the two sexes becomes nonsensical. At most, equalization of the relations between the sexes is possible only within the public sphere. The private sphere remains sexually polarized insofar as sex roles, especially reproductive roles, remain binarily differentiated. Beauvoir and Firestone relish the development of new technological means of regulating reproduction and eliminating the effects of women's specific biologies on women's roles as social, economic, cultural, and sexual beings. Such a position remains ambiguously and paradoxically connected to the in-vitro fertilization programs so strongly advocated by some feminists (and so strongly criticized by others, e.g., Rowland) insofar as it sees the reproductive imperative as a major or defining feature of femininity as we know it, while at the same time, regarding female bodies as inadequate, in need of (this time surgical) supplementation or supersession. Their difference resides in the fact that for such feminists of equality, maternity is what must be overcome, while for the advocates of in-vitro programs, maternity is the or an ultimate goal of femininity. They are the negative and positive sides of women's childbearing capacities.[18]

Members of this first, egalitarian category share several beliefs: a notion of the body as biologically determined and fundamentally alien to cultural and intellectual achievement; a distinction between a sexually neutral mind and a sexually determinate (and limited) body (it is significant, though, that the maleness of the male body is never seen as a limit to man's transcendence; at most, the humanity of his body—its facticity and mortality—are abstract and universal characteristics that may restrict man's potential for transcendence);[19] an idea that women's oppression (in agreement with patriarchs) is a consequence of their containment within an inadequate, i.e., a female or potentially maternal, body (it is not simply the social and historical context of the body, the social restraints imposed on an otherwise autonomous body but the real vulnerability or fragility of the female body that poses the problem of women's social subordination); and a notion that women's oppression is, at least to some extent, biologically justified insofar as women *are* less socially, politically, and intellectually able to participate as men's social equals when they bear or raise children. Thus biology itself requires modification and transformation.

Social Constructionism

The second category includes probably the majority of feminist theorists today: Juliet Mitchell, Julia Kristeva, Michèle Barrett, Nancy Chodorow, Marxist feminists, psychoanalytic feminists, and all those committed to a notion of the social construction of subjectivity. This group has a much more positive attitude to the body than the first group, seeing it not so much as an obstacle to be overcome as a biological object whose representation and functioning is political, socially marking male and female as distinct. Instead of being coded by a nature/culture opposition, as it is for egalitarian feminists, the mind/body opposition is now coded by the distinction between biology and psychology and the opposition between the realms of production/reproduction (body) and ideology (mind). This coding is not directly correlated with the male/female opposition for clearly both men and women participate in material and ideological realms; but *within* each of these domains, the positions of men and women are distinct. In the material realm of production, for example, men function within the mode of production while women, even if they function in production, are, as women, largely located in a mode of reproduction; and within the ideological domain, women are produced as passive and feminine and men as active and masculine.

Like egalitarian feminists, social constructionists share several commitments, including a biologically determined, fixed, and ahistorical notion of the

gender/sex

body and retention of the ~~mind/body~~ dualism (even if mind cannot exist without body, the mind is regarded as a social, cultural, and historical object, a product of ideology, while the body remains naturalistic, precultural; bodies provide the base, the raw materials for the inculcation of and interpellation into ideology but *Althusser* are merely media of communication rather than the object or focus of ideological production/reproduction). Political struggles are thus directed toward neutralization of the sexually specific body. This neutralization is not so much the result of the intervention of the medico-technological forces as it is the consequence of a program of equalization through the social reorganization of childraising and socialization, as Chodorow makes explicit. So while male and female bodies remain untouched by and irrelevant to such programs, the associated gender traits of masculinity and femininity would, ideally, be transformed and equalized through a transformation in ideology.

In contrast to the egalitarian position, the constructionists hold a number of distinctive commitments, including the belief that it is not biology per se but the ways in which the social system organizes and gives meaning to biology that is oppressive to women. The distinction between the "real" biological body and the body as object of representation is a fundamental presumption. There is thus no question of superseding the body or biological functions; the task is to give them different meanings and values. Correlatively there is a presumption of a base/superstructure model in which biology provides a self-contained "natural" base and ideology provides a dependent parasitic "second story" which can be added—or not—leaving the base more or less as is. For constructionists, the sex/gender opposition, which is a recasting of the distinction between the body, or what is biological and natural, and the mind, or what is social and ideological, is still operative. Presuming that biology or sex is a fixed category, feminists have tended to focus on transformations at the level of gender. Their project has been to minimize biological differences and to provide them with different cultural meanings and values. There also remains the possibility of the equalization of relations between the two sexes only if the psychological functioning of each—gender—can be understood and transformed. Equalization does not require a transformation or supersession of the body. The body itself, in the strongest version of this position, is irrelevant to political transformation, and in the weakest version is merely a vehicle for psychological change, an instrument for a "deeper" effect. What needs to be changed are attitudes, beliefs, and values rather than the body itself.

Sexual Difference

In contrast with both egalitarianism and social constructionism, a third group can be discerned. Its participants include Luce Irigaray, Hélène Cixous, Gayatri Spivak, Jane Gallop, Moira Gatens, Vicki Kirby, Judith Butler, Naomi Schor, Monique Wittig, and many others. For them, the body is crucial to understanding woman's psychical and social existence, but the body is no longer understood as an ahistorical, biologically given, acultural object. They are concerned with the *lived body*, the body insofar as it is represented and used in specific ways in particular cultures. For them, the body is neither brute nor passive but is interwoven with and constitutive of systems of meaning, signification, and representation. On one hand it is a signifying and signified body; on the other, it is an object of systems of social coercion, legal inscription, and sexual and economic exchange. This diverse group tends to be more suspicious of the sex/gender distinction and to be less interested in the question of the cultural construction of subjectivity than in the materials out of which such a construct is forged.[20]

This group shares several features, which clearly distinguish it from its intellectual predecessors. There is a refusal or transgression of the mind/body dualism, which may be replaced by monism or a more uneasy yet noncontradictory relation between the binarized terms, or possibly even a head-on confrontation of the polarized terms. It is not clear that the holism implied by monist positions really solves the question of the relations between mind and body. For example, seeking resonances and parallels between mind and body (as dualists tend to do) may be less interesting than raising the question of their dissonances, cases of breakdown, failure, or disintegration (this will be explored in a later chapter). The body is regarded as the political, social, and cultural object par excellence, not a product of a raw, passive nature that is civilized, overlaid, polished by culture. The body is a cultural interweaving and production of nature. This group shares a commitment to a notion of the fundamental, irreducible differences between the sexes (which does not amount to essentialism, for there is a wholehearted acknowledgment, even valorization of differences between members of the same sex rather than an uncritical acceptance of universalist essences or categories). Whatever class and race differences may divide women,[21] sexual differences demand social recognition and representation, and these are differences no amount of technological innovation or ideological equalization can disavow or overcome. These differences may or may not be biological or universal. But whether biological or cultural, they are ineradicable. They require cultural marking and inscription. There also is a wariness of the sex/gender distinction. It is in any case not clear how one can eliminate the effects of (social) gender to see the contributions of (biological) sex. The body cannot be understood as a neutral screen, a biological *tabula rasa* onto which masculine or feminine could be indifferently projected. Instead of seeing sex as an essentialist and gender as a constructionist category, these thinkers are concerned to undermine the dichotomy. The concept of the social body is a major strategy in this goal. As sexually specific, the body codes the meanings projected onto it in sexually determinate ways.[22] These feminists thus do not evoke a precultural, presocial, or prelinguistic pure body but a body as social and discursive object, a body bound up in the order of desire, signification, and power.

That may help explain the enormous investment in definitions of the female body in struggles between patriarchs and feminists: what is at stake is the activity and agency, the mobility and social space, accorded to women. Far from being an inert, passive, noncultural and ahistorical term, the body may be seen as the crucial term, the site of contestation, in a series of economic, political, sexual, and intellectual struggles.

Body Traces

If women are to develop autonomous modes of self-understanding and positions from which to challenge male knowledges and paradigms, the specific nature and integration (or perhaps lack of it) of the female body and female subjectivity and its similarities to and differences from men's bodies and identities need to be articulated. The specificity of bodies must be understood in its historical rather than simply its biological concreteness. Indeed, there is no body as such: there are only *bodies*—male or female, black, brown, white, large or small—and the gradations in between. Bodies can be represented or understood not as entities in themselves or simply on a linear continuum with its polar extremes occupied by male and female bodies (with the various gradations of "intersexed" individuals in between) but as a field, a two-dimensional continuum in which race (and possibly even class, caste, or religion) form body specifications.

There are always only specific types of body, concrete in their determinations, with a particular sex, race, and physiognomy. Where one body (in the West, the white, youthful, able, male body) takes on the function of model or ideal, the human body, for all other types of body, its domination may be undermined through a defiant affirmation of a multiplicity, a field of differences, of other kinds of bodies and subjectivities. A number of ideal types of body must be posited to ensure the production, projection, and striving for ideal images and body types to which each individual, in his or her distinct way, may aspire. Only when the relation between mind and body is adequately retheorized can we understand the contributions of the body to the production of knowledge systems, regimes of representation, cultural production, and socioeconomic exchange. If the mind is necessarily linked to, perhaps even a part of, the body and if bodies themselves are always sexually (and racially) distinct, incapable of being incorporated into a singular universal model, then the very forms that subjectivity takes are not generalizable. Bodies are always irreducibly sexually specific, necessarily interlocked with racial, cultural, and class particularities. This interlocking, though, cannot occur by way of intersection (the gridlike model presumed by structural analysis, in which the axes of class, race, and sex are conceived as autonomous structures which then require external connections with the other structures) but by way of mutual constitution. Moreover, (if) subjectivity cannot be made to conform to the universalist ideals of humanism, if there is no concept of "the human" that includes all subjects without violence, loss, or residue, (then) the whole of cultural life, including the formation and evaluation of knowledges themselves, must be questioned regarding the sexual (and cultural) specificity of their positions. Knowledges, like all other forms of social production, are at least partially effects of the sexualized positioning of their producers and users; knowledges must themselves be acknowledged as sexually determinate, limited, finite.

If feminists are to resuscitate a concept of the body for their own purposes, it must be extricated from the biological and pseudo-naturalist appropriations from which it has historically suffered. The body must be understood through a range of disparate discourses and not simply restricted to naturalistic and scientistic modes of explanation. There are other ways in which sexually specific corporeal differences may be understood than those developed in more conventional and scientific representational contexts. Given the investment in restricting or containing studies of the body within the biological and life sciences and disavowing all traces of corporeality that appear elsewhere (i.e., in epistemic, artistic, social, and cultural concerns—the rest of life outside of the sphere of simple biology), developing alternative accounts of the body may create upheavals in the structure of existing knowledges, not to mention in the relations of power governing the interactions of the two sexes. If the body functions as the repressed or disavowed condition of all knowledges (including biology), then providing new bases to rethink the body may share the unarticulated assumptions of these knowledges. Other forms of knowledge, other modes of knowing than those which currently prevail, will need to be undertaken. This means, among other things, not only contesting the domination of the body by biological terms but also contesting the terms of biology itself, rethinking biology so that it too is able to see the body in terms other that those thus far developed.

For example, to develop a philosophy which refuses to privilege mind at the expense of body would, as (Nietzsche) discovered, completely change the character of the philosophical enterprise; and presumably the same would be true of all other knowledges insofar as the body is the disavowed condition of them all. If, as feminists have claimed, "our politics starts with our feelings" and if the very category of experience or feeling is itself problematized through a recognition of its ideological production—if, that is, experience is not a raw mode of access to some truth—then the body provides a point of mediation between what is perceived as purely internal and accessible only to the subject and what is external and publicly observable, a point from which to rethink the opposition between the inside and the outside, the private and the public, the self and other, and all the other binary pairs associated with the mind/body opposition. Finally, if we take seriously the antiessentialist decentering of identity and if, correlatively, we are committed to an antihumanist notion of "the production or construction of subjectivity," then unless the "raw materials" of the process of subject construction can be explained and problematized as raw or preinscriptive materials, the analogy between the production of subjects and the production of commodities—so crucial to a Marxist notion of ideology—breaks down. As pliable "raw materials" it is only an account of the body that gives this model any plausibility. Incidentally, this does not imply that the body is in any sense natural or raw, i.e., non- or presocial. Nor, on the contrary, can the body itself be regarded as *purely* a social, cultural, and signifying effect lacking its own weighty materiality. The very interaction and engagement of the natural with the cultural, the production of the natural in the (specific) terms of the cultural, the cultural as the (reverse) precondition of the natural—in short, the binary opposition between the cultural and the natural—needs careful reconsideration. It is not adequate to simply dismiss the category of nature outright, to completely retranscribe it without residue into the cultural: this in itself is the monist, or logocentric, gesture par excellence. Instead, the interimplication of the natural and the social or cultural needs further investigation—the hole in nature that allows cultural seepage or production must provide something like a natural condition for cultural production; but in turn the cultural too must be seen in its limitations, as a kind of insufficiency that requires natural supplementation. Culture itself can only have meaning and value in terms of its own other(s): when its others are obliterated—as tends to occur within the problematic of social constructionism—culture in effect takes on all the immutable, fixed characteristics attributed to the natural order. Nature may be understood not as an origin or as an invariable template but as materiality in its most general sense, as destination (with all the impossibilities, since Derrida, that this term implies). Their relation is neither a dialectic (in which case there is the possibility of a supersession of the binary terms) nor a relation of identity but is marked by the interval, by pure difference.

How, then, is a different analysis of the body to proceed? By what techniques and presumptions is a nondichotomous understanding of the body possible? Without preempting the more concrete analyses to follow, it can at least be pointed out more explicitly what must be overcome, negotiated, in order to create alternative, more positive accounts of the body. What, ideally, would a feminist philosophy of the body avoid, and what must it take into consideration? What criteria and goals should govern a feminist theoretical approach to concepts of the body?

First, it must avoid the impasse posed by dichotomous accounts of the person which divide the subject into the mutually exclusive categories of mind and body. Although within our intellectual heritage there is no language in which to describe such concepts, no terminology that does not succumb to versions of this polarization, some kind of understanding of *embodied subjectivity*, of *psychical corporeality*, needs to be developed. We need an account which refuses reductionism, resists dualism, and remains suspicious of the holism and unity implied by monism—a notion of corporeality, that is, which avoids not only dualism but also the very problematic of dualism that makes alternatives to it and criticisms of it possible. The narrow constraints our culture has imposed on the ways in which our materiality can be thought means that altogether new conceptions of corporeality— those, perhaps, which use the hints and suggestions of others but which move beyond the overall context and horizon governed by dualism—need to be developed, notions which see human materiality in continuity with organic and inorganic matter but also at odds with other forms of matter, which see animate materiality and the materiality of language in interaction, which make possible a materialism beyond physicalism (i.e., the belief that reality can be explained in terms of the laws, principles, and terms of physics), a materialism that questions physicalism, that reorients physics itself.

Second, corporeality must no longer be associated with one sex (or race), which then takes on the burden of the other's corporeality for it. Women can no longer take on the function of being *the* body for men while men are left free to soar to the heights of theoretical reflection and cultural production. Blacks, slaves, immigrants, indigenous peoples can no longer function as the working body for white "citizens," leaving them free to create values, morality, knowledges. There are (at least) two kinds of body. Sex is not merely a contingent, isolated, or minor variation of an underlying humanity. It is not trivial to one's social and political status in a way in which it is conceivable that eye color is: it is integral to the status and social position of the subject. It has a pervasive influence on and effects for the subject. One's sex cannot be simply reduced to and contained by one's primary and secondary sexual characteristics, because one's sex makes a difference to *every* function, biological, social, cultural, if not in their operations then certainly in significance.

Third, it must refuse singular models, models which are based on one type of body as the norm by which all others are judged. There is no one mode that is capable of representing the "human" in all its richness and variability. A plural, multiple field of possible body "types," no one of which functions as the delegate or representative of the others, must be created, a "field" of body types—young and old, black and white, male and female, animal and human, inanimate and animate—which, in being recognized in their specificity, cannot take on the coercive role of singular norm or ideals for all the others. Such plural models must be used to define the norms and ideals not only of health and fitness but also of beauty and desire.[23] But in positing a field of body types, I do not want to suggest that there is a single homogeneous field on which all sorts of body types can, without any violence or transcription, be placed so that they can now be assessed fairly and equally. This is nothing but the liberal paradigm, which leaves unacknowledged the criteria by and the interests through which the field is set up. A field may be a discontinuous, nonhomogenous, nonsingular space, a space that admits of differences, incommensurability, intervals or gaps between types, a field, in short, that is established and regulated according to various perspectives and interests.

Fourth, while dualism must be avoided, so too, where possible (though this is not always the case—one is always implicated in essentialism even as one flees it), must biologistic or essentialist accounts of the body. The body must be regarded as a site of social, political, cultural, and geographical inscriptions, production, or constitution. The body is not opposed to culture, a resistant throwback to a natural past; it is itself a cultural, *the* cultural, product. The very question of the ontological status of biology, the openness of organic processes to cultural intervention, transformation, or even production, must be explored. In particular this implies the difficult task of producing or exploring a range of possible metaphors other than the mechanistic ones which have dominated the history of philosophy, metaphors which postulate or make recognizable different relations between the biological and the social than those represented by the machine, by the base-superstructure or building model and the model of binarized opposition. These metaphors have all presumed a certain mastery of and exteriority to the object—the body, bodies—that, I claim, is not possible. What is needed are metaphors and models that implicate the subject in the object, that render mastery and exteriority undesirable.

Fifth, whatever models are developed must demonstrate some sort of internal or constitutive articulation, or even disarticulation, between the biological and the psychological, between the inside and the outside of the body, while avoiding a reductionism of mind to brain. Any adequate model must include a psychical representation of the subject's lived body as well as of the relations between body gestures, posture, and movement in the constitution of the processes of psychical representations. Both psychical and social dimensions must find their place in reconceptualizing the body, not in opposition to each other but as necessarily interactive.

Sixth, instead of participating in—i.e., adhering to one side or the other of—a binary pair, these pairs can be more readily problematized by regarding the body as the threshold or borderline concept that hovers perilously and undecidably at the pivotal point of binary pairs. The body is neither—while also being both—the private or the public, self or other, natural or cultural, psychical or social, instinctive or learned, genetically or environmentally determined. In the face of social constructionism, the body's tangibility, its matter, its (quasi) nature may be invoked; but in opposition to essentialism, biologism, and naturalism, it is the body as cultural product that must be stressed. This indeterminable position enables it to be used as a particularly powerful strategic term to upset the frameworks by which these binary pairs are considered. In dissolving oppositional categories we cannot simply ignore them, vowing never to speak in their terms again. This is neither historically possible nor even desirable insofar as these categories must be engaged with in order to be superseded. But new terms and different conceptual frameworks must also be devised to be able to talk of the body outside or in excess of binary pairs.

PART II

The Inside Out

2 | Psychoanalysis and Psychical Topographies

> ... the repressed of today is the body, the sensory and motor body. In the era
> of the third industrial revolution, the revolution of information, nuclear energy,
> and the video, the repressed is the body.
>
> Didier Anzieu, *The Skin Ego* (1990: 64)

The Inside Out

IN THIS AND the next chapter, I propose to explore the ways in which the body's
psychical interior is established as such through the social inscription of bodily
processes, that is, the ways in which the "mind" or psyche is constituted so that
it accords with the social meanings attributed to the body in its concrete historical, social, and cultural particularity. Psychoanalysis will be discussed in terms
of its radical presumption of a correspondence or correlation between the forms
of the body and the forms of mind or psyche (an argument with major implications insofar as mind or psyche, until the advent of contemporary feminism, had
been regarded as sexually neutral and indifferent to the particularities of the
body); and conversely, that the constitution of the subject as an integrated and
functional psychical totality is an active ingredient in the constitution of the
body, for it provides the subject with a body which has particular, socially distinctive, and culturally determined attributes and abilities, individual idiosyncra-
sies and styles of behavior.

This chapter will focus on the contributions psychoanalytic theory has made
to understanding how the body functions, not simply as a biological entity but
as a psychical, lived relation, and the ways in which the psyche is a projection of
the body's form. Given the vastness of Freud's writings and the major if largely
unrecognized role of the body in his understanding of the psyche, I will have
space to focus on only three aspects of his understanding of psychical functioning: his notions of the ego, his conception of sexual drives, and his accounts of
psychical topography. These are at the center of his radical understanding of the
body. I will also spell out the refinements, modifications, and detailed developments of his work undertaken by a number of theorists inspired by psychoanalysis, especially the French psychoanalyst Jacques Lacan, with his formulation of
the mirror stage and the genesis of the ego, his notion of the imaginary anatomy,

and the signifying function of the drives. Finally I will look at some of the implications a notion of the psychical body has for feminists interested in rethinking concepts of female subjectivity, sexuality and corporeality.

Models of the Psyche

From the beginnings of psychoanalysis, Freud was fascinated with the relations between neurology and psychology. Although he soon abandoned any hope of being able to reduce psychological discourses and treatments to those of neurology or psychological terms to those of chemistry, he nevertheless retained an interest in the ways in which the two domains might interact. Perhaps without even being aware of it, Freud problematized the ways in which both the psychical and the biological have been conceived, showing that each, in its very existence and operations, implies the other. It is therefore not surprising that he returned again and again in his psychological writings to the question of the integration of psychology with biology.[1] He frequently relied on models and metaphors derived from biology, and his notions of energy, libido, drive, and force are clearly and directly borrowed from biological models. Yet, as I will argue, he effects a series of displacements of the biological, modifying the ways in which biology is generally conceived, showing its susceptibility to the psychological rather than assuming a rift between them, as occurs in Cartesian notions of mind and body. Rather than seeing biology or neurology as the groundwork, substratum, bedrock, or master plan for psychological models and processes, Freud transforms our understanding of biology so that it can no longer be seen as a determining factor in psychical life. Biology must be understood as psychologically pliable. If anything, a two-way determination or overdetermination, a clear interaction of the biological and the psychological, is forged in his writings.

Freud's interest in theorizing the interface between the soma and the psyche, between biology and psychology, is clear in his concern with the role of perception in psychical life (for another feminist reading and refiguring of the mind/body relation that reworks psychoanalytic theory, see Brennan, 1992). Perception is a concept that already exists in the breach between the mind and the body, being the psychical registration of the impingement of external and internal stimuli on the body's sensory receptors. It is a term, as Merleau-Ponty was to recognize (see chapter 4), that requires a transgression of the binarism of the mind/body split. It shows the ineliminable dependence of the inside and the outside, mind and matter, on each other. Freud makes perception the cornerstone of his notion of the ego and psychical agencies and, especially in *The Ego and the Id* (1923), the site of his second notion of the ego. An earlier understanding is developed in "On Narcissism: An Introduction" (1914); it forms the basis of what might be called his narcissistic model of the ego. This narcissistic model, in which the ego's origin is described in terms of the subject's ability to take itself or part of its own body as a love object, is, contrary to the account in *The Ego and the Id*, a description of the subject's libidinal investment in its own body. In *The Ego and the Id*, however, the ego is seen as a mediator between two contradictory terms rather than the circulation of libidinal cathexes, the instinctual and corporeal strivings of the id on one hand and the demands and requirements of "reality" or "civilization" for the modification, control, or postponement of instinctual satisfaction on the other.[2]

Freud is curious to know how the subject becomes cognizant of thought processes and what the distinction between thought and perception is, given that endogenous sensations are not received by various sense receptors in the way exogenous stimuli are. How is consciousness of our own thoughts possible? Freud had approached this issue in a metapsychological paper, "The Unconscious" (1915a), in which he asked how a perception is successively registered in unconscious, preconscious, and conscious agencies. He asked whether one and the same perception is registered in several successive agencies in the psyche and is thus represented in a number of locations simultaneously or whether, instead, it undergoes a functional change as it proceeds from one agency to another on its path to motility, in which case it exists only in a singular but mobile location. There, as in *The Ego and the Id*, Freud eventually resorts to a linguistic model, claiming that the difference between a conscious registration of a perception and its unconscious registration is not a difference in the location of the perception or a functional transformation so much as a difference between a perception which has access to linguistic expression ("word presentations") and one which has been refused access to verbalization, thus remaining purely perceptual ("thing-presentations"):

> We now seem to know all at once what the difference is between a conscious and an unconscious presentation. The two are not, as we supposed, different registrations of the same content in different psychical localities; nor yet different functional states of cathexis in the same locality, but the conscious representation comprises the presentation of the thing plus the presentation of the word belonging to it, while the unconscious presentation is the presentation of the thing alone. (Freud 1915a: 201–2)

Freud presents a more complex analysis of the processes of a perception's coming to consciousness in *The Ego and the Id*. If internal processes such as thinking are to become conscious, they must first of all function like external perceptions. This occurs through memory traces. But these memory traces are themselves not (or not yet) external perceptions unless they are located close to the system Freud calls the "Pcpt-Cs" system. The memory trace differs from hallucination and perception because its cathexis is contained within the mnemic system. The hallucination can pass itself off for a current perception only insofar as it is able to transfer its intensity to the conscious system. How, then, can a memory trace function as a current perception, that is, in hallucinatory fashion? This question of the veracity of perceptual impingements is crucial if Freud is to explain how the ego is a vehicle of the adaptation of the id's impulses to the requirements of reality—which is his aim in developing his view of the ego in *The Ego and the Id*.

The conscious system automatically furnishes "indications of reality," which Laplanche (1976: 59) likens to a bell lighting up on a pinball machine every time a certain spot is hit by the perception. When in contact with a veridical perception, the organism receives two kinds of messages, one from the sensory periphery of the nervous system, the other from consciousness, the second message confirming the veracity of the first. This means that the ego does not have direct access to reality even on this so-called "realist" view of the ego. Its function here is to discriminate between endogenous and exogenous stimuli, that is, between reality and what, being internal, passes as reality. A stimulus may present itself as a perception and be received by consciousness. This is true for internal excitations and thought processes as much as for external perception. It is for this reason that the internal excitation, the thought, must accede to language. Only by acquiring a mode of reality, not unlike that of hallucination, can thought become conscious:

> The part played by word-presentations now becomes perfectly clear. By their interposition, internal thought-processes are made into perceptions. It is like a demonstration of the theorem that all knowledge has its origin in external perception. When a hypercathexis of the process of thinking takes place, thoughts are *actually* perceived—as if they came from without—and are consequently held to be true. (Freud 1923: 23)

By being expressed in language, thought processes can become perceptual contents available for consciousness. It is only through such a mode of externalization that these thoughts have any "reality," that is, any stability, longevity, or identity. Otherwise they remain fleeting, momentary events. In asking the question of how to distinguish internal from external excitations, Freud is really asking about how to distinguish the "objective" from the "subjective," veridical perception from hallucinatory states, mind from body. As he makes clear, however, this kind of definitive separation is never possible: the psychical cannot be unambiguously separated from the perceptual.

This issue of the achievement of some kind of unity and identity over and above the mere momentary impingements of stimuli (whether internal or external) is one of the guiding themes in Freud's theorization of the ego. Freud locates the ego at the center or nucleus of the perceptual-conscious system. I will return to the question of psychical topographies shortly but will now concentrate on the ways in which Freud understands the ego in corporeal terms.

The Ego as Corporeal Projection

In *The Ego and the Id*, Freud presents a startling, enigmatic account of the structure and form of the ego as a corporeal projection, a notion which has been frequently mentioned in the secondary literature but which nonetheless remains relatively undeveloped.[3] This view confirms his claims in "On Narcissism" that the subject acquires an underlying sense of unity and identity only as the end result of a series of processes which construct the ego as such. The subject only gradually acquires a sense of unity and cohesion over and above the disparate, heterogeneous sensations that comprise its experiences. If the subject were merely a perceiving and experiencing being—as naive empiricism presumes—then there could be no way of unifying the subject's experiences as the experiences of a single being, no way of asserting some kind of propriety over those experiences, no way of taking responsibility for them. The subject would simply be an aggregate of otherwise disconnected perceptual events, which could give it no index of the existence of objects or the world. Objects and the world have an abiding, even if changing, set of characteristics, an ongoing identity independent of but confirmable by perception. All that exists for the neonate is a whirring, ever-changing flux of experiences, which are not yet organized in terms of patterns, groupings, identities, and objects. In the preobject stage, before the advent of primary narcissism, the child is a (passive) conglomerate of fleeting experiences, at the mercy of organic and social excitations to which it may respond but over which it has no agency or control.

Confirming and expanding on Freud's implicit characterization of this earliest period of development, Henri Wallon argues that the child's perceptual experiences vacillate between a phenomenalism in which only the most visible and striking features of an object are registered and a syncretism in which there is a diffused but holistic image with few or no clear-cut conceptual features. Only through a prolonged process of development does the child succeed in integrating its phenomenality with its syncretism, thus approximating what in the adult would be the perception of an object:

> . . . two types of thought emerge that seem to be in competition, though both stem from the same causes. One is a kind of perceptual realism that retains only those aspects or features of a given thing that make particularly vivid or striking impressions on the senses, a pure phenomenalism which reduces reality to an infinite mutability of diverse forms of objects. The other is a kind of confused image, in which the part played by impressions derived directly from things and the part originating in the subject . . . remain undifferentiated: the practical merges with the perceptual. Experience is no more than a succession of situations to which the subject reacts. His representation of this experience is the image of these global wholes, while specific features and details are

merely circumstances surrounding an act that have no distinct individuality of their own. . . . The opposition between phenomenalism and syncretism seems obvious; nevertheless, they alternate and coexist. (Henri Wallon, in G. Voyat 1984: 75–76)

For Freud, the ego is what brings unity to the vast and overwhelming diversity of perceptions which, to begin with, overwhelm the child. The ego is a consequence of a perceptual surface; it is produced and grows only relative to this surface. In his initial formulations, Freud argues that the ego does not result from a preordained biological order but is the result of a psychosocial intervention into the child's hitherto natural development:[4]

We are bound to suppose that a unity comparable to the ego has to be developed. . . . there must be something added to auto-eroticism—a new psychical action—in order to bring about narcissism. (Freud 1914: 77)

This new action engenders primary narcissism (or what Lacan calls the mirror stage) at around six months of age. It consists in the relative stabilization of the circulation of libido in the child's body, so that the division between subject and object (even the subject's capacity to take itself as an object) becomes possible for the first time. This emerges as a result of two complementary processes. First, the ego is the result of a series of identificatory relations with other subjects, particularly the mother or even its own image in the mirror. These identifications are introjected into the ego in the form of the ego ideal, the idealized model of itself for which the ego strives. And second, the ego is a consequence of a blockage or rechanneling of libidinal impulses in the subject's own body in the form of a narcissistic attachment to a part or the whole of its body. In this sense, the ego is the meeting point, the point of conjunction, between the body and the social. The narcissistic genesis of the ego entails that the subject cannot remain neutral or indifferent to its own body and body parts. The body is libidinally invested. The subject always maintains a relation of love (or hate) toward its own body because it must always maintain a certain level of psychical and libidinal investment. No person lives his or her own body merely as a functional instrument or a means to an end. Its value is never simply or solely functional, for it has a (libidinal) value in itself. The subject is capable of suicide, of anorexia (which may in some cases amount to the same thing), because the body is *meaningful*, has significance.

Schilder cites the example of the wasp and the dog. When impaired by a broken limb, both animals will gnaw off the extremity because it hampers their movements. He also notes that "according to Vexküll, a dragonfly starts to eat up its own body when its rear end is pushed between its jaws" (Schilder 1978: 195). It could be argued that the creature values life above corporeal wholeness. This of course is not entirely different from the subject who sells his or her organs for financial reasons or from the processes of self-mutilation and self-amputation that sometimes occur in prisons or other institutions of detention. I am reminded of an extraordinary series of mutilations and self-mutilations that occurred in New South Wales, Australia, in the late 1980s, which when reported in the newspapers seemed to intensify. In the first episode, the papers reported the discovery of an amputated penis in a public toilet. Within weeks there were daily reports of wives severing their husbands' penises, of prisoners' self-castrations, of men arriving at the hospital emergency room with a penis wrapped in ice, and so on. There was a veritable fad of adult castrations which seemed to diminish only when the press lost interest in reporting them. Nonetheless, even in these cases, it is not that the penis is without significance or value for the self-castrator; on the contrary, it is because these kinds of mutilation are considered so horrendous and disturbing that they are able to function as a mode of violent protest, resistance, or escape.

It seems likely that animals too have something like a body image, even if it is a relatively rudimentary one. Sacks, in *A Leg to Stand On*, cites the case of the dog who forgets to use its once-broken leg, in an experience analogous to Sacks's own experience of his broken leg. Every body, in order to be operational, must be invested within the sociality of animal "culture" itself. This seems to be Lacan's point (and Caillois's too, as we shall soon see) regarding migratory locusts and gregarious pigeons, which do not take on an "identity" as a member of their species except through the internalization of the image of another relatively similar species:

> ... it is a necessary condition for the maturation of the gonad of the female pigeon that it should see another member of its species, of either sex; so sufficient in itself is this condition that the desired effect may be obtained merely by placing the individual within the reach of the field of reflection of a mirror. Similarly, in the case of the migratory locust, the transition within a generation from the solitary to the gregarious form can be obtained by exposing the individual, at a certain stage, to the exclusively visual action of a similar image, provided it is animated by movements of a style sufficiently close to that characteristic of the species. (Lacan 1977a: 3)

Freud claims that the genesis of the ego is dependent on the construction of a psychical map of the body's libidinal intensities. In *The Ego and the Id*, he claims that the ego is not so much a self-contained entity or thing as a kind of bodily tracing, a cartography of the erotogenic intensity of the body, an internalized image of the degrees of the intensity of sensations in the child's body. He backs up his claims with reference to the "cortical homunculus," a much-beloved idea circulating in neurological and medical circles in the nineteenth century:[5]

> The ego is first and foremost a bodily ego: it is not merely a surface entity, but is itself the projection of a surface. If we wish to find an anatomical analogy for it we can best identify it with the "cortical homunculus" of the anatomists,

which stands on its head in the cortex, sticks up its heels, faces backwards and as we know, has its speech-area on the left hand side. (Freud 1923: 26)

This confirms a claim Freud made in "On Narcissism" that the ego is a mapping, not of the real or anatomical body but of the degree of libidinal cathexis the subject has invested in its own body:

> We can decide to regard erotogenicity as a general characteristic of all organs and may then speak of an increase or decrease of it in a particular part of the body. For every such change in the erotogenicity of libidinal zones there might be a parallel change in the ego. (Freud 1914: 84)

In spite of the apparent agreement regarding the ego as a psychical mapping of the libidinally invested body in both these papers, there is still a tension between the two positions. In the 1914 paper, Freud claims that the amount of libidinal intensity cathecting erotogenic zones parallels changes that occur at the level of the ego. If the ego is a libidinal reservoir, as he claims in this paper, its "shape" and contours vary according to its libidinal investments in other objects and according to the quantities of libidinal excitation that circulate in the body which are available for object-love through the sexual drives and find their sources in the different erotogenic zones of the body. Freud does not specify which erotogenic zones he has in mind here, although it is usually presumed that he is referring to the primacy of the pre-Oedipal psychosexual zones singled out for special attention as a result of the infant's development. In *The Ego and the Id*, however, he is explicit in saying that the ego is a projection or map of the surface of the body, implying that it is a "skin ego" (using Anzieu's phrase) that he has in mind. In a footnote added to the text in 1927, Freud clarifies:

> The ego is ultimately derived from bodily sensations, chiefly from those springing from the surface of the body. It may thus be regarded as a mental projection of the surface of the body, besides, as we have seen above, representing the superficies of the mental apparatus. (1923: 26)

We need not choose between these specialized sites of libidinal investment in deciding how this psychical map, which later becomes the site of the ego, first emerges. It is clear that elements of both the earlier and later views are necessary and that the two conceptions are compatible. Freud follows the older generation of neurologists in attributing a privileged role to the erotogenic zones, for it is clear that they play a disproportionately significant role in the formation of the sensorimotor homunculus. The homunculus, the tiny "manikin" registered in the cerebral cortex, is inverted like a mirror image. Instead of being a point-for-point projection of the outside of the body in its entirety, it stresses certain points of intensity above all others and leaves little or no room for the registration of other bodily zones. For example, the homunculus is usually regarded as highly overdeveloped in oral, manual, and genital representations, and it is significant that the homunculus has no brain, because the brain is the object of neither motor nor sensory relations (precisely because it is the locus for the registration of sensory and motor factors).[6] Moreover, it is particularly significant that no mention is made of the female homunculus or the ways in which it differs from the male. In much of the relevant literature, the homunculus is *explicitly* described as male, and there is no mention of what this means for women.

In spite of his manifest sexism, Gorman makes it clear that the homunculus is largely, though not exclusively, based on the information afforded by visual perception:

> The homunculi . . . stimulate the eye, for their visual appearance is that of *distorted little male persons*, whose deformities are arresting to the studious as well as the curious. The face and the mouth of the homunculus are huge, his forehead is barely present, his hands gargantuan and his *genitals gross*. He has a respectably large intra-abdominal area, but he possesses not even a trace of a brain area. . . . Those parts of the body which can neither be seen nor felt do not appear in the motor homunculus and those parts which do not yield sensations of perceived touch are denied a position in the sensory homunculus. Since the brain is hidden from vision, and imperceptive of touch to its matter, we must reluctantly grant that our cherished but imaginary manikins are not able to represent our brains. (Gorman 1969: 193; emphasis added)

Gorman gives no explanation of the maleness of the homunculus and no account of the shape or form of the homunculus for women. Seeing that his view strongly privileges the information provided by vision—presumably this is why he does not accord female sexual organs any place on the homunculus—he is inconsistent, in a way that Freud is not, in assuming a universal set of homunculi for both sexes. Given the major role visual, tactile, and kinesthetic sensations provide in women's sexual arousal, there must be some kind of psychical registration of female genitalia on the homunculus. The question is, in what terms, using what kinds of projections, are women's bodies inscribed, and with what effects?

Although sensory information can be provided by any of the sense organs, the surface of the body is in a particularly privileged position to receive information and excitations from both the interior and the exterior of the organism. This may help explain why the orifices are especially privileged in the establishment of erotogenic zones and why the infant's psychosexual stages are part of the process of maturation, which relies disproportionately on the cutaneous openings of the body's surface. In any case, however, the skin and the various sensations which are located at the surface of the body are the most primitive, essential, and constitutive of all sources of sensory stimulation. The information provided by the surface of the skin is both endogenous and exogenous, active and passive, receptive and expressive, the only sense able to provide the "double sensation." Double sensations are those in which the subject utilizes one part of the body to touch another, thus exhibiting the interchangeability of active and passive sensations, of those positions of subject and object, mind and body. The other senses can elicit the double sensation only on the ground already set up by tactility, a point that will prove to be significant for feminist readings of Merleau-Ponty (chapter 4). This is the twisting of the Möbius strip, the torsion or pivot around which the subject is generated. The double sensation creates a kind of *interface* of the inside and the outside, the pivotal point at which inside will become separated from outside and active will be converted into passive (a line of border which is not unlike the boundary established by the duplicating structure of the mirror, which similarly hinges on the pivotal plane represented by the tain of the mirror).

This neuro- and psychophysiological process is both the precondition and the correlate of the ego's ability to distinguish between itself and others (at first developed in only rudimentary form at the mirror stage), between internal and external stimuli, and between subject and object:

> . . . you find human beings who suffer from blindness or deafness, or no sense of smell, and this does not prevent them from living, nor from succeeding in communicating, perhaps in a somewhat more complicated way, but they do communicate. By contrast, there is no human being without a virtually complete envelope of skin. If one seventh of the skin is destroyed by accident, lesion, or burns, the human being dies. One can find a symbolic mode of communication even with a child who is both deaf and blind at birth, starting from increasingly differentiated tactile contacts. The skin is so fundamental, its functioning is taken so much for granted, that no one notices its existence until the moment it fails. (Anzieu 1990: 63–64)

The surface of the body, the skin, moreover provides the ground for the articulation of orifices, erotogenic rims, cuts on the body's surface, loci of exchange between the inside and the outside, points of conversion of the outside into the body, and of the inside out of the body. These are sites not only for the reception and transmission of information but also for bodily secretions (as will be discussed in the last chapter), ongoing processes of sensory stimulation which require some form of signification and sociocultural and psychical representation. These cuts on the body's surface create a kind of "landscape" of that surface, that is, they provide it with "regions," "zones," capable of erotic significance; they serve as a kind of gridding, an uneven distribution of intensities, of erotic investments in the body.

In *The Ego and the Id* Freud shows the ego emerging from out of the id through a gradual process of differentiation initiated by the organism's confrontation with reality. It is in contact with the external world only through the mediation of various forms of sense perception.[7] Freud shows the crucial role that bodily perception plays in the establishment of these agencies and in their modes of operation. The ego is only gradually distinguished from the id through the impact of perceptual stimuli on the surface of the organism. As Freud explains it, the ego is something like a "psychical callous" formed through the use of the body, and particularly its surface, as a screen or sieve for selecting and sorting the sensory information provided by perception. But although perception is crucial in the establishment of the psychical agencies, Freud implies that the body itself, or at least certain privileged bodily zones and organs, particularly those with heightened reception of sensory inputs, is even more significant. It is in this sense that the ego must be understood as a bodily ego:

> Another factor, besides the influence of the system Pcpt, seems to have played a part in bringing about the formation of the ego and its differentiation from the id. A person's own body, and above all its surface, is a place from which both external and internal perceptions may spring. It is seen like any other object, but to the touch it yields two kinds of sensations, one of which may be equivalent to an internal percept. . . . Psychophysiology has fully discussed the manner in which a person's own body attains its special position among other objects in the world of perception. Pain, too, seems to play a part in the process, and the way in which we gain new knowledge of our organs during painful illnesses is perhaps a model of the way in which in general we arrive at the idea of our body. (Freud 1923: 25–26)

The ego, then, is something like an internal screen onto which the illuminated and projected images of the body's outer surface are directed. It is the site for the gathering together and unification of otherwise disparate and scattered sensations provided by the various sense organs, in all their different spaces and registers. It is also a mapping of the body's inner surface, the surface of sensations, intensities, and affects, the "subjective experience" of bodily excitations and sensations.

This means that the ego is not a veridical diagram or representation of the empirical and anatomical body; nor is it an effect of which the body or the body's surface is a cause (this would make the ego and other relevant psychical agencies as rigidly determined by biology and biological processes as they would be if they were innate). The ego is not a point-for-point projection of the body's surface but an outline or representation of the degrees of erotogenicity of the bodily zones and organs. The ego is derived from two kinds of "surface." On one hand, the ego is on the "inner" surface of the psychical agencies; on the other hand, it is a projection or representation of the body's "outer" surface. In both cases, the surface is perceptual. Perception thus provides both the contents of the ego and, to begin with, the earliest sexual "objects" for the child. Moreover, in the establishment of the ego, perceptual processes are themselves sexualized, libidinally invested.

The ego is a representation of the varying intensities of libidinal investment in the various bodily parts and the body as a whole. Significantly, this notion of the body as a whole is dependent on the recognition of the totality and autonomy of the body of the other. The ego is thus both a map of the body's surface and a reflection of the image of the other's body. The other's body provides the frame for the representation of one's own. In this sense, the ego is an image of the body's significance or meaning for the subject and for the other. It is thus as much a function of fantasy and desire as it is of sensation and perception; it is a taking over of sensation and perception by a fantasmatic dimension. This significatory, cultural dimension implies that bodies, egos, subjectivities are not simply reflections of their cultural context and associated values but are constituted as such by them, marking bodies in their very "biological" configurations with sociosexual inscriptions.

Freud illustrates the blurring of the psychical and the physical, the mind and the body, with reference to hypochondria. In "On Narcissism" Freud tries to distinguish between hypochondria and organic disorders but finds that it is unclear where one can place the dividing line:

> Hypochondria, like organic disease, manifests itself in distressing and painful bodily sensations, and it has the same effect as organic disease on the distribution of libido. The hypochondriac withdraws both interest and libido . . . from objects in the external world and concentrates both of them upon the organ that is engaging his attention. The difference between hypochondria and organic diseases now becomes evident: in the latter, the distressing sensations are based upon demonstrable (organic) changes; in the former, this is not so. But it would be entirely in keeping with our general conception of the processes of neurosis if we decided to say that hypochondria must be right: organic changes must be supposed to be present in it, too. (Freud 1914: 83)

It is significant, although Freud does not discuss it here, that the two neuroses traversing the mind/body split, hysteria and hypochondria, which both involve a somatization of psychical conflicts, are sexually coded, are "feminine" neuroses in which it is precisely the status of the female body that is causing psychical conflict. Why is it that women are more likely to somatize their conflicts than men? Does this have anything to do with the female body image? With the problematic rift of mind and body which women are even less able than men to live out and live with?

The ego is not simply bounded by the "natural" body. The "natural" body, insofar as there is one, is continually augmented by the products of history and culture, which it readily incorporates into its own intimate space. In this, "man" must be recognized as a "prosthetic god," approaching the fantasy of omnipotence, or at least of a body well beyond its physical, geographical, and temporal immediacy. If the ego is a mapping of the body and if the body is able to incorporate a host of instrumental supplements, the ego (or at least its ideal) aspires to a megalomania worthy of gods:

> With every tool [man] is perfecting his own organs, whether motor or sensory, or is removing the limits to their functioning. Motor power places gigantic

forces at his disposal, which, like his muscles, he can employ in any direction; thanks to ship and aircraft neither water nor air can hinder his movements; by means of spectacles he corrects defects in the lens of his own eyes; by means of the telescope he sees into the far distance; by means of the microscope he overcomes the limits of visibility set by the structure of his retina. . . . Man has, as it were, become a kind of prosthetic God. When he puts on all his auxiliary organs he is truly magnificent, but these organs have not grown onto him and they still give him much trouble at times. (Freud 1929: 90–92)

The once-clear boundary between the mind and the body, nature and culture, becomes increasingly eroded. The very organ whose function is to distinguish biological or id impulses from sociocultural pressures, the ego, is always already the intermingling of both insofar as it is the consequence of the cultural, that is, significatory effects of the body, the meaning and love of the body as the subject lives it.

Lacan and the Imaginary Anatomy

Like Freud, Lacan claims that the ego has no a priori status. It comes into being in the mirror stage. The mirror stage provides the matrix or ground for the development of human subjectivity. Lacan describes the formative effect on the child's ego of the fascination with and introjection of an (externalized) image of its own body. For Lacan as for Freud, the ego is a kind of mapping or tracing of the subject's perceived and perceiving corporeality. It is a lived, corporeal identity that is at stake: the mirror stage functions to "establish a relation between the organism and its reality or, as they say, between the *Innenwelt* and the *Umwelt*" (Lacan 1977a: 24). And he seems to take Freud's comments about the ego being a bodily extension or projection very seriously. For Lacan, the ego is not an outline or projection of the real anatomical and physiological body but is an imaginary outline or projection of the body, the body insofar as it is imagined and represented for the subject by the image of others (including its own reflection in a mirror). The mirror stage provides the child with an anticipatory image of its own body as a *Gestalt*. The earliest recognition by the child of its bodily unity, that is, the recognition that its skin is the limit of its spatial location, is at the same time a misrecognition, insofar as the image with which the child identifies belies the child's own sensory and motor incapacities. Lacan makes it clear that the mirror stage institutes "an essential libidinal relationship with the body-image" (Lacan 1953: 1).

Lacan derives many of his insights regarding what he calls the "imaginary anatomy" from the work of a number of his predecessors and contemporaries, neurophysiologists, neuropsychologists, and psychoanalysts,[8] on the concept of the body image or body schema. I will return to them in more detail in the following chapter. The imaginary anatomy is an internalized image or map of the meaning that the body has for the subject, for others in its social world, and for the symbolic order conceived in its generality (that is, for a culture as a whole). It is an individual and collective fantasy of the body's forms and modes of action. This, Lacan claims, helps to explain the peculiar, nonorganic connections formed in hysteria and in such phenomena as the phantom limb.

It also helps to explain why there are distinct waves of particular forms of hysteria (some even call them fashions), i.e., why hysteria commonly exhibited forms of breathing difficulty (e.g., fainting, tussis nervosa, breathlessness, etc.) in the nineteenth century which, by comparison today, have relatively disappeared (perhaps with the exception of asthma and various "allergic" reactions) and yet why, taking their place as the most "popular" forms of hysteria today, are eating disorders, anorexia nervosa and bulimia in particular.[9]

Anorexia, for example, is arguably the most stark and striking sexualization of biological instincts: the anorexic may risk her very life in the attainment of a body image approximating her ideal. Neither a "disorder" of the ego nor, as popular opinion has it, a "dieting disease" gone out of control, anorexia can, like the phantom limb, be a kind of mourning for a pre-Oedipal (i.e., precastrated) body and a corporeal connection to the mother that women in patriarchy are required to abandon. Anorexia is a form of protest at the social meaning of the female body. Rather than seeing it simply as an out-of-control compliance with the current patriarchal ideals of slenderness, it is precisely a renunciation of these "ideals."

Lacan argues that instead of observing and following the neurological connections in organic paralyses, hysterical paralyses reproduce various naive or everyday beliefs about the ways the body functions. In an hysterical paralysis, it is more likely that limbs which are immobilized are unable to move from a joint, whereas in organic paralyses, the immobilization extends farther upward and encompasses many nerve and muscular connections not apparent to the lay observer. Hysterical paralyses follow commonsense views of the way the body works, especially those based on observation, visual appearance, rather than exhibiting any understanding of the body's underlying physiology:

> To call these symptoms functional is but to profess our ignorance, for they follow a pattern of a certain imaginary Anatomy which has typical forms of its own. In other words, the extraordinary somatic compliance which is the outward sign of this imaginary anatomy is only shown within certain limits. I would emphasize that the imaginary anatomy referred to here varies with the ideas (clear or confused) about bodily functions which are prevalent in a given culture. It all happens as if the body-image had an autonomous existence of its own, and by autonomous I mean here independent of objective structure. (Lacan 1953: 13)

Like Freud, Lacan refers to the notion of the cortical homunculus, seeing it as a neurological equivalent to the phenomenon of the child's mapping of the ego through the subject's identification with and internalization of the *Gestalt* of its mirror image. Although he is, not atypically, very vague on this point and gives no references to other research in the area, he does seem to have in mind the anatomists' notion of the cortical homunculus. He attributes the origins of the "intraorganic mirror" to "Man's" specific prematurity at birth, to a foundational lack at the origin of human subjectivity and desire. He implies that there is a cortical and psychical mapping of the body:

> In man . . . this relation to nature is altered by a certain dehiscence at the heart of the organism, a primordial Discord betrayed by the signs of uneasiness and motor uncoordination of the neonatal months. The objective notion of the anatomical incompleteness of the pyramidal systems and likewise the absence of certain humoral residues of the maternal organism confirm the view that I have formulated as the fact of a real *specific prematurity at birth* in man.
>
> It is worth noting, incidentally, that this is a fact recognized as such by embryologists, by the term *foetalization*, which determines the prevalence of the so-called superior apparatus of the neurax, and especially the cortex, which psycho-surgical operations lead us to regard as the intraorganic mirror. (Lacan 1977a: 4)

Lacan does not make explicit what kinds of surgery he is referring to here. Nonetheless, his insights do seem to make sense of such peculiar phenomena as the phantom limb and some of its neurological relatives.[10] In the phantom limb, the diseased limb that has been surgically removed continues to induce sensations of pain in the location that the limb used to occupy. In such cases, which occur with near universality in the surgical removal of mobile limbs,[11] the absence of a limb is as psychically invested as its presence. The phantom can indeed be regarded as a kind of libidinal memorial to the lost limb, a nostalgic tribute strongly cathected in an attempt to undermine the perceptual awareness of its absence. It does not completely undermine the experience of the absence of the limb but results in the phantom feeling "shell-like," "empty," merely formal and abstract, different from the way other limbs feel to the subject. The subject's healthy limbs, for example, exert a certain weight or gravity which is absent when the limb is amputated. The phantom limb exhibits many curiosities and seems to follow "laws" of its own very different from those regulating the rest of the body. While I will return in more neurological detail to the phantom limb later, it is significant that the phenomenon attests to the more or less tenacious cohesion of the imaginary anatomy or body schema. Like hysteria, hypochondria, and sexuality itself (see the next section), the phantom limb testifies to the pliability and fluidity of what is usually considered the inert, fixed, passive biological body. The biological body, if it exists at all, exists for the subject only through the mediation of an image or series of (social/cultural) images of the body and its capacity for movement and action. The phantom limb is a libidinally invested part of the body phantom, the image or *Doppelgänger* of the body the subject must develop if it is to be able to conceive of itself as an object and a body, and if it is to take on voluntary action in conceiving of itself as subject.

In the first instance, the imaginary anatomy begins to emerge only at the mirror stage, when the infant first comes to recognize itself as distinct and separate from the mother. At about six months of age, the child gradually comes to recognize its mirror reflection as an image of itself. For Lacan, this relation of imaginary identification is fraught with tensions and contradictions insofar as the child identifies with an image that both is and is not itself. It is itself in the sense that the mirror image is an inverted, virtual representation of the exterior of the body, an exteriority to which the child would have no other access except through a mirror (or through an equally problematic identification with the image of another, usually the mother).

Human subjects are able to see or feel only parts of their bodies. While the extremities are most readily visible, clearly there are many parts of the body to which the subject has no direct visual or tactile access, mainly the back. And although the subject can feel many parts of its body which are not normally visible, it can at best gain a serial notion of its own bodily parts, unless it has access to a unified and unifying image of the body as a whole. This, Lacan suggests, occurs as a result of the mirror phase. Lacan stresses that what the child sees in the mirror is a *Gestalt*, a totalized image of itself: this *Gestalt* forms the basis of an imaginary anatomy or body phantom which, although it will undergo modifications and transformations throughout the child's life, will nevertheless derive its stability (or lack of it) from the earliest stages of the child's self-representations. What it sees as a unified exteriority, however, belies the turbulence and chaos occasioned by its motor and sensory immaturity. The child feels disunified at exactly the same moment that it perceives an image of (possible) unity for itself:

> The fact is that the total form of the body by which the subject anticipates in a mirage the maturation of his powers is given to him only as *Gestalt*, that is to say, in an exteriority in which this form is certainly more constituent than constituted, but in which it appears to him above all in a contrasting size that fixes it and in a symmetry that inverts it, in contrast with the turbulent movements that the subject feels are animating him. Thus, this *Gestalt*—whose pregnancy should be regarded as bound up with the species, though its motor style remains scarcely recognizable—by these two aspects of its appearance, symbolizes the mental permanence of the *I* at the same time as it prefigures its alienating destination; it is still pregnant with the correspondences that unite the *I* with the statue in which man projects himself, with the phantoms that dominate him, or with the automaton in which, in an ambiguous relation, the world of his own making tends to find its completion. (Lacan 1977a: 2–3)

The mirror image provides an anticipatory ideal of unity to which the ego will always aspire. This image, preserved after the Oedipus complex as the ego ideal, is a model of bodily integrity, of outsideness, which the subject's experiences can never confirm. The ego is split between two extremes: a psychical interior, which requires continual stabilization, and a corporeal exterior, which remains labile, open to many meanings. Lacan suggests that this desire for a solid, stable identity may help explain our fascination with images of the human form.[12]

There is confirmation of the structure of the imaginary anatomy not only in the dreams of so-called normal (i.e., neurotic) subjects but also in the symptoms and hallucinations of psychotics, which contain residues of the pre-Oedipal body image, for example in the dreams and fantasies of the dissolution or "fragilization" of the body, which is an hallucinatory reactivation of memory traces of the primitive motor and sensory apparatus of the mirror-stage child. These reach their most extreme form in psychotic depersonalization, in which the subject's ego is no longer centered in its own body, and the body feels as if it has been taken over by others or is controlled by outside forces.[13] When autoscopy occurs, the subject may see itself as it were from the outside or may be haunted by the most terrifying of images, the *Doppelgänger*.[14] Autoscopy is commonly preceded by depersonalization in epileptic seizures, and in this case the subject may experience itself as outside its own boundaries, looking on in a detached manner. Here the phantom appears in bright and vivid detail, and may be perceived not only visually but also in auditory and tactile terms, as if emotionally and kinesthetically attached to the subject.[15]

These diverse forms of body-image disintegration or reorganization are possible only because the body image established in the mirror stage contains all the ingredients, which are stretched one way or distorted in another. They recall the complex dialectic the infant strives to resolve in its identifications, the tensions that Lacan locates between the image of the body-in-bits-and-pieces, the child's reconstruction of the body fragmented and divided by its diverse and scattered experiences, and by the body's compartmentalized sensations in the earliest stages of life, in which experience is serialized, momentary, fleeting, without any ongoing unity:

> Such typical images appear in dreams, as well as in fantasies. They may show, for example, the body of the mother as having a mosaic structure like that of a stained glass window. More often, the resemblance is to a jig-saw puzzle, with the separate parts of the body of a man or an animal in disorderly array. Even more significant for our purposes are the incongruous images in which strange trophies, trunks, are cut up in slices and stuffed with the most unlikely fillings, strange appendages in eccentric positions, reduplications of the penis, images of the cloaca represented as a surgical excision, often accompanied in male patients by fantasies of pregnancy. (Lacan 1953: 13)

In other words, the stability of the unified body image, even in the so-called normal subject, is always precarious. It cannot be simply taken for granted as an accomplished fact, for it must be continually renewed, not through the subject's conscious efforts but through its ability to conceive of itself as a subject and to separate itself from its objects and others to be able to undertake willful action. The dissolution or disintegration of the unified body schema risks throwing the subject into the preimaginary real, the domain inhabited by the psychotic.[16] In such a state, the sense of autonomy and agency that accompanies the imaginary and symbolic orders is lost, being replaced by the fantasies of being externally controlled, which are images of fragmentation, and being haunted by part objects derived from earlier, more primitive experiences.[17]

> This fragmented body—which term I have also introduced into our system of theoretical references—usually manifests itself in dreams when the movement of analysis encounters a certain level of aggressive disintegration in the individual. It then appears in the form of disjointed limbs, or of those organs represented in exoscopy, growing wings and taking up arms for intestinal persecutions—the very same that the visionary Hieronymus Bosch has fixed, for all time, in painting, in their ascent from the fifteenth century to the imaginary zenith of modern man. But this form is even tangibly revealed at the organic level, in the lines of "fragilization" that define the anatomy of phantasy, as exhibited in the schizoid and spasmodic symptoms of hysteria. (Lacan, 1977a: 4–5)

The imaginary anatomy, then, is at work not only in the everyday functioning of neurotic and perverse subjects, where it operates most commonly at the level of the sexualization of parts or the whole of the body, but also in the operation of drives and their privileged objects. It is also crucial in explaining the symptomatology of psychosis. It is the precondition and raw material of a stable, that is, symbolic, identity which the child acquires as a result of the resolution of the Oedipus complex. Its reorganization or decomposition witnesses psychotic breakdown.

The constitution of the subject's imaginary identity in the mirror phase establishes a provisional identity which still requires the stabilization, ordering, and placement of the subject in a sociosymbolic position where it can engage in symbolic and linguistic exchange with others. It also creates the conditions of possibility for the child's earliest and most primitive notions of milieu, context, environment, or location. In other words, it conditions and makes possible the child's earliest notions of spatiality and temporality. Reduplicated in the specular image is the child's environment. For the first time, the child is not absorbed by its environment (which means both occupying no space at all and being all-pervasive—which amounts to the same thing in this context) but is now part of space, taking up a place or location in space. Its multifarious forms of lived spatiality are generally dominated by vision. Spatiality comes to conform to a spatiality dominated by vision, a spatiality of hierarchized perspective. This notion of spatiality and, correlatively, temporality, insofar as the mirror stage is the midposition between the retrospective fantasies of incompleteness and lack and the anticipatory fantasies of unity and wholeness,[18] is a mutual condition or accompaniment of the acquisition of the body image.

In his studies of the earliest years of the child's development, Stern argues that the child's first notion of space is "buccal," a "space that can be contained in, or exploited by his [the child's] mouth. Not only the mouth but the whole respiratory apparatus gives the child a kind of experience of space. After that, other regions of the body intervene and come into prominence" (Merleau-Ponty 1965: 122). In the mirror stage, the child supersedes this buccal, enclosed spatiality with the first notions of a binarized space capable of being divided into real and virtual planes. The image becomes categorized as a reflection of itself and not simply as another object located within a single and homogeneous space. It is only under this assumption that the child recognizes the frame or border dividing the real from the virtual, the image from the object:

> The child knows well that he is there where his introceptive body is, and yet in the depth of the mirror he sees the same being present, in a bizarre way, in a visible appearance. There is a mode of spatiality in the specular image that is altogether distinct from adult spatiality. In the child, says Wallon, there is a kind of space clinging to the image. All images tend to present themselves in space, including the image of the mirror as well. According to Wallon, this spatiality of adherence will be reduced by intellectual development. We will learn gradually to return the specular image to the introceptive body, and reciprocally, to treat the quasi-locatedness and pre-spatiality of the image as an appearance that counts for nothing against the unique space of real things. . . . An ideal space would be substituted for the space clinging to the image, since for the child it is a question of understanding that what seems to be in different places is in fact in the same place. This can occur only in passing to a higher level of spatiality that is no longer the intuitive space in which the images occupy their own place. (Merleau-Ponty 1965: 129–30)

Lacan describes the kind of primitive spatiality that the child develops in the mirror phase as "kaleidoscopic." He claims that this subjective or imaginary sense of spatiality is the precondition of the intersubjective or shared (social) space required for all symbolic interactions and for an objective or scientific (i.e., measurable, quantifiable) form of space. The virtual duplication of the subject's body, the creation of a symmetry measured from the mirror plane, is necessary for these more sophisticated, abstract, and derivative notions of spatiality:

> The notion of the role of spatial symmetry in man's narcissistic structure is essential in the establishment of the bases of a psychological analysis of space— however, I can do no more here than simply indicate the place of such an analysis. Let us say that animal psychology has shown us that the individual's relation to a particular spatial field is, in certain species, mapped socially, in a way that raises it to the category of subjective membership. I would say that it is the subjective possibility of the mirror projection of such a field into the field

of the other that gives human space its original "geometrical" structure, a structure that I would be happy to call *kaleidoscopic*. Such, at least, is the space in which the imagery of the ego develops, and which rejoins the objective space of reality. (Lacan 1977a: 27)

Caillois and the Space of Legendary Psychasthenia

In his paper "Mimicry and Legendary Psychasthenia" (1984), Caillois explores the notion of spatiality manifested in the phenomenon of mimicry within the natural world. His analysis is clearly a powerful influence on Lacan's notions of the mirror stage, the order of the imaginary, and psychosis. Caillois presents a sociological and ethological analysis of the behavior of insects which mimic other insects or their own natural environment, which "feign" their surroundings or other creatures. Mimesis is particularly significant in outlining the ways in which the relations between an organism and its environment are blurred and confused—the way in which its environment is not distinct from the organism but is an active internal component of its "identity." Caillois claims that mimicry does not serve any adaptive function. Its purpose is not to ensure the survival of the species through disguising the insect, hiding it from its predators. Mimicry does not have survival value, for most predators rely on the sense of smell rather than of vision.[19] Mimicry has no value in the dark. Caillois considers mimicry a "luxury" or excess over natural survival, inexplicable in terms of self-protection or species survival. He abandons naturalistic explanations to seek some kind of answer in psychology. The mimesis characteristic of certain species of insects has to do with the distinctions it establishes between itself and its environment, including other species. Mimicry is a consequence not of space but of the *representation* of and captivation by space.

Caillois likens the insect's ability for morphological imitation to the psychosis Pierre Janet described as "legendary psychasthenia," in which the psychotic is unable to locate himself or herself in a position in space:

> It is with represented space that the drama becomes specific, since the living creature, the organism, is no longer the origin of the coordinates, but one point among others; it is dispossessed of its privilege and literally *no longer knows where to place itself*. One can recognize the characteristic scientific attitude and, indeed, it is remarkable that represented spaces are just what is multiplied by contemporary science: Finsler's spaces, Fermat's spaces, Riemann-Christoffel's hyperspace, abstract, generalized, open and closed spaces, spaces dense in themselves, thinned out and so on. The feeling of personality, considered as the organism's feeling of distinctness from its surroundings, of the connection between consciousness and a particular point in space, cannot fail under these conditions to be seriously undermined; one then enters into the psychology of psychasthenia, and more specifically of *legendary psychasthenia*, if we agree to

use this name for the disturbance in the above relations between personality and space. (Caillois 1984: 28; emphasis in original)

For Caillois, psychasthenia is a response to the lure posed by space for the subject's identity. For the subject to take up a position as a subject, it must be able to be situated in the space occupied by its body. This anchoring of subjectivity in its body is the condition of coherent identity, and, moreover, the condition under which the subject *has a perspective* on the world, and becomes a source for vision, a point from which vision emanates and to which light is focused. In certain cases of psychosis, this coincidence or meshing of the subject and the body fails to occur. Some psychotics are unable to locate themselves where they should be. They may look at themselves from outside, as another might; they may hear the voices of others in their heads. The subject is captivated and replaced by space, blurred with the positions of others:

> *I know where I am, but I do not feel as though I'm at the spot where I find myself.* To these dispossessed souls, space seems to be a devouring force. Space pursues them, encircles them, digests them. . . . It ends by replacing them. Then the body separates itself from thought, the individual breaks the boundary of his skin and occupies the other side of his senses. He tries to look at *himself* from any point whatever in space. He feels himself becoming space, *dark space where things cannot be put.* He is similar, not similar to something, but just *similar.* And he invents spaces of which he is "the convulsive possession." (Caillois 1984: 30; emphasis in original)

Psychosis is the human analogue of mimicry in the insect world (which may perhaps be conceived as a kind of "natural psychosis"): both represent what Caillois describes as the "depersonalization by assimilation to space" (30). Both the psychotic and the insect renounce their rights to occupy a perspectival point, abandoning themselves to being spatially located by/as others. The primacy of one's own perspective is replaced by the gaze of another, for whom the subject is merely a point in space and not the focal point organizing space. The representation of space is thus a correlate of one's ability to locate oneself as the point of reference of space: the space represented is a complement of the kind of subject who occupies it.[20]

The idea of space, the child's notion of location and positionality, then, is acquired only gradually and through various phases of neurological and psychological development. It is both derived from and makes concrete experience possible. The disorganized and as yet unintegrated information available to the infant at the sensorimotor level provides it with a diverse series of spaces—sensorial, postural, prehensile, and locomotive—which are hierarchically subordinated to a singular space at the time when spatiality becomes independent of the bodily gestures and movements of the child. These very different modes of spatiality and spatial representation become ordered and unified according to the space of vision, the perspectival space that has dominated perception at least since the Renaissance. Only through the resolution of the mirror-stage dilemmas of identity, when the child becomes able to distinguish itself definitively from objects and above all from others, can this space be attained. The child's relation with others is exceedingly complex, and its confusion and identification with others remain blurred and indistinct until the resolution of a form of infantile transitivism, as outlined in the work of child psychologists. The researches of Charlotte Bühler and the Chicago school are vital here, and are carefully augmented and developed in the writings of Lacan, Wallon, Guillaume, and Spitz.

Wallon describes this as a phase of alternation, in which the child becomes not only able to distinguish the roles of agent and spectator (active and passive) but, more interesting, to play at both roles, giver and receiver, actor and audience, switching from one role to the other. This transitivism positions the child in a role of spatial reciprocity with the other, a space in which its position is attained only relative to the position of the other, yet where the position of the other is reciprocally defined by the position of the subject. From such a transitivism, the child first gains access to a notion of the social field, a field within which it is to find its identity and whose parameters, according to Lacan, are defined and guaranteed only with reference to the Other, the symbolic.

> [The child] plays the active and passive roles alternately: the one who hits and the one who hides, the one who seeks; the one who throws the ball, the one who catches it. These games of role alternation allow the child to recognize himself, though still in a neutral and anonymous way. He inhabits the two poles of a single situation without yet choosing one or the other and making that his personal locus. He is no more able to identify himself consistently, than he is to identify his antagonist. He remains prey to uncertain fluctuations and full of ambivalence. All this, however, leads up to the moment when he will, in fact, take up one position or the other, often for no other reason than the need to do so. (Wallon, in Voyat 1984: 26)

A stabilized body image or imaginary anatomy, a consistent and abiding sense of self and bodily boundaries, requires and entails understanding one's position vis-à-vis others, one's place at the apex or organizing point in the perception of space (which, in turn, implies a knowledge that one could also be an object in the spatial fields of others), as well as a set of clear-cut distinctions between the inside and the outside of the body, the active and passive positions, and, as we will see, a position as a sexually determinate subject.

Psychology and Biology

Freud's preoccupation with the relations between biology and psychology, his attempt to link the operations of bodily functions to the operation of psychical functions, is most directly expressed in the various attempts he made to present a model of psychical topography. Although it is clear that Freud devised a number of different, sometimes incompatible, representations of the organization of the psyche,[21] I will concentrate here on his earliest formulations of the psyche, developed in 1895 in the posthumously published "Project for a Scientific Psychology" and later elaborated in "The Unconscious" (1915a) and "Instincts and Their Vicissitudes" (1915b).

Freud makes clear in the introduction to "The Project" that his goal is "to furnish a psychology that shall be a natural science: that is, to represent psychical processes as quantitatively determinate states of specifiable material particles" (1895: 295). These elementary material particles Freud identifies as neurones. Although many have disqualified Freud's model insofar as they claim it relies on an anachronistic nineteenth-century view of neurophysiology (e.g., Reiser 1984: 95–96), others have claimed that not only is his argument's validity to be judged independently of the accuracy of nineteenth-century biology but, moreover, his views actually challenge and transform this biology so that they closely anticipate modern views (e.g., Laplanche 1976). Laplanche does not find nineteenth-century biology so problematic as Freud's inaccurate reading of nineteenth-century physics and Freud's attempt to apply a mechanistic neuronal model—a psychophysics—to biology. His working hypothesis in this neuronal model is that there are a vast number of identical neurones whose only differentiation comes from the position they occupy in the neurological system. Those nearer the periphery or surface function differently from those at the center, given the different functions each must perform. Neurones tend to divest themselves of energy as rapidly as possible. This he calls, following Fechner, the "constancy principle," which, much later in his career, he will term the death drive. In deriving the death drive from Fechner's "constancy principle," Freud conflates it with the principle of inertia, and it is only through such a confusion that he "scientifically" legitimates the postulation of the death drive. There is a tendency for the organism as a whole, as well as at its most elementary level, to minimize its states of excitation, retaining only the barest levels of energy. The constancy principle functions not only in the case of stimuli received from the external world but also in relation to endogenous stimuli or needs. With external stimuli, the organism has the capacity to utilize its sensory and motor skills either to psychically register the stimulus or, in the case of danger, to flee. This is of course not possible with endogenous stimuli, which require the attainment of suitable objects to satisfy those needs.

The nervous system is comprised of a vast network of identically structured neurones—like horizontal Ys webbed together—each of which is connected to three other neurones. These neurones form a system insofar as the energy received at one end of the neurone must be discharged at the other end, through a bifurcated choice of pathways. An excitation is thus transmitted through the nervous system, one neuronal pathway at a time. Because each energetic impulse has at least two possible paths of discharge, the effects of various stimuli are differentiated, depending on which neuronal pathways they traverse. Between each neurone is a contact barrier, which exerts a resistance, a kind of friction, in the automatic transmission of energy from one cell to the next. The presence of this point of resistance means that if the neurone is to discharge the energy that has been invested in it, the quantity of this energy must be greater than the quantity of resistance. When this is not the case, the energy is discharged from the neurone in trying to overcome the contact barrier but is not registered in the next successive neurone. Presumably this occurs with the vast majority of perceptual stimuli, the plethora of trivial details that do not gain access to memory systems or to consciousness. Only those stimuli which are invested with a strong enough affect and are repeated a number of times gain the force to acquire mnemic or conscious registration.

This is the neuronal system in its absolute simplicity. Freud distinguishes two kinds of neurones, or at least two kinds of location or function for neurones. Those at the "surface," or periphery, of the nervous system, closest to sensory inputs, allow the passage of energy through them as if there were no contact barriers, exerting no resistance to energetic inputs. If they exert no resistance, they are not permanently modified by the stimulation they receive. They are permeable, serving the function of registering but not recording perceptual impressions. Perceptions pass through these neurones without predisposing them for future perceptions. This nonconscious perceptual system is distinguished from those neurones closer to the core of the neurological system which comprise the mnemic systems, for these are impermeable. They exert considerable resistance to perceptual impingements. Thus when the quantity of energy is cathected strongly enough to traverse the contact barriers, these neurones are permanently modified and in this sense can be regarded as a mnemic record of perceptions. Each such impermeable neurone has several contact barriers and thus creates what in Freud's later work are described as associative networks with other neurones, a trace or frayage of pathways. Here Freud identifies the permeable neurones with the brain and the impermeable neurones with gray matter (1895: 303).

For Freud, the crucial question in establishing a scientific psychology is that of translation. How are the quantitative and neurological characteristics of the neurones translated into the terms of psychological and qualitative theory?

> . . . a place has to be found for the content of consciousness. . . . Consciousness gives us what are called *qualities*—sensations which are *different* in a great multiplicity of ways and whose *difference* is distinguished according to its relations with the external world. Within this difference, there are series, similarities and so on, but there are in fact no quantities in it. It may be asked how qualities originate and where qualities originate. (308.)

This question is crucial, for it amounts to the question of how psychical or mental qualities can emerge from purely neurological quantities of excitation. It asks about the genesis of the psychical from the biological, which Freud himself has described as "the mysterious leap" from the body to the mind. Freud claims, following Locke, that qualities do not originate in the external world. Conscious and unconscious perceptions are qualitatively colored. If this is the case, then somewhere in between the neurological registration of perception and its conscious registration, qualities must arise. He excludes the permeable and the impermeable (perceptual and mnemic) neuronal systems, for these systems are by definition sensitive only to quantities of excitation. To account for the genesis of qualities, Freud postulates a third neuronal system, beyond perception and memory, which is excited along with perception but not along with reproduction or memory and whose states of excitation give rise to qualities, i.e., conscious sensations (308). In Freud's conception this third neuronal system is the result not only of the transmission of quantities of energy but also of their frequency or periodicity. This periodicity, which is unaffected by contact barriers or resistances, originates, Freud claims, in the sense organs, in which qualities are also represented by "different periods of neuronal motion" (310).

> It is only by means of such complicated and far from perspicuous hypotheses that I have hitherto succeeded in introducing the phenomenon of consciousness into the structure of quantitative psychology. No attempt, of course, can be made to explain how it is that excitatory processes in [the third neuronal perceptual system] brings consciousness along with them. It is only a question of establishing a coincidence between the characteristics of consciousness that are known to us and processes in [the third neuronal system] which vary in parallel with them. (311)

Although Freud resorts to a psychophysical parallelism in which consciousness is not identified with the third neurological system but simply accompanies it, his own hypotheses allow him a stronger claim: that consciousness or the perception of qualities is the result of a particular modality of quantitative excitations, that it *is*, and not just accompanies, the periodicity of excitations. This third neuronal system is capable of distinguishing between perceptions which arise directly from the sense organs and indirectly from the external world and ideas, which are endogenous in origin, through "the indication of reality" which Freud later calls "reality testing." While this indication of reality breaks down in the case of an hallucinatory reactivation of a memory trace, the discharge through consciousness and the action of the energy traversing the psychical systems demonstrate the congruence of the perceptual contents of consciousness with the world from which the perception arose.

In this earliest topographical account of the psyche, Freud has outlined the progression of a perceptual impingement from its first neurological registration, through its facilitation of mnemic systems, on its path to conscious registration. This model, which also accounts for the functioning of the ego and the mechanisms of psychical defense,[22] leaves relatively unclear the intervening psychical agencies between the memory systems and consciousness. This Freud has elaborated in considerably more detail in chapter seven of *The Interpretation of Dreams* (1900). He augmented this model in "The Unconscious" (1915a), where he claims that, interceding between the mnemic systems and consciousness, are the two psychical systems of the unconscious and the preconscious, divided by the barrier of censorship. The transformation of quantitative to qualitative excitations thus occurs well before the conscious registration of the perception. The movement occurs in the translation of terms between the mnemic systems, which involve quantitative transformations of the neurone, and the unconscious, which is composed of nothing but perceptions which strive for conscious expression, i.e., wishes. This is thus the threshold point between neurological and psychological processes, the point at which the outer material impingements deflect into an internal, psychical order.

Freud denies any causal relation between the physiological process and the psychological process. This is clear, he claims, because if the cause is logically and temporally distinct from its effects (this is part of the very definition of causation), physiological processes do not cease when the psychological processes emerge. Instead, physiological causes have their own physiological effects. Rather than causal relations, he sees a relation of correspondence or parallelism.[23] But it is not clear that this isomorphism is a necessary postulate: it places psychoanalysis firmly in the tradition of Cartesian dualism, which Freud's work seems at other places to strongly contest. His assault on dualism is perhaps most readily perceived in his notion of sexual drives, the drive being a concept that lies midway between the mind and the body, irreducible to either. In understanding how his notion of the drives resists the imperatives of dualism, we may be in a better position to understand the processes of translation between quantity and quality that distinguish neurological from psychological processes while nevertheless maintaining their intimate connections. As Freud says, the instinct or drive is "a concept at the frontier between the mental and the somatic" (1915b: 122).

Drives and Instincts

In "Instincts and their Vicissitudes" (1915b), Freud returns to the neurological model he elaborated in "The Project." The most elementary postulate is that the nervous system functions to rid itself of excitations. Freud claims that instincts function in quantitative rather than qualitative terms (1915b: 123); and he distinguishes between exogenous and endogenous stimuli. He lists three characteristics which differentiate the endogenous excitations arising from instincts or drives from the exogenous perceptions arising from the external world. First, an instinct/drive arises from internal rather than external sources; second, whereas a perceptual or sensory stimulus is a momentary force, an instinct/drive exerts a constant, relentless pressure; and third, this pressure ceases only when the appropriate objects put an end to the internal source of stimulation—in other words, unlike an external stimulus or perception, an instinct/drive requires an object of satisfaction. Rather than chart the progress of perceptual stimuli through the various psychical exigencies, as Freud does in "The Project" and elsewhere, in "Instincts" he focuses on the psychical mechanisms and processes involved in dealing with an endogenous force.

The notion of the sexual drive is close to, but needs to be differentiated from, the notion of biologically determined instincts. If the instinct can be defined as a biologically universal, preformed set of processes and behaviors, endogenous in origin and necessary for the maintenance of life (in its simplest form it is usually represented on the model of the reflex),[24] then it can be argued that even apparently incontestable processes such as hunger, thirst, and the need to urinate or defecate—which are generally regarded as instincts par excellence—are not biologically fixed but are amenable to a psychosymbolic takeover, in which they are retraced, taken over, as sexualized drives. From the moment this sexualization occurs, instincts can no longer remain purely programmed: the drive transforms and transcends the instincts.

In *The Three Essays on the Theory of Sexuality* (1905), Freud proposes three general characteristics which define all sexual drives (infantile and adult). Here he refers to the oral drive and its relation to the hunger instinct, and he also acknowledges that some non-organ-based drives do not conform to this model: "the drives of scopophilia, exhibitionism and cruelty, which appear in a sense independently of erotogenic zones" (1905: 191).

> Our study of thumb-sucking or sensual sucking has already given us the three essential characteristics of an infantile sexual manifestation. At its origin it *attaches itself to* one of the vital somatic functions [i.e., instincts]; it has as yet no sexual object, and is thus *auto-erotic*; and its sexual aim is dominated by an *erotogenic* zone. (1905: 182–83)

The drives are thus attached to biological processes; they are autoerotic and regulated by an erotogenic zone. The notion of propping, or anaclisis, is what seems to interest Laplanche the most: this movement of propping[25] describes the complex derivation and departure of drives from biological instincts. The drive leans upon the instinct, is supported by it, or, more accurately, retraces the neurological and biological pathways across the subject's body that the instinctual and biological processes took, thus mimicking them and taking on the same attributes of preformed instincts (this may explain why the sexual drives are assumed to be instinctive in popular imagination). The drive, however, deviates from the instinct insofar as it takes for itself not a real object—food—but a fantasmatic object, an object defined primarily through the lack or absence of a real object. Freud describes this in the advent of sensual sucking, the first (oral) sexual drive to emerge out of the hunger instinct. Sensual sucking emerges at that point where milk is no longer the sought-after object; instead the child now seeks the pleasure of the sucking movements themselves, a repetition of the processes (or some of them) involved in feeding, in the absence or as a displacement of the need for food. The child will now suck on a wide variety of objects, none of which can satisfy its hunger:

> In orality . . . two phases may be delineated: one consisting in sucking of the breast, and a second, quite different from the first, which is characterized as "sensual sucking." In the first phase, breast-sucking for nourishment—we are faced with a function or . . . with a total instinctual pattern of behavior, one which is, in fact, so complete . . . that it is precisely hunger, the feeding pattern, which the "popular conception" assumes to be *the model of every instinct*. . . . Simultaneous with the feeding function's achievement of satisfaction in nourishment, a sexual process begins to appear. Parallel with feeding there is a stimulation of lips and tongue by the nipple and the flow of warm milk. The stimulation is initially modelled on the function, so that between the two, it is at first barely possible to distinguish a difference. (Laplanche 1976: 17)

The drive is able to imitate or prop itself on the instinct because it is able to borrow the sites, sources, and aims of the instincts, inserting a new fantasy object in place of the object of need, enervating the circuit or flow between the external object, the bodily erotogenic source, and the fantasmatic link between them. This is possible only because the erotogenic zone functions both as a biological and as a sexual organ. But this is true not only of the mouth and digestive system but of every one of the biological processes and all organs, which, through the processes necessary for the preservation of life (instincts) or perhaps through some accident or organic disorder, may function to provide a biologically registered marking of the body. Freud describes this as "somatic compliance," by which he means that by being singled out as different from, as significant relative to, other biological processes or organs, an organ becomes susceptible to a psychical takeover. If, for example, the subject breaks a limb, undergoes an operation, or is subjected to recurring illnesses, the region of the body most affected, depending on the point in the subject's life history when it occurs, may become loaded with significances which make it ripe for sexualization.

It may be for this reason that Freud claims that every orifice, every external organ, and possibly even the internal organs—including the brain itself—are capable of becoming an erotogenic zone.[26] Any part of the body is capable of sexualization, although which parts become eroticized is determined by the individual's life history (and especially the history of its corporeality). There is a complete plasticity in the body's compliance with sexual meanings.

Sexuality insinuates itself in the various biological and instinctual processes because there is, as it were, a space which it can occupy, an incompleteness at the level of instincts that it can harness for its own purposes. Lacan links this incompleteness to biological prematurity at birth, in other words, to the failure or immaturity of instincts to serve the purposes of survival in the neonatal period. The child's instincts are unable to support the child's needs because of its sensory and motor incapacities. It is naturally dependent, not only for its well-being but also for its barest survival, on the active good will of others. In this sense, paradoxically, human subjects are biologically social, social out of biological necessity. A lack at the level of instincts distinguishes the advent of human desire from animal need. This lack requires the augmentation of language and representation understood more broadly: when the child is unable for many years to fend for and to take care of itself, it is able to supplement its needs, indeed to replace them or cover them over, with its capacity for representation.

Any corporeal process, event, or experience is capable of sexualization. Freud regards sexuality as a "concomitant effect" (his very phrase in discussing psychophysical causality) of a vast range of bodily experiences:

> Sexual excitation arises as a concomitant effect as soon as the intensity of those processes passes beyond certain quantitative limits. What we have called the component drives of sexuality are either derived directly from these internal sources or are composed of elements both from those sources and from the erotogenic zones. (Freud 1905: 204–5)

The sexual drives displace the reality of the objects, aims, and bodily sources of the instincts and biological processes. In the case of orality, for example, there is a metonymic shift from the biological orientation to milk to a sexual orientation which takes the breast, thumb, or their potentially infinite substitutes as sexual objects. This is true of all the sexual drives. The biological processes or instincts seem to provide the ground or preconditions for the emergence of sexual impulses, but they must not be too closely identified with them: without these biological processes tracing a path through the body, the raw materials for sexuality would not exist. But these biological processes are not enough. What must be added to them is a set of meanings, a network of desires which, in the first instance, emanate from and are transmitted by the mother or nurturer. These desires and significances impose a set of (pliable and usually inarticulable) meanings on the child's bodily processes. In this sense, it is not surprising that in the case of so-called wild children, children raised outside the constraints and significances, there is neither sexual drive nor language.[27]

Sexual drives result from the insertion of biological or bodily processes into networks of signification and meaning; through this immersion, they become bound up with and intimately connected to the structure of individual and collective fantasies and significations. The drive is a result of corporeal significances, the binding of bodily processes and activities to systems of meaning.[28] This signifying and fantasmatic dimension is necessary for the sexual to emerge as such and for the establishment of desire. The domain of sexual drives is doubly implicated in representation and signification. On one hand, it is bound up with the signifying order of parental desire and meanings, which are projected onto the child's body and bodily processes. In this sense, sexuality is imposed from without. But the child must be seen not only as a passive victim of this imposition (a powerful tendency in many current feminist preoccupations with child abuse and incest) but also as an active agent trying to find its place in the web of meanings into which it is born. On the other hand, the child's sexuality as it is subjectively experienced is a retracing, a psychical transcription, of biological processes, organs, and pathways. The body is quite literally rewritten, traced over, by desire. Desire is based on a veritable cartography of the body (one's own as well as that of the other). The sexual is able to displace the biological only because there is a lack at the level of the biological. Sexuality, contrary to popular opinion, is thus not the result of (a pubertal) exuberance or excess of biological processes; it is a consequence of an insufficiency, an inadequate match between the child and its "nature."[29]

We may now return to the radical notion of psychical topography Freud theorized, to indicate the kinds of subversion of the mind/body dualism his model effects. In the same way that sexuality is derived from instinctual processes through a deviation from and retranscription of their modes of corporeality, so too the psyche is not identical with or merely the correlate of physiological and neurological processes but is their retracing and retranscription. Neither simply in continuity with the neurological (as reductionism implies) nor radically divided from it by an unbridgeable chasm (as dualism implies), the psychical agencies are the translation into different terminology of a "language" of neuronal activity. Lacan has plausibly reinterpreted Freud's neurological model in the terms of Saussurean linguistics: if the neurone is a metaphor of the signifier (and as a material, this time an energetic rather than a graphic or auditory trace, this is not an implausible supposition) and if the relation between cathected neurones and facilitated pathways is a metaphor of the signifying chain, then neurology is always already a mode of signification (Lacan suggests as much in his claim that even the chromosomal structure can be regarded as a form of linguistic double articulation, a primitive or elemental language).[30] The psyche is, then, the transliteration of neurological structures. Neurology and biology do not provide a base for a psychological superstructure: a base exists independent of a superstructure rather than in a relation of mutual influence or dependence. Rather, they are the material constraints from which psychical and sexual phenomena are the deviation and completion. This neurological model finds its closest analogy and material illustration (ironically, in terms of the charge of anachronism leveled at Freud's neurology) in the digital or binarized functioning of the computer. The bifurcated neuronal pathways, the various "paths" traced across the neural system, represent the various "choices" or "decisions" functioning in the computer.

> Sexuality, in effect, leaves life out of its field of operation, borrowing from it only prototypes of its fantasies. The ego, on the contrary, seems to take over the vital order as its own; it takes it over in its essence: constituted as it is on

the model of a living being with its level, its homeostasis, and its constancy principle. In addition, it assumes charge of the vital order by virtue of the fact that it replaces and compensates for the vital functions. (Laplanche 1976: 83)

Masculine and Feminine

The question of biology and of the mind/body relation is raised once again, and in a most crucial and complex fashion, in Freud's account of the differences between the sexes. This is clearly the location of the most controversial and, in feminist terms, most contested elements of his work. Yet even here, in spite of Freud's clear biologism, there are also concepts and ideas which indicate a considerably more sophisticated understanding of sexual difference than many views commonly attributed to him. This is not, of course, to deny that there are still major problems from a feminist point of view regarding his understanding of the differences between the sexes, and particularly female sexuality. Although this cannot be examined in any thoroughgoing detail, it is nevertheless worthwhile indicating some of the major areas of feminist concern as well as those places in Freud's writing where his position entails much that could be of value to feminist theory regarding the body and sexual difference.

Considerable feminist labor has already been devoted to an analysis and interrogation of Freud's account of the Oedipus complex and of the psychical implications of anatomical sex differences, and I do not want to rehearse those arguments again.[31] Whether feminists evaluate Freud's work with critical commitment, as in the case of de Lauretis, Silverman, Gallop, and Irigaray, or with wholehearted acceptance, as in the case of Mitchell, Ragland Sullivan, and others, they seem to agree that his account of sexual difference, with its references to the phallic mother, the castration complex, and the Oedipus complex, provides an accurate description of the processes which produce masculine and feminine subjects within our Western, patriarchal, capitalist culture. Their disagreements arise regarding the universality of Freud's account and its value in the prognosis of future social relations—that is, regarding the necessity of the domination of the phallus.

Freud's account of the acquisition of masculine and feminine psychical positions can be interpreted plausibly as an account of the ways in which the male and female bodies are given meaning and structured with reference to their relative social positions. While it is clear that Freud himself is not really concerned with the question of anatomy per se, seeking instead the psychical implications of anatomical differences, and while it is also clear that he nevertheless justifies his claims regarding the order of psychical events with recourse to a kind of confrontation the child has with (the meaning of) anatomy, his position can be understood in terms of how meanings, values, and desires construct male and female bodies (and particularly how their differences are represented). His postulation of the Oedipus complex and the castration threat can be read as an analysis and explanation of the social construction of women's bodies as a lack and the correlative (and dependent) constitution of the male body as phallic.

The notions of phallic and castrated are not simply superimposed on pre-given bodies, an added attribute that could, in other cultural configurations, be removed to leave "natural" sexual differences intact. Rather, the attribution of a phallic or a castrated status to sexually different bodies is an internal condition of the ways those bodies are lived and given meaning right from the start (with or without the child's knowledge or compliance). There is no natural body to return to, no pure sexual difference one could gain access to if only the distortions and deformations of patriarchy could be removed or transformed. The phallus binarizes the differences between the sexes, dividing up a sexual-corporeal continuum into two mutually exclusive categories which in fact belie the multiplicity of bodies and body types.[32]

I have already outlined the ways in which pre-Oedipal forms of sexuality are a retracing of biological zones and tracts. There is no reason to believe that the processes of retracing do not occur in all the psychosexual stages and with all bodily organs and activities. Moreover, although most psychoanalysts do not attribute sexual difference and specificity to the pre-Oedipal stages and most theorists of and experimenters on the body image do not discuss the question of the sex of the body image or the ways in which the body image does or does not include the sex of the body, it seems incontestable that the type of genitals and secondary sexual characteristics one has (or will have) must play a major role in the type of body image one has and that the type of self-conception one has is directly linked to the social meaning and value of the sexed body. Indeed, an argument could be made that the beloved category of "gender," so commonly used in feminist theory to avoid the problems of essentialism, could be understood not as the attribution of social and psychological categories to a biologically given sex but in terms that link gender much more closely to the specificities of sex. Gender is not an ideological superstructure added to a biological base. Masculine or feminine gender cannot be neutrally attributed to bodies of either sex. Therefore, in agreement with Gatens (1990), it becomes clear that the "masculinity" of the male body cannot be the same as the "masculinity" of the female body, because the kind of body inscribed makes a difference to the meanings and functioning of gender that emerges.

Lacan says explicitly what is implied in Freud's understanding of sexual difference: while it makes perfect sense for the young boy, before he understands the anatomical differences between the sexes, to see others (animate and inanimate), as in the case of Little Hans,[33] on a model derived from his own body morphology, it makes no sense at all to claim, as Freud and Lacan do, that the girl too sees the whole world on a model derived from the boy's experience. This makes no sense, and indeed it is the site of an amazing blindness on the part of these founding fathers of psychoanalytic feminism, to explain why both the boy and the girl regard themselves, each other, and the others in their world as phallic unless the phallus has an a priori privilege in the constitution of the body image. This is precisely Lacan's claim:

> All the phenomena we are discussing [that is, the various manifestations of the body image in psychical life] seem to exhibit the laws of *Gestalt*; the fact that the penis is dominant in the shaping of the body image is evidence of this. Though this may shock the sworn champions of the autonomy of female sexuality, such dominance is a fact and one moreover which cannot be put down to cultural influences alone. (Lacan 1953: 13)

Among Lacan's most deliberately provocative statements (in a body of work that abounds in provocation), it is unclear that the "laws of *Gestalt*" entail the dominance of the penis in the body image *unless* female sexuality is already, even in the pre-Oedipal stages when the body image is being formed according to the "laws of *Gestalt*," construed as castrated. Now, in one sense this is true. If patriarchy requires that female sexual organs be regarded more as the absence or lack of male organs than in any autonomous terms, then for the others in the child's social world, the child's female body is lacking. But for the child herself to understand her body as such requires her to accept castration long before the castration complex. What Lacan says is clear for the boy: insofar as the body image is a unified, externalized, and totalizing representation of the body and insofar as the penis is "part" of the male body, it clearly plays some role, even if not yet a dominant one, in shaping the boy's body image. But how it does so in the case of the girl is entirely obscure. When the penis takes on the function of the phallus, which is only possible as a result of the Oedipal classification of female sexuality as castrated, as lacking the phallus, only then can it be said to be dominant in the shaping of the body image for girls as well as boys. And even then, whether penis or phallus—Lacan seems to confuse them here—it does not have the same meaning for the girl as it does for the boy. At best, for the girl it represents a form of nostalgic fantasy for her pre-Oedipal and precastrated position; but for the boy it represents the social valorization of the penis, an actual and not simply a fantasized part of the body.

Why is it that both Freud and Lacan adopt only the boy's point of view? Is it simply an effect of their ignorance and lack of interest in the specificities of female morphology and sexuality—an effect of their misogyny? Or is it motivated by a desire to represent female sexuality and anatomy according to its current-day social position? And why is it that the mother's status must shift from phallic to castrated? The phallic mother must be understood as a fantasy, as the (boy's) fantasy of omnipotence and omniscience. She is represented by psychoanalytic theory as sexually neutral, insofar as the questions of sexual difference and sexual specificity make no sense for the pre-Oedipal child. Freud implies that the child (boy) bestows on the mother the attributes he acknowledges in himself, idealizing them in the process. It is for this reason, apparently, that Freud describes her as phallic. But given that even the boy is not yet aware of his own position as phallic, it is not simply that the boy accords the mother a genital organ like his own (although this seems confirmed by the case of Little Hans [1911]); children of both sexes, he claims, attribute to the mother a position in which she holds the power of life and death. The phallic mother is the fantasy of the mother who is able to grant the child everything, to be its object of desire. And, in turn, the child of either sex desires to be the mother's object of desire. But if Freud simply means that the mother is construed as all-powerful, it is not clear why he describes her as phallic. This description is hardly a sexually neutral characterization of her position, and if Freud wanted to insist on her sexually indifferent status, she could just as readily and much less contentiously be described as all-powerful. Something more is at stake here.

It is only on condition that the mother's all-powerful phallic status is transferred to the (symbolic) father that the child is able to abandon its intensive attachment to her and turn instead to the father. He is the heir to her phallic position, and it is not clear where the child's idea of his (castrating, all-powerful) position comes from, if not on loan from the mother. The child's resolution—or lack of it—of the Oedipus complex, his or her position as masculine or feminine, depends on the way in which this transference of status is effected, and particularly on the alignment of maleness with the powerful and femaleness with the powerless positions that results from this transfer. In short, the condition under which patriarchy is psychically produced is the constitution of women's bodies as lacking.

If women do not lack in any ontological sense (there is no lack in the real, as Lacan is fond of saying), men cannot be said to have. In this sense, patriarchy requires that female bodies and sexualities be socially produced a lack. This, in some social contexts, is taken literally[34] but also occurs at an imaginary and symbolic level, that is, at the level of the body's morphology and the body image. Psychoanalysis describes how this mutilated body image comes about, thus explaining the socially authorized social and sexual positions and behaviors appropriate to and expected from women; but it is unable to explain how this occurs (because it not only unable to see that its analyses find their context in patriarchal culture and not just neutral "civilization" but above all because it is unable to see that its own pronouncements and position are masculine).

What psychoanalytic theory makes clear is that the body is literally written on, inscribed, by desire and signification, at the anatomical, physiological, and neurological levels. The body is in no sense naturally or innately psychical, sexual, or sexed. It is indeterminate and indeterminable outside its social constitution as a body of a particular type. This implies that the body which it presumes and helps to explain is an open-ended, pliable set of significations, capable of being rewritten, reconstituted, in quite other terms than those which mark it, and consequently capable of reinscribing the forms of sexed identity and psychical subjectivity at work today. This project of rewriting the female body as a positivity rather than as a lack entails two related concerns:[35] reorganizing and reframing the terms by which the body has been socially represented (a project in which many feminists are presently engaged in the variety of challenges feminism poses in literary, visual, and filmic representational systems) and challenging the discourses which claim to analyze and explain the body and subject scientifically—biology, psychology, sociology—to develop different perspectives that may be able to better represent women's interests.

3 | Body Images
Neurophysiology and Corporeal Mappings

> Put briefly, perhaps the entire evolution of the spirit is a question of the body;
> it is the history of the development of a higher body that emerges into our
> sensibility. The organic is rising to yet higher levels.
>
> Friedrich Nietzsche, *The Will to Power* (1968: 357–58)

THE NOTION OF the body image has figured strongly in psychoanalytic conceptions of subjectivity as a third term intervening between and requiring the operations of both mind and body. Freud and Lacan utilize this idea in explaining
the genesis and functioning of the ego and in linking the operations of the various psychical systems to the subject's access to bodily motility and to conscious
behavior. Freud's notion of the cortical homunculus and Lacan's account of the
imaginary anatomy have shown that although biological and neurophysiological
inputs are crucial to understanding psychological processes, biology and neurophysiology are themselves dependent on psychical processes of transcription and
signification for their "completion" and effective functioning. This chapter will
continue the psychological and neurological investigations of the preceding chapter, outlining more directly the sources of the body image or corporeal schema
developed in the work of psychologists and neurophysiologists. The following
chapter (chapter 4) will explore the ways in which this research has been developed in Maurice Merleau-Ponty's phenomenological studies of subjectivity,
which counter prevailing philosophical dualisms and the preeminence of empiricist or idealist accounts of perceptual processes. This phenomenological and experiential orientation confirms and augments psychoanalytic insights regarding
the interactions of biology and psychology and the status of the body as a problematic and uncontainable term in both sets of discourses.

The Body Image

The concept of the body image has had a long and illustrious history in Western medicine. Perhaps its earliest anticipations date back to ancient Egypt, where
the word *ka* was used to indicate a copy of the human body, a copy that is more
ethereal and less dense than the physical body, an invisible but still material analogue of the living being, the soul. This soul-like double inhabited and animated

the material body but was logically distinct from it. It left the body at the point of death. Unlike the formlessness of the Cartesian notion of soul or mind, the double bears the image of the body, being a ghostlike icon of the subject. In Greek antiquity there seems to be a similar conception of the body image in, for example, Aristotle's theory of the *pneuma* and Epicurean conceptions of the *soma leptomeres*, the "finer" or more subtle body than the coarsely material and materialistic body. These conceptions clearly form the basis of the development of the Christian notion of soul, which also bears a close resemblance to the material body, being a particular soul emanating from a particular body and life. Its resemblance to the material body is what serves as a quasi-guarantee of its abiding identity. The very possibility of resurrection implies some privileged and formative link between the morphology of the soul and the morphology of the body.

While the ancients provided philosophical, religious, and ritualized contexts for the medically oriented views, probably the earliest technical references to the body image occur in the writings of the renowned sixteenth-century physician and surgeon Ambroise Paré. Paré, a remarkable figure in the history of medicine, not only devised a major classificatory scheme for teratological disorders according to their presumed causes;[1] he also introduced the use of ligature (which he used to separate Siamese twins), artificial limbs, and even artificial eyes. Like the work of many surgeons who followed him in their researches on the body image, Paré's work was primarily developed in the field of war injuries, which gave him a great deal of experience with amputations. It was from this knowledge that he wrote the first descriptions of the phantom limb. He explained the experience of the phantom limb after "mortification" as being produced by the continuity and "consentiment" of the dead parts with the living ones. As an example of the phantom sensation, he suggested an analogy with the feeling of being pulled by the shirt, where the body is being acted upon, and acts, with reference to an absent or intangible force.

A century later, in *The Meditations*, Descartes used the example of the phantom limb as an illustration of the deception to which the inner senses are prone, just as he used arguments from illusion to illustrate the deception of the outer senses. In his *Principles*, he used the painful sensations of the phantom hand as proof that only the soul experiences what is in the brain. He acknowledged the importance of peripheral stimulation, and in *The Passions of the Soul* he claimed that the mind is connected to the whole of the body and not simply to the brain. But the phantom phenomenon is a crucial "test case" in his psychophysical dualism and in his mechanistic account of the body's functioning. Although he refuses to identify the mind with the brain, nonetheless the major site for the interactions of the mind and the body is identified by him as the brain. Sensations are the consequences of "movements" in the brain, which are themselves the results of stimuli coming from internal or peripheral parts of the body. The internal stimuli are represented in the mind as having their origin and location in a particular part of the body through the movement of "animal spirits."

S. Weir Mitchell, a physician working with patients injured in the United States Civil War, treated large numbers of amputees. He noted that the phantom limb could be changed through treatment and experimentation and presented detailed descriptions of the experiences of the phantom limb. The treatment of war injuries seems to have provided the strongest stimulus to the exploration of anomalies of the body image. Not only was the phenomenon of the phantom limb most readily and frequently observable in war injuries, but clearly war provided huge numbers of "experimental" subjects for medical observation, under both controlled and, commonly, long-term conditions.[2] Weir Mitchell gave a detailed description of a number of disorders that were later classified as distortions of or disruptions to the body image: the (absence of) knowledge of the position of limbs when the patient's eyes are closed, and the loss of awareness of the movements of fingers. In fact it was Weir Mitchell who coined the term *phantom limb*. He concluded that "there is a mental condition which represents to the consciousness the amount of motion, its force and ideas of the change of place in the parts so willed to move" (Weir Mitchell 1965: 347).

If the phantom limb provoked a first impetus to postulate a notion of the body image, then other war injuries, particularly brain lesions of various kinds, provided another set of motivations for further research on the image of the body. This is true of the various researches on aphasia and related disorders undertaken by John Hughlings Jackson (whose work strongly influenced Freud), Sir Henry Head, A. R. Luria, Gelb and Goldstein, Pick, and many others.

Hughlings Jackson, a prominent British neurologist working at the end of the nineteenth century, believed that neurological disorders tend to reverse the direction of neurological "evolution" in the sense that in physiological crises the higher-order functions are more readily abandoned than the lower-order processes, which are clearly more necessary for the preservation of life and are preconditions for higher-order thought activities. These higher-order activities develop later, and break down sooner, than the lower-order functions. The breakdown of these higher-order functions has its effects on the lower-order processes as well, insofar as the destruction of these functions removes inhibitions on the lower centers and these also tend to become "more excitable," more readily able to discharge themselves. In the case of aphasia, for example, with the breakdown of the higher-level language functions, particularly the ability to use language in propositional form, lower linguistic forms such as swearing, which Hughlings Jackson considered to be automatic or emotional/expressive speech functions, nonetheless commonly remained.

From the early 1870s, a number of neurologists were committed to a project of finding exact localizations or correlations between speech and behavioral disturbances and injuries to specific parts of the brain. They hoped to provide a complete map of the regions in the brain which correlated with and connected to behavior. While it became increasingly difficult to provide these correspondences, particularly because the lesions discovered at the stage of autopsy did not confirm those areas postulated as the point of localization for particular disorders, the vast majority of neurologists were still interested in the problem of the cerebral location of aphasic disorders. Hughlings Jackson was less concerned with establishing exact locations of particular behavioral and psychological events in the brain or nervous system than in identifying the various neurological functions and behavioral processes disrupted by brain lesions. His pioneering contributions in the study of aphasia were made in 1864, the year Trousseau coined the term *aphasia*.[3] It was largely as a result of Hughlings Jackson's psychological or functional approach that the work of Pick, Goldstein, Head, and others became possible. Hughlings Jackson's careful researches did not reveal a regular or predictable correlation between clinical observation and cerebral pathology. Although Hughlings Jackson claimed that the right hemisphere was crucial in the functioning of speech and comprehension centers and that the "faculty" of language could not be localized anywhere in the left hemisphere "or anywhere except in the whole brain or the whole body" (quoted in Weisenberg and McBride 1935: 16), many psychologists today still believe that language is localized in the left hemisphere.

It is significant that even in the case of the apparently "disinterested" objective observational approach undertaken by the locationists, many have argued about the functional and anatomical differences between male and female brains. It has been argued—and this is a trend still observable today—that women's brains, like children's, are less localized, more fluid and plastic (and thus less developed or lower in evolutionary terms), with functions dispersed more widely through the cortex. Such speculation was largely based on clinical evidence that women are less likely to lose speech after a stroke or cerebral lesion. The assumption is that the speech functions or centers in women are not so discretely localized and thus are less vulnerable to attack. While localizationist accounts are less powerful today as a theoretical force, in practice most neurophysiological work is implicitly localized, commonly investigating the "psychological capacity" of certain areas of the brain.[4]

Sir Henry Head's work on aphasia provides the first modern account of aphasia, and he is also responsible for providing the earliest technically rigorous notion of the body image, which he called the "postural model of ourselves" or the "postural schema." From the sensory and behavioral changes in patients suffering from cerebral lesions, he argued that there must be a postural recognition based on the coordination of various sensory impulses in "normal" subjects. This coordination or integration cannot be conscious, but neither is it purely neurological. It requires both neurological and psychological explanation:

> By means of the perpetual alterations in position we are always building up postural models of ourselves, which constantly change. Every new posture or

movement is recorded on this plastic schema, and the activity of the cortex brings every fresh group of sensations evoked by altered posture in relation with it. . . .

It is to the existence of these "schemata" that we owe the power of projecting our recognition of posture, movement, and locality beyond the limits of our own bodies to the end of some instrument held in the hand. Without them we could not probe with a stick, nor use a spoon unless our eyes were fixed upon the plate. Anything which participates in the conscious movement of our bodies is added to the model of ourselves and becomes part of these schemata: a woman's power of localization may extend to the feather in her hat. (Head and Holmes 1911: 188)

By the postural model of the body, Head understands a three-dimensional image that both registers and organizes the information provided by the senses regarding the subject's body, its location in space (i.e., its posture or comportment), and its relations to other objects. The body image registers current sensations but also preserves a record of past impressions and experiences against which its present sensations and movements can be compared. It is a spatiotemporally structured and structuring model of the subject, a "schema," which mediates between the subject's position and its behavior. Damage to or destruction of the body schema by cortical lesions results in the subject's failure to be able to recognize the postural positions of parts or the whole of its body, or to be unable to locate various stimulated positions on its own body. Head mentions the case of a patient who had a leg amputated some time before suffering a cerebral lesion. After the amputation, the patient experienced the usual phantom leg sensations, but the phantom abruptly disappeared from the time of the lesion.

The postural model of the body has, in Head's view, several characteristics. The body schema is plastic. It is comprised both of a record of past bodily postures and movements and of the last posture or movement undertaken. On the basis of this history, it provides the context or horizon of current or future actions. It is thus able to function as a "standard" against which all subsequent changes of posture are measured. Head distinguishes between two kinds of body image or at least between two modalities of the body image, one of which may survive a lesion that impairs or destroys the other. The first is a model of the body's general posture and orientation in space; the second is a model of the locality of certain regions of or spots on the body. The body schema is composed both of physiological dispositions in the central nervous system (which have some psychological equivalent) and physiological processes (which do not have a psychical equivalent). In other words, many transformations or disturbances of the body schema occur without any conscious awareness or registration on the part of the subject. Although vision does play a significant role in the establishment of the postural model of the body, its form is largely multisensory, and the visual elements of the schema are positioned and integrated into kinesthetically and synergetically organized sensations.

Head's notion of this mobile, changing, organizing body schema provided the terms and framework contemporary neurologists and neuropsychologists have adopted—whether negatively or positively—in dealing with postural and locational disorders caused by lesions of the frontal lobes.

Schilder and the Body Image

Schilder's landmark work in the 1920s and 1930s on the body image is strongly influenced by Head's conception of the postural model of the body. But there are a number of differences between their conceptions. Schilder's conception of the body image relies much more strongly on psychology than it does on neurophysiology. Freud's work, particularly his analysis of narcissism and his conception of the libidinal drives, forms a major part of Schilder's understanding. On Schilder's model, social and interpersonal attachments and investments, as well as libidinal energy, form a major part of one's self-image and conception of the body.[5] This concept is thus more amenable to the kinds of sociohistorical and cultural analysis of the body feminists are interested in than Head's more austere neurophysiological approach. And where Head provides a kinesthetically structured body image, Schilder stresses much more firmly the optical or visual aspects of the schematic representation of the body. For Schilder, every touch is already oriented in a visual register, for it evokes a mental (that is to say visual) image of the spot touched. Schilder, however, stresses that the body schema, unlike the schema in Head's model, does not have two parts, one optical and the other tactile. This notion cannot explain how the two can be integrated to link our ability to see an object with our ability to touch it. The body image is synesthetic, just as every sensation, visual or tactile, is in fact synesthetically organized and represented:

> This means that there does not exist any primary isolation between the different senses. The isolation is secondary. We perceive and we may with some difficulty decide that one part of the perception is based upon the optic impressions. The synaesthesia is therefore a normal situation. The isolated sensation is the product of an analysis. In the scheme of the body, tactile, kinaesthetic and optic impulses can only be separated from each other by artificial methods.
>
> What we have studied is the change in the unity of the postural model of the body by change in the sensation of the tactile and optic sphere. The nervous system acts as a unit according to the total situation. The unit of perception is the object which presents itself through the senses and through all the senses. Perception is synaesthetic. (Schilder 1978: 38–39)

The body image, for him, is formed out of the various modes of contact the subject has with its environment through its actions in the world. In this sense, the body schema is an anticipatory plan of (future) action in which a knowledge of the body's current position and capacities for action must be registered. It is also comprised of various emotional and libidinal attitudes to the body, its parts and its capacity for certain kinds of performance; and finally, it is a social relation, in which the subject's experience of its own body is connected to and mediated by others' relations to their own bodies and to the subject's body.

> The image of the human body means the picture of our own body which we form in our mind, that is to say, the way in which the body appears to ourselves. There are sensations given to us. We see parts of the body-surface. We have tactile, thermal, pain impressions. . . . Beyond that there is the immediate experience that there is a unity of the body. . . . We call it a schema of our body or bodily schema, or, following Head . . . the postural model of the body. . . . There is a self-appearance of the body. It indicates . . . that, although it comes through the senses, it is not a mere perception. There are mental pictures and representations involved in it . . . (Schilder 1978: 11)

Combining Head's largely neurological model with Freud's notion of libidinal investment, Schilder's position on the relations between neurological and psychological interactions is similar to Freud's notion of the psychical mimicry or the anaclisis of biological processes. Schilder claims that there is a thoroughgoing community between psychical and organic processes such that "every change in the organic function is liable to bring forth with it psychical mechanisms which are akin to this organic function." (1978: 33). Here Schilder is signaling, this time from a neurological perspective, the phenomenon that Freud referred to as "somatic compliance," the organic body's amenability to psychical takeover. To illustrate, he refers to cases of hemiasomatognosia, in which an organic disturbance, a cortical lesion, makes the subject unable to recognize one-half of the body, which "will readily develop an unconscious and conscious wish in addition to this primitive urge" (1978: 33). Here it is almost as if, impelled by the organic disturbance, psychological processes take over and adopt the biological disturbance as their own and utilize it to express psychical wishes and significances, both conscious and unconscious.

In the first part of his *Image and the Appearance of the Human Body*, Schilder concerns himself with the physiological bases of the body image. From his observation of the consequences of various kinds of cerebral lesions, Schilder argues, following Head, that the body image has (at least) two components. One concerns the ability to localize and orient sensations, generally manifested in a loss of the ability to distinguish between right and left sides (alloesthesia). Significantly, though, this occurs not only with respect to the patient's own body but also with respect to the bodies of others. The postural model of the subject's own body is thus demonstrably linked to the model that the subject has of other bodies and, in turn, that other bodies have of the subject's body. In some cases, the subject can with great accuracy describe or localize a particular sensation on a limb but is unable to describe or position the limb in space and relative to the rest of the body. Schilder also cites examples of the patient's ability to transfer sensations from one, healthy, side of the body to its symmetrical position on the other, impaired, side (allochiria). Sensations on the left-hand side provoke hallucinations of sensations on the right-hand side. While this clearly points to a major psychical and anatomical significance of the body's (quasi-)symmetry,[6] it also indicates that the ability to recognize the locality of a sensation must be differentiated from the ability to recognize the position of that location relative to the rest of the body. On the other hand, there are neurological disorders that indicate the ability to locate positions in space but not to be able to localize them.[7]

These two modes of body image are closely related to perception and action respectively. Schilder, unlike Head, stresses that these are not two distinct kinds of body image but more like two poles or extremes of a single integrated and integrating image. Alloesthesia, the transference of sensations from one side of the body to the other, and hemianasomatognosia, the nonperception of one-half of the body, are closely related, demonstrating the psychical-physiological axis of symmetry running through the subject's body. The interrelations of these two aspects or features of the body image, while frequently manifested in disorders which render either one or the other dysfunctional, can also, more rarely, occur together, in which case the patient loses the ability to distinguish between a passive sensation and an active movement, that is, between experiencing a movement that has been performed (by someone else) on the subject's body and one in which the subject has moved his or her own limbs. Perceptions themselves do not have an inherent qualitative aspect that can lead to clear-cut and unmistakable sensations of reception or movement (Schilder 1978: 39; Head and Holmes 1911). These patients, it is clear, do not suffer from optic or tactile disturbances per se: the visual or tactile sensations regarding the external world and objects remain intact and functional. Rather, what takes place is a disturbance of body image. This is evidenced by the fact that whenever difficulty occurs regarding the recognition of different parts of the body or the position of the body, it occurs not only in the subject's self-perception but also always in the perception of others' bodies as well.

More strikingly, given the central role of the body image in initiating movement, there is a marked impairment in behavior as well. This inability to undertake the movements necessary for specific action is called apraxia. The apractic will usually know what to do in order to achieve certain results and may even be able to articulate this in language, but he or she is unable to act on that knowledge.[8] In these cases the body image, which is not only a picture of the body but also an anticipatory plan for the detailed movements the body must undertake in order to act, breaks down. The body image includes both the representation of the movements necessary to attain a specific goal and all the various intermediary actions required to move the body from its present position to this goal. This plan is not of course entirely conscious (nor for that matter is it unconscious, for it is not repressed); it is preconscious, that is, capable of being made conscious.

Thus body-image disturbances may affect either the ways in which the subject perceives and experiences his or her own body, sensations, or movements, or it may affect the ways in which the subject is able to relate his or her present postural position to wished-for goals of actions (this may involve either difficulties in initiating action or disordering of the necessary temporal arrangement of actions, which lead from one to the other in the attainment of a goal); and finally, it may affect the ways in which the subject is able to position his or her body relative to the bodies of others:

> In this plan the knowledge of one's own body is an absolute necessity. There must always be a knowledge that I am acting with my body, that I have to start the movement with my body, that I have to use a particular part of my body. But in the plan there must also be the aim of my actions. There is always an object towards which the action is directed. This aim may be one's own body or it may be an object in the outside world. In order to act, we must know something about the quality of the object of our intention. And, finally, we must know in what way we want to approach the object. The formula contains therefore the image of the limb or of the part of the body which is performing the movement. (Schilder 1978: 52)

The Phantom Limb

Perhaps the most convincing evidence regarding the existence of the body image is what Weir Mitchell referred to as the phantom limb. After the amputation of movable, functional extremities, the phantom limb seems to be experienced in close to 100 percent of the cases (the exceptions are mentally retarded subjects and children under the age of about seven years). The phantom most commonly appears shortly after the amputation but may take up to two years to fully emerge. Body phantoms are not limited to limbs. In adults, phantoms have been noted to occur in almost every part of the body. After mastectomy, for example, there is usually the experience of the phantom breast (Hopwood and MacGuire 1988: 47–50). Phantoms have been noted after the loss of the eyes, the rectum, the larynx, parts of the face, the penis—which may experience phantom erections and even phantom orgasms—and the internal organs: phantom ulcer pains have been noted in the case of gastrectomies (Gorman 1969: 99). It is, however, significant that a hysterectomy, while often leading to depression and feelings of lower self-worth for many women, is not usually addressed in terms of a body phantom. And there is a significant silence regarding the effects of medical clitoridectomies, which were used to cure "chronic masturbation" in women in the nineteenth century and are still performed regularly today. Can it be that the psychoanalytic understanding of female sexuality as castrated means that the surgical removal of an organ (or set of them) already designated as lacking is not registered (the lack of a lack)? The enigmatic, indeed paradoxical, status of the female body, the silence of neurophysiology on the question of the sexual determinacy of the body image, signals a point of resistance that feminists need to address. It is a remarkable oversight which indicates that the notion of "the" body that is generally addressed by neuro- and psychophysiology is implicitly the male body. It is not clear why hysterectomy does not carry with it the kind of phantom effects that even the removal of other internal organs, organs not usually consciously perceived, such as the appendix, have as scar tissue. Is this because the vagina, cervix, clitoris, and other female sexual organs are already codified paradoxically as "missing" organs?

The body phantom is not really an image of the limb which is now absent. In contrast to the recollection of a missing limb or to the experience of a fully functional limb or body part, the body phantom is very commonly distorted. In the case of missing extremities, for example, the phantom is invariably shorter than the limb; often the proximal portions of the phantom are missing; it is commonly perceived as flatter than the healthy limb; it usually feels light and hollow; and the perception of its mobility is extremely impaired (often to such an extent that its movements are experienced as the change from one cramped position to another), losing its ability to perform finer, more nuanced acts of dexterity which the intact limb was able to undertake.

The phantom moves spontaneously in accordance with the movements of the rest of the body and is sometimes amenable to voluntary movement. Indeed, this seems to be a prerequisite for the amputee's ability to use prosthetic replacements, artificial limbs. It is only through the controlled use of the phantom that the artificial limb can (gradually) take the place of the lost limb, even if only for functional purposes. But the movement of the phantom is fundamentally different from the movement of the healthy limb insofar as the weight and gravity of the real limb is considerably stronger than that of the phantom. Patients refer to its "husklike," weightless, and floating character.

The phantom limb changes quite dramatically over time. The closer in time to the amputation, the more realistic is its appearance and (usually but not always) the more painful are the sensations coming from it; the greater the passage of time since the amputation, the more distorted and phantomlike the sensations become. Schilder explains that these body representations follow their own kinds of psychological and physiological laws:

> The phantom in the beginning usually takes the shape of the lost extremity but in the course of years it begins to change its shape and parts of it disappear. When there is a phantom of the arm, the hand comes nearer to the elbow, or in extreme cases may be immediately on the place of amputation. Also the hand may become smaller and be like the hand of a child. Similar phenomena occur on the leg. The position of the phantom is often a rigid one, and . . . it

is often the position in which the patient lost his limb. It is as if the phantom were trying to preserve the last moment in which the limb was still present.

The phantom follows its own laws. When the arm is moved towards a rigid object, the phantom goes into the rigid object. It may even go through the patient's own body. . . . We can be sure that we are dealing with central processes in all these processes of shaping, or disappearing of parts, in the changes of the position of the hand and the feet to the stump. (Schilder 1978: 64)

In the experience of the phantom limb, there is always a complex interaction of various psychical mechanisms. Not only is there a displacement of sensory experience from the limb (now missing) and the phantom, there is also a denial that the amputation has taken place—or, rather than an unambiguous denial, there seems to be a process of disavowal. Plügge notes an experiment which highlights this ambiguity of attitude on the part of the subject to the missing limb:

The basic experiment required a mid-forearm amputee who has developed a differentiated and impressive phantom limb to bring the stump of his arm to within one or two centimeters of a wall, say of a room, at an angle of 90 degrees.

If one then unexpectedly asks the subject whether the phantom might have penetrated the wall, or whether it has become shorter in being compressed by the approach of the stump to the wall, or whether, pushed out of its original direction, it has been deflected or has disappeared . . . his first spontaneous . . . expression is one of perplexity. (Plügge, in Spicker 1970: 300)

The patient is perplexed because he has two simultaneous experiences which are equally real to him: on one hand, the "reality" of the phantom sensations; on the other, the perceptual reality of the experiences of the stump. The patient has ambivalent, contradictory experiences regarding both the phantom and the stump (this is hardly surprising given that both are a compromise between death and the healthy limb): the phantom is felt to be a living, moving, "organic" part of the body, in broad coordination with the rest of the body's movements. But at the same time, it behaves as if it were autonomous, with qualities and requirements of its own that impinge upon the subject and remain out of the subject's volitional control. Similarly, the stump comes to behave like a sense receptor whose sensitivity approaches that of the lost extremity. It is the site for various perceptions, and, of course, it is the object of sensory, tactile, optical attention. Yet it is commonly experienced as thinglike, passive, inert, a mere object with no animating or receptive interiority. The amputee avows two contradictory realities simultaneously: the reality of a living limb and the reality of its destruction. These two "limbs" occupy the same space and time, one the ghostly double of the other's absence.

Schilder resorts to psychological and libidinal terms to explain the peculiar laws and tendencies regulating the transformations which the body phantom undergoes, seeing the phantom as a kind of extension of the rest of the subject's psychical life ("It is a model of how psychic life in general is going on" (68). The phantom is not so much a regression to infantile experiences (although this is a common explanation) as an attempt on the part of the subject to keep the limb in the closest proximity to the meaning that the real limb had in its presence.

> We are accustomed to have a complete body. The phantom of the amputated person is therefore a reactivation of a given perceptive pattern by emotional forces. The great variety in phantoms is only understood when we consider the emotional reactions of individuals towards their own body. One of Betlheim's patients felt that his right arm was preserved somewhere and would be given back to him. (Schilder 1978: 67)

The phantom is an expression of nostalgia for the unity and wholeness of the body, its completion. It is a memorial to the missing limb, a psychical delegate that stands in its place. There is thus not only a physical but also a psychical wound and scar in the amputation or surgical intervention into any part of the body.[9] The phantom limb is the narcissistic reassertion of the limb's presence in the face of its manifest biological loss, an attempt to preserve the subject's narcissistic sense of bodily wholeness (an image, as Lacan points out, developed through the mirror stage). While clearly not purely psychical in its operations (otherwise its uniformity would be considerably broken up and contingent on psychological variations), the psychical systems of meaning within which the subject operates nonetheless have taken over as their own the organic disturbance that has broken the unity of the biological body. The phantom limb is a sometimes cumbersome narcissistic compensation for the loss of the limb or bodily unity, a psychical attempt to reactivate a past body image in place of the present reality. This is not unlike Freud's analysis of hysteria and the secondary narcissism he attributes to women—a kind of nostalgic reaffirmation of the body of women outside of (phallic) genitality. And that raises the general question of the status of the body image of women insofar as women are considered and consider themselves to have suffered an amputation more debilitating than most—the amputation implied by castration. Do women have a phantom phallus? What is the status of a fantasized amputation (such as is required by castration) and a real one? Do women experience the castration complex as a bodily amputation as well as a psychosocial constraint? If so, is there, somewhere in woman's psyche, a representation of the phallus she has lost? Is this what makes the masculinity complex possible?

Insofar as women's body images are clearly different from men's and are modeled on lack and castration, are the amputee's relations to the phantom limb similar to the woman's mourning for what has been lost (the freedom, self-determination, and autonomy accorded to the male body)? Until female genitals and women's bodies are inscribed and lived (by the subject and by others) as a positivity, there will always remain paradoxes and upsetting implications for any notion of femininity.

The body image is derived to a large extent from the perceptions, sensations, and movements of the organic body, yet sensation alone is not adequate to build up the body image or to explain its characteristics and attributes. There are psychical and fantasmatic dimensions which also need to be accounted for if the body image is to be explained in the depth and detail it requires. Schilder stresses, in a way that his neurophysiological predecessors did not, that the body image is a psychical, and primarily libidinal, construct, a representation (or series of them) cathected with libidinal intensity. Schilder, in other words, utilized Freud's insights about the structure of narcissism—especially primary narcissism—in explaining the peculiarities of the form and structure of the body image. He refers to the infantile and developmental model of narcissism that Freud developed in "On Narcissism." But like Freud himself, Schilder does not go on to connect the narcissistically invested body image with the question of sexual difference. He links sexual difference, like psychoanalytic orthodoxy, to the later Oedipus complex, while ignoring the major effects that the sexually inscribed body and body image must have for the narcissistic/pre-Oedipal subject.

Schilder argues that the first object of primary narcissism is the image of the body, and in this sense his work coalesces with Lacan's insights regarding the mirror stage. This is not entirely unexpected: it seems clear that Lacan was aware of Schilder's research and utilized many of his insights in developing his account of the mirror stage. The image of the body is psychically invested insofar as the infant's body is not yet a self-contained entity, distinct and separate from the world. The body and its various sensations are projected onto the world, and conversely the world and its vicissitudes are introjected into the body of the subject-to-be. Schilder argues, following Freud, that the image of the body is built up gradually, according to the stages of libidinal development the child undergoes. The body image is constructed and invested according to the different emphases of libidinal intensities the child experiences. The oral stage, for example, is centered on the mouth, the anal stage on the anus, and so on for all the libidinal phases. Each successive stage adds to and redefines the preceding stages, augmenting and reorienting them. From the time of oral sexuality, the mouth and digestive tract remain narcissistically invested, and even when the anal stage takes over the intensity of the oral, the mouth remains significant, even if it no longer dominates the child's sensations. Each psychosexual stage and drive involves an investment and thus participates in the production and differentiation of the body image.

All the orifices, which play a major role in the transmission and reception of information from the inside to the outside of the body and from the outside to the inside, together with the sexual drives, which find their sources in these bodily openings, induce the sensitivity and thus the privilege of the erotogenic zones for the body image. It is through the libidinalization of bodily zones, organs, and functions that the body image is built up and takes on its particular form:

> ... difference in the libidinous structures is reflected in the structure of the postural model of the body. Individuals in whom a partial desire is increased will feel the particular point of the body, the particular erogenic zone belonging to the desire, in the centre of the body-image. It is as if the energy is amassed on these particular points. There will be lines of energy connecting the different erogenic points, and we shall have a variation in the structure of the body-image according to the psychosexual tendencies of the individual. (Schilder 1978: 125–26)

Like Freud, Schilder emphasizes the crucial role played not only by the child's own corporeal sensations but also by the activities of those who tend and care for the child during its earliest years. Freud discusses the essentially seductive role played by the mother's care for the child and the child's reliance on her support for survival (Freud 1905c). This necessary dependence implies that the child's body and its bodily experiences are not simply the product of its own endogenous sensations and its various experiments with its bodily capacities; the child's body, particularly as an already sexually designated body onto which a culture's fantasies of sexual difference are etched, is like a screen onto which the mother's—and culture's—desires, wishes, fears, and hopes are projected and internalized. Its orifices are well suited for sexualization not only because they are conduits between the inside and outside of the body (i.e., not simply in terms of their "natural" or adaptative functions) but because they are the sites from which the mother's or nurturer's successes and failures, ambitions and disappointments, are most readily projected and played out; they are the sources for criteria of her self-worth and sexual value in the sense that the mother's own unconscious desires must play a significant role for each successive generation.

The body image is in a continuous process of production and transformation. It changes orientation or inflection as the child develops into adolescence and adulthood. Adolescence is also of significance in understanding the development of the body image, for this is a period in which the biological body undergoes major upheavals and changes as an effect of puberty. It is in this period that the subject feels the greatest discord between the body image and the lived body, between its psychical idealized self-image and its bodily changes. Experientially, the philosophical desire to transcend corporeality and its urges may be dated from this period. The adolescent body is commonly experienced as awkward, alienating, an undesired biological imposition. Moreover, although the child's sexuality is structured primarily in pre-Oedipal and Oedipal development, it is only in adolescence that its sexuality acquires social recognition and value; it is only in adolescence that it becomes clear that the subject has a sexual, i.e., a genital, position, whether this is wanted or not. In pubertal development the genitalia and secondary sexual characteristics become definitive objects of consciousness and only bit by bit acquire representation in the body image.

The body image undergoes major modifications in the case of organic or psychological disorders. In the refusal of sexual roles ordained by heterosexuality, for example, gay men and lesbians may perversely cling to preadolescent body images, which may remain ambiguous regarding the differences between the sexes; or, perhaps more provocatively, they may invest even greater intensity in erotogenic sites, making them the center of libidinal attention and narcissistic investment, in effect reinscribing them in a mode of resistance. Bodily zones, regions, activities, and practices which perhaps should be repressed if the penis-vagina, coital model of sexual gratification is to develop—most notably oral, anal, and sadistic impulses, tactility, scopophilia, and the other "sexual perversions"—may tend to be emphasized, indeed, cultivated, in a mode of defiance to heterosexist requirements.

In the case of illness or pain, the effected zones of the body become enlarged and magnified in the body image. Freud describes the transference of libido from the external world and love objects to the subject's own body in illness. Perhaps another way of expressing this is to say that the illness engorges specific regions of the body image. This also occurs in hypochondria and hysteria, where the motivation for changes in body image comes from psychical rather than organic sources. But even here, as I argued earlier, the psychical and libidinal investments in their turn also effect bodily changes. Changes in the body image tend to become changes at the level of the body itself, just as corporeal changes are registered in changes in the body image. Hypochondria hypercathects a particular region of the body treating nongenital zones as if they had taken on genital meaning. This is also true in the case of hysteria, in which the hysterogenic zone takes on a sexual, usually a phallic, function. Like the phallus, the hypochondriacal zone shows an autonomy from, an existence independent of, the normal conscious control the subject exerts over body images:

> Hypochondria is a fight against narcissism; the individual defends himself against the libidinous overtension of the hypochondriac organ; he tries to isolate the diseased organ, to treat it like a foreign body in the body-image. (Schilder 1978: 142)

Depersonalization is a much more severe psychical transformation of the body image. Schilder is credited with providing depersonalization with its now commonly recognized role of mediating between notions of self and the external world.[10] It takes to extremes the hypochondriac's attitude to the erotogenic zone which the hypochondriac tried to expel from the body image but cannot because the zone is overinvested with libido. In depersonalization, subjects lose interest in the whole body. They refuse or are afraid to invest any narcissistic libido in the body image. They may feel a dramatic change in self-conception and in relations to the external world. Self-observations seem completely disinterested or disinvested, viewed from the point of a spectator or outsider. Not only is the subject's own body treated with disinterest, but the outside world is also experienced as flat and disinvested. Depersonalization may in fact account for the phenomenon of out-of-body experiences. The body, or its various parts, is set at a distance from the subject. The greater the libidinal investment in the organ or bodily zone before depersonalization, the more alienated the subject feels from that zone in the various manifestations of the disorder.[11] These symptoms may well result from severe sexual abuse, although Schilder does not discuss this. Significantly, Schilder claims that the particular phenomenon of depersonalization, like all disturbances of the body image, shares a pathology with an organic disorder, using its characteristics for its own purposes. This psychical disturbance, Schilder claims, is almost always accompanied by dizziness:

> Depersonalization and organic dizziness have the same psychological nucleus, though it is expressed in different levels of organization. Dizziness due to organic causes often provokes phenomena which are akin to the psychic phenomena of depersonalization of the body. (Schilder 1978: 140)

Depersonalization is a kind of psychical mimicry of the organic structure of dizziness. Its disinvestment in the processes of self-observation is a function of the narcissistic decathexis of the subject's own inclinations to voyeurism. The subject denies its own voyeuristic impulses, withdrawing from the pleasure of seeing so that seeing no longer has any value. The subject is now seen, or sees itself, with little or no libidinal investment in looking (or being looked at).

In hypochondria there is a transposition of libidinal intensity from the genitals to other parts of the body. In depersonalization, there is a withdrawal of libido from privileged zones, often from the whole of the subject's body image. In hysteria, as in hypochondria, there is a process of transference of the meaning of sexual zones and organs to other organs which are not usually associated with sexuality, or at least with genitality. Like the two other cases, hysteria clearly exhibits transformations in the subject's body image. In hypochondria, there is a displacement or transposition of libido from one organ to another; this also occurs in the case of hysteria, but added to it is the primary process of condensation. The intensity of one zone is displaced onto another bodily zone; but the meaning and value of a zone, or more than one, are also transferred to another bodily zone. Dora's hystericization of the throat and breathing apparatus, her shortness of breath and *tussis nervosa*, Freud claims, exhibit an upward transposition from a genitally experienced set of sensations that must be repressed. Her throat and vocal cords take on the meaning of the phallus, for they are the heirs, as Freud suggests, to the whole of the patient's sexual life. Particular regions of the body image may take on the meaning of other repressed sexual zones of the body.

This implies that there is a lability of meaning for the various bodily organs, zones, and processes. Any zone of the body can, under certain circumstances, take on the meaning of any other zone. This occurs more or less continually in normal mental life but is particularly striking in neurotic and psychotic disorders. In neurosis and psychosis, the subject's sexual life is transposed from its socially expected locations, aims, and objects to elsewhere, either to different erotogenic sources or to different objects with different aims. The life history of the subject (the systems of psychical meaning and the events rendered meaningful in the subject's history) and of the body (the history of its explorations and practices, on one hand, and its various accidents and illnesses, on the other) may provide some index of which organs are likely to be rendered significant in the body image, which are likely to transfer their intensity and meaning to other organs, and which organs are the preferred sites of this transfer.[12]

In the case of hysteria, Schilder, unlike Freud, distinguishes two kinds of hysterical symptoms which have two different effects on the body image. The first group is related to the surface of the body and its outward appearance (presumably here Schilder has in mind such symptoms as skin disorders—rashes, infections, eczema). Anzieu argues that the scratching of skin disorders may be an archaic reactivation of aggressive impulses (1989: 20). The second group is connected to the inner bodily processes and organs, those which are not generally visible (choking, breathing difficulties, paralyses, etc.). This division indicates both the psychical significance of the public/private division and the division between inside and outside. Disorders visible on the surface of the body have different kinds of effects on others than those which are not visible. In the first case, some kind of message to others is being transmitted, while in the second case, the message is of a different order, being directed not to another subject but, as Lacan says, to another signifier.

Hypochondria, depersonalization, and hysteria indicate the overlap and the interchange between the organic and the psychical bodies through the mediation of the body image. They show that the biological or organic body is open to psychical meanings, able to take on meanings and accommodate intensities, to comply with and be of use to psychical systems. And in turn the psychical order shows a "respect" for the morphology of body processes insofar as it takes them as its raw materials and accepts the forms and processes as its models of expression. Psychic processes rely on various organic connections.[13] And conversely, psychical factors may make the subject more liable to organic disorders (particularly gastric ulcers, angina, influenza, and viral infections).[14]

Without the mediating position of the body image, these interactions with the organic and the psychical would not be possible. It is by affecting, modifying, transforming the body image, on one side or the other, that each is able to effect transformations in the other. Organic diseases, for example, provoke sensations that transform the body image. The organs or parts of the body affected are thus intensified through both the increase and the change in the sensations to which it is sensitive, and these are registered and experienced at the level of the body image, which in turn affects the subject's psychological states and general attitudes. Psychical or narcissistic investments in organs, bodily zones, or activities are also registered on the body image and may, depending on the general health of the subject, provoke irritation at the organic level, causing organic transformations. Both psychical and organic experiences are amenable to changes effected in the other.

Social Extensions of the Body

Freud had predicted that "man" would become a "prosthetic god" through the supplementary use of tools and the instruments of civilization to compensate for "his" biological defects and the limits of "his" facticity. Schilder shows that the body image cannot be simply and unequivocally identified with the sensations provided by a purely anatomical body. The body image is as much a function of the subject's psychology and sociohistorical context as of anatomy. The limits or borders of the body image are not fixed by nature or confined to the anatomical "container," the skin. The body image is extremely fluid and dynamic; its borders, edges, and contours are "osmotic"—they have the remarkable power of incorporating and expelling outside and inside in an ongoing interchange.

Schilder points out that even on an organic level the feelings and sensations we have of the body do not exactly correspond with anatomy. He discusses what he calls the "zones of sensitivity" in connection with the phenomenology of the various bodily orifices. The sensations a subject has of these bodily openings are experienced about one centimeter from the opening (Schilder 1978: 88). It seems as if, even on the most elementary level of introspection, the ways in which the body is experienced, the morphology provided by these zones of sensitivity, are moderately smaller than the body itself. Even problems or diseases of internal organs are not experienced in their precise anatomical locations; sensations appear to emanate from about one or two centimeters below the skin for both internal sensations and those occurring on (or immediately below) the body's outer surface. Ironically, though, this seems less true of the vagina. Once again, Schilder, like Goldstein and others, leaves the question of women's specific body images aside.

Just as there is a zone of sensitivity concerning the body's openings and surfaces, so too there is a zone outside the body, occupying its surrounding space, which is incorporated into the body. Intrusion into this bodily space is considered as much a violation as penetration of the body itself. The size and form of this surrounding space of safety is individually, sexually, racially, and culturally variable. But even for one and the same subject, the space surrounding the body is not uniform: it is "thinner" in some places (for example, the extremities, which more readily tolerate body contact than other zones) and "thicker" in others (which are particularly psychically, socially, and culturally "privatized"). Moreover, some people's behavior is regarded as obtrusive while the same behavior in others is welcome.[15] Spatiality, the space surrounding and within the subject's body, is thus crucial for defining the limits and shape of the body image: the lived spatiality of endogenous sensations, the social space of interpersonal relations, and the "objective" or "scientific" space of cultural (including scientific and artistic) representations all play their role.[16]

But perhaps more significantly and less abstractly, the body image is capable of accommodating and incorporating an extremely wide range of objects. Anything that comes into contact with the surface of the body and remains there long enough will be incorporated into the body image—clothing, jewelry, other bodies, objects. They mark the body, its gait, posture, position, etc. (temporarily or more or less permanently), by marking the body image: subjects do not walk the same way or have the same posture when they are naked as when they wear clothing. And the posture and gait will, moreover, vary enormously, depending on what kind of clothing is worn:

> The body image can shrink or expand; it can give parts to the outside world and can take other parts into itself. When we take a stick in our hands and touch an object with the end of it, we feel a sensation at the end of the stick. The stick has, in fact, become part of the body-image. In order to get the full sensation at the end of the stick, the stick must be in a more or less rigid connection with the body. It then becomes part of the bony system of the body, and we may suppose that the rigidity of the bony system is an important part in every body-image. (Schilder 1978: 202)

External objects, implements, and instruments with which the subject continually interacts become, while they are being used, intimate, vital, even libidinally cathected parts of the body image. These objects and implements need not be small: objects ranging from the smallest tools to jets, ships, and cars are all capable of becoming part of the body image. Part of the difficulty of learning how to use these implements and instruments is not simply the technical problem of how they are used but also the libidinal problem of how they become psychically invested. In driving, the car becomes part of the body image, a body shell for the subject; its perils and breakdowns, chasing another car or trying to fit into a small parking spot, are all experienced in the body image of the driver (and sometimes, to their horror, in that of the passengers as well). The surgeon would be unable to operate without the scalpel and medical implements being incorporated into the surgeon's body image. The writer would be unable to type, the musician unable to perform, without the word processor or musical instrument becoming part of the body image. It is only insofar as the object ceases to remain an object and becomes a medium, a vehicle for impressions and expression, that it can be used as an instrument or tool.

If discrete objects form part of the subject's body image, depending on how they are used and the performances the body must undergo to use them, there is an "intermediate" category of objects, midway between the inanimate and the bodily. These are the various "detachable" parts of the body, its excretions, waste products, and bodily by-products, which Lacan describes as *objet a*, and Kristeva refers to as the abject (Kristeva 1982). I will return to the abject and to bodily fluids and their relation to the question of sexual difference in the final chapter. For now, we need to concentrate on the role they play in the constitution of the body image. These "objects," which were once part of the subject's body and body image, are never as distinct and separable from the subject's body as inorganic objects are:

> . . . objects which were once connected with the body always retain something of the quality of the body-image in them. I have specifically pointed out the fact that whatever originates in or emanates out of our body will still remain a part of the body-image. The voice, the breath, the odour, faeces, menstrual blood, urine, semen, are still parts of the body image even when separated in space from the body. (Schilder 1978: 213)

Detachable, separable parts of the body—urine, faeces, saliva, sperm, blood, vomit, hair, nails, skin—retain something of the cathexis and value of a body part even when they are separated from the body. There is still something of the subject bound up with them—which is why they are objects of disgust, loathing, and repulsion as well as envy and desire. They remain (peripheral, removable) parts of the body image, magically linked to the body.[17] They illustrate the narcissistic investment in the body image: these body products can only be negatively coded (with disgust or horror) because there is also the possibility (and the prior actuality) of a love of the body and all its substances. No part of the body is divested of all psychical interest without severe psychical repercussions. Human subjects never simply *have* a body; rather, the body is always necessarily the object and subject of attitudes and judgments. It is psychically invested, never a matter of indifference. Human beings love their bodies (or, what amounts libidinally to the same thing, they hate them or parts of them). The body never has merely instrumental or utilitarian value for the subject. It is significant that the investment in and the various shapes of different parts of the body image are uneven, for clearly some regions are far more libidinally invested than others. Which regions are invested and the kinds of investments that animate them are functions of the subject's psychical, interpersonal, and sociohistorical relations and are malleable and continually changing, always potentially open to new meanings and investments.

The investments and significances attributed to the different regions of the body image are not simply the consequence of the subject's sensations or the subject's relations to others but also result from the significance of body parts for others (their own as well as the subject's). In this sense, they are never self-determined, voluntarily adopted, or easily shaken off, for they are to a large extent a function of socially shared significances. No matter how much the individual may wish or will it, male and female genitals have a particular social meaning in Western patriarchal cultures that the individual alone—or even in groups—is unable to transform insofar as these meanings have been so deeply etched into and lived as part of the body image. The reinscription of sexual morphology in terms more conducive to women's corporeal and sexual autonomy, beyond the problematic of lack, would entail a thoroughgoing transformation of the social meanings of sexual difference, and consequently the constitution of different body images for the two sexes. Consequently, it implies a very different self-conception and a very different organic body than the dichotomous division of sexed bodies into two types, with their particular characteristics, in patriarchy today.

Before summarizing Schilder's notion of the body image, it might be worth mentioning a single reservation I have about Schilder's otherwise enormously useful rethinking of mind/body relations. It has to do, not surprisingly, with the question of sexual difference. In *The Image and Appearance of the Human Body* he writes in terms of a sexually neutral subject who experiences cerebral lesions and neurological or psychological disorders in a sexually neutral way. But at times, particularly in his discussion of case studies and individual life histories, he refers to the Freudian model of sexual difference, with its emphasis on the castration threat and the Oedipus complex. Even where he discusses sexual impulses and feelings, he does not elaborate what this means for each of the sexes. He develops a single frame of reference, which is clearly appropriate for men and male sexuality but not so clearly relevant for women and female sexuality. Under the form of sexually neutral statements, Schilder, like virtually all the theorists of the body image, does not specify that male experience is taken as the norm and women's experience is discussed only insofar as it deviates from or compares to this referential framework. This is strikingly true for all the relevant literature on neurophysiology, which is hardly surprising, given the influence that studies of war injuries had on the development of this field and the vast disproportion of male subjects in active war service relative to females, even at present.

> It cannot be denied that our discussion of the body image . . . is a contribution to one of the general principles of psychoanalysis, namely that the development of genital sexuality is necessary for a full appreciation of other persons and our appreciation of their somatic integrity. . . . But the development from pre-genitality to genitality is also of fundamental importance for our attitude towards our own body. We experience our body as united, as a whole, only when the genital level is harmoniously reached. Fully developed genital sexuality is indispensable for the full appreciation of our own body-image. (Schilder 1978: 173)

In discussing the libidinal structure of the body image, Schilder states that the unification of the body image and the cohesion of our self-identities is dependent on the attainment of a stable, genital form of sexuality. While this seems true for men and male sexuality—insofar as genital, phallic sexuality hierarchically subordinates but does not eliminate the pregenital drives—it is not even clear what this would mean for women and female sexuality—insofar as female sexuality is already *genitally* multilocational, plural, ambiguous, polymorphous, and not clearly able to subordinate the earlier stages.[18] It is not clear what "genital development" entails for women in the way that it *is* clear what it means for men.

To sum up Schilder's understanding of the body image, several points may be relevant. The body image unifies and coordinates postural, tactile, kinesthetic, and visual sensations so that these are experienced as the sensations of a subject coordinated into a single space; they are the experiences of a single identity. This image is the necessary precondition for undertaking voluntary action, the point at which the subject's intentions are translated into the beginning of movement, the point of transition in activating bones and muscles. While undertaking involuntary action or merely reactive behavior need not imply a body image, any willful action requires a plan of bodily action—precisely the function of the body image.

The body image is a map or representation of the degree of narcissistic investment of the subject in its own body and body parts. It is a differentiated, gridded, and ever-changing registration of the degrees of intensity the subject experiences, measuring not only the psychical but also the physiological changes the body undergoes in its day-to-day actions and performances. It is the condition under which synesthesia and the transposition of organs and bodily functions becomes possible: it is by means of the body image that the information provided by the different senses functions together on one hand; but on the other hand, it is the means by which the significances of one of the senses or organs can be displaced onto another.

The body image determines both the localization of sensations in different concrete regions of the body and the position of the body as a whole within space, the relative positions of two simultaneous stimuli and the differences between movements on the surface of the skin and the movements of limbs. It establishes a series of differentiations of bodily zones, orifices, curves, convex and concave spaces, including the line of lateral symmetry that divides up the body into a series of interacting parts. Instead of being built up from the sensations of the various parts, the body image always functions as a unity, moving from a state of amorphousness to increasing differentiation and specialization.

The body image is necessary for the distinction between the figure and ground, or between central and peripheral actions. Relative to its environment, the body image separates the subject's body from a background of forces; but also within the body, the body image establishes the distinctions—between movements of limbs, say, and the rest of the body—which provide it with its corporeal context. A single movement reorients the whole of the body, creating what might be called a gait or posture, an individual and cultural bodily style.

The body image establishes the distinctions by which the body is usually understood—the distinctions between its outside or skin, and its inside or inner organs; between organs and processes; between active and passive relations; and between the positions of subject and that of object. The psychic investment in the body as a whole and in its various parts is as much a function of the subject's relations with others as it is of the subject's own sensations and libido. In this sense, the body image is the result of shared sociocultural conceptions of bodies in general and shared familial and interpersonal fantasy about particular bodies.

Changes to the body and its organs as a result of illness or disease are reflected, even if indirectly, in changes to the body image. For example, even if the cancer of a subject is not experienced as such, there is nonetheless a set of accompanying changes in the strength and state of tiredness of the body. Each physiological and psychological change in the body has concomitant effects on changes in the body image.

Even when the subject's body image is an effect in part of its relations to others, the effects others have on the body image is more far-reaching: appersonization involves the transfer of the meaning which other people's body parts have for them onto the subject's own body image, resulting in the treatment of one's own body as an outside object. It may also involve identification with the symptoms, actions, and fantasies of other people, a kind of psychical vampirism. This occurs primarily through identification, incorporation, and introjection. The subject's body image begins, in the earliest phases of life, by being confused with others (in syncretism and later in transitivism) and their perceptions of themselves and of the child. Others continue to influence the child's perceptions of its own body and the bodies of others.

The body image is always slightly temporally out of step with the current state of the subject's body. The earliest infantile experiences are formative of the parameters and nature of the body image, which is in a condition of continual transformation, but there seems to be a time lag in the perception and registration of real changes in the body image. This may be illustrated in the case of anorexia, where the body image remains at the level of the preanorexic subject's weight, or in the case of aging, where the body image seems resistant to the changes brought about by aging (this may account for the shock one gets in seeing friends after a considerable period—they seem to have aged, whereas the subject feels as if he or she has not). The logic governing registered changes in the body image functions according to different principles than those regulating biological transformations.[19] In the psychogenic disorders of hypochondria, depersonalization, and hysteria, various organs and parts of the subject's body are experienced as separate and discrete, with their own relative independence and autonomy.

The body image is not an isolated image of the body but necessarily involves the relations between the body, the surrounding space, other objects and bodies, and the coordinates or axes of vertical and horizontal. In short, it is a *postural* schema of the body. The body image is the condition of the subject's access to spatiality (including the spatiality of the built environment).

As a result of the work of neurologists, psychologists, and psychoanalysts, a new term, *body image*, now mediates the mind/body polarization, a term which necessarily entails input from both poles in order to function and be effective. This term signals the impossibility of conceiving the polar terms as binaries, as mutually exclusive. But perhaps more interesting, these theorists and clinicians have demonstrated the extreme pliability, the inherent amenability, of the body image to immense transformations, upheavals, and retranscriptions according to psychical, behavioral, biological, social, and signifying changes. The body image does not map a biological body onto a psychosocial domain, providing a kind of translation of material into conceptual terms; rather, it attests to the necessary interconstituency of each for the other, the radical inseparability of biological from psychical elements, the mutual dependence of the psychical and the biological, and thus the intimate connection between the question of sexual specificity (biological sexual differences) and psychical identity.

Lived Bodies
Phenomenology and the Flesh

Corporeal Phenomenology

Merleau-ponty begins with a fundamental presumption, not of a Cartesian dualism of mind and body but of their necessary interrelatedness. He claims that phenomenology wants to understand the relations between consciousness and nature and between interiority and exteriority. The body and the modes of sensual perception which take place through it are not mere physical/physiological phenomena; nor are they simply psychological results of physical causes. Rather, they affirm the necessary connectedness of consciousness as it is incarnated; mind, for him, is always embodied, always based on corporeal and sensory relations.[1] Unlike Sartre, for whom consciousness and reflective self-consciousness (being-for-itself) assert a priority over and are transcendent of the inertia of the immanent body (being-in-itself), Merleau-Ponty begins with the negative claim that the body is not an object. It is the condition and context through which I am able to have a relation to objects. It is both immanent and transcendent. Insofar as I live the body, it is a phenomenon experienced by me and thus provides the very horizon and perspectival point which places me in the world and makes relations between me, other objects, and other subjects possible. It is the body as I live it, as I experience it, and as it shapes my experience that Merleau-Ponty wishes to elucidate. Phenomenological reflection on the body reveals that I am not a subject separated from the world or from others, a mind somehow cut off from matter and space. Unlike Sartre, whose idealism grants a primacy to mind or consciousness, Merleau-Ponty claims to reveal a subject as a "being-to-the-world" (1962: viii), a "subject committed to the world," a subject of perception and behavior as well as cognition and reflection. I am not able to stand back from the body and its experiences to reflect on them; this withdrawal is unable to grasp my body-as-it-is-lived-by-me. I have access to knowledge of my body only by living it.

Instead of conceiving of the human subject as a mind housed or encapsulated in a (quasi-mechanical) body, the "captain of the ship"—a postulate which leads to the related problems of solipsism, the existence of other minds, and the existence of an independent material reality—Merleau-Ponty begins with the postulate that we perceive and receive information of and from the world through our bodies:

The perceiving mind is an incarnated body. I have tried . . . to re-establish the roots of the mind in its body and in its world, going against the doctrines which treat perception as a simple result of the action of external things on our body as well as against those which insist on the autonomy of consciousness. These philosophies commonly forget—in favor of a pure exteriority or of a pure interiority—the insertion of the mind in corporeality, the ambiguous relation with our body, and correlatively, with perceived things. . . . And it is equally clear that one does not account for the facts by superimposing a pure, contemplative consciousness on a thing-like body. . . . Perceptual behavior emerges . . . from relations to a situation and to an environment which are not merely the working of a pure, knowing subject . . . (Merleau-Ponty 1963: 3–4)

For Merleau-Ponty, although the body is both object (for others) and a lived reality (for the subject), it is never simply object nor simply subject. It is defined by its relations with objects and in turn defines these objects as such—it is "sense-bestowing" and "form-giving," providing a structure, organization, and ground within which objects are to be situated and against which the body-subject is positioned. The body is my being-to-the-world and as such is the instrument by which all information and knowledge is received and meaning is generated. It is through the body that the world of objects appears to me; it is in virtue of having/being a body that there are objects for me:

Classical psychology . . . stated that my body is distinguishable from the table or the lamp in that I can turn away from the latter whereas my body is constantly perceived. It is therefore an object which does not leave me. But in this case is it still an object? . . . an object is an object only insofar as it can be moved away from me, and ultimately disappear from my field of vision. Its presence is such that it entails a possible absence. Now the permanence of my body is entirely different in kind. . . . It defies exploration and is always presented to me from the same angle. Its permanence is not the permanence in the world, but a permanence from my point of view. . . . Insofar as it sees or touches the world, my body can therefore be neither seen nor touched. What prevents it ever being an object, ever being "completely constituted," is that it is that by which there are objects. It is neither tangible nor visible insofar as it is that which sees and touches. (Merleau-Ponty 1962: 90–92)

The relation between the subject and objects is thus not causal but based on sense or meaning. The relations of mutual definition governing the body and the world of objects are "form-giving" insofar as the body actively differentiates and categorizes the world into groupings of sensuous experience, patterns of organization and meaning.

Merleau-Ponty attempts to demonstrate this with reference to a series of neurological disturbances, including the complementary yet opposite symptoms of the phantom limb and agnosia; he also outlines details from Goldstein and Gelb's famous case study of the brain-damaged aphasic Schneider.[2] Merleau-Ponty refers to Schneider in a number of texts, starting with *The Structure of Behavior* and culminating in *The Phenomenology of Perception*. Schneider's cerebral lesion entails a series of apparently unrelated disorders in perceptual/visual relations, memory, the perception of tactile spaces, various motor disorders, and the breakdown of language and intellectual skills. He is unable to undertake abstract actions; at most he can participate only in the concrete. Schneider is unable to take on genuinely goal-directed behavior or any actions which rely on abstract functions:

> . . . our patients are unable to imitate or copy anything that is not part of their immediate concrete experience. . . . they have the greatest difficulty in repeating a sentence which is meaningless for them. . . . To say such things . . . demands . . . the ability to live in two spheres, the concrete sphere where "real" things take place and the non-concrete, the merely "possible" sphere, for in saying meaningless things we must shift from one to the other. This the patient is unable to do. He can live and act only in the concrete sphere. He is therefore always himself. He is unable to place himself in the situation of other people nor is he able to impersonate as an actor does. . . . In normal life we are rarely forced into action by the stimulus situation itself. Usually we have to place ourselves . . . in the appropriate situation. The outside world merely gives us the impulse to do this. Thus even the initiation of an action demands the abstract attitude. . . . We may say that the patient has no world at all outside himself and opposed to him in the sense that we do; he is impaired in his capacity for separating himself from the world. His inability to achieve performances which demand an abstract attitude means not only a shrinkage of his personality but also a shrinkage of the world in which he lives. (Goldstein 1963: 53–67)

Schneider's self-identity, his absolute self-coincidence, implies that he is unable to perform the most everyday and taken-for-granted actions. He lives entirely in the concrete. It is not that he has lost motor or sensory or even relevant intellectual abilities, although he does exhibit some impairment. Rather, he lacks an abstract context in which to make use of these skills. For example, he is able to take out his handkerchief from his pocket and blow his nose but is unable to perform these same actions with his eyes shut. He is unable to perform any action or respond to any situation which is not currently present. He can only perform actions by watching his limbs in movement. He is incapable of initiating any action unless he is called to do so by something external. In other words, he is unable to project his wishes, hopes, and plans for the future onto a present situation. Consequently, the world in its abstractness does not give him cues for action, as goal-seeking behavior usually requires. He can grasp and touch objects but not point to them; he cannot draw by imitation, cannot repeat statements. He cannot follow conversations, although he may respond to concrete questions. He cannot understand that single words may be joined to form phrases and sentences; he cannot break down words into letters. He is unable to listen to two conversations at once and cannot tell the difference between a riddle and a problem. He has no capacity to survey or reflect on his past or his future, and he can only see in the direction in which he is looking: "He never sings or whistles of his own accord . . . he never takes an initiative sexually. He never goes out for a walk but always on an errand" (Merleau-Ponty 1962: 134). Merleau-Ponty has argued that a causal explanation, an explanation in terms of physiological or psychological causes, is not possible.

> Thus all of Schneider's troubles are reducible to a unity, but not the abstract unity of the "representative function"; he is "tied" to "actuality," he "lacks liberty," that concrete liberty which comprises the general power of putting oneself in a situation. (Merleau-Ponty 1962: 135)

Schneider's disorders are neither purely bodily nor purely conceptual but result from the breakdown or disintegration of the passage or interconnections between these two spheres.

The irreducibility of psychology to biology and of biology to psychology can be illustrated with the two opposite disorders of the phantom limb and agnosia. In the phantom limb, as explained in the preceding chapter, the patient still suffers a pain in a location where the limb once used to be, before its amputation; agnosia, on the other hand, is the nonrecognition of a part of the body as one's own. The phantom limb illustrates an organ or bodily part within a total body image that is no longer there; agnosia by contrast is the nonrecognition of a body part that should occupy a position within the body image. In traditional psychological and physiological terms, the phantom limb is treated as a memory, a past experience reactivated in the present (hence, an hallucination), and agnosia is seen as a forgetfulness, a refusal or negative judgment. Yet for Merleau-Ponty both demonstrate a fundamental ambivalence on the part of the subject. On one hand, there is a recognition of the loss or possession of the real limb; on the other hand, the actions which the arm, say, would or could have performed are still retained as possible actions for the subject. It is as if the subject refuses to close off the possibilities of actions of which the body is capable. The phantom limb is not a memory or an image (of something now absent). It is "quasi-present." It is the refusal of an experience to enter into the past; it illustrates the tenacity of a present that remains immutable.

By means of these and other neurological disorders, Merleau-Ponty demonstrates that traditional psychology and physiology presume a fundamentally passive body, one on which the sensuousness or perceptuality of objects impinges. Instead, he shows that it is active insofar as it gives form and sense to its own component parts and to its relations with objects in the world. The phantom limb and agnosia indicate that our experiences are organized not by real objects and relations but by the expectations and meanings objects have for the body's movements and capacities. They indicate a "fictional" or fantasmatic construction of the body outside of or beyond its neurological structure, which he explains with reference to the notion of the body schema, which is clearly strongly influenced by Schilder's researches.

The body is fundamentally linked to representations of spatiality and temporality. This relation to space and time is a precondition of the subject's relations with objects. Merleau-Ponty's point is that we grasp the idea of external space only through certain relations we have to our body or corporeal schema. His suggestion is that we acquire motor skills and a system of possible actions or corporeal projects spanning the gulf and spectrum of possibilities, which range from our subjectivity to the external environment:

> Our body is not in space like things; it inhabits or haunts space. It applies itself to space like a hand to an instrument, and when we wish to move about we do not move the body as we move an object. We transport it without instruments . . . since it is ours and because, through it, we have access to space. (Merleau-Ponty 1963: 5)

In other words, we do not grasp space directly or through our senses but through our bodily situation. Space is not understood as a series of relations between different objectively located points, points of equal value; for one thing, this flattens and neutralizes the positive contribution we ourselves make in the perception of objects. Rather, space is understood by us as a relation between these points and a central or organizing perspective which regulates perceptions so that they occupy the same perceptual field. This perspective has no other location than that given by the body:

> . . . these relations are different ways for external stimuli to test, to solicit, and to vary our grasp on the world, our horizontal and vertical anchorage in a place and in a here-and-now. We find that perceived things, unlike geometrical objects, are not bounded entities whose laws of construction we possess *a priori*, but that they are open, inexhaustible systems which we recognize through a certain style of development, although we are never able, in principle, to explore them entirely, even though they never give us more than profiles and perspectival views of themselves. (Merleau-Ponty 1963: 5–6)

Schneider can scratch his nose more readily than point to it; he lives in a space narrowly circumscribed by the spatiality of his practical needs. The space within which he is able to effectively operate is heterogeneous, a set of distinct and significant locations defined by his bodily impulses (the place where it itches or hurts). He does not understand the qualitatively and quantitatively distinct space of physics; for him, space is a continuum of homogeneous points in which no point has greater value than any other.

It is as an embodied subject that the subject occupies a perspective on objects. Its perspective represents the position within space where it locates itself. Its perspective dictates that its modes of access to objects are always partial or fragmentary, interacting with objects but never grasping or possessing them in their independent and complete materiality. The object posed before a subject, a subject engaged with objects, must be a subject situated in space as the (virtual) point of central organization of perspective, the point which organizes a manifold into a field.

The body for Merleau-Ponty is the very condition of our access to and conception of space:

> The "here" applied to my body does not refer to a determinate position in relation to other positions or to external coordinates, but the laying down of the first coordinates, the anchoring of the active body in an object, the situation of the body in the face of its tasks. Bodily space can be distinguished from external space and envelop its parts instead of spreading them out. . . . the body image is . . . a way of stating that my body is in the world. . . . one's own body is the third term . . . in the figure-background structure and every figure stands out against the double horizon of external and bodily space.
>
> By considering the body in movement, we can see better how it inhabits space (and possibly time) because movement is not limited to submitting passively to space and time, it actively assumes them, it takes them up in their basic significance which is obscured in the commonplace of established situations. (Merleau-Ponty 1962: 100–102)

If my consciousness is not spatially located and if external objects are always located in space, how is it possible for consciousness to establish a space or distance between itself and its objects? For Merleau-Ponty, the mediating term necessary to explain their interaction is the "corporeal schema," or body image. He asks us to reflect on how we move our bodies and do things: the body "knows" what its muscular and skeletal actions and posture are in any movement or action, quite independent of any knowledge of physiology or how the body functions. I am able to pick up a pebble and throw it without reflecting on how I am to do it. The movements I make are not simply the addition of various successive mechanical movements of a Cartesian or Hobbesian body-machine: the pebble and my picking it up and throwing it are integrated into a unified relation to my body as a whole. For example, it is not by means of access to a Cartesian abstract or geometrical space that one knows where to scratch in order to satisfy an itch on one's back. I know exactly where it itches and am able, if I can reach it, to scratch without having to locate my hand in relation to the itch. This is true even if I use an instrument like a stick. From this point, Merleau-Ponty claims, the stick is no longer an object for me but has been absorbed or incorporated into my perceptual faculties or body parts. Here he affirms Schilder's notion of the plasticity of the body image, adding to it the philosophical idea of the body image's crucial function in establishing the lived space and time of the subject.

The corporeal or postural schema of the body is what enables us to develop a practical relation to objects in the world and a psychic attachment to our bodies and body parts. Because my body is not seen as a mere object by me, I necessarily have a different relation to it than to any other objects. It is by means of my body that I am able to perceive and interrelate with objects; it is my mode of access to objects. And unlike my perspectival access to all other objects, my own body is not accessible to me in its entirety. I cannot take up a perspective on my body because it is the vantage point from which I have a perspective: "as for my body, I do not observe it itself: in order to do that it would be necessary to have the disposal of a second body which itself would not be observable" (Merleau-Ponty, 1962: 107).

As Merleau-Ponty acknowledges in "The Child's Relations to Others" (in Merleau-Ponty 1963) he owes his understanding of the postural schema of the body to a number of neurologists and psychoanalysts working in the 1920s and 1930s on the first year of life—Head, Wallon, Guillaume, Schilder, Stern, Spitz, Lacan, and others. Merleau-Ponty begins with questions already posed by Wallon and Guillaume. How do I become aware of my body and distinguish it from the bodies and sensations of others? What enables me to identify my body as my own? How do I locate my experiences? All maintain that at first there is a phase of confusion and indistinction, in which the child does not recognize the "otherness" of the other—that is, it does not recognize any boundaries separating itself from the world. Merleau-Ponty describes this as a phase of "anonymous collectivity" or an "undifferentiated group" (1963: 119). René Spitz, in *The First Year of Life* (1965), suggests that there is no distinction between the "psyche and soma, between inside and outside, between drive and object, between "I" and "non-I," and not even regions of the body" (Spitz 1965: 35).

At birth and for the first several days, the outside world is virtually nonexistent for the baby. All its perceptual functions are directed to internal, introceptive processes; they continue to be mediated through introception until several months later, even when the child comes to distinguish itself from its environment. Only at the end of the first week of life does it respond to cues with reflex actions, such as turning its head to the breast when held in a suckling position. The child, however, recognizes the nipple only when it is put in his or her mouth. If anything distracts the child, including its own crying, it will not react to the nipple, even if it is inserted into the child's mouth. Only after the first month do other human beings acquire a special status distinct from other objects; and within a few weeks of this period, it begins to recognize the human face in particular, following its movements with close attention.

The mouth, as Freud recognized, is especially privileged in terms of its sensitivity to sensations. It functions both introceptively and extroceptively. It is a primordial link or bridge connecting perceptions from the inside and the outside of the body. There is a gradual shift from such contact perception to more distance-oriented perception, especially hearing and seeing, but to begin with the various senses are not all operational, not organized or integrated to form a coherent set of synesthetic perceptions. It must learn to link the sensation of sucking at the breast and the visual perception of the mother's face. The cohesiveness of perceptions needs to be built up not by aggregation but by integration. By three months, the child will respond to an adult's face with a smile; but even now the face must be presented front on so that the child can see both eyes and other features; a profile will not elicit the infant's recognition: "At this age level, nothing else, not even the baby's food, provokes this response. . . . 98% of infants smiled during this period in response to any individual, friend or stranger, regardless of sex or colour" (Spitz 1965: 88).

Up to about the third month, the child doesn't really distinguish between introception and extroception. There is no clear evidence that it recognizes the otherness of others. Merleau-Ponty claims that if the child cries when someone goes away, it is not that the child recognizes the other's absence; it is rather that the child has "a sensation of incompleteness," experienced as an internal sensation (1963: 124). These writers seem to agree that the first active processes of extroception occur when the child reacts to the voice of others. This may provoke pleasure, delight, surprise, even fright. The child at the same time becomes aware of its own voice and listens to the various sounds it makes, differentiating them from other sounds. The child will experiment with monologues of sound, repeating the labials and linguals in rhythmic variations.

Probably the most significant link between the introceptive and extroceptive perceptual functions is the child's acquisition of organized visual perception. This too begins in a fragmentary way, and is built up into cohesive perception bit by bit (the subclasses of vision it gains over time include color vision, spatial or depth perception, perceptions of movement, variations of luminosity). We should note that the visual perception of oneself (e.g., in a mirror) is derived from the gradual unification of visual capacities. The recognition of its specular image as an image of itself is the most significant contribution to the acquisition of the corporeal schema. The specular image, while extroceptively perceived, is also still introceptively internalized as a kind of double of itself:

> Until the moment when the specular image arises, the child's body is a strongly felt but confused reality. To recognize his image in a mirror is for him to learn that *there can be a viewpoint taken on him*. . . . By means of the image . . . he becomes capable of being a spectator of himself. Through the acquisition of the specular image, the child notices that he is *visible*, for himself and for others. (Merleau-Ponty 1963: 136)

The Visible and the Invisible

Merleau-Ponty has always seen his work in opposition to and as an attempt to destabilize the structure of binary oppositions dominating so much of Western thought. Rather than valorize one or the other side of a dichotomous pair, rather than affirm their unity and oneness in some kind of global or local holism (which always entails some kind of reductionism) or accept the bifurcation and mutually exclusive and exhaustive status of such pairs, Merleau-Ponty's work, in ways that surprisingly anticipate Derrida's supplementary readings of dichotomous polarizations, attempts to take up and utilize the space in between, the "no-man's land" or gulf separating oppositional terms. This impossible, excluded middle predates and makes possible the binary terms insofar as it precedes and exceeds them, insofar as it is uncontainable in either term. Perception is, as it were, midway between mind and body and requires the functioning of both. Neither empiricism nor idealism, neither pure physiology nor pure psychology, have been able to produce terms to adequately account for the complex interactions and implications involved in perceptual processes. To explain or analyze perception requires an understanding not only of physiological and psychological processes but above all of the ways in which each is mutually implicated with the other.[3]

His defiance of and challenge to binary polarizations places his interests close to those of many feminists, especially those who regard logocentrism as inherently complicit with phallocentrism. His philosophical aims and methods of rendering binary polarization problematic accord quite well with the goals of many feminists—and perhaps most strikingly Luce Irigaray—of making explicit the unspoken assumptions of and debt to femininity and maternity that founds philosophy as we know it. What Merleau-Ponty seems to offer feminists like Irigaray is not simply a common theoretical struggle but, more positively, elements that may augment or enrich feminist theory itself. His emphasis on lived experience and perception, his focus on the body-subject, has resonances with what may arguably be regarded as feminism's major contribution to the production and structure of knowledges—its necessary reliance on lived experience, on experiential acquaintance as a touchstone or criterion of the validity of theoretical postulates. But it is clear that experience cannot be taken as an unproblematic given, a position through which one can judge knowledges, for experience is of course implicated in and produced by various knowledges and social practices. Nevertheless, I would contend that without some acknowledgment of the formative role of experience in the establishment of knowledges, feminism has no grounds from which to dispute patriarchal norms.

As one of the few more or less contemporary theorists committed to the primacy of experience, Merleau-Ponty is in a unique position to provide a depth and sophistication to feminist attempts to harness experience in political evaluation. His understanding of lived experience has three crucial insights from which many feminists could learn. First, he refuses to relegate experience to an ineffable, unquestionable, given category, as some feminists have tended to do. Experience cannot be unproblematically taken as a source of truth, an arbiter of theory (although clearly it must play some role in them). Experience is not outside social, political, historical, and cultural forces and in this sense cannot provide an outside vantage point from which to judge them. Merleau-Ponty's understanding of the constructed, synthetic nature of experience, its simultaneously active and passive functioning, its role in both the inscription and subversion of sociopolitical values, provides a crucial confirmation of many feminists" unspoken assumptions regarding women's experiences. Second, in contrast to the bracketing off of experience in much of poststructuralism and antihumanism, Merleau-Ponty still takes experience seriously, not as something to be explained away as simply untrustworthy or "ideological" but as something to be explained. He renders experience of immediate and direct relevance to philosophy and the production of knowledge. It is not only the starting point of analysis but also a kind of measure against which the vagaries of theory can be assessed. Third, Merleau-Ponty locates experience midway between mind and body. Not only does he link experience to the privileged locus of consciousness; he also demonstrates that experience is always necessarily embodied, corporeally constituted, located in and as the subject's incarnation. Experience can only be understood between mind and body—or across them—in their lived conjunction.

Toward the end of his life, particularly in the unfinished text *The Visible and the Invisible* (1968), Merleau-Ponty shifted the terms in which he understood perception and the mind/body problem, changing the orientation though not the motivating interests guiding his earlier writings. In this last text, his object of theoretical speculation is the concept of "the flesh," a term providing the preconditions and the grounds for the distinctions between mind and body, subject and object, and self and other.[4]

The notion of the body schema or postural model of the body outlined by Merleau-Ponty in *The Phenomenology of Perception* anticipates or provides the origins of the concept of the flesh in *The Visible and the Invisible*. The body is able to move, to initiate and undertake actions, because the body schema is a series, or rather a field, of possible actions, plans for action, maps of possible movements the body "knows" how to perform. The body schema is also the field in which the subject's cohesion and identity as a subject and its intimate incarnation in and as a particular body take place. The concept of the flesh is developed as an "ultimate notion" (Merleau-Ponty 1968: 140), not the union or compound of two substances, but "thinkable by itself," an elementary or foundational term, which "has no name in any philosophy" (139, 147), an "*exemplar sensible*." While it does not displace perception as the thematic object of investigation, it is a more elementary and prior term, the condition of both seeing and being seen, of touching and being touched, and of their intermingling and possible integration, a commonness in which both subject and object participate, a single "thing" folded back on itself.

Whereas in his earlier works Merleau-Ponty stresses the fundamental interimplication of the subject in the object and the object in the subject, in his last text he explores the interrelations of the inside and the outside, the subject and the object, one sense and another in a common flesh—which he describes as the "crisscrossing" of the seer and the visible, of the toucher and the touched, the indeterminacy of the "boundaries" of each of the senses, their inherent transposability, their refusal to submit to the exigencies of clear-cut separation or logical identity. What is described as flesh is the shimmering of a *différance*, the (im)proper belongingness of the subject to the world and the world as the condition of the subject. He attempts a return to prediscursive experience before the overlay of reflection, before the imposition of metaexperiential organization and its codification by reason. A "return" to or reconstitution of such prediscursive experience, a "wild being," an uncultivated or raw sensibility, is necessary to produce a nondualist, nonbinarized ontology. In returning to a prereflective sensible, however, he is not seeking a pure datum uninfluenced by the social; instead, his goal is to find the preconditions within sensibility itself, within the subject that makes the subject open up to and be completed by the world. Neither subject nor object can be conceived as cores, atoms, or nuggets of being, pure presence; not bounded entities, they "interpenetrate," mingle.

Merleau-Ponty illustrates this with reference to the relations between the visible (sensible) and the invisible (intelligible), the seer and the seen, although it is significant that at crucial points in his argument he turns to the relations between the toucher and the touched.[5] The visible is a kind of palpitation of being, never self-identical or absolutely dispersed, a series of fluctuations and differences. It is

> a concretion of visibility, it is not an atom. . . . in general a visible is not a chunk of absolutely hard, indivisible being, offering all naked to a vision which could only be total or null, but is rather a sort of straits between exterior horizons and interior horizons, ever gaping open, something that comes to touch lightly and makes diverse regions of the colored or visible world resound at the distances, a certain differentiation, an ephemeral modulation of this world—less a color or a thing, therefore, than a difference between things and colors, a momentary crystallization of colored being or of visibility. Between the alleged colors and visible, we would find anew the tissue that lines them, sustains them, nourishes them, and which for its part is not a thing, but a possibility, a latency, and a flesh of things. (Merleau-Ponty 1968: 132–33)

The relevance of the visual model to the other senses needs to be carefully assessed, given that there are clear characteristics which can be attributed only to the visual and other sensual features which are relevant to the other senses but not to vision.[6]

To understand the radical departure from other phenomenologies which Merleau-Ponty proposed in his chapter entitled "The Intertwining—the Chiasm" (in *The Visible and the Invisible*), it may be worthwhile to describe briefly the more traditional accounts of perception and vision, including Merleau-Ponty's own earlier writings. Throughout *The Phenomenology of Perception*, Merleau-Ponty describes vision in terms of an activity undertaken by a subject in relation to a distinct and separate object. To this bare presumption—shared equally by empiricists and idealists—Merleau-Ponty adds two other factors: the claim that subjects are always and necessarily embodied, incarnate, corporeal beings and the claim that vision is always composed not of a given sense datum but of a set of relations between figure and ground, horizon and object. In short, vision is always a function of establishing a (visual) field. The conditions of having a visual field, then, involve the constitution of an horizon and the taking up of a perspective:

> The horizon is what guarantees the identity of the object throughout the exploration; it is the correlative of the impending power which my gaze retains over the objects which it has just surveyed, and which it already has over the fresh details which it is able to discover. . . . The object-horizon structure, or the perspective, is no obstacle to me when I want to see the object; for . . . it is the means whereby they are disclosed. (Merleau-Ponty 1968: 67–68)

The Senses

Merleau-Ponty's view in *Phenomenology* made clear the simplicity of traditional modes of isolation in accounts of sense perception and the relations between the information provided by the senses to the production of knowledges. Since the earliest days of Greek philosophy, vision was considered superior to the other senses. Knowledge itself was generally described in metaphors derived from vision and optics. Thus it has tended to function not only as the model for knowledge but also as representative of all the other senses. It is incomplete in itself, and being the most "developed" sense, it requires the support and functioning of other senses. Its role is generally regarded as that of unifying and hierarchically ordering the other senses, taming or honing them.

The epistemological value of sight is based on the clarity and precision of the images of which it is composed. An image, traditionally, has three characteristics: it presents a manifold field or set of events in terms of simultaneity (it is the only nontemporal or synchronous sense); it functions at a distance, setting up a space or field between the seer and the seen, the physical and the psychical; and it does not imply or presume causality (because the other senses are momentary and occasioned by events, vision is ongoing and need not be focused on or caused by any object). These characteristics serve to distinguish vision from the other senses and to place it in a privileged position in terms of the access it yields to what are believed to be the raw elements, the data necessary for the production of knowledge.

> Sight is par excellence the sense of the simultaneous or the coordinated, and thereby of the extensive. A view comprehends many things juxtaposed, as coexistent parts of one field of vision. It does so in an instant: as in a flash, one glance, an opening of the eyes, discloses a world of co-present qualities spread

out in space, ranged in depth, continuing into indefinite distance, suggesting, if any direction on their static order, then by their perspective a direction away from the subject rather than toward it . . . (Jonas, in Spicker 1970: 313)

Just as sight is usually regarded as a spatial sense, dominated by a field more than an object, hearing is usually understood as a temporal sense, in which duration is a major characteristic. In this opposition between sight and hearing, it is believed that sound discloses not an object but the region or location of an object. Rather than producing iconic representations, as does vision, it functions indexically. There must be a cause, object, or event producing a sound, although sound in no way resembles it. As sight holds together and unifies various disparate objects, cotemporal sounds are unified into a single sound no longer resembling its components (for example, stronger sounds drown out weaker sounds). Only a few sounds can be followed simultaneously, and beyond a certain narrow limit, sound rapidly becomes noise. Unlike the activity sight bestows on the seer, hearing is entirely conditional on being exposed to a noise-emitting event. Admittedly the subject can actively attend to sound or choose to ignore it as much as possible, but even so, the subject must wait for something to stimulate the hearing organs. To provide a temporal continuity, hearing alone is not adequate, for it must rely on memory. In other words, whereas vision is inscribed as an activity, hearing is characterized as a passivity. If, however, sight and hearing are set up as polar opposites—sight being spatial and active and hearing being temporal and passive—this cannot be understood as an effect or necessity of nature but as the ways in which the senses have been transcribed, incised, and rendered functional. There is no logical necessity—and indeed, given the ways in which temporality and spatiality or activity and passivity define and are implicated in each other, there is no physiological reason for these couplings or associations.

Touch shares with hearing the successiveness of its impressions, their momentary impact. It also shares with vision the presumption of a static or given object (in this sense, touch is also iconic). Touch may well prove to be the most difficult and complex of all the senses to analyze because it is composed of so many interacting dimensions of sensitivity, involving a number of different functions (touch, pressure, texture, frequency, pain, and heat). In other words, touch, like seeing and hearing, is overlaid and constituted through transcriptions, retracings, modes of dimensionality that involve a kind of cultural writing which both (provisionally) separates the senses and entails the possibility of their realignments and retranscriptions into other terms.

Touch is regarded as a contact sense. First, it provides contiguous access to an abiding object; the surface of the toucher and the touched must partially coincide. Second, touch may produce (along with vision) the notion of shape or form, but (unlike vision, which gives shape its simultaneity or synchronicity) touch only yields successive or additive, diachronic notions of shape. Third, touch grants the subject access to the texture of objects (which vision only intimates). Texture, like shape, is not given in a single contact but is a differential notion and depends on a comparison of different textures. Fourth, touch yields access to the surface—and, in some cases at least, to the depth—of objects, depending on their composition. Fifth, touch provides information (again, differentially or comparatively). It has many sense receptors, including the body's entire surface, but the hand is probably the most refined and sensitive. Touching, like hearing, is limited in the amount of simultaneous information that can be processed. Like hearing and sight, it is a modality of difference:[7]

> It appears in the embryo before the other sensory systems (towards the end of the second month of gestation), preceding the two other proximal systems— the olfactory and gustatory—the vestibular apparatus, and the two distal systems (the auditory and the visual), obeying the biological law that the earlier a system develops, the more likely it is to be fundamental. It has a great density of receptors (50 per 1000 square millimetre). . . . The skin can judge time (less well than the ear) and space (less well than the eye), but it alone combines the spatial and temporal dimensions . . . (Anzieu 1989: 14)

Even in *The Phenomenology of Perception* Merleau-Ponty argues that the senses cannot be so readily separated off from each other in the attempt to understand their specific modalities and properties, for in lived experience the senses interact, form a union, and yield access to a singular world. Sight and touch are able to communicate with each other, to provide confirmations (or contradictions) of each other, because they are the senses of one and the same subject operating simultaneously, within one and the same world. The senses not only communicate with each other, adding to or enriching each other; they are transposable, within certain limits, onto each other's domains, although they remain irreducible in their differences. Sight, touch, hearing, and smell function contemporaneously and combine their effects. The senses are transposable only because each lays claim to a total world, a world in fact defining the subject's sensory state; each world is able to mesh with, be gridded in terms of, the other "sensory worlds":

> The senses communicate with each other. Music is not in visible space, but it besieges, undermines and displaces that space. The two spaces are distinguishable only against the background of a common world and can compete with each other only because they both lay claim to total being.
> The sight of sounds and the hearing of colors comes about in the same way as the unity of the gaze through the two eyes: in so far as my body is not a collection of adjacent organs, but a synergic system, all the functions of which are exercised and linked together in the general action of being in the world, in so far as it is the congealed face of existence. . . . When I say that I see a sound, I mean that I echo the vibration of the sound with my whole sensory being, and particularly with that sector of myself which is susceptible to colors. (Merleau-Ponty 1962: 232–34)

In short, for Merleau-Ponty, the senses are able to be "translated" into each other, or at least understood in the terms of the other senses, only because of the unity provided by the body image. It is through the mediation of the body image that the information provided by the different bodily senses can be integrated, unified, coordinated, or even put into comparison or conflict: "My body is the fabric into which all objects are woven, and it is, at least in relation to the perceived world, the general instrument of my 'comprehension' " (235).

Merleau-Ponty is not the only phenomenologist interested in the question of the integration and transposition of the senses. Levinas too addresses this question of establishing a kind of "kinesthetic intertranslation" between one perceptual system and another or at least a transposition of the senses. The visual resonates with the sayable; the light is capable of eliciting a tactile, textured response; hearing can be visualized.

The Reversibility of the Flesh

Flesh is the term Merleau-Ponty uses to designate being, not as a plenitude, self-identity, or substance but as divergence or noncoincidence. Flesh is no longer associated with a privileged animate category of being but is being's most elementary level. Flesh is being's reversibility, its capacity to fold in on itself, a dual orientation inward and outward, which Merleau-Ponty has described—not unproblematically—as "invagination."[8] The flesh is reflexivity, that fundamental gap or dehiscence of being that Merleau-Ponty illustrates with a favorite example, the "double sensation," an example that clearly illustrates the various gradations between subjectivity and objectuality. Between feeling (the dimension of subjectivity) and being felt (the dimension of objectuality) is a gulf spanned by the indeterminate and reversible phenomenon of the being touched of the touching, the crossing over of what is touching to what is touched, the ambiguity which entails that each hand is in the (potentially reversible) position of both subject and object, the position of both phenomenal and objectual body.

Between touching and being touched, between seeing and being seen, there is a fundamental reversibility. In the case of touch, for example, Merleau-Ponty points out that there are three modalities or manifestions of touch: touching of an object, touching of the properties or qualities of an object, and touching of the touch, or what in *The Phenomenology of Perception* he refers to as the "double sensation." In the double sensation my right hand is capable of touching my left hand as if the latter were an object. But in this case, unlike an object, my left hand feels the right hand touching it. My left hand has the double sensation of being both the object and the subject of the touch. It is not the case that I have two contrary sensations at the same time (as one might feel two objects at the same time); rather each hand is in the ambiguous position of being capable of taking up the positions of either the toucher or the touched. If the double sensation makes it clear that at least in the case of tactile perception, the subject is implicated in its objects and its objects are at least partially constitutive of the subject, Merleau-Ponty wants to argue that such a model is just as relevant for vision.

It is on the basis of the double sensation that Merleau-Ponty frames his arguments regarding the seer and the visible: it is in an analogy with and in the interlocking of the tangible and the visible that he demonstrates the implication of the seer in the visible, the shared participation of the subject and object in a generalized visibility. The example of touch is in fact more convincing, for the gulf between subject and object is never so distant as in vision, where the crossing of the subject into the object is more easily recognizable because access to either the inside or the outside is simply a matter of shifting focus rather than literally changing positions. Merleau-Ponty wishes to apply the same principles of folding back or invagination that mark his discussion of the double sensation. While it is clear that in the case of touch, the toucher is always touched, in traditional understandings of vision, the seer sees at a distance and is unimplicated in what is seen. But for Merleau-Ponty the seer's visibility conditions vision itself, is the ground the seer shares with the visible, the condition of any relation between them.

To see, then, is also, by implication, to be seen. Seeing entails having a body that is itself capable of being seen, that is visible.[9] This is the very condition of seeing, the condition of embodiment:

> . . . he who looks must not himself be foreign to the world that he looks at. As soon as I see, it is necessary that the vision . . . be doubled with a complementary vision or with another vision: myself seen from without, such as another would see me, installed in the midst of the visible, occupied in considering it from a certain spot . . . he who sees cannot possess the visible unless he is possessed by it, unless he is of *it*, unless . . . he is one of the visibles, capable by a singular reversal, of seeing them—he who is one of them. (1968: 134–35)

Merleau-Ponty is making a stronger claim than that every person who sees is capable of being seen by other subjects. His point is ontological and not interpersonal: the painter sees trees; but the trees also, in some sense, see the painter (his example, 1968: 167). This attribution of visibility as well as vision to the seer is not the result of a problematic anthropomorphism on Merleau-Ponty's part; rather, it is a claim regarding the seer's mode of material existence. While it is clear in the case of touch that the toucher is always touched, on the classical conception of vision, the seer, in seeing at a distance, is unimplicated in what is seen. But on his account, the seer's visibility conditions vision itself. Instead of any anthropomorphism or animism, Merleau-Ponty is claiming not an actual but only an in-principle reversibility of seer and seen or toucher and touched:

> To begin with, we spoke summarily of a reversibility of the seeing and the visible, of the touching and the touched. It is time to emphasize that it is a *reversibility always immanent and never realized in fact*. My left hand is always

on the verge of touching my right hand touching things, but I never reach co-incidence; the coincidence eclipses at the moment of realization . . . likewise I do not hear myself as I hear others, the sonorous existence of my voice is for me as it were poorly exhibited; I have rather an echo of its articulated exis-tence, it vibrates through my head rather than outside. I am always on the same side of my body, it presents itself to me in one invariable perspective. (1968: 147–48)

Although all perception, all sensible existence, entails a reversibility based on the belongingness of the material subject to its material world, this reversibility is asymmetrical. It is in this sense that the trees can be said to "see" the painter: as visible, trees and the painter are of the same "matter," flesh. The trees are a mirror of my visibility, as is anything I see.[10]

There is always a slippage in the double sensation because one's two hands are part of the same body. They remain irreducible to each other (the left hand feeling the right hand is not the same as the right hand feeling the left), split between touching and being touched, in spite of their potential interchangeabil-ity. The subject can at best experience the transformation of one position into another, but never their identity. The subject brings to the world the capacity to turn the world back on itself, to fold it over itself and the world, introducing that fold in which the subject is positioned as a perceiving, perspectival mobility. To explain this asymptotic self-coincidence Merleau-Ponty experiments with a series of metaphors which he gradually modifies. This relation, he claims, shows the human body as a "being of two leaves," one of which is an object in a world of other objects, the other of which is a perceiver of these objects. It is doubled back on itself. But to leave the metaphor at this point is to reassert simply another form of dualism, a union of incompatible properties:

> If one wants metaphors, and it would be better to say that the body sensed and the body sentient are as the obverse and the reverse, or again, as two segments of one sole circular course which goes above from left to right and below from right to left, which is but one sole movement in its two phases. . . . if the body is one sole body in its two phases, it incorporates into itself the whole of the sensible and with the same movement incorporates itself into a "sensible in itself." (Merleau-Ponty 1968: 138)

Language too is understood by Merleau-Ponty according to the self-enfold-ing of the flesh. Language is not dependent on any voice but is what gives voice to the world itself. He writes that "language is everything since it is the voice of no one, since it is the very voice of the things, the waves and the forests" (155). Language, in short, is the result of or is made possible by the dehiscence or fold-ing back of the flesh of the world. In this sense, language too is "another flesh" (153), another "wild being."

Perception involves neither keeping the self-contained object at a distance nor the purely perceptual functioning of a self-identical subject. Each is implicated in and necessary for the existence of the other as such. The flesh is that elementary, precommunicative domain out of which both subject and object, in their mutual interactions, develop. The subject can no longer be conceived as an enclosed nucleus of identity or as an empty receptivity ready to take in the contents provided by objects. And objects can no longer be viewed as a pure positivity or simply as an aggregate of sensations. Subject and object, mind and body, the visible and the invisible, are intercalated; the "rays," the lines of force, indelibly etch the one into the other. The flesh is composed of the "leaves" of the body interspersed with the "leaves" of the world: it is the chiasm linking and separating the one from the other, the "pure difference" whose play generates persons, things, and their separations and unions.

The subject and the object are inherently open to each other, for they are constituted in the one stroke dividing the flesh into its various modalities. They are interlaced one with the other, not externally but through their reversibility and exchangeability, their similarity-in-difference and difference-in-similarity. Things solicit the flesh just as the flesh beckons to and as an object to things. Perception is the flesh's reversibility, the flesh touching, seeing, perceiving itself, one fold (provisionally) catching the other in its own self-embrace.

Feminist Phenomenology?

Many feminists have found support for their various projects in Merleau-Ponty's particular brand of phenomenology, but it is significant that of all the feminist writings on his works with which I am familiar, even those feminists strongly influenced by him remain, if not openly critical, then at least suspicious of his avoidance of the question of sexual difference and specificity, wary of his apparent generalizations regarding subjectivity which in fact tend to take men's experiences for human ones. It is significant too that generally, with the exception of Irigaray, most feminists have little to say about his last works and about his notion of the flesh, concentrating instead on either his understanding of sexuality (as in Judith Butler's critical reading [1990]) or his notions of embodiment (as Iris Young does in her demonstration of phenomenology's incapacity to adequately account for female corporeality and pregnancy [1990]). I will return to these critical readings shortly but for the moment would like to concentrate on Irigaray's analysis of "The Intertwining—The Chiasm," as she presents it in *Ethique de la différence sexuelle* (1984).

Merleau-Ponty does not explicitly address the question of sexual difference in *The Visible and the Invisible*, but if Irigaray's reading is appropriate, it is clear that his work derives much from an implicit sexualization of ontology, the utilization of a whole series of metaphors embedded in and derived from relations between the sexes. These metaphors underlie and make possible his notion of the flesh and of reversibility. In this sense, the feminine may be understood as the unspoken, disembodied underside of the flesh: the flesh, Irigaray argues, has a point-for-point congruence with the attributes of both femininity and maternity.

To rather drastically oversimplify her elliptical style, her objections to Merleau-Ponty's reworking of being in terms of the flesh revolve around three major claims: first, that the privileged, indeed dominant, position of vision in his writings, in overpowering and acting as a model for all other perceptual relations, submits them to a phallic economy in which the feminine figures as a lack or a blind spot; second, that the concept of the flesh is implicitly coded in terms of the attributes of femininity; and third, a related point, that Merleau-Ponty disavows the debt that the flesh owes to maternity. I will turn briefly to each of these issues.

Irigaray claims that Merleau-Ponty privileges vision in terms of metaphors of fluidity and absorption; for example, he compares the intimacy of the relations between the seer and the visible to the indeterminacy of the relations between "the sea and the strand" (1968: 131). For Irigaray this metaphorics of fluids, emblematic of femininity in *This Sex Which Is Not One* (1985b) and *Marine Lover* (1991), signifies not only the "formlessness" of feminine *jouissance* but more particularly the amniotic element that houses the child in the mother's body and continues to be a "watermark" etched on the child's body. In this sense the womb and the earliest relations between mother and child, those relations between the operations of a fully constituted vision, must remain in darkness, a kind of nocturnal state that precludes but preconditions vision, an invisible that Merleau-Ponty can never acknowledge:

> If it was not the visible that is in question here, it would be possible to believe that Merleau-Ponty alludes here to intrauterine life. After all, he employs the "images" of the sea and the strand. Of the immersion and the emergence? And he speaks of the risk of disappearance of the seer/seeing and the visible. What doubly corresponds to an existence in the intrauterine nesting: who is still in this night does not see and remains without any visible. . . . Especially without memory of that first event where he is enveloped-touched by a tangible invisible out of which even his eyes are formed but which he will never see: without seeing, neither visible nor visibility in this place. (Irigaray 1984: 144–45)

This darkness or invisibility of the maternal sojourn conditions and makes vision possible. It cannot be understood simply as an absence of vision, a lack of light, for it is a positivity. This tactility is not entirely obscured by Merleau-Ponty's account of vision, for it infiltrates his very first example, that of seeing colors. In confronting a color, the subject is not confronted with a "pellicle" or atom of being but with a field of differences—differences between colors, shapes, and textures and differences between colors and that which is colored. As Irigaray notes, color here must function as a fluidity; it presumes a metaphorics of the tactile and the feminine:

> [Color] pours itself out—stretches itself out, escapes itself . . . imposes itself upon me as a recall of what is most archaic in me, the fluid. That through

which I have received life, have been enveloped in my prenatal sojourn, have been surrounded, dressed, fed, in another body. That by the grace of which I could see the light, could be born, and, moreover, see: the air, the light. . . . Color resuscitates, in me, the whole of anterior life . . . (Irigaray 1984:147)

Perhaps more important is her claim that the visible and the tactile do not, as Merleau-Ponty asserts, have a relation of reciprocity and mutual dependence. As I noted earlier, Merleau-Ponty turns to the tactile to illustrate the thesis of reversibility even though he has thus far restricted his claims to the visual. This reversion to the tactile is not simply a lapse or a more simple example: Merleau-Ponty needs to invoke the tactile at this point because its characteristics are not generalizable for all the senses—vision operates differently.

To illustrate this claim, Irigaray ever so slightly transforms his example. It will be recalled that Merleau-Ponty invokes the phenomenon of the double sensation, the case of one hand feeling another which is itself feeling an object. Refashioning these two hands, Irigaray instead evokes the image of the two hands joined at the palms, with fingers stretched: a relation of symmetry between the two hands rather than the kind of structural domination or hierarchy that Merleau-Ponty describes in giving one hand access to the other without in its turn being touched by the other. For him, there is always a slippage in the double sensation: they remain irreducible to each other. At best the subject can experience the transformation of one position into the other, but not their simultaneity. This other kind of touching, Irigaray suggests, cannot presume the dominance of one or the other hand, for it is a mutual and reciprocal touching, one, of course, not unlike the touching of the "two lips" which serves as her most consistent description of female sexuality.

> We must habituate ourselves to think that every visible is cut out in the tangible. Every tactile being in some manner promised to visibility and that there is encroachment, infringement, not only between the touched and the touching but also between the tangible and the visible, which is encrusted in it, as conversely, the tangible itself is not a nothingness of visibility, is not without visual existence. . . . Every vision takes place somewhere in the tactile space. There is a double and crossed situating of the visible in the tangible and the tangible in the visible; the two maps are complete and yet they do not merge into one. The two parts are total parts and yet are not superposable. (Merleau-Ponty 1968: 134)

In opposition to Merleau-Ponty, Irigaray claims that the map provided by the tactile is not congruous with that provided by the visual. In her understanding, the visual and the tactile function according to different logics and rhythms, although it is clear that there is some interchange between them. There is, she claims, a surreptitious reclamation and reordering of the tactile by the visual, which subordinates all the other senses to its exigencies and forms. Irigaray denies that the visible can be situated within the tangible or that the tangible is situated through the visual: theirs is not a relation of reciprocity, for the tangible provides the preconditions and the grounds of the visible. In brief, her claim is that the visible requires the tangible but the tangible is perfectly capable of an existence autonomous from the visible (a case that is perhaps best illustrated in the existence of blindness—one cannot conceive of a case of a tangible equivalent to blindness, where touch no longer functions while the other senses remain operative; if the tangible does not function, the subject is in a state of unconsciousness). In her understanding, the tangible is the unacknowledged base or foundation, the source of the visible that renders any comparison between them false: they are not comparable, for they occupy different logical positions—one is the foundation and origin of the other. The tangible is the invisible, unseeable milieu of the visible, the source of visibility; it precedes the distinction between active and passive and subject and object: "I see only through the touching of the light" (Irigaray 1984: 155).

Most particularly, Irigaray suggests, along lines similar to her reading of the psychoanalytic privileging of vision in the story of Oedipus, that the visual is the domain in which lack is to be located; it is the order of plenitude, gestalt, and absence: the order which designates female genitals as missing, an order which is incompatible with the plenitude, enfolding and infinite complexity of the tactile and the tangible. What remains invisible within phallocentrism is both the prenatal condition of corporeal existence, the child's inability to see the mother as source or origin of its existence, and the existence of the other sex, a sex different from and incommensurable with the subject: "If I cannot see the other in its alterity, and if the other cannot see me, my body no longer sees anything in the difference. I become blind as soon as it is about a body that is sexed differently" (Irigaray 1984: 157). It is not, for Irigaray, simply a matter of opening one's eyes and having a good look. The kind of invisibility of the other sex for the self-same is not curable through vision itself. Her claim seems to be more ontological: that when it comes to the otherness of the other (whether woman for man, man for woman, or any others) the subject is necessarily unable to see that otherness. We see nothing in the difference because difference itself cannot be grasped, made present; hence I remain blind to—but equally unable to hear or feel—a body that is sexed differently.

For Irigaray, it is significant that Merleau-Ponty, perhaps without being aware of what he commits himself to in this maneuver, describes the reversal of the seer and the visible in terms of the two lips.[11] These two lips are not those lived and experienced by women as such, although his metaphor may be an attempt to reappropriate this carnal intimacy of female corporeality: his lips remain each with their own identity and place, one on the side of the seer, the other on the side of the visible; neither can touch itself through touching the other—the point of Irigaray's self-enfolding metaphor—for neither is able to dissolve its boundaries through its intimacy with the other.

More primordial than vision, the tangible is also the necessary accompaniment of the earliest sensations, those in the blackness of the womb, those to do with hearing, which, for Irigaray, is necessarily bound up with the maternal voice. Chronologically between the touch and seeing, hearing, while relying on tactility, cannot hide its earliest feminine/maternal origins: the music of the womb, the precondition of both sound and meaning. The tactile is related by Irigaray to the concept of the mucus, which always marks the passage from inside to outside, which accompanies and lubricates the mutual touching of the body's parts and regions. The mucus is neither the subjective touching of the toucher nor the objectivity of the touched but the indeterminacy of any distance between them. It escapes control, not being subject to the kind of voluntary slippage by which the touching hand becomes the touched. She suggests that the mucus may represent the toucher/touched indeterminacy more precisely than one hand grabbing the other.

Her argument is that Merleau-Ponty's theoretical paradigm owes a debt—indeed, its conceptual foundations—to femininity and maternity, a debt whose symptoms reside in the kind of language of pregnancy he continually invokes to articulate the emergence of that torsion within the flesh that constitutes and unites the seer and the visible. The world remains isomorphic with the subject, existing in a complementary relation of reversibility. The perceiving, seeing, touching subject remains a subject with a proprietorial relation to the visible, the tactile: he stands over and above while remaining also within his world, recognizing the object and the (sexed) other as versions or inversions of himself, reverse three-dimensional "mirrors," posing all the dangers of mirror identifications:[12]

> If there is no cutting of the cord and of osmotic exchanges with the maternal world and its substitutes, how could sublimation of the flesh take place? It continues becoming in closed circuit, within sorts of nourishing relationships to the other. Does it sublimate itself in order to accede to the alliance with the other? It does not seem so. It perpetuates a state, entertains it in its permanence, absorbing its cuttings and shocks? What is called reversibility here is perhaps also that by which the subject producing some mucus at the exterior re-envelops itself in it. Some elaboration of the carnal takes place there. But always in its solipsistic relationships to the maternal. There *is not a single trace of a carnal idea of the other woman nor of a sublimation of the flesh with the other*. At most an alchemy of substitution of a placentary nourishment. (Irigaray 1984: 168; emphasis in original)

Sexuality and the Lived Body

If Merleau-Ponty does not address the question of sexuality or the sex of the body in *The Visible and the Invisible*, he does devote chapter five of *The Phenomenology of Perception* to the question of the body in its sexual being. Although there is much of value in his discussion—Judith Butler (1990), for example, strongly praises some facets of his notion of sexuality for his commitment to seeing sexuality not as a drive or a cause of behavior but as a modality of existence, infusing all aspects of the ways we face and act in the world, part of our situation in the world—at the same time, and particularly in his analysis of Schneider's sexuality, he is clearly representing sexuality on the model of male sexual experiences while ignoring female sexuality.[13]

Iris Young, although developing a quite different account of embodiment than that represented by Butler's discussion of Merleau-Ponty's work, seems to come to a similiar broad conclusion: that while Merleau-Ponty provides a number of crucial insights about the forms and structure of human embodiment, he nevertheless excludes or cannot explain those specific corporeal experiences undergone by women. Young elaborates in considerable detail the specificities of female embodiment and lived experience in her explorations of women's corporeal comportment and ways of compartmentalizing their bodily unity to undertake physical tasks. In the experience of breasted existence in a sexist society, for example, breasts are an inherent bodily attribute subjectively lived and at the same time function as objects, both for men and for women. And in the ambiguous and unbounded experiences of pregnancy, we can no longer definitively specify whether it is one subject/body or two that is in question. The relations between immanence and transcendence, between owning and being a body, between subject and object or one subject and another, are not the same for women as for men, in ways that Merleau-Ponty seems unaware of.

Significantly, Merleau-Ponty opens his discussion of the sexuality of the lived body with reference to the breakdown of sexual interest and activity in the case of Schneider. Schneider has little if any interest in sexual activities. Indeed, sexual desires, activities, and relations seem to have lost all meaning for him. For other persons in sexual situations—a caress, a kiss—contact with the erotogenic zones induces (and results from) sexual desire, a desire to continue and prolong itself through intimate contact with another. But for Schneider, all sexual contact with others is momentary and localized, lasting only as long as the contact:

> [Schneider] no longer seeks sexual intercourse of his own accord. Obscene pictures, conversations on sexual topics, the sight of a body, do not arouse desire in him. The patient hardly ever kisses, and the kiss for him has no value as sexual stimulation. Reactions are strictly local and do not begin to occur without contact. . . . At every stage it is as if the subject did not know what is to be done. There are no active movements, save a few seconds before the orgasm which is extremely brief. (Merleau-Ponty 1962: 154)

Exactly how and why a man who has no interest in sex has an orgasm, however brief, neither Goldstein and Gelb nor Merleau-Ponty explain. But leaving that aside, Merleau-Ponty uses Schneider's case to argue against the prevailing beliefs that sexuality is an instinct modeled on the reflex, in which sexual organs respond to appropriate stimuli, as it were, automatically. If this were the case then a cerebral injury of the kind Schneider sustained would have no effect on the subject's sexual responsiveness (as indeed is the case with hunger). For those without Schneider's injuries, the sexual object is not perceived like any other perceptual object. The desexualized object does not beckon or entice the subject with its secret recesses as does the sexual object, inducing greater intimacy. Schneider lacks sexual desire because he has no context or is incapable of producing a context, a set of future possibilities, for current caresses.

This erotic and eroticizing perception, in which the subject is open to and partially productive of the intimate exploration of and attachment to a sexual object, is a projection of possible futures onto the structure of the lived present. This eroticized perception is neither objective (in the sense of shared or intersubjective) nor purely conceptual, intellectual, based on ideas, because, as Merleau-Ponty states, desire "understands blindly in binding a body to a body." To perceive the other's body as desirable means converting the other's sexual "physiognomy" into a set of signs addressed to the subject, reorienting movements, activities, and behaviors with other significances, reordering erogenous zones so that they are privileged not only in the body of the other but above all in the subject's body (through the intercommunication of body images). The subject perceives the outer surface and behavior of the other in terms of its own inner animations, its vibrant sensitivity.[14]

It is only the sensory, perceiving subject, the corporeal subject, who is capable of initiating (sexual) desire, responding to and proliferating desire. The libido is not an effect of instincts, biological impulses, or the bodily reaction to external stimuli. It emanates from the structure of sensibility, a function and effect of intentionality, of the integrated union of affectivity, motility, and perception. Sexuality is not a reflex arc but an "intentional arc" that moves and is moved by the body as acting perceiver.

Merleau-Ponty's integration of the mind/body duality and his attempts to accord perception a primacy in psychical and biological life have provided a crucial set of strategic terms which feminists can use as they will in their attempts to think a radical notion of sexual difference. Although, like psychoanalytic theory, Merleau-Ponty's work provides a set of powerful insights and a broad methodological framework in which to rethink the body outside of dualism, his work remains inadequate for understanding the differences between the sexes. And if the reservations of Alphonso Lingis are to be taken seriously regarding Merleau-Ponty's understanding of sexuality in particular, it remains inadequate for rethinking male, let alone female, sexuality, for it is incapable of accounting for or adequately conceiving voluptuous passion.

Lingis claims that in spite of Merleau-Ponty's attempts to render sexuality as part of the meaningful and meaning-producing intentionality of subjects, he reduces desire too readily to significance and consequently leaves out of account its affectivity, force, or drive. Where Freud perhaps too strongly emphasizes desire (enabling it to be readily equated with instincts), Merleau-Ponty does not provide it with a central enough role, with a disturbing, disquieting, and disruptive role, in perceptual life:

> Does not the orgasmic body figure as a body decomposed, dismembered, dissolute, where postures and dynamic axes form and deform in the limp indecisiveness of the erotic trouble? Is it not a breaking down into a mass of exposed organs, secretions, striated muscles, systems turning into pulp and susceptibility? The orgasmic body is . . . the body drifting toward a state on the far side of organization and sense, a state where action loses its seriousness and becomes play . . . (Lingis 1985a: 55–56)

If we can for the moment ignore the sexual specificity of Lingis's remarks—he seems to have no awareness that what he provides is not a description of the dissolution of the orgasmic body but only the dissolution of the male body after the man's orgasm—we may agree that sexuality may be that arena in which intentionality breaks down, no longer functions adequately, but where its breakdown is positively sought and relished with pleasure.

Perhaps more serious than Lingis's objections is the claim that in discussing the question of sexuality and the body image, Merleau-Ponty leaves out—indeed, is unable to address—the question of sexual difference, the question of what kind of human body he is discussing, what kind of perceptual functions and what kind of sexual desire result from the sexual morphology and particularity of the subject. Never once in his writings does he make any suggestion that his formulations may have been derived from the valorization and analysis of the experiences of only one kind of subject. The question of what other types of human experience, what other modalities of perception, what other relations, subjects may have with objects is not, cannot be, raised in the terms he develops. Along with Lingis and others, he seems unaware of the masculinity and phallocentrism of their various (phenomenological) analyses of the lived body, the fact that these may be able to be described in terms quite other than and possibly alien to their own. Each presents a discussion of sexuality as if it were the same dynamical force, with the same psychological structures and physiological features, for any sexed subject.

It is not simply a matter of providing women with a "genuine recognition" of their sexual specificity, as if there is the possibility of a direct and unmediated relation between the two sexes, or between any two individuals. Irigaray seems to be arguing against any notion of self-sufficiency or self-identity, against "a reversal of the gift of flesh, maternal, into the self-sufficiency of the subject of and in language" (1984: 167). Sexual specificity is possible only if there is already an unrecognizable and ungraspable sexual difference. Identity is itself the solidification or coagulation of these potentially volatile and unstable differences. We can affirm this interval by which we are incessantly remade only if we acknowledge the unrecognizable difference of the other sex.[15] Feminists need to seriously question whether phenomenological descriptions are appropriate for women's experience and, if they are not, whether it is desirable that they should be or whether, instead, altogether new and different theoretical terms are necessary—and how such terms may be developed.

PART III

The Outside In

5 | Nietzsche and the Choreography of Knowledge

"If the skin were parchment and the blows you gave me were ink . . . "
Dromio the slave to Antipholus his master, in *The Comedy of Errors*

IN THE THREE preceding chapters I examined psychoanalytic, neurological, and phenomenological accounts of the subject's lived experience and the psychical structuring of its corporeal exterior. I explored the ways in which various models and theories explain how the body's outside, or exteriority, is lived and experienced, the ways in which the inside constitutes and accepts itself as an outside, how experience itself structures and gives meaning to the ways in which the body is occupied and lived. I looked at how the subject's psychical interior can be understood as an introjection, a form of internalization of (the meaning and significance of) the body and its parts, and conversely, how the body is constituted through projection as the boundary, limit, edge, or border of subjectivity, that which divides the subject in the first instance from other subjects and in the second, from objects in the world. I suggested that in psychoanalytic and phenomenological terms, the psychical attitudes and experiences of the body are necessary ingredients of the subject's acquisition of a unified and cohesive body image and a functional, activity-generating, and responsive body. In discussing various psychological and neurophysiological breakdowns and disturbances, I argued that these entail major and in many cases unpredictable psychical effects which may dramatically alter the subject's body image, changing psychological processes as well as motor and sensory actions and reactions. I explored the ways in which the psychical interior has made the body its forms of exteriority, as it were from the inside out. In this and the following chapters, I propose to explore the ways in which the social inscriptions of the surface of the body generate a psychical interiority—the movement from the outside in. With this aim in mind, I intend to examine a broad movement in the history of philosophy, beginning with Nietzsche, which has interrogated the primacy of consciousness or experience in conceptions of subjectivity and displaced the privilege of these terms by focusing on the body as a sociocultural artifact rather than as a manifestation or externalization of what is private, psychological, and "deep" in the individual. This chapter will be profoundly superficial in the sense that questions of internality, of psychical or affective operations, will be temporarily put to one side. In their place, I will examine a number of philosophical positions on the body, from Nietzsche to Foucault, Deleuze, and Lingis, which outline the procedures and powers which carve, mark, incise—that is, actively produce—the body as historically specific, concrete, and determinate.

In psychical notions of the body or body image, the body can be understood as the site of the intermingling of mind and culture; it can also be seen as the symptom and mode of expression and communication of a hidden interior or depth. In this part of the book, comprising this and the next two chapters, however, the body is seen as a purely surface phenomenon, a complex, multifaceted surface folded back on itself, exhibiting a certain torsion but nevertheless a flat plane whose incision or inscription produces the (illusion or effects of) depth and interiority.

Whereas psychoanalysis and phenomenology focus on the body as it is experienced, rendered meaningful, enmeshed in systems of significations, Nietzsche, Foucault, Deleuze, Lingis, and others whose work I will analyze, focus on the body as a social object, as a text to be marked, traced, written upon by various regimes of institutional, (discursive and nondiscursive) power, as a series of linkages (or possibly activities) which form superficial or provisional connections with other objects and processes, and as a receptive surface on which the body's boundaries and various parts or zones are constituted, always in conjunction and through linkages with other surfaces and planes. To briefly illustrate: oral sexuality can be retranscribed in corporeal terms. Instead of describing the oral drive in terms of what it feels like, as an endogenously originating psychical representation striving for an external, absent, or lost object (the fantasmatic and ultimately impossible object of desire), orality can be understood in terms of what it does: creating linkages with other surfaces, other planes, other objects or assemblages. The child's lips, for example, form connections (or in Deleuzian terms, machines, assemblages) with the breast or bottle, possibly accompanied by the hand in conjunction with an ear, each system in perpetual motion and in mutual interrelation. Instead of seeing the obsessional person's desire for impenetrability as a yearning for what is absent and lost (a staving off of the castration threat and the expression of the desire to occupy the position of the symbolic father), the obsessional person's toes can be seen to make machinic connections with sand, with rocks, with grass, such that these "external objects" can no longer be considered either an internalized part of the subject or an expelled external residue of the subject; rather, they exist on the same level as the subject's body parts (in this case, feet), neither inside nor outside but functional alongside of and with the subject's body.

These interactions and linkages can be seen as surface effects, relations occurring on the surface of the skin and various body parts. They are not merely superficial, for they generate, they produce, all the effects of a psychical interior, an underlying depth, individuality, or consciousness, much as the Möbius strip creates both an inside and an outside. Tracing the outside of the strip leads one directly to its inside without at any point leaving its surface. The depth, or rather the effects of depth, are thus generated purely through the manipulation, rotation, and inscription of the flat plane—an apposite metaphor for the undoing of dualism. No longer understood on the model of the clock or the machine, as Descartes and la Mettrie understood it, or on the computer, cybernetic, or virtual models much beloved by theorists of artificial intelligence. We will instead explore the other side, the outer becoming the inner side, of the Möbius metaphor. In spite of its obvious limits, limits that will be discussed later, the metaphor of the body as a page or strip on which a social text (or several texts) is written will be useful in reconfigurations of the body.

In many recent texts, the body has figured as a writing surface on which messages, a text, are inscribed. This metaphorics of body writing posits the body, and particularly its epidermic surface, muscular-skeletal frame, ligaments, joints, blood vessels, and internal organs as corporeal surfaces, the blank page on which engraving, graffiti, tattooing, or inscription can take place. This metaphor of the textualized body asserts that the body is a page or material surface, possibly even a book of interfolded leaves (one of Merleau-Ponty's favorite metaphors), ready to receive, bear, and transmit meanings, messages, or signs, much like a system of writing. This analogy between the body and a text remains a close one: the tools of body engraving—social, surgical, epistemic, disciplinary—all mark, indeed constitute, bodies in culturally specific ways; the writing instruments—pen, stylus, spur, laser beam, clothing, diet, exercise—function to incise the body's blank page. These writing tools use various inks with different degrees of permanence, and they create textual traces that are capable of being written over, retraced, redefined, written in contradictory ways, creating out of the body text a palimpsest, a historical chronicle of prior and later traces, some of which have been effaced, others of which have been emphasized, producing the body as a text which is as complicated and indeterminate as any literary manuscript. The messages or texts produced by this body writing construct bodies as networks of meaning and social significance, producing them as meaningful and functional "subjects" within social ensembles.

If psychoanalysis and phenomenology can be regarded as knowledges concerned with the psychical inscription and coding of bodies, pleasures, sensations and experiences, then this mode of psychical (re)tracing or writing marks the "inside" of the Möbius surface; what marks its "outside" surface is more law, right, requirement, social imperative, custom, and corporeal habits. If the psychical writing of bodies retraces the paths of biological processes using libido as its marker pen, then the inscription of the social surface of the body is the tracing of pedagogical, juridical, medical, and economic texts, laws, and practices onto the flesh to carve out a social subject as such, a subject capable of labor, of production and manipulation, a subject capable of acting as a subject and, at the same time, capable of being deciphered, interpreted, understood. Michel de Certeau argues that juridical inscriptions constitute the body as part of social or collective order, structuring the broad category of subjectivity required in particular epochs, while, by contrast, modes of medical inscription constitute the body as individualized, particularized:

> This machinery transforms individual bodies into a social body. It brings to bear in these bodies the text of a law. Another machinery doubles itself, parallel to the first, but of medical or surgical, and no longer of the juridical type. It uses an individual, and no longer collective therapeutics. The body that it treats is distinguished from the group. Only after having been a "member"—arm, leg or hand of the social unit, or a meeting place of forces or cosmic "spirits," it gradually stood out as a totality with its diseases, its stabilities, its deviations and its own abnormalities. A long history has been necessary, from the fifteenth to the eighteenth centuries, for this individual body to be "isolated," in the way in which one "isolates" a body, in chemistry or in microphysics; for it to become the basic unit of a society . . . in which it appeared as a miniaturization of the political and celestial order—a "microcosm." (De Certeau 1979: 4–5)

Flesh, a raw, formless, bodily materiality, the mythical "primary material," through corporeal inscriptions (juridical, medical, punitive, disciplinary) is constituted as a distinctive body capable of acting in distinctive ways, performing specific tasks in socially specified ways, marked, branded, by a social seal. Bodies are fictionalized, that is, positioned by various cultural narratives and discourses, which are themselves embodiments of culturally established canons, norms, and representational forms, so that they can be seen as living narratives, narratives not always or even usually transparent to themselves. Bodies become emblems, heralds, badges, theaters, tableaux, of social laws and rights, illustrations and exemplifications of law, informing and rendering pliable flesh into determinate bodies, producing the flesh as a point of departure and a locus of incision, a point of "reality" or "nature" understood (fictionally) as prior to, and as the raw material of, social practices. De Certeau conceives of this intextuation of bodies as meeting limits imposed from two directions. On one hand, there must be a certain resistance of the flesh, a residue of its materiality left untouched by the body's textualization; on the other hand, there is another limit imposed by the inability of particular texts or particular languages to say or articulate everything—a resistance from the side of the flesh and from the functioning of representation:

> This discursive image must inform an unknown "real," formerly designated as "flesh." From the fiction to the unknown that will embody it, the relay is effected by instruments multiplying and diversifying the unforeseeable resistances of the body to (con)formation. Between the tool and the flesh, there is . . . a play which is translated on the one hand by a change in the fiction . . . and on

the other, by a cry, an inarticulate, unthought suffering of corporeal difference. (De Certeau 1979: 8)

This model will help explain how the body, once it is constituted as such, is transcribed and marked by culture; but on its presumption of the body as a blank page, an unmarked text, a *tabula rasa*, it cannot explain how incision and inscription actively produce the body as such. They cannot explain what it is that produces the blank page, what the stuff of this page may be. Here de Certeau posits an "inarticulate, unthought suffering," a carnality or flesh outside of or prior to inscription, something which somehow, being unthought, resists determinate production. This is a clear consequence of his reduction of textuality or inscription to discourse, and more particularly to narrative. With a narrow or, in Derrida's terms, "vulgar" reading of textuality, one which reduces it to speech, to representation, a message or communication, there must be an outside, a noninscribed or nontextual framing and context for every text. The non- or preinscribed corporeality of the flesh provides just such a frame or context for body writing. The question then remains: how and in what terms to think that writing which is prediscursive, that writing or trace which produces the page to be inscribed?

According to de Certeau, the subject is marked as a series of (potential) messages or inscriptions from or of the social (Other). Its flesh is transformed into a body organized, and hierarchized according to the requirements of a particular social and familial nexus. The body becomes a "text" and is fictionalized and positioned within myths and belief systems that form a culture's social narratives and self-representations. In some cultural myths, this means that the body can be read as an agent, a laboring, exchanging being, a subject of social contracts, and thus of rights and responsibilities; in others, it becomes a body shell capable of being overtaken by the other's messages (for example, in shamanism or epilepsy). Social narratives create their characters and plots through the textualization of the body's contours and organic outlines by means of the tools of body writing. Writing instruments confine and constitute corporeal capacities, both stimulating and stifling social conformity (the acting out of these narratives as "live theater" and a corporeal resistance to the processes of social inscription). The consequences of this are twofold: the "intextuation of bodies," which transforms the discursive apparatus of regimes of social fiction or knowledge, "correcting" or updating them, rendering them more "truthful" and ensuring their increasingly microscopic focus on the details of psychical and corporeal life; and the incarnation of social laws in the movements, actions, behaviors, and desires of bodies—a movement of the text into the body and the body outside of itself and into sociocultural life.

Whereas models of the subject as psychical interior introduce the dimension of social relations and the external world through modes of introjection and incorporation—the social "enters" the subject through the mediation and internalization of social values and mores (usually by means of some kind of identification with social representatives such as the parents)—the model of social inscription I will elaborate here, by contrast, implies that social values and requirements are not so much inculcated into the subject as etched upon the subject's body. This may explain why the problematic of socialization, which provides the model for understanding the transmission and reproduction of social values, is replaced in models of social inscription with the problematic of punishment, that is, why law and constraint replace the model of desire and lack. Whereas on these earlier models desire, through its constitutive lack, induces the subject from within to accept the mediation of social regulations in its attempts to gain gratification (Freud's distinction between the pleasure principle and the reality principle), whereas, in other words, there is something already inside the subject (need, desire) that impels it toward others and, through others, to the social, on the inscriptive model it is the social exterior, or at least its particular modes of inscription, that commands or induces certain kinds of behavior and practices. Punishment is the "externalized" counterpart of socialization; both are forms of codification of the social onto the corporeal, though from two different directions.[1]

The various notions of the body to be explored here and in the following chapters are in many ways antithetical to those explored in the previous chapters. The notion of corporeal inscription of the body-as-surface rejects the phenomenological framework of intentionality and the psychoanalytic postulate of psychical depth; the body is not a mode of expression of a psychical interior or a mode of communication or mediation of what is essentially private and incommunicable. Rather, it can be understood as a series of surfaces, energies, and forces, a mode of linkage, a discontinuous series of processes, organs, flows, and matter. The body does not hide or reveal an otherwise unrepresented latency or depth but is a set of operational linkages and connections with other things, other bodies. The body is not simply a sign to be read, a symptom to be deciphered, but also a force to be reckoned with. The energetics, or rather the politics, of signification must here be recognized. The ways in which (fragments of) bodies come together with or align themselves to other things produce what Deleuze has called a machine: a nontotalized collection or assemblage of heterogeneous elements and materials. In itself, the body is not a machine; but in its active relations to other social practices, entities, and events, it forms machinic connections. In relation to books, for example, it may form a literary machine; in relation to tools, it may form a work machine. The body is thus not an organic totality which is capable of the wholesale expression of subjectivity, a welling up of the subject's emotions, attitudes, beliefs, or experiences, but is itself an assemblage of organs, processes, pleasures, passions, activities, behaviors linked by fine lines and unpredictable networks to other elements, segments, and assemblages:

We will ask what it functions with, in connection with what other things it does and does not transmit intensities, in which other multiplicities its own are inserted and metamorphosed, and with what bodies without organs its own converges. (Deleuze and Guattari 1987: 4)

Instead of relying on a model of sense, of the tracing of the body's surface on the subject's psyche (a relation that remains always in the order of signification), Deleuze and others remain interested in cartographies and in surveying, that is, in representations that do something, that refer outside themselves in non- or extradiscursive relations. One does not need to read meaning onto bodies and their behavior; rather, one can survey the linkages between bodies of different kinds. Instead of aspiring to a model of signification, which links the subject's psyche to signifying chains, to the order of the signifier, that is, in which the body is the medium of signification, Deleuze sees his project as that of the mapmaker, the drawer of lines and spaces on a flat surface. This may explain why Deleuze and Guattari privilege the map over the tracing, the rhizome over the tree:

The map is open and connectable in all its dimensions; it is detachable, reversible, susceptible to constant modification. It can be torn, reversed, adapted to any kind of mounting, reworked by an individual, group or social formation. It can be drawn on the wall, conceived as a work of art, constructed as a political action or as a mediation. . . . The map has to do with performance, whereas the tracing always involves an alleged "competence." (Deleuze and Guattari 1987: 12–13)

If the body is the external expression of an interior in the first or psychical view, it is seen as a pure surface in the second. In the first case, metaphors of latency, depth, interiority, inside are crucial, while the image of the flat surface (or "plane of consistency") is central to the second. For the first, the body needs to be interpreted, read, in order to grasp its underlying meaning; for the second, the body is a surface to be inscribed, written on, which can be segmented, dissolved into flows, or seen as a part (or parts) of a larger ensemble or machine, when it is connected to other organs, flows, and intensities. However, rather than turn immediately to the texts of Foucault and Deleuze and Guattari, it will be worthwhile to discuss the contributions of their predecessors—especially Nietzsche and Kafka—to understanding terms that represent the body as a social surface of inscription.

Nietzsche, Knowledge, and the Will to Power

Nietzsche does not have a coherent theory of the body as such. However, there are abundant references to the body in his writings, and from them it may be possible to extract an account (even if not a coherent theory) of his understanding of the body. Here I propose to explore the body's role in the production of knowledge and truth on one hand and its relations to the will to power on the other. Nietzsche's conception of the body, it should be noted, is considerably more positive and productive than Foucault's. For Foucault, the body is penetrated by networks and regimes of power-knowledge that actively mark and produce it as such: the body seems to be the passive raw data manipulated and utilized by various systems of social and self-constitution, an object more or less at the mercy of nonintentional or self-directed, conscious production (this will be discussed in more detail in the next chapter). In Nietzsche, by contrast, it is the body, both at an intraorganic or cellular level and as a total, integrated organism, an animal, that is active, the source and site for the will to power and the movement of active (as well as reactive) forces.[2] Knowledge and power are, for Nietzsche, the results of the body's activity, its self-expansion and self-overcoming. The will to power involves a struggle to survive, to grow, to overcome itself on the level of cells, tissues, organs, where the lower-order bodily functions are subordinated to and harnessed by higher-order bodily processes and activities (the brain being considered the highest (1968: 348–49). This hierarchization Nietzsche seems to share with the neurophysiologists discussed in chapter 3. The forces and energies comprising the body are not in any sense reducible to atoms, elementary particles, objects, or organs (Nietzsche strongly opposes atomism) but is made up of forces, micro-wills, which struggle among themselves for supremacy. Nietzsche likens them to aristocratic nobles, social equals.

> The assumption of a single subject is perhaps unnecessary: perhaps it is just as permissible to assume a multiplicity of subjects whose interaction and struggle is the basis of our thought and our consciousness in general? A kind of "aristocracy of cells" in which dominion resides? To be sure, an aristocracy of equals, used to ruling jointly and understanding how to command?
> *My hypothesis*: The subject as multiplicity. (Nietzsche 1968: 270)

Here Nietzsche suggests a kind of parallelism between the organic and the subjective, for just as the subject is a multiplicity of forces, the organism is not singular and unified. It too is a series of interacting and conflicting energies which struggle among themselves, which gain dominion or become subordinated through the dominance of others. The unity (of either subject or body), if it is possible at all, is the result of the suppression or subordination of the multiple conflicting forces, the result of cruelty. For Nietzsche, these organs, bodily processes, muscles, and cells do not, indeed cannot, as the empiricist presumes, yield knowledge or even error; rather, the body necessarily generates and presumes interpretations, perspectives, partial and incomplete acquaintance, which serve its needs in the world and may enhance its capacity and hunger for life. They enable the organism to function pragmatically in the world but do not yield truth or knowledge. The will to power is the drive toward self-expansion, the movement of becoming, for it increases the body's quantity and quality of forces and energies, a drive toward "vigorous, free, joyful activity" (Nietzsche 1969: 33).

Instead of seeing the body in terms of the mind/body distinction or regarding it as a substance to which various attributes, such as consciousness, can be added, Nietzsche sees it more in terms of a political/social organization, but one in which there is a kind of chaos of whirling forces, defined in terms of their quantities and intensities more than in terms of distinct characteristics. These forces or energies (at the levels of both organic and inorganic matter) are divided into dominant or active and subordinated or reactive forces:

> A quantum of power is designated by the effects it produces and that which it resists. The adiaphorous state is missing. . . . It is a question of struggle between two elements of unequal power: a new arrangement of forces is achieved according to the measure of power in each of them. (1968: 633, 634)

Active forces "care" for, concern themselves with, only their own well-being and expansion; reactive forces, by contrast, give primary concern to active forces, finding their principle of action outside themselves. As Deleuze stresses in his reading of Nietzsche,

> even by getting together reactive forces do not form a greater force, one that would be active. They proceed in an entirely different way—they decompose; they *separate active force from what it can do*; they take away a part or almost all of its power. In this way reactive forces do not become active, but, on the contrary, they make active forces join them and become reactive in a new sense. (Deleuze 1983: 57)

The active forces, within and outside the body, are noble, aristocratic, for they govern, they expand. Reactive forces are not weaker than active ones (on the contrary, they tend to overpower active forces and convert them into reactive forces); they are slavish insofar as they are adapted toward the active forces, reacting to their initiative and impetus:

> . . . reactive force is: 1) utilitarian force of adaptation and partial limitation; 2) force which separates active force from what it can do, which denies active force . . . ; 3) force separated from what it can do, which denies or turns against itself. . . . And, analogously, active force is: 1) plastic, dominant and subjugating force; 2) force which goes to the limit of what it can do; 3) force which affirms its difference, which makes its difference an object of enjoyment and affirmation. Forces are only concretely and completely determined if these three pairs of characteristics are taken into account simultaneously. (Deleuze 1983: 61)

Given the plasticity and mobility of active forces, and given that these forces are not governed by or directed toward preordained objects, the body itself must be seen as a pliable and potentially infinitely diverse set of energies, whose capacities and advances can never be predicted. In this sense, Nietzsche's conception directly inherits the tradition propounded by Spinoza in his assertion that we do not know, cannot know, what the body is capable of doing or achieving. For Nietzsche, as for Spinoza, the body's capacity for becoming cannot be known in advance, cannot be charted; its limits cannot be definitively listed. The body itself, in its microforces, is always in a position of self-overcoming, of expanding its capacities.

Out of the chaos of active and reactive forces comes a dominating force that commands, imposes perspective, or rather perspectives (there is no implication of singularity here). Consciousness can be regarded as the direct product or effect of reactive forces in the governance of the body. For Nietzsche, consciousness is a belief, an illusion: on one hand useful for life, a convenient fiction, and on the other an effect of the inwardly inflected, thwarted will to power or force that, instead of subduing other bodies and other forces, has sought to subdue itself.[3] The subject's psychical interior, or "soul," can be seen as nothing but the self-inversion of the body's forces, the displacement of the will to power's continual self-transformation back onto the body. In this sense, there is and has always been only body. Consciousness, soul, or subjectivity is nothing but the play of the body's forces that, with the help of metaphysics, have been congealed into a unity and endowed as an origin. The body's forces, instincts, are not simply part of nature or essence (both nature and essence are metaphysical descriptions of the play of forces in the will to power); they are entirely plastic, fluid, capable of taking any direction and any kind of becoming:

> All instincts that do not discharge themselves outwardly *turn inward*—this is what I call the *internalization* of man: thus it was that man first developed what was later called his "soul." The entire inner world, originally as thin as if it were stretched between two membranes, expanded and extended itself, acquired depth, breadth and height, in the same measure as outward discharge was *inhibited*. (Nietzsche 1969: 84–85)

Consciousness or psyche is an effect or consequence of the modulations and impulses of the body. It is for this reason Nietzsche suggests that looking inward, as is ordained by introspection or psychology, self-consciousness or self-reflection, is both illusory and misleading. Illusory, because the psychical interior is in fact a "category," project, or product of the body that, for various reasons (grammatical, cultural, habitual), has been mistaken for mind; and misleading, insofar as self-reflection, the goals of self-knowledge, mistake an effect for a cause, confuse an instrument or tool with its producer:

> We psychologists of the future—we have little patience with introspection. We almost take it for a sign of degeneration when an instrument tried "to know itself": we are instruments of knowledge and would like to possess all the naivete and precision of an instrument—consequently we must not analyze our-

selves, "know" ourselves. First mark of the great psychologist: he never seeks himself, he has no eyes for himself, no interest or curiosity in himself . . . (Nietzsche 1968: 230)

Knowledge, mind, philosophy, as that activity supposedly concerned with reason, is the discipline most implicated in a will to ignorance. It has resolutely ignored the body, leaving physiology to the medical disciplines. If it is true that "belief in the body is more fundamental than belief in the soul: the latter arose from unscientific reflection [on the agonies] of body" (Nietzsche 1968: 271), then philosophy is based on a disavowal of its corporeal origins and its status as corporeal product. The body is the intimate and internal condition of all knowledges, especially of that knowledge which sees itself as a knowledge of knowledges—philosophy. But to see themselves as objective, true, valid for all, independent of formulation and context, outside of history, and immutable, knowledges must disavow or deny that they are the consequence not only of particular bodies but, even more narrowly, of particular, dominant forces or passions of bodies. A genealogy of various epistemological attitudes and ontological commitments could be devised such that their origin in bodily states, carnal motives, and physiological processes may be discerned.

> All virtues are physiological *conditions:* particularly the principal organic functions considered as necessary, as good. All virtues are really refined *passions* and enhanced states.
>
> Pity and love of mankind as development of the sexual drive. Justice as the development of the drive to revenge. Virtue as pleasure in resistance, will to power. Honor as recognition of the similar and equals-in-power. (Nietzsche 1968: 148)

In this sense, philosophy can be seen as a reactive force, a *ressentiment,* a certain fleeing before life and the world in which we live, a fear of and reaction to the body's activity, its constitutive role in the production of language, values, morals, truths or knowledges:

> *Why philosophers are slanderers.*—The treacherous and blind hostility of philosophers towards the senses—how much of mob and middle class there is in this hatred! . . . if one wants a proof of how profoundly and thoroughly the actually barbarous needs of man seek satisfaction, even when he is tamed and "civilized." One should take a look here at the "leitmotifs" of the entire evolution of philosophy:—a sort of revenge on reality, a malicious destruction of the valuations by which men live, an unsatisfied soul that feels the tamed state as a torture and finds a voluptuous pleasure in a morbid unravelling of all the bonds that tie it to such a state.
>
> The history of philosophy is a secret raging against the preconditions of life, against the value feelings of life, against partisanship in favor of life. Philosophers have never hesitated to affirm a world provided it contradicted this world . . . (1968: 253)

Just as all moral values are in fact bodily passions and energies which are misrepresented as the products of mind or reason, so too knowledges, including the sciences, are functions and effects of the knower's corporeality:

> Through the long succession of millennia, man has not known himself physiologically: he does not know himself even today. To know, e.g., that one has a nervous system (—but no "soul"—) is still the privilege of the best informed. . . . One must be very humane to say "I don't know that," to afford ignorance. (1968: 132)

Philosophy, and knowledge more generally, not only depend for their conceptual origins on the body and its forces, but must disown or disinvest themselves of this debt; they are also necessarily indebted to language. Philosophy, and its privileged object, truth, are ultimately dependent on language. Truth is, for Nietzsche, nothing but a set of congealed or frozen metaphors whose metaphorical status has been mistaken for the literal: "What is truth but a mobile army of metaphors?" And language itself, he suggests, is at base corporeal. Words are doubly metaphorical: they are transcriptions or transpositions of images, which are themselves transpositions of bodily states. For Nietzsche, bodily forces underlie language and its possibility of representation:

> One designates only the relations of things to man, and to express them, one calls on the boldest metaphors. A nerve stimulus, first transposed into an image—first metaphor. The image, in turn, imitated by a sound—second metaphor. *(On Truth and Lie in an Extra-Moral Sense,* 1.)

Philosophy is not, in spite of its self-representation, a rational, intellectual system of inquiry and knowledge acquisition, based purely on truth considerations and the requirements of conceptual coherence. It is practice, a strategy, and thus part of a struggle, a battle. Philosophy is not a reflection on things or concepts from a transcendent position; it is a practice that does things, legitimizing and challenging other practices, enabling things to happen or preventing them from occurring. For Nietzsche, knowledges in general and philosophy in particular are drives for mastery—consequences of the will to power. Far from contemplative reflection, philosophy is a consequence of the drive to live, to conquer, a will to power that is primarily corporeal. Philosophy is a product of the body's impulses that have mistaken themselves for psyche or mind. Bodies construct systems of belief, knowledge, as a consequence of the impulses of their organs and processes. Among the belief systems that are the most pervasive, long-lived, and useful are those grand metaphysical categories—truth, subject, morality, logic—which can all be read as bodily strategies, or rather resources, which contribute to the will to power. For example, to posit a "doer" beyond the "deed" is a useful or enabling fiction, a fantasy that helps to explain the body's drive to expansion, to life, to joy.

If knowledge is or has been unable to acknowledge its own history, origin, or genealogy in the history and functioning of the body, nonetheless it can be judged and assessed, not in terms of its truth, its internal consistency, its parsimony, or its use of minimal ontological commitments—that is, in terms of the consistency of own self-representations—but rather in terms of its effects, what it does, what it enables bodies, powers, to do. If its "origin" and history are the consequences of reactive forces, then, nevertheless, it can be actively affirmed, positively retrieved and used for self-expansion, if its limits, its corporeal status, and its ends are more clearly, powerfully, understood: "Truth is the kind of error without which a certain species of life could not live. The value for life is ultimately decisive" (1968: 272).

Beliefs are adjuncts to the senses, modes of augmentation of their powers and capacities; and, like the senses, they yield interpretations, not truths, perspectives which may be life-enhancing, which may favor movement, growth, vigor, expansion. Knowledge has survival value rather than truth value. These perspectives are not, however, as they were for Merleau-Ponty and other phenomenologists, a partial view of an abiding, inert, unchanging object; they are the modes of differential production of the "object"; they are all that there is. The appearance discerned, constituted though perspective, is a generative, differential power or force.[4] Where knowledge exists, it is not a transparent reflection, a meditative proposition, pure ideality, but an ability or resource. It is for this reason that it can be said that the body has a "great intelligence," that muscles, tissues, cells, have knowledge, can remember:

> I want to speak to the despisers of the body. I would not have them learn and teach differently, but merely say farewell to their own bodies—and thus become silent.
>
> "Body am I, and soul"—thus speaks the child. And why should one not speak like children?
>
> But the awakened and knowing say: body am I entirely and nothing else; and soul is only a word for something about the body.
>
> The body is a great reason, a plurality with one sense, a war and a peace, a herd and a shepherd. An instrument of your body is also your little reason, my brother, which you call "spirit"—a little instrument and toy of your great reason.
>
> "I," you say, and are proud of the word. But greater is that in which you do not wish to have faith—your body and its great reason: that does not say "I," but does "I."
>
> Behind your thoughts and feelings, my brother, there stands a mighty ruler, an unknown sage—whose name is self. In your body he dwells; he is your body. (Nietzsche 1985: 34)

The will to power animates, moves, energizes and strives to proliferate. This may explain why Nietzsche insisted on a new type of philosophy or knowledge, one which, instead of remaining sedentary, ponderous, stolid, was allied with the arts of movement: theater, dance, and music. Philosophy itself was to be written walking—or, preferably, dancing. This is because philosophy is a bodily activity and is, if wrenched from the hands of the most reactive forces (ascetics, priests of various kinds), capable of dynamizing and enhancing life. Philosophy and truth are capable of affirming active power when they, in their turn, return power and force to the body from which they derive. Philosophy is capable of providing resources for the lifting of the body higher, the elevation of its forces and perspectives; it is capable of reversing its reactive status:

> In the main, I agree more with the artists than with any philosopher hitherto: they have not lost the scent of life, they have loved the things of "this world"— they have loved their senses. To strive for "desensualization": that seems to me a misunderstanding or an illness or a cure, where it is not merely hypocrisy or self-deception. I desire for myself and for all who live, *may* live, without being tormented by a puritanical conscience, an ever-greater spiritualization and multiplication of the senses: indeed, we should be grateful to the senses for their subtlety, plenitude, and power and offer them in return the best we have in the way of spirit. What are priestly and metaphysical calumnies against the senses to us! (1968: 434)

Where philosophy, or what counts as truth, enhances the body's capacities, enlarges its powers of becoming, intensifies the body's sensations, makes it able to do other things in the world, such a philosophy is affirmative and productive of the overcoming of man, the production of new, hitherto unimagined possibilities, the transformation of man into the higher man:

> Put briefly: perhaps the entire evolution of the spirit is a question of the body; it is the history of the development of a higher body that emerges into our sensibility. The organic is rising to yet higher levels. Our lust for knowledge of nature is a means through which the body desires to perfect itself or rather: hundreds of thousands of experiments are made to change the nourishment, the mode of living and of dwelling of the body: consciousness and evaluations in the body, all kinds of pleasure and displeasure, are signs of these changes and experiments. It is not a question of man at all: he is to be overcome. (1968: 358)

A knowledge that could acknowledge its genealogy in corporeality would also necessarily acknowledge its perspectivism, its incapacity to grasp all, or anything in its totality. Perspectives cannot simply be identified with appearance, underlying which there is an abiding and stable reality. Rather, there are only perspectives, only appearances, only interpretations. There is nothing beyond the multiplicity of perspectives, positions, bodily forces; no anchor in the real. The body itself is a multiplicity of competing and conflicting forces which, through the domination of one or a few, comes to have a perspective and position, one among a number of competing, or complementary, perspectives vying for ascendancy.

Nietzschean Body Writing

Although Nietzsche defines and understands the body with reference to a concept of instincts that may at first sight appear ahistorical or naturalistic, it is clear that he has a complex notion of nature that precludes associating instincts with their usual biologistic and nonhistorical connotations. Nature is not the origin, source, or designer of instincts; nature itself is a destination, product, or effect. In man, there is nothing natural, if by nature is understood what is inert, transhistorical, governed by law, conquerable:

> How man has become more natural in the nineteenth century (the eighteenth century is that of elegance, refinement, and *sentiments*)—Not "return to nature"—for there has never yet been a natural humanity. The scholasticism of the un- and the anti-natural value is the rule, is the beginning; man reaches nature only after a long struggle—he never "returns"—Nature: that is, daring to be immoral like nature. (1968: 73)

In *The Genealogy of Morals* Nietzsche outlines the rudiments of an account of body inscription as the cultural condition for establishing social order and obedience. This account is not disconnected from his epistemological researches, his notion of the will to power, or his understanding of active and reactive forces. Active and reactive forces are personified in *The Genealogy of Morals* through the figures of the aristocratic noble and the base slave, respectively. It should be noted here that Nietzsche is not advocating feudal relations of power and domination in any straightforward way; he is not simply identifying these two types or categories of individual with preexisting class-based models. On the contrary, there are aristocratic and base impulses within all individuals, and those individuals who may belong to one class or another (by accident of birth or environment) may exhibit base and noble impulses. The values characterizing the noble assume a will to "powerful physicality, a flourishing, abundant, even overflowing health, together with that which serves to preserve it: war, adventure, hunting, dancing, war games, and in general all that involves vigorous, free, joyful activity" (1969: 33). These values are self-directed and self-affirming—and, of course, most notably, virile: the noble impulse is concerned with self-production and self-expansion independent of the other. It has no other binding ties, no connections or commitments to the weak, the underprivileged, or children. It affirms its own capacities as well as whatever contingencies may affect it; it looks not to the past but only to the future (the past tends to tie and limit it to what has been, to what grounds and contains it, while the future is open, limitless, capable of being infinitely characterized); it affirms its own possibilities of becoming, joyously and without fear; it aspires to height, to power, to intoxication, reveling in its corporeality. Because the past is of little concern, the noble impulse is forgetful, retaining no memory, no nostalgia, no resentment. This leaves it always open to the intensities of the present, unclouded by previous impressions and impulses; it is Dionysiac, dynamic, playful, celebratory. By contrast, the slavish impulse is always reactive: its position is always dictated by *ressentiment* of the other, a desire for revenge, a mortal and self-converting hatred of the other, against which all its activities are measured. It functions surreptitiously, thwarted in acts, and is thus enticed by imaginative wishes and fantasies. Slavish impulses are fundamentally negative; they always say no to "what is 'outside', what is 'different', what is 'not itself'; and this No is its creative deed" (1969: 36). It is thus always embittered and disappointed by the world, by the activity of others, and by its own frustrations. This resentment and spirit of hostility means that reactive or slavish forces are devious, deceptive, indirect, clever: "His soul *squints*; his spirit loves hiding places, secret paths, and back doors, everything covert entices him . . . " (38). The slavish impulse never forgets; it is bound up with the past, and thus is incapable of openness to the present and future; all past incidents and events are recorded, stored, brooded over, and well up into an unsatisfied hostility. Whereas the noble soul has no memory, has cultivated forgetfulness, the soul of *ressentiment* cannot erase, cannot overcome.

If the aristocratic impulse can be illustrated with three privileged figures from Nietzsche's writings, they would be the artist, the noble, and the sovereign individual, for they actively affirm the pleasures of life and the body, the power to forget, and the power of will in making promises, respectively.[5] Each figure affirms "his" power to intensify corporeal experiences, dreams, the past and the future. Counterposed to these figures of affirmation are the exemplars of *ressentiment*: the priest, the nihilist, and the philosopher. The priest, the object of Nietzsche's most scathing condemnation, is the figure of hatred, hatred of this world; passive in the face of the world, the priest devises all manner of rationalizations to justify inertia, passivity, and acceptance; like the nihilist and the philosopher, the priest turns away from the world, is disappointed with it, and yearns for something other. The nihilist, the philosopher, and the priest despise the body, the other, and themselves.

In the second essay of *The Genealogy of Morals*, Nietzsche focuses on the question of what kind of force is necessary to constrain and train reactive forces before culture can reach its pinnacle, the active "man," the sovereign individual. What must culture resort to if it is always a struggle between the forces of action and those of reaction? How is the active, affirmative force capable of subduing the forces of reaction so that they can be acted out, converted into action, reversed in their very reversal of action into reaction, so that they can (re)turn to activity? Nietzsche's genealogy of morals is an attempt to read morality from the point of view of the confrontation of active and reactive forces, indeed, to explain their genesis in terms of corporeality:

> ... every table of values, every "thou shalt" known to history or ethnology, requires first a *physiological* investigation and interpretation, rather than a psychological one; and every one of them needs a critique on the part of medical science. (Nietzsche 1969: 55)

Nietzsche wants to locate the primordial or mythical origins of culture in the ability to make promises, the ability to keep one's word, to propel into the future an avowal made in the past or present. This ability to make promises is dependent on the constitution of an interiority, a moral sense, a will. The will to remember, which Nietzsche characterized in this case as an active desire, a desire not to rid oneself, "a desire for the continuance of something desired once, a *real memory of the will*" (1969: 58), is counterposed with and in opposition to the active will to forget, that mode of forgetfulness, necessary for "robust health" (58), which enables subjects to ingest and incorporate experience but also to digest and expel it (the alimentary metaphor is Nietzsche's), ready and open for new stimulation (this model is surprisingly close to Freud's neurological characterization of memory and perception in "The Project for a Scientific Psychology"). The ability to make promises involves renouncing forgetfulness, at least in part, and, in spite of intervening events, being able to put intention or commitment into action. A counterforgetfulness needs to be instituted.

Nietzsche's insight is that pain is the key term in instituting memory. Civilization instills its basic requirements only by branding the law on bodies through a mnemonics of pain, a memory fashioned out of the suffering and pain of the body:

> One can well believe that the answers and methods for solving this primeval problem [the problem of how to instill a memory in the subject] were not precisely gentle; perhaps indeed there was nothing more fearful and uncanny in the whole prehistory of man than his *mnemotechnics*. "If something is to stay in the memory it must be burned in: only that which never ceases to hurt stays in the memory"—this is a main clause of the oldest (unhappily also the most enduring) psychology on earth. One might even say that wherever on earth solemnity, seriousness, mystery and gloomy coloring still distinguish the life of man and a people, something of the terror that formerly attended all promises, pledges and vows on earth is *still effective*. . . . Man could never do without blood, torture, and sacrifices when he felt the need to create a memory for himself; the most dreadful sacrifices and pledges (sacrifices of the first-born among them), the cruelest rites of all—the religious cults and all religions are at the deepest level systems of cruelties—all this has its origin in the instinct that realized that pain is the most powerful aid to mnemonics. (Nietzsche 1969: 61)

The degree of pain inflicted, Nietzsche suggests, is an index of poverty of memory: the worse memory is, the more cruel are the techniques for branding the body. It is almost as if the skin itself served as a notebook, a reminder of what was not allowed to be forgotten. Where this procedure is internalized to form what is known as conscience, less pain or sacrifice is required. The "unforgettable" is etched on the body itself:

> The worse man's memory has been, the more fearful has been the appearance of his customs; the severity of the penal code provides an especially significant measure of the degree of effort needed to overcome forgetfulness and to impose a few primitive demands of social existence as *present realities* upon the slaves of momentary affect and desire. (1969: 61)

The establishment of a memory is the key condition for the creation of social organization; it is also a cornerstone in the creation and maintenance of economic and contractual relations and systems of justice. For example, economic and social relations function only if the relation that bonds debtors to creditors is founded on some sort of contractual guarantee which ensures that debts, in some way or other, will always be paid. The presumption founding economic, social, and judicial relations is that every debt and obligation has an equivalence in the last instance, an equivalence between the debt owed and the pain the creditor can extract from the debtor. Pain becomes, in Deleuze's words "a medium of exchange, a currency, an equivalent" (1983: 130). The cost or price of an unkept promise, an unpaid debt, an act of forgetfulness, is the debtor's pain. This system of equivalences, which is very often carefully codified in terms of the precise value of body organs and intensities of pain, is the foundation of systems of justice, and the means justice uses to achieve such an equivalence is punishment. This equivalence ensures that even in the case of economic bankruptcy, the debt is still retrievable from the body of the debtor; in some sense at least, the debt can always be repaid. Nietzsche cites a number of examples from Roman law where

> the creditor could inflict every kind of indignity and torture upon the body of the debtor; for example, cut from it as much as seemed commensurate with the size of the debt and everywhere and from early times one had exact evaluations, all evaluations, of the individual limbs and parts of the body from this point of view, some of them going into horrible and minute detail. I consider it an advance, as evidence of a freer, more generous, more *Roman* conception of law when the Twelve Tables of Rome decreed it a matter of indifference how much or how little the creditor cut off in such cases. (1969: 64)

Damages are not measured by equivalent, that is, substitutable, values, as occurs in economic exchange, but by the extraction of organs, parts, forces, and energies from the debtor's body. This is clearly a system of recompense through socially and juridically sanctioned cruelty. Contractual relations thus found justice—contrary to legal idealizations which based contractual connections on a prior system of justice—and both of these are themselves founded on blood, suffering, and sacrifice. The equivalence of the pain caused to the debtor and the amount owed on the debt is the formula of the social contract. Any contract is thus ultimately founded on a kind of bodily collateral. The social order is not, contrary to Lévi-Strauss, founded on exchange, but on credit, on the rule that, at bottom, the body can be made to pay, to guarantee. The injury caused by the failure to keep promises, by the failure to pay off debts, by the failure to remember to what one is committed, is rendered commensurate with the degree of pain extracted from the body. This equivalence is rendered possible by, is itself founded on, the prior equivalence of the degree of suffering (of the debtor) with the degree of pleasure in causing suffering (for the creditor)—a kind of primitive, aristocratic urge to sadism:

> Let us be clear as to the logic of this form of compensation: it is strange enough. An equivalent is provided by the creditor's receiving, in place of a literal compensation for an injury (thus in place of money, land, possessions of any kind), a recompense in the form of a kind of *pleasure*, the pleasure of being allowed to vent his power freely upon one who is powerless, the voluptuous pleasure *"de faire le mal pour le plaisir de la faire"*, the enjoyment of violation. This enjoyment will be the greater the lower the creditor stands in the social order, and can easily appear to him as a most delicious morsel, indeed as a foretaste of the higher rank. In punishing the debtor, the creditor participates in a *right of the masters:* at last he, too, may experience for once the excited sensation of being allowed to despise and mistreat someone as "beneath him." . . . The compensation, then, consists in a warrant for and title to cruelty. (1969: 64–65)

Significantly, a compensatory recourse not only to the debt owed but also to class and social (though clearly not sexual) privilege is implied for the creditor here—a pleasure in the exercise of will alone, a pleasure sanctioned and approved, in which the debtor is now forced to participate and to share the memory of the creditor. As far as Nietzsche is concerned, this debtor-creditor relation and its lust for cruelty is the basis of all other social relations, moral values, and cultural production. Morality and justice share a common genealogy in barter and cruelty: memory, social history, and cultural cohesion are branded onto the flesh:

> It was in *this* sphere, the sphere of legal obligations, that the moral conceptual world of "guilt," conscience," "duty," "sacredness of duty" had its origin: its beginnings were, like the beginnings of everything great on earth, soaked in blood thoroughly and for a long time. And might one not add that, fundamentally, this world has never since lost a certain odor of blood and torture? (Not even in good old Kant: the categorical imperative smells of cruelty.) . . . To . . . what extent can suffering balance debts and guilt? To the extent that to *make* suffer was the highest degree pleasurable, to the extent that the injured party exchanged for the loss he had sustained, including the displeasure caused by the loss, an extraordinary counterbalancing pleasure: that of *making* suffer—a genuine *festival*.

> Without cruelty, there is no festival: thus the longest and most ancient part
> of human history teaches—and in punishment there is so much that is *festive*.
> (1969: 65–67)

Although this socially validated system of cruelty and coercion stands at the
(mythical) origins of civilization as the system which institutes trust, faith, and
a common bond between individuals who share a culture, the advances of civilization are themselves no less cruel or corporeal: there has been a kind of social
sublimation, a desensualization, and a series of refinements to these processes of
social engraving of the law on bodies, but it remains more or less a requirement
of the social taming of the will to power. The law today is no less corporeal, no
more cerebral, just, or fair than it has ever been; nor is it necessarily any kinder
or more humane (a point Foucault stresses throughout his analysis of the history
of punishment: there is no discernible "enlightenment" in the various historical
transformations punishment has undergone):

> Perhaps the possibility may even be allowed that this joy in cruelty does not
> really have to have died out; if pain hurts more today, it simply requires a cer-
> tain sublimation and subtilization, that is to say, it has to appear translated
> into the imaginative and psychical and adorned with such innocent names that
> even the tenderest and most hypocritical conscience is not suspicious of them.
> (Nietzsche 1969: 68)

This emblematic of body writing, and the necessary investment of punishment in systems of body writing, while clearly developed in Nietzsche's writings,
are elaborated and developed in a number of directions in the work of his intellectual heirs Kafka, Foucault, Deleuze, and Lingis, to whom we must now turn
in order to explain the various body-writing practices comprising our own culture.

Kafka's Punishment Machine

Whereas Nietzsche understands all cultural achievements as conditioned by
an institutionalized system of torture, as forms of socially controlled barbarity,
probably the finest evocation of the inscriptive infiltration of the body's surface
at the behest of the law regulating punishment occurs in Kafka's brilliant short
story "The Penal Settlement." While other writings of Kafka's hauntingly describe a system of justice or judgment gone out of control, where the individual
is, for some unknown reason, thrown to the mercy of vast bureaucracies, cast up
into nets of power over which he has no control and no redress, and while Kafka's writings have been elevated to the category of what Deleuze calls a "minor
literature," a kind of revolutionary literary nomadism,[6] in "The Penal Settlement" he is not merely describing an anachronistic punitive system which has
trapped its victim in a frightening passivity; although it is at the point of breakdown and decay, it nonetheless is a system which has exquisite appropriateness,

a system which reveals very clearly the origins and function of punishment as regulated revenge and calculated blood lust.

Kafka describes a "perfect" punishment machine, a machine with an entire legal system, that openly acknowledges the body of the prisoner as its target and objective and clearly positions consciousness and conscience as the by-products, effects, or results of corporeal inscriptions in a theater of cruelty. The punishment machine is basically a system of writing: it is not a creative system, but more like a printing technique in which the machine blindly executes the sentence that has been decided elsewhere. The punishment machine is simultaneously a machine which executes a sentence by inscribing it on the body of the prisoner and a system of textualization, a system which brings "enlightenment," meaning, a statement of the crime, to the prisoner's consciousness. It executes a sentence in both senses of the word. The condemned individual is part of the writing system: his body is the parchment on which the text is written, and his blood provides the ink to write the message. The machine remains analogous to the stylus or pen, an automated device for reproducing a juridical template. But in this case (unlike the case of psychical inscription) it is only the body and not the subject which knows the sentence being inscribed—and even this occurs retrospectively.

Kafka's machine is an ingenious device made of three parts: a "Bed" onto which the prisoner is tied; a "Designer," which provides the template or model for the message to be inscribed, a program for the machine to follow, which distinguishes one sentence from another; and a "Harrow," which executes the sentence on the prisoner's body, using a moving layer of needles to print the Designer's message. The last officer left at the colony describes the machine to a stranger who has come to observe:

> As soon as the man is strapped down, the bed is set in motion. It quivers in minute, very rapid vibrations. . . . You will have seen similar apparatus in hospitals; but in our Bed, the movements all correspond very exactly to the movements of the Harrow. . . . Our sentence does not sound very severe. Whatever commandment the condemned man has disobeyed is written on his body. "Honour thy superiors." . . . [Although he doesn't know the sentence] he'll learn it corporeally, on his person. . . . An ignorant onlooker would see no difference between one punishment and another. The Harrow appears to do its work with uniform regularity. . . . the actual progress of the sentence can be watched, [for] the Harrow is made of glass. . . . When the Harrow . . . finishes its first draft of the inscription on the back, the layer of cotton wool [on the Bed] begins to roll and slowly turns the body over, to give the Harrow fresh space for writing. Meanwhile the raw part that has been written on lies on the cotton wool, which is especially prepared to staunch the bleeding and so makes all ready for a new deepening of the script. . . . So it keeps on writing deeper and deeper for the whole twelve hours. . . . But how quiet he grows at just about the sixth hour! Enlightenment comes to the most dull-witted. It begins around the eyes. From there, it grows, it radiates. A moment that might even

tempt one to get under the Harrow with him. Nothing more happens after that, the man only begins to understand the inscriptions. . . . You have seen how difficult it is to decipher the script with one's eyes; but our man deciphers it with his wounds. To be sure, that is a hard task; he needs six hours to accomplish it. By that time, the Harrow has pierced him quite through and casts him into the grave. . . . Then the judgement has been fulfilled and we bury him. (Kafka 1969: 68–73)

Three features of Kafka's description of the punishment machine, its design and functioning, are of significance in the context of Nietzsche's understanding of the body. Kafka positions punishment within a fine network which links together the inscription of bodies and the production of knowledges. The former commandant, the man who designed and built the machine, is a compressed emblem of expertise and knowledge, combining in one personage the various mechanical, technical, juridical, and medical forms of expertise that are usually divided across different institutions and authorized positions of knowledge. He is a "soldier, judge, mechanic, chemist, and draftsman," situated at the interstices of legal, medical, moral, penitential, and educational institutions. As Kafka describes it, penal punishment requires an epistemic backup—for knowledges are both the preconditions of power and subject to revision and modification according to the information and possible enlightenment of the prisoner, a point we will have occasion to discuss further in dealing with Foucault. Not only must we note the complicity of apparently neutral and disinvested knowledges, "sciences," in the most barbaric of social practices—the practice of punishment; the highly individualized knowledge of the prisoner, on whose body the sentence (of whatever kind) is always enacted as a crucial ingredient in the punishment. It seems crucial to the procedures of punishment that the prisoner is, sooner or later, enlightened by the punishment. The Harrow requires six hours of suffering to make up the pain and punishment of the subject, of consciousness and conscience, for only in this final phase of the punishment is the condemned aware of the sentence and the penalty.

This leads directly to a second implication: the machine etches its message directly on the prisoner's body. This message, which cannot be read with the eyes and therefore cannot be understood from the outside by any observer, is written to be read in tactile terms, a kind of braille for the skin. The message is tailored to suit the crime, and also to suit the criminal's body and individuality. His consciousness is the end result, an effect, of the deepening inscription of the surface of the body. Without knowledge of the crime with which he has been charged or of the sentence imposed on him, the machine creates the possibility of enlightenment, of conscious awareness and indeed guilt, in the face of the crime purely through this outer inscription. A body writing has come to replace speech and verbal communication just as the body-subject replaces or displaces consciousness. The judicial system at most produces consciousness as an effect of body writing and, at the least, would function as it does quite independent of consciousness. Consciousness is a by-product, perhaps even an epiphenomenon, of the inscription of the body.

Kafka explicitly describes the machine as an instrument of writing, as a material means of inscription through which propositions, texts, and sentences are etched onto the prisoner's skin, and through it, his subjectivity. This writing machine is the mechanism of transfer through which an abstract, or rather a textually based, law is rendered incarnate, living. But ironically, it is only at the moment of death that the prisoner is a living exemplar of the law. For that split second before death, the prisoner knows, and indeed accepts and embodies, law; others, observers, see the perfect match between the judgment and the sentence. But the law cannot be incarnate, it cannot be fixed, for it is abstract, intangible, and fleeting. The body, that of the prisoner and of the social subject, is indeed always etched, inscribed. There is no preinscribed body; but it is always excessively etched. Whatever of the social is written there is fundamentally open to reinterpretation, to reinscription, to transformation through context, situation, and position.

Kafka's story shows us that the Nietzschean model of corporeal inscription need not be regarded simply as a metaphorical description of processes that occur largely psychologically. On the contrary, processes of body inscription must be understood as literal and constitutive.

6 | The Body as Inscriptive Surface

Lingis and Body Tattoos

ALPHONSO LINGIS SKETCHES an account of the body as a surface of erotogenic intensity which combines elements of the Nietzschean notion of the body as a surface of social incision, the Freudian and phenomenological conceptions of the libidinal investments in narcissistically privileged bodily zones and organs, and elements of Deleuze's understanding of the body as a site for the circulation of energetic intensities. Lingis's chapter "Savages" in *Excesses: Eros and Culture* (1984), addresses the notion of the body as a surface of libidinal and erotogenic intensity, a product of and material to be further inscribed and reinscribed by social norms, practices, and values. Lingis compares and contrasts so-called primitive or savage rituals of body inscription with the so-called civilized or modern forms. While his discussion of modes of "savage" body marking remains problematic in its exoticism and in the sometimes touristlike position of spectatorship Lingis uses to divide the savage from the civilized, his work can be used not as a truthful depiction of the "savage" other but as a symptomatic expression of a certain Western anxiety about and risking of the borders which Western society shares with its various others.[1] While this does not justify or validate his analysis, it does mean that his text can be used for purposes other than those for which it was written, in this case, for revealing what may be at stake in specifying a general, cross-culturally valid notion of body writing and for distinguishing our culture from its others and from its own past.

Lingis claims that the processes by which the primitive body is marked or scarred seem to us, in the West, to be painful and barbaric. Like the tattooing of the Western body, there is something facile and superficial about the permanent etching on the body's surface. It offends Western sensibility (at least the white, and especially middle-class, sensibility, although Lingis doesn't specify this) that a subject would voluntarily undertake the permanent inscription of a verbal or visual message on its skin. Its superficiality offends us; its permanence alarms us. We are not so much surfaces as profound depths, subjects of a hidden interiority, and the exhibition of subjectivity on the body's surface is, at least from a certain class and cultural perspective, "puerile" (his word).

Primitive inscriptions on the body surface function, he claims in *Excesses*, to intensify, proliferate, and extend the body's erotogenic sensitivity. Instead of being read simply as messages, that is, as signifiers of a hidden or inferred signified which is the subject's interiority, these incisions function to proliferate, intensify, and extend the body's erotogenic sensitivity. Welts, scars, cuts, tattoos, perforations, incisions, inlays, function quite literally to increase the surface space of the body, creating out of what may have been formless flesh a series of zones, locations, ridges, hollows, contours: places of special significance and libidinal intensity. What he is describing is the constitution of erotogenic orifices, rims, and libidinal zones, producing intensities unevenly over the entire surface of the body and within the body's muscular-skeletal frame, a kind of interweaving of incisions and perforations with the sensations and sexual intensities, pleasures, and pains of the body. These incisions and various body markings create an erotogenic surface; they create not a map of the body but the body precisely as a map. They constitute some regions on that surface as more intensified, more significant, than others. In this sense they unevenly distribute libidinal value and forms of social codification across the body:

> The savage inscription is a working over the skin, all surface effects. This cutting in orifices and raising tumescences does not contrive new receptor organs for a depth body [as, for example, the prosthetic additions to the civilized body do] . . . it extends an erotogenic surface . . . it's a multiplication of mouths, of lips, labia, anuses, these sweating and bleeding perforations and puncturings . . . these warts raised all over the abdomen, around the eyes . . . (Lingis 1984: 34)

These puncturings and markings of the body do not simply displace or extend from already constituted, biologically pregiven libidinal zones; they constitute the body in its entirety as erotic, and they privilege particular parts of the body as self-constituted orifices. They make the very notion and sensations of orifices and erotogenic rims possible. This provides, according to Lingis, one of the key distinguishing features separating primitive forms of inscription from civilized ones. "Civilized" inscriptions imply and are read in terms of psychical depths. In this case, bodily markings can be read as symptoms, signs, clues to unraveling a psychical set of meanings. To take the case of anorexia, which many argue—not entirely convincingly—is a fear of pregnancy: the subject cannot swallow, ingest, or expel food; her self-starvation not only inscribes the oral but also the anal tract with the meaning of the reproductive system, whose functioning she has also indirectly altered (as the common symptom of amenorrhoea attests). The mouth and the anus acquire the significance of the womb that she wishes to protect from impregnation. In this sense, the hysteric can be seen as the polar opposite of the "savage": she displaces one erotogenic zone onto the position of another, thereby reducing the sites of erotogenic sensation, while "savage" scarification extends and proliferates them, creating the whole abdomen, arm, back, neck, leg, or face—whichever surface is tattooed or marked—as an erotogenic site ex nihilo.

Lingis's savages—he refers in particular to the people of Kau, in Kenya, who were so artfully and captivatingly caught on film by Leni Riefenstahl[2]—do not displace a pregiven sexual zone onto another site of the body but multiply sensations (both pleasurable or painful) in their inextricable intermingling. The erotic dimensions attributed by us to genitality are spread in varying intensities over the surface of the body, along the lines of perforation or incision. The mapped, ordered, regulated sequences of patterns, carefully laid out in ritual form, do not, like a name tag, map a particular psyche or subjectivity but designate a position, a place, binding the subject's body to that of the social collective:

> . . . these incisions, these welts and raised scars, these graphics are not signs; they are intensive points. They . . . do not refer to intentions in an inner individual psychic depth, not to meaning or concepts in some transcendent beyond. They reverberate one another . . . they are lined up. Warts and scarifications in rows, circles, in swastikas, in zigzags. . . . These are for the most part, not representations. . . . It is the incision and tumescence of new intensive points, pain-pleasure points, that first extends the erotogenic surface. What we have then is a form of spacing, a distributive system of marks. They do not form representations and not signifying chains, but figures, figures of intensive points, whose law of systematic distribution is lateral and immanent, horizontal and not traverse. (1984: 38)

Cicatrizations and scarifications mark the body as a public, collective, social category, in modes of inclusion or membership; they form maps of social needs, requirements, and excesses. The body and its privileged zones of sensation, reception, and projection are coded by objects, categories, affiliations, lineages, which engender and make real the subject's social, sexual, familial, marital, or economic position or identity within a social hierarchy. Unlike messages to be deciphered, they are more like a map correlating social positions with corporeal intensities.

Lingis counterposes this savage mode of body inscription to the civilized production of the body, not as surface pattern but as depth, latency: the civilized body is marked by and as signs, legible, meaning-laden interiorities, subjectivities capable of experiencing themselves in and as a determinate form, with particular qualities and capacities. The primitive body is distinguished from the civilized body not by degrees of barbarism, pain, or cruelty; our social system is no more or less cruel than any other. Both their modes and distributions of cruelty and the specific effects they have on the bodies they constitute differ. They do not differ in terms of the writing implements and tools used, although clearly there is a wide cultural variation in which instruments are capable of writing bodies. What differentiates savage from civilized systems of inscription is the sign-ladenness of the latter, the creation of bodies as sign systems, texts, narratives, rendered meaningful and integrated into forms capable of being read in terms of personality, psychology, or submerged subjectivity. Ours, we believe, is not a superficial identity but an enigma, a mystery to be uncovered, a secret to be explored through a reduction of the body to a symptom of the self:

> All that is civilized is significant. . . . We find the ugliness of tattooed nakedness puerile and shallow. . . . The savage fixing his identity on his skin. . . . Our identity is inward, it is our functional integrity as machines to produce certain civilized, that is, coded types of action. (1984: 43)

Inscriptions on the subject's body coagulate corporeal signifiers into signs, producing all the effects of meaning, representation, depth, within or subtending our social order. The intensity and flux of the sensations traversing the body become fixed into consumable, gratifiable needs and desires. The indefinite and ever-changing impetus and force of bodily sensations can now be attributed to an underlying psyche or consciousness. Corporeal fragmentation, the unity or disunity of the perceptual body, becomes organized in terms of the implied structure of an ego or consciousness, marked by and as a secret and private depth, a unique individuality. The civilized body is constituted as a use value and its dimensions and capacities become purchasable commodities, capable of selective augmentation, replacement, or transformation.

Whatever the merits or problems of Lingis's account of the savage as the other of the civilized subject, his work makes it clear that in our own culture as much as in others, there is a form of body writing and various techniques of social inscription that bind all subjects, often in quite different ways according to sex, class, race, cultural and age codifications, to social positions and relations. These modes of scarification are no less permanent or more removable than tattooing or epidermic or muscular lesions, although they may be less readily observed or directly readable. The civilized body is marked more or less permanently and impermeably. In our own culture, inscriptions occur both violently and in more subtle forms. In the first case, violence is demonstrable in social institutions of correction and training, prisons, juvenile homes, hospitals, psychiatric institutions, keeping the body confined, constrained, supervised, and regimented, marked by implements such as handcuffs, the traversing of neural pathways by charges of electricity in shock therapy, the straitjacket, the regimen of drug habituation and rehabilitation, chronologically regulated time and labor divisions, cellular and solitary confinement, the deprivation of mobility, the bruising of bodies in police interrogations, etc.[3] Less openly violent but no less coercive are the inscriptions of cultural and personal values, norms, and commitments according to the morphology and categorization of the body into socially significant groups—male and female, black and white, and so on. The body is involuntarily marked, but it is also incised through "voluntary" procedures, life-styles, habits, and behaviors. Makeup, stilettos, bras, hair sprays, clothing, underclothing mark women's bodies, whether black or white, in ways in which hair styles, professional training, personal grooming, gait, posture, body building, and sports may mark men's. There is nothing natural or ahistorical about these modes of corporeal inscription. Through them, bodies are made amenable to the prevailing exigencies of power. They make the flesh into a particular type of body—pagan, primitive, medieval, capitalist, Italian, American, Australian. What is sometimes loosely called body language is a not inappropriate description of the ways in which culturally specific grids of power, regulation, and force condition and provide techniques for the formation of particular bodies.

Not only does what the body takes into itself (diet in the first instance) effect a "surface inscription" of the body; the body is also incised by various forms of adornment. Through exercise and habitual patterns of movement, through negotiating its environment whether this be rural or urban,[4] and through clothing and makeup, the body is more or less marked, constituted as an appropriate, or, as the case may be, an inappropriate body, for its cultural requirements. It is crucial to note that these different procedures of corporeal inscription do not simply adorn or add to a body that is basically given through biology; they help constitute the very biological organization of the subject—the subject's height, weight, coloring, even eye color, are constituted as such by a constitutive interweaving of genetic and environmental factors.

The more or less permanent etching of even the civilized body by discursive systems is perhaps easier to read if the civilized body is decontextualized, stripped of clothing and adornment, behaviorally displayed in its nakedness. The naked European/American/African/Asian/Australian body (and clearly even within these categories there is enormous cultural variation) is still marked by its disciplinary history, by its habitual patterns of movement, by the corporeal commitments it has undertaken in day-to-day life. It is in no sense a natural body, for it is as culturally, racially, sexually, possibly even as class distinctive, as it would be if it were clothed.[5]

Every body is marked by the history and specificity of its existence. It is possible to construct a biography, a history of the body, for each individual and social body. This history would include not only all the contingencies that befall a body, impinging on it from the outside—a history of the accidents, illnesses, misadventures that mark the body and its functioning; such a history would also have to include the "raw ingredients" out of which the body is produced—its internal conditions of possibility, the history of its particular tastes, predelictions, movements, habits, postures, gait, and comportment.[6]

The various procedures for inscribing bodies, marking out different bodies, categories, types, norms, are not simply imposed on the individual from outside; they do not function coercively but are sought out. They are commonly undertaken voluntarily and usually require the active compliance of the subject. Body building, to take one rather stark example, is not imposed from without (even if it may be argued that the norms and ideals governing beauty and health do not always serve the interests of those who identify with them) but is actively undertaken; it could not possibly be effective otherwise. It is what Foucault might call a "technique of self-production" in its most literal sense.

The body builder—either male or female (and I would suggest that body building means different things for men and for women within the present health fad)[7]—is involved in actively reinscribing the body's skeletal frame through the inscription of muscles (the calculated tearing and rebuilding of selected muscle groups according to the exercises chosen) and of posture and internal organs. But body building does not simply add to an already functional, nonmuscular body; rather, it operates according to a logic that Derrida describes as supplementary[8]—in which the primary term, in this case the "natural," preinscriptive body, always makes possible, through the impossibility of its own full presence, its binary opposite, the term which has been expelled in order to constitute it, in this case the "worked-over" muscular body. There must be some shortfall of nature in order to make possible an augmentation of nature; there must already be a plastic and pliable body in order for it to be possible to mold and sculpt it according to the canons and dictates of body-building protocols. There is no "natural" norm; there are only cultural forms of body, which do or do not conform to social norms. The problem is not the conformity to cultural patterns, models, or even stereotypes, but which particular ones are used and with what effects. My point is different from the more common feminist concern with the "ideology" of the norms of beauty and the desire for self-control that patriarchal power relations impose on women, with or without women's knowledge.

Susan Bordo, for example, discusses body building and the body image of the anorexic in terms of a psychology of self-control:

First, there is the reassurance that one can overcome all physical obstacles, push oneself to any extremes in pursuit of one's goals. . . . Second, and most dramatic . . . is the thrill of being in total charge of the shape of one's body. (Bordo 1988: 99)

While such a psychological approach, an approach in terms of role models, images, ideals, and fantasies of the body beautiful, is perfectly valid and, in many contexts, extremely useful, nonetheless it leaves unexplored an entire dimension of the ontology and sociopolitical status of the body itself. The very status of the body as product—the question is whose product?—remains at stake here. While psychological investigations are clearly useful and necessary in accounting for women's—and, less frequently, men's—entwinement with dietary and exercise procedures, such approaches risk duplicating the mind/body dualism and taking the body as a kind of natural bedrock on which psychological and sociological analyses may be added as cultural overlays. The extreme formlessness and plasticity of any concept even resembling the natural body must also be taken into account in discussing the positive productivity of systems of diet and exercise—not to mention the strategic use of these systems by women—or men—in the day-to-day negotiations over their lives and life-styles.

Less solid, permanent, and tangible than the transformations effected by the body writing of muscular exertion but no less inscriptive is the habitual marking of the body by clothing, ornamentation, prosthetic devices, and makeup. I do not want to suggest, as Sandra Lee Bartky does, that adherence to and investment in these techniques of body marking signal women's acceptance of and absorption into prevailing patriarchal paradigms:

> The woman who checks her makeup half a dozen times a day to see if her foundation has caked or her mascara has run, who worries that the wind or the rain may spoil her hairdo, who looks frequently to see if her stockings have bagged at the ankle or who, feeling fat, monitors everything she eats, has become, just as surely as the inmate of the Panopticon, a self policing subject, a self committed to a relentless self-surveillance. This self-surveillance is a form of obedience to patriarchy. (Bartky 1988: 81)

While she also stresses the production of pleasure in feminine practices and preoccupations, this seems more a by-product than the adoption of a strategically resistant use of self-surveillance. The practices of femininity can readily function, in certain contexts that are difficult to ascertain in advance, as modes of guerrilla subversion of patriarchal codes, although the line between compliance and subversion is always a fine one, difficult to draw with any certainty. All of us, men as much as women, are caught up in modes of self-production and self-observation; these modes may entwine us in various networks of power, but never do they render us merely passive and compliant. They are constitutive of both bodies and subjects. It is not as if a subject outside these regimes is in any sense more free of constraint, less amenable to social power relations, or any closer to a state of nature. At best such a subject remains indeterminate, nonfunctional, as incapable of social resistance as of social compliance. Its enmeshment in disciplinary regimes is the condition of the subject's social effectivity, as either conformist or subversive. Women are no more subject to this system of corporeal production than men; they are no more cultural, no more natural, than men. Patriarchal power relations do not function to make women the objects of disciplinary control while men remain outside of disciplinary surveillance. It is a question not of more or less but of differential production, a question to which we will return in a later chapter.

Foucault and the Regimes of Knowledge-Power-Bodies

Foucault's genealogical writings[9] can be seen as the culmination of one particular line of thought in Nietzsche's work concerning the body and its inscription through procedures of punishment. In "Nietzsche, Genealogy, History" (in 1977b), Foucault credits Nietzsche with formulating the notion of a history capable of being analyzed and recovered by a procedure known as genealogy. Genealogy does not seek out the origin of things or events, or the "exact essence of things, their purest possibilities and their carefully protected identities" (142). If, instead of retaining a metaphysical faith in the identity and recoverability of historical events, the historian "listens to history, he finds that there is something altogether different behind things: not a timeless secret, but the secret that they have no essence or that their essence was fabricated in a piecemeal fashion from alien forms" (142).

It is not by accident that Foucault should choose to label his own methods genealogical, following Nietzsche's use of that term. Genealogy is what provides a "history of the present," a history of the various events that lead up to or make possible various struggles in the present—the prisoners' movement, sexual liberation movements, Marxism, and so on—a history that in no way pretends to be neutral, disinterested, and objective or to describe historical events as they really occurred. Genealogy is a history of events, here understood as discrete, disparate, often randomly connected material conjunctions of things or processes. Genealogy makes no presumptions about the metaphysical origins of things, their final teleology, the continuity or discontinuity of temporally contiguous elements, or the causal, explanatory connections between events. Instead, genealogy can be seen as the study of elements insofar as they are already interpreted, a study aimed at unsettling established models of knowledge and epistemological presumptions involved in the production of history, philosophy, and morality. Like Nietzsche, Foucault is concerned with the material, corporeal costs of historical events and transformations, their investments in and reliance on systems of power:

> Examining the history of reason, [Nietzsche] learns that it is born in an altogether "reasonable" fashion—from chance; devotion to truth and the precision of scientific methods arose from the passions of scholars, their reciprocal hatred, their fanatical and unending discussions, and their spirit of competition—the personal conflicts that slowly forged the weapons of reason. . . . What is found at the historical beginnings of things is not the inviolable identity of their origin, it is the dissension of other things. It is disparity. (1977b: 142)

An affirmation of knowledge about the impossibility of pure knowledge, a celebration of the unsettling nonfinality of all knowledges, genealogy in Foucault's reading of Nietzsche is about the ways in which history affects bodies, the interface between bodies and knowledges, how knowledges are extracted from and in their turn help to form bodies:

> The body—and everything that touches it: diet, climate, and soil—is the domain of [descent: the object of a genealogical investigation]. The body manifests the stigmata of past experiences and also gives rise to desires, failings and errors. . . .
> The body is the inscribed surface of events (traced by language and dissolved by ideas), the locus of a dissociated Self (adopting the illusion of a substantial unity), and a volume in perpetual disintegration. Genealogy, as an analysis of descent, is thus situated within the articulation of the body and history. Its task is to expose *a body totally imprinted by history* and the processes of history's destruction of the body. (1977b: 148; emphasis added)

Yet if Foucault derives his own genealogical techniques from Nietzsche and shares the latter's fascination with the fictitious origins of knowledge and the inscription of social power on bodies, nevertheless the particular concepts of history, knowledge, power, and the body in Foucault's writings differ significantly from Nietzsche's use of these concepts. In Foucault, the body is the object, target, and instrument of power, the field of greatest investment for power's operations, a stake in the struggle for power's control over a materiality that is dangerous to it, precisely because it is unpredictable and able to be used in potentially infinite ways, according to infinitely variable cultural dictates.[10] Especially under the forms of disciplinary normalization prevalent today, power, according to Foucault, utilizes, indeed produces, the subject's desires and pleasures to create knowledges, truths, which may provide more refined, improved, and efficient techniques for the surveillance and control of bodies, in a spiral of power-knowledge-pleasure. The body is that materiality, almost a medium, on which power operates and through which it functions. By contrast, in Nietzsche's understanding the formation of knowledges is the unrecognized product of bodies. Bodies are the agents of knowledge, but physiological causes have been mistaken for their conceptual, intellectual, or moral effects. Where for Foucault the body is the field on which the play of powers, knowledges, and resistances is worked out, for Nietzsche the body is the agent and active cause of knowledge.[11] In short, Foucault takes the body as a resistant yet fundamentally passive inertia whose internal features and forces are of little interest to the functioning of power. The body itself functions almost as a "black box" in this account:[12] it is acted upon, inscribed, peered into; information is extracted from it, and disciplinary regimes are imposed on it; yet its materiality also entails a resilience and thus also (potential) modes of resistance to power's capillary alignments. It is a kind of passivity, capable of being mobilized according to the interests of power or in the forms of subversion, depending on its strategic position. In Nietzsche, however, the body is the site for the emanation of the will to power (or several wills), an intensely energetic locus for all cultural production, a concept I believe may be more useful in rethinking the subject in terms of the body. Foucault's antihumanism dismisses consciousness as a mode of active resistance to power's alignments; but at the same time he seems to strip corporeality itself of its multiplicity of forces. Nietzsche's bodies, like Foucault's, are inscribed by power, branded to create a memory, but this is precisely because the body's forces, the forces of forgetfulness, are so strong. For Nietzsche the body's forces are the site for resistance because of their impetus and energy, not simply because of their location or recalcitrance.

Corresponding to this inflection in the notion of the body from Nietzsche to Foucault, the notions of power and knowledge are also transformed. Knowledge, in Foucault's understanding, is not simply an illusory aspiration, a mode of survival, of pure use value (these seem to be the two tendencies in Nietzsche); it is a body of propositions and texts, together with their accompanying institutions and protocols. Knowledge is what is socially recognized as knowledge. Remaining uncommitted regarding the ontological status of truth, Foucault instead prefers a more sociohistorical and pragmatic understanding: knowledge and truth are what a particular culture counts as true, what functions as true.[13] In Nietzsche's account of it, power is manifested most directly as will, the will to power, a force or series of forces animating and activating animate life, a pseudo- or quasi-biological life force which strives to enhance itself, to survive and grow. It is an energy, an activity, a series of directions. Foucault, by contrast, sees power more as a fine network, whether it functions by global or mass structures or takes on micro or capillary forms, that brings things and events into interrelations, even remote ones, a series of linkages differentially investing certain relations, leaving others less invested. For him, power is a "mobile substrate of force relations which, by virtue of their inequality, constantly engender states of power" (1978: 93). Power is an impersonal set of negotiations between practices, discourses, nondiscursive events, a mode of management of a multiplicity of relations, a set of technologies linking the most massive cultural movements to the most minute day-by-day events in interpersonal life. Power has no specifiable or universal goal, no pregiven shape or form, no privileged maneuvers, no generally preferred targets or privileged representations:

> By power, I do not mean "Power" as a group of institutions and mechanisms that ensure the subservience of the citizens of a given state. By power, I do not mean, either, a mode of subjugation which, in contrast to violence, has the form of the rule. Finally, I do not have in mind a general system of domination exerted by one group over another, a system whose effects through successive derivations, pervade the entire social body. . . . Power must be understood . . . as the multiplicity of force relations immanent in the sphere in which they operate and which constitute their own organization; as the process which, through ceaseless struggles and confrontations, transforms, strengthens

or reverses them; as the support these force relations find in one another, thus forming a chain or a system, or on the contrary, the disjunctions and contradictions which isolate them from one another; and lastly, as the strategies in which they take effect, whose general design or institutional crystallization is embodied in the state apparatus, in the formulation of the law, in the various social hegemonies. (1978: 92)

For Foucault, knowledge is a major instrument and technique of power; knowledge is made possible and functions only through its alignments with regimes of power; and conversely, power in its turn is transformed, realigned, shifted with transformations in the order and functioning of knowledges. It is not simply that power uses knowledge; power and knowledge are both made possible and actively feed into each through shifts and realignmens in those mobile forces that are their conditions of existence. Power and knowledge are mutually conditioning. Power does not function to distort knowledge, to produce illusion or ideology, for power's most privileged vein of functioning is within the order of truth. Power, in its capacity to bring together or to sever words and things, is the condition under which truth can be distinguished from falsehood[14] and truth elevated at the expense of falsehood, error and fiction. But, in its turn, knowledge is one of the conduits by which power is able to seize hold of bodies, to entwine itself into desires and practices: knowledge devises methods for the extraction of information from individuals which is capable of being codified, refined, reformulated in terms of and according to criteria relevant to the assessment of knowledge. As legitimized and sanctioned knowledge, discourses are then able to feed back into the regimes of power which made them possible and to enable power to operate in more subtle or systematic, more economical or vigilant, forms.

Turning now more directly to Foucault's conception of the role of the body in the nexus of knowledge-power relations, in his earlier archaeological writings[15] Foucault already foreshadows the concept of the body he will develop in his later texts. He states:

The body is molded by a great many distinct regimes; it is broken down by the rhythms of work, rest and holidays; it is poisoned by food or values, through eating habits or moral laws; it constructs resistances. . . . Nothing in man—not even his body—is sufficiently stable to serve as a basis of self-recognition or for understanding other men. (1977b: 153)

The body is not outside of history, for it is produced through and in history. Relations of force, of power, produce the body through the use of distinct techniques (the feeding, training, supervision, and education of children in any given culture) and harness the energies and potential for subversion that power itself has constructed (regimes of order and control involved in modern disciplinary society need the creation of a docile, obedient subject whose body and movements parallel and correlate with the efficiency of a machine or a body whose desire is to confess all about its innermost subjectivity and sexuality to institutionally sanctioned authorities). The body is indeed the privileged object of power's operations: power produces the body as a determinate type, with particular features, skills, and attributes. Power is the internal condition for the constitution and activity attributed to a body-subject. It is power which produces a "soul" or interiority as a result of a certain type of etching of the subject's body ("The soul is the effect and instrument of a political anatomy; the soul is the prison of the body," 1977a: 30). Power does not control the subject through systems of ideas—ideologies—or through coercive force; rather, it surveys, supervises, observes, measures the body's behavior and interactions with others in order to produce knowledges. It punishes those resistant to its rules and forms; it extracts information from its punitive procedures—indeed, through all its institutions and processes—and uses this information to create new modes of control, new forms of observation, and thus new regimes of power-knowledge as well as, necessarily, new sites of resistance. Foucault is concerned to explore the coproduction of bodies in their materiality and energetic force, and the machineries of power. He has published a number of texts on the encounters of what might be called anomalous minor individuals whose various transgressions thrust them into a direct corporeal encounter with the machineries of power. "The Life of Infamous Men," for example, chronicles the collision of petty criminals, deserters, wife beaters, and adulterers with the networks of power, bringing these individuals into the discursive calculations of police, clergy, surgeons, schoolmasters, and other officials or bureaucrats:[16]

> . . . the body is . . . directly involved in a political field; power relations have an immediate hold upon it; they invest it, mark it, train it, torture it, force it to carry out tasks, to perform ceremonies, to emit signs. This political investment of the body is bound up, in accordance with complex reciprocal relations, with its economic use; it is largely as a force of production that the body is invested with relations of power and domination; but, on the other hand, its constitution as labor power is possible only if it is caught up in a system of subjection (in which need is also a political instrument meticulously prepared, calculated and used); the body becomes a useful force only if it is both a productive body and a subjected body. . . . there may be a "knowledge" of the body that is not exactly the science of its functioning, and a mastery of its forces, that is more the ability to conquer them: this knowledge and this mastery constitute what might be called the political technology of the body. . . . What apparatuses and institutions operate is, in a sense, a micro-physics of power, whose field of validity is situated in a sense between the great functionings and the bodies themselves with their materiality and their forces. (1977a: 26)

For Foucault, power deploys discourses, particularly knowledges, on and over bodies, establishing knowledges as the representatives of the truth of those bodies and their pleasures. Discourses, made possible and exploited by power, intermesh with bodies, with the lives and behavior of individuals, to constitute them as particular bodies. Power is the condition of possibility of these true discourses, the motivating force behind their profusion and the energy which inscribes them on bodies and pleasures.

In *Discipline and Punish*, Foucault begins his exploration of the interface of corporeality and the power to punish with a graphic description of the horrifying and spectacular punishment of the regicide Damiens in 1757. Damiens's body is quite literally torn to pieces in the most calculated and precise way, in full public view, with all the ceremony and ritual of a public spectacle. His torture and execution are not unlike the descriptions both Nietzsche and Kafka use in outlining the law's inscription on bodies. Four significant points can be made regarding the form of spectacular punishment marking the criminal body early in the eighteenth century. First, punishment can be seen as a form of spectacle in which there is a socially sanctioned equivalence established between the crime committed and the punishment enacted; second, punishment involves procedures for carving, marking, even dismembering the body in proportion to the gravity of the crime; third, punishment can be regarded as a carefully regulated, socially acceptable form of torture, codified and regulated by law in accordance with the requirements of the sovereign's body politic; and fourth, these ritualized forms for the public display of punishment established their own modes of truth (in confessions, curses, repentance, or lack of remorse):

> If torture was so strongly embedded in legal practice, it was because it revealed truth and showed the operation of power. It assured the articulation of the written on the oral, the secret on the public, the procedure of investigation on the operation of the confession; it made it possible to reproduce the crime on the visible body of the criminal; the same horror had to be manifested and annulled. It also made the body of the condemned man the place where the vengeance of the sovereign was applied, the anchoring point for a manifestation of power. (1977a: 55)

Within a remarkably short time—seventy years—this system of spectacular and unusual punishment was replaced by what Foucault calls our modern or "disciplinary" form of punishment. Counterposed to the four characteristics describing sovereign punishment are the four features of disciplinary punishment. First, torture and highly individualized forms of punishment were replaced by a single, regimented system whose distribution varied by degree rather than kind (in other words, whatever the crime or its particular savagery, one form of punishment—prison—was meted out to all; what varied was the length of the sentence); second, as the final phase in the process of criminal justice (temporally following the processes of apprehension and judgment), punishment, from being the most public feature of the juridical process becomes its most private, being secreted behind the walls of the penitentiary; third, correlatively, the emphasis within the processes of judgment shifts from an assessment of the crime to a judgment about the criminal, the personality or subject "behind" the deed; and consequently, fourth, the soul rather than the body becomes the object of punitive practices. Revenge is no longer the motive of punishment, which instead now aims for the redemption of the criminal.

The history of punishment can, Foucault claims, be seen as a variable series of technologies of the body, procedures for the subjugation, manipulation, and control of the body. He shows how transformations in conceptions of subjectivity or self are a consequence of changing investments of power in the body. For him, punishment is a "political technology" of the body. As the object of sovereign forms of justice, punishment, and torture, the body is a frail and pathetic object capable of being broken, the converse of the king's body—an object which has attacked the sovereign's might and requires the severest retribution. In the projected but never actualized system of representational punishment proposed during the 1830s, where punishment is envisaged as a system of clearly legible signs to be read by the populace, the criminal's body must become "literary," capable of bearing meanings and of being deciphered as a sign of prevention. No longer a force against which the sovereign's might is pitted, as in the earlier system, the body becomes a book of instruction, a moral lesson to be learned. Within disciplinary technologies, the body is an intricate yet pliable instrument, capable of being trained, tuned to better, more efficient performance, a fine machinery of parts to be regulated, segmented, put to work, reordered, and replaced where necessary. In brief, there is a dramatic transformation in the concepts of subject and body, from a concern for the well-being of the king's body to the maintenance and well-being of the social body. This is a shift from the right over death to a power to regulate life through a micropolitical regulation of the body, the power to actively foster life:

> It is a question of situating the techniques of punishment whether they seize the body—in the ritual of public torture and execution or whether they are addressed to the soul—in the history of this body politic; of considering penal practices less as a consequence of legal theories than as a chapter of political anatomy.
>
> The history of this "micro-physics" of the punitive power would then be a genealogy or an element in a genealogy of the modern "soul." Rather than seeing this soul as the reactivated remnants of an ideology, one would see it as the present correlative of a certain technology of power over the body. It would be wrong to say that the soul is an illusion, or an ideological effect. On the contrary. It exists, it has a reality, it is produced permanently around, on, within the body by the functioning of a power that is exercised on those punished. . . . This real, noncorporal soul is not a substantive; it is the element in which are articulated the effects of a certain type of power and the reference of a certain type of knowledge, the machinery by which the power relations give rise to a possible corpus of knowledge, and knowledge extends and rein-

forces the effects of this power. On this reality reference, various concepts have been constructed and domains of analysis carved out: psyche, subjectivity, personality, consciousness, etc; on it have been built scientific techniques and discourses, and the moral claims of humanism . . . (1977a: 28–30)

The institutionalization of penal punishment is symptomatic of a more widespread entwinement of modern social institutions, knowledge of the human subject, and coercive social practices. Foucault alludes to the ways in which the prison both makes possible and is symptomatic of the disciplinary or carceral society. Penal discipline provides a generalizable set of procedures for the containment and control of unpredictable social events and individual actions. The alignments between such disciplinary institutions as family, army, school, workshop, factory, and prison and the networks of global surveillance allow us to discern a more global carceral power at work.

Foucault specifies more clearly the distinction between the sovereign power of death and the disciplinary power of the management of life in the final section of the first volume of *The History of Sexuality*. There he defines the disciplinary power over life as biopower, a power to regulate the minute details of daily life and behavior in both individuals and populations. His argument throughout this volume is that sex and discourses on sexuality are crucial ingredients in the operations of biopower, itself a concept at the heart of conceptions of both individuality and populations. Sexuality is a particularly privileged locus of the operations of power because of its strategically advantageous position at the core of individualizing processes of discipline and training, which intensify or realign bodily energies and pleasures. It is also at the heart of the management of the population (for example, in birth statistics, architectural plans, town planning, etc.). Sexuality is not a pure or spontaneous force that is tamed by power; rather, sexuality is deployed by power to enable it to gain a grip on life itself. Sex becomes not just something people do but the secret heart of life:

> [Sex] was at the pivot of the two axes along which developed the entire political technology of life. On the one hand it was tied to the disciplines of the body; the harnessing, intensification and distribution of forces, the adjustment and economy of energies. On the other hand, it was applied to the regulation of populations, through all the far reaching effects of its activity. It fitted in both categories at once, giving rise to infinitesimal surveillances, permanent controls, extremely meticulous ordering of space, indeterminate medical or psychological examination, to an entire micro-power concerned with the body. . . . Sex was a means of access both to the life of the body and the life of the species. (1978: 145–46)

If the history of the prison and of the treatment of the prisoner's body highlights and illustrates a mode of social control and order that also characterizes many other institutional sites—school, barracks, workshop, etc.—that is, if the prison illustrates a "carceral" power that functions throughout a social organization, then the history of (true discourses on) sexuality also serves as an illustration or exemplification of the development of the techniques of biopower, the modern form of regulation of the bodies of individuals and groups. The biopolitical investment of the body's function is not really an invention of the nineteenth century, although it flourished and gained precedence as the major investment of power in bodies only from that time onward. Techniques and procedures from considerably earlier periods—the techniques of the Christian confessional, the practices of medical investigation, the procedures of legal and punitive practices—became of strategic use in the biopolitical management of bodies and formed part of a systematic regime of powers when they coalesced into a coherent orientation in the nineteenth century.

Foucault outlines a number of lines of proliferation and specification of sexuality which emerged gradually during the eighteenth century, in particular the twofold movement centrifugally circling the heterosexual, monogamous couple. On one hand, there is a proliferation and dispersion of sexuality and of sexual "types," which are defined in terms of their deviation or departure from the heterosexual, marital norm. In this movement there is an increasing specification and focus on the sexuality of children, the mad, the criminal, homosexuals, perverts, etc. On the other hand, there is an increasing discretion granted to the heterosexual couple, who, while remaining the pivot and frame of reference for the specification of these other sexualities, are less subject to scrutiny and intervention, are granted a form of discursive privacy. One must assume that in the era of AIDS, it is still the sexuality of marginalized groups—gay men, intravenous drug users, prostitutes—that is increasingly administered, targeted, by public health policy, while the sexuality of the reproductive couple, especially of the husband/father, remains almost entirely unscrutinized, though his (undetected) secret activities—his clandestine bisexuality or drug use—may be responsible for the spread of the virus into hitherto "safe" (heterosexual) populations.

The dispersion of sexualities into multiple forms (as opposed simply to the specification of a range of perverse sexual acts) and the increasing medicalization of the observation and control of these perverse sexualities, together with the creation of psychological "types," "personalities," or characters, create the necessary conditions for the intense investment of power in the implantation of a sexual "profile" or history at the heart or as the secret of each individual. When sexuality can be acknowledged as the innermost secret of our being, a secret not only from others but also possibly from ourselves, then its analysis and regulation become not only necessary but also desirable enterprises, ones in which we willingly participate:

> Imbedded in bodies, becoming deeply characteristic, the oddities of sex relied on a technology of health and pathology. And conversely, since sexuality was a medical and medicalizable object, one had to try and detect it . . . in the depth of the organism, or on the surface of the skin, or among all the signs of be-

havior. The power which thus took charge of sexuality set about contacting bodies, caressing them with its eyes, intensifying areas, electrifying surfaces, dramatizing troubled moments. It wrapped the sexual body in its embrace. There was undoubtedly an increase in effectiveness and an extension of the domain controlled; but also a sensualization of power and a gain of pleasure. This produced a two-fold effect: an impetus was given to power through its very exercise; an emotion rewarded the overseeing control and carried it further; the intensity of the confession renewed the questioner's curiosity; the pleasure discovered fed back to the power that encircled it. (1978: 44–45)

Power does not oppose sexuality like a prohibition, confronting it from the outside. Sexuality, for Foucault, is nothing other than the effect of power. Power is able to gain a hold on bodies, pleasures, energies, through the construction and deployment of sexuality. The act or event of sex is not simply a lived, experienced reality, outside of power. If sexuality is a discursive-technological complex, a unity of knowledge, pleasure, and power, then sex is not simply the material reality of sexuality. Foucault suggests that sex is itself a product of the deployment of sexuality, a coherent integration or artificial unity of quite disparate elements, sensations, attitudes, practices, that a range of knowledges like anatomy, biology, and psychology take as their respective objects of investigation. Sexuality enables sex to become the object of these knowledges, linking sexual pleasure to the largely normalizing aims of power. Sex, the deployment of sexuality, enables the power produced by their material energies to intensify its hold on bodies, forces, their sensations and pleasures, binding subjects, in their very desires, to the operations of power.

Sex is a kind of conglomeration of elements of varying consistency and composition—physiological processes, hormonal secretions, muscular activities, wishes, hopes, desires, sensations, attitudes—which have historically been attributed a status as a unified, even natural, entity. The unification of these disparate elements is an effect of a particular investment of power:

Sexuality must not be thought of as a kind of natural given which power tries to hold in check, or as an obscure domain which knowledge tries gradually to uncover. It is the name that can be given to a historical construct: not a furtive reality that is difficult to grasp, but a great surface network in which the stimulation of bodies, the intensification of pleasures, the incitement to discourse, the formation of special knowledges, the strengthening of controls and resistances, are linked to one another, in accordance with a few major strategies of knowledge and power. (1978: 105–106)

Foucault makes it clear that if sexuality is the "artificial" or social construction of a unity out of a heterogeneity of processes, sensations, and functions, sex is no more real, primordial, or prediscursive than sexuality. Indeed, as far as he is concerned, sex is a "complex idea formed inside the deployment of sexuality," "an imaginary point determined by the deployment of sexuality" (1978: 152, 155).

> The notion of "sex" made it possible to group together, in an artificial unity, anatomical elements, biological functions, conducts, sensations, and pleasures, and it enabled one to make use of this fictitious unity as a causal principle, an omnipresent meaning, a secret to be discovered everywhere: sex was thus able to function as a unique signifier and as a universal signified. (1978: 154)

Thus both sex and sexuality are, for Foucault, social constructs, effects or results of the micropolitical investment in the minute regulation of bodies. The deployment of sexuality, as one of the finer and more successful threads that bind knowledge-power to bodies, is not the promise of liberation but a way of tying individuals and groups ever more firmly to the biopolitical control of bodies.

Sexuality and Sexually Different Bodies

At this point it may be pertinent to raise two kinds of concerns regarding Foucault's work and the general relevance of the model of surface inscription in Nietzsche and others, from the point of view of their relevance to feminist attempts to provide an autonomous notion of female subjectivity, sexuality, and corporeality.

The first question regards what might be called Foucault's corporeal ontology. If both sex and sexuality are effects of the deployment of sexuality, is there a more basic, possibly even foundational, commitment to a primordial materiality evident in his writings? In other words, if sex and sexuality are the results of the inscription of particular kinds of power, on what are these inscriptions articulated? Foucault, like Nietzsche, seems to require the meeting of (at least) two antagonistic forces in order for his "analytics of power" to function: on one hand, the particular procedures and techniques of social institutions (prison, hospital, asylum, factory, school); on the other hand, the resisting and resistant bodies and pleasures of individuals. "Bodies and pleasures" are the objects and targets of power; in a sense, Foucault seems to imply that they preexist power, that they are or may be the raw materials on which power works and the sites for possible resistance to the particular forms power takes. It is only according to such a presupposition that Foucault can rather enigmatically suggest that the deployment of sexuality may be vulnerable to a counterattack from the point of view of bodies and pleasures: "The rallying point for the counterattack against the deployment of sexuality ought not to be sex-desire, but bodies and pleasures" (157). It is unclear to me what this could possibly mean: is it that bodies and pleasures are somehow outside the deployment of sexuality? Or are they neuralgic points within the deployment of sexuality that may be strategically useful in any challenge to the current nexus of desire-knowledge-power? Why are bodies and pleasures a source of subversion in a way that sex and desire are not? Perhaps more important, whose bodies and which pleasures are to be such a "rallying point"? Foucault's implicit answer seems clear, seeing that he rarely discusses female bodies and pleasures, let alone women's sex and desires: in lieu of any specification, one must presume, along with rest of patriarchal culture, that the neutral body can only be unambiguously filled in by the male body and men's pleasures.

The issue of the ontological and political status of the body (and pleasures) in Foucault's genealogical writings raises a more general feminist concern about the model of social inscription: do sexually different bodies require different inscriptive tools to etch their different surfaces? Or rather, is it the inscription of power on bodies that produces bodies as sexually different? Is it that there is a sexual continuum—a (quasi-biological or even natural) continuum of (sexual) differences between bodies, which power divides and organizes in historically and culturally variable forms? Or does power help constitute the very biologies, and pleasures, of bodies? Does the concept of a field or continuum of bodies serve to homogenize bodies in a single terrain, neutralizing the spacing or intervals, the difference, that (politically) marks every field? These crucial questions find no ready answer in any of the theorists examined in this chapter, because each rarely, if ever, talks about the issue of sexual difference or specifies that the objects of his investigation are implicitly male bodies and subjectivities, men's practices and modes of social organization.

I am suggesting that, in feminist terms at least, it is problematic to see the body as a blank, passive page, a neutral "medium" or signifier for the inscription of a text. If the writing or inscription metaphor is to be of any use for feminism—and I believe that it can be extremely useful—the specific modes of materiality of the "page"/body must be taken into account: one and the same message, inscribed on a male or a female body, does not always or even usually mean the same thing or result in the same text. The elision of the question of sexual (and racial) specificity of the inscribed surface occurs throughout the history of accounts of the body. Yet all of the theorists examined here are committed in some sense to a "natural given," something outside of or before the processes of inscription, a preinscriptive surface, which, it could be argued, takes on the function of the feminine, in its support of the writing metaphor. In Nietzsche, it is the "instincts," pregiven—indeed, "pre-natural"—forces or impulses that require to be tamed and given representation and memory by social inscriptions; in Foucault, it is bodies and pleasures that either preexist the sociopolitical deployments of power or resist them; and Lingis, too, in spite of his dazzling evocation of corporeal inscriptions, remains paradoxically committed to a sexual, experiencing body, but one that is rendered neuter.

For Lingis it is as if the pure body, before its social incision, is a form of pure plenitude, a series of undifferentiated processes and functions that become erotic and sexually specific only by social marks. It is this presumption of a sexually neutral or indeterminate, universal body that enables him to render circumcision as equivalent to clitoridectomy:

> ... circumcision castrates the male of the labia about his penis, as the clitori-dectomy castrates the female of her penis. It is through *castration of the natural bisexual* that the social animal is produced. (Lingis 1984: 40; emphasis added)

The body is "naturally" bisexual for Lingis, and it is a form of social, inscriptive "castration" that creates the division between the sexes. There is no sensitivity to or awareness of the major sexual dysymmetry of circumcision and clitoridec-tomy, for both function for him as support to the phallus. Circumcision does not by any means remove the male sexual organ—on the contrary, many cultures and individuals affirm that it enhances men's sexual sensitivity in a way that clitoridectomy clearly does not. Clitoridectomy implies the entire subordination or, ultimately, the annihilation of the bodily sources of women's genital pleasure, in the interests of men. It is the excision of the possibility of a certain kind of genital sexual gratification for women, according to what men perceive as their own interest. There is not and can never be symmetry between the two sexes here. It is not circumcision but removal of the penis (with the preservation of the testicles) which is the physiological (if not the cultural) counterpart of clitoridectomy.

Whereas my first concern is addressed to the status of the sexually differen-tiated body on the various models of social inscription outlined here, my second is addressed to the status and form these inscriptions take in being directed to different types of body. If we take Foucault as representative of this tradition in philosophical thought, it is significant that until his last writings, the concept of the body that he utilized is a "neutral," sexually indifferent, and thus abstract body. Implicitly, or without adequately acknowledging it, Foucault talks only about the male body—with the exception of one or two paragraphs. The treat-ment of prisoners is especially clearly sexually linked—the kinds of punishment received, the kinds of crimes committed, the kinds of judgments (and what it is that is judged) are clearly different for the two sexes in ways that he does not explain. Given that he is correct about the investments of power in the produc-tion and incarceration of the criminal personality, why is it that there is in fact a dual production—two kinds of punishment, two types of prisoner, two types of incarceration, depending on the sex of the prisoner?

In *The History of Sexuality*, Foucault outlines only one specific program of sexualization directed toward women: "the hystericization of women's bodies." In treating hysteria as an effect of power's saturation of women's body, he ig-nores the possibility of women's strategic occupation of hysteria as a form of resistance to the demands and requirements of heterosexual monogamy and the social and sexual role culturally assigned to women. Like homosexual or any other sexual practices, the hystericization of women's bodies is a procedure that, depending on its particular context, its particular location, and the particular subjects, may function as a form of complicity with or refusal of patriarchal sexual relations.

In *The Use of Pleasure* (1985), the second volume of *The History of Sexuality*, Foucault has shifted his attention from the genealogy of modern social institutions and knowledges to an analysis of the ancient Greek techniques of self-regulation, the ways in which individuals value their conduct and perform their duties. His concern shifts from a genealogy of knowledge-power to a system of ethical self-production. He is now interested in "the practices which led individuals to focus their attention on themselves, to decipher, recognize, and acknowledge . . . a certain relationship that allows them to discover, in desire, the truth of that being" (1985: 5). Whereas his object of analysis in the genealogical texts was the nexus of knowledge, power, and bodies, now he is primarily concerned with the genesis or self-creation of subjectivity. His preoccupation with ethical concerns over sexual conduct is not entirely alien to his earlier interests, although it does not accord with his announcement of a proposed six-volume history of sexuality. The "techniques of self" with which he is now concerned form part of the genealogy of the modern concern with pinning down and knowing subjectivity assumed by the "sciences of man."

By the time he writes *The Use of Pleasure*, Foucault is quite open about the fact that his privileged object of investigation, the "techniques of self," refers only to men:

> women were generally subjected (excepting the liberty they could be granted by a status like that of courtesan) to extremely strict constraints, and yet this ethics was not addressed to women, it was not their duties or obligations that were recalled, justified or spelled out. It was an ethics for men: an ethics thought, written and taught by men and addressed to men—to free men, obviously. (1985: 22)

His openness about women's exclusion is not or need not be, in itself, a political problem for feminists, especially those who take seriously his critique of the politics of representation, of speaking on behalf of others,[17] if his work has, in spite of this exclusion, not closed off the possibility of others, women, talking about the birth of the women's prison, the history of women's sexuality, or women's ethic of self-production—however different these might look from men's. Foucault himself closes off this possibility, however, by implying that there was not a corresponding ethics of women's self-production during the classical age: he claims that women had to wait until the advent of an "ethics of marital relations" in the Middle Ages, as if questions of moral self-regulation were not relevant to women up to this period. His work has not left a space for the inclusion of women's accounts and representations of the various histories of their bodies that could be written. That does not mean that the metaphor of the social inscription of corporeal surfaces must be abandoned by feminists but that these metaphors must be refigured, their history in and complicity with the patriarchal effacement of women made clear, if there is to remain something of insight or strategic value in these texts.

7 | Intensities and Flows

There is no ideology and never has been.
(Gilles Deleuze and Felix Guattari, *A Thousand Plateaus* (1987: 4))

W E ARE NOW well along the path of the inversion of the Möbius strip, at that point of twisting or self-transformation in which the inside flips over to become the outside, or the outside turns over on itself to become the inside. The crucial question around which much of this book has revolved is about whether the terms in which the conceptual order, reason, knowledge, subjectivity, and interiority are thought—and in this book they have been paradigmatically represented in the frameworks and terms of psychology, psychoanalysis, and phenomenology—can be transcribed into the frameworks and terms appropriate for corporeality. Can accounts of subjectivity and the psychical interior be adequately explained in terms of the body? Can depths, the interior, the subjective, and the private instead be seen in terms of surfaces, bodies, and material relations? Can the mind/body dualism be overcome using the concepts associated with the devalued term of the binary pair of mind and body, that is, are the body and corporeality the (disavowed) grounds and terms on which the opposition is erected and made possible? What happens to conceptual frameworks if the body stands in place of the mind or displaces it from its privileged position defining humanity against its various others? What happens in the bifurcation of sexed bodies—which is, in my opinion, an irreducible cultural universal—that is inevitably part of our understanding of bodies? If mind or subjectivity can be adequately and without reduction explained in terms of bodies, bodies understood in their historicocultural specificity, does this mean that sexual specificity—sexual difference—will be finally understood as a necessary (even if not sufficient) condition of our understanding of subjectivity? Can various key issues and concepts in feminist theory—including women's experience, subjectivity, desire, pleasure—be reconceived in corporeal terms, whether these are provided by the theoretical frameworks of Nietzsche, Foucault, Deleuze, or others? Is there a possibility of transposing the terms of consciousness and the entire psychical topography into those of body mapping and social tattooing? What is lost in this process? Or gained? Why is it necessary to transform these terms? These are among the central issues to be raised in this chapter. Here I propose a provisional reconstruction of Deleuze and Guattari's understanding of corporeality in *A Thousand Plateaus*—a text that could be regarded as their (anti-)opus—in terms of the flatness, surfaces, intensities, investments, i.e., in the terms other than those provided by dichotomous thought, capable of outstripping, overturning, or exceeding binary logics.

Feminism and Rhizomatics

It is significant that all the male theorists of the body I have explored here have a highly contentious position in feminist theory; all of them have generated considerable debate regarding their ostensibly sexist remarks, their apparent derision of women or femininity; and all of them have been defended by other feminists in terms of their strategic and provisional usefulness in explaining the operations of a phallocentric culture and patriarchal representational models. Deleuze and Guattari's status in feminist evaluations seems rather more shaky than others'. Most feminists have said virtually nothing about them, although there are a few significant exceptions.[1] They seem to have been generally ignored by those who are otherwise quite sympathetic to French theory: their works have thus far generated little of the controversy and impact accorded to the writings of Lacan, Foucault, or Derrida. This is rather surprising given the privileged position they—or at least Deleuze—holds in radical French thought. And even those feminists who do engage with their writings have tended to be critical or at least suspicious of their apparent appropriations of feminist theory and politics, in similar ways to feminist suspicions regarding Derrida's metaphorics of invagination.

Alice Jardine, for example, expresses a series of misgivings about their work and its possible value or usefulness for feminist purposes. She claims that

> to the extent that women must "become woman" first . . . might that not mean that she must also be the first to disappear? Is it not possible that the process of "becoming woman" is but a new variation of an old allegory for the process of women becoming obsolete? There would remain only her simulacrum: a female figure caught in a whirling sea of male configurations. A silent, mutable, head-less, desireless spatial surface necessary only for *his* metamorphosis? (Jardine 1985: 217)

The notion of the flattening of subjectivity, the disorganization of the organism ("head-less"), the destabilization of political order and social organization, poses a theoretical anxiety for Jardine that, in this passage at least, is almost as strong as her worries about the appropriation of the metaphorics of "becoming woman" as a new label for male self-expansion. Jardine articulates clearly the anxieties posed for feminists by Deleuze's radical refiguring of ontology in terms of planes, intensities, flows, becomings, linkages, rather than being, objects, qualities, pairs, and correlations, through the figure of woman and femininity. Her anxieties seem related to the apparent bypassing or detour around the very issues with which feminist theory has tended to concern itself: "identity," otherness, gender, oppression, the binary divisions of male and female—all central and driving preoccupations of feminist thought.

The suspicion that "becoming woman, "desiring machines," and related concepts are covers or excuses for yet another male appropriation of whatever is radical or subversive in feminist politics (including the politics of theory production) is hinted at, although Deleuze and Guattari are not mentioned by name, in Irigaray's writings as well. Irigaray claims that women are once again subsumed under the neut(e)rality of concepts such as desire, machinic functioning, assemblages, connections, and are thus made the props or supports of men's fantasies about themselves and about humanity:

> . . . doesn't the "desiring machine" still partly take the place of woman or the feminine? Isn't it a sort of metaphor of her that men can use? Especially in terms of their relation to the techno-cratic?
>
> Or again: can this "psychosis" be woman's? If so, isn't it a psychosis that prevents them from acceding to sexual pleasure? At least to *their* pleasure? That is, to a pleasure different from an abstract neutral pleasure of sexualized matter. That pleasure which perhaps constitutes a discovery for men, a supplement to enjoyment, in a fantasmatic "becoming-woman," but which has long been familiar to women. For them isn't the [Body-without-Organs] a historical condition? And don't we run the risk once more of taking back from woman those as yet unterritorialized spaces where her desire might come into being? Since women have long been assigned the task of preserving "body-matter" and the "organless," doesn't the [Body-without-Organs] come to occupy the place of their own schism? of the evacuation of women's desire in women's body? . . . To turn the [Body-without-Organs] into a "cause" of sexual pleasure, isn't it necessary to have had a relation of language and sex to the organs—that women have never had? (Irigaray 1985b: 140–41)

While Rosi Braidotti is considerably more sympathetic to Deleuze and Guattari's broad project, she expresses similar reservations about their recuperation of the impetus and insight of feminist politics. She is clear in her ambivalences, her unresolved relation to and against Deleuze's writings—as, it seems to me, feminists must be if they are on one hand to benefit from men's modes of production of knowledges while on the other hand moving beyond them in recognizing their limitations. Her relations to Deleuze's texts vacillate between criticism and utter fascination, both equally strong:

> Although I see the consistency in Deleuze's argument—from his global rejection of binary oppositions to the rejection of the man/woman dichotomy in favour of the continuum of interacting embodied subjectivities—I am puzzled by the consequences that this may have for women. Can feminists, at this point in their history of collective struggles aimed at redefining female subjectivity,

actually afford to let go of their sex-specific forms of political agency? Is the bypassing of gender in favour of a dispersed polysexuality not a very masculine move? . . . Deleuze's multiple sexuality assumes that women conform to a masculine model which claims to get rid of sexual difference. What results is the dissolution of the claim to specificity voiced by women. . . . Only a man would idealize sexual neutrality. (Braidotti 1991: 120–21)

Between them, Jardine, Irigaray, and Braidotti voice a number of reservations that seem to chart a more general attitude on the part of many feminists toward the project Deleuze has described as rhizomatics. I will briefly list these objections, adding that it is not always clear to me that these objections are justified.

First, the metaphor of "becoming woman" is a male appropriation of women's politics, struggles, theories, knowledges, insofar as it "borrows" from them while depoliticizing their radicality. At the least, Deleuze and Guattari can be accused of aestheticizing and romanticizing women's struggles,[2] while in stronger terms, they may be accused of depoliticizing women's various political struggles and using them precisely to neutralize, to render human (and thus to rephallicize), women's specificity, which they have struggled so hard to produce and represent.

Second, these metaphors not only neutralize women's sexual specificity, but, more insidiously, they also neutralize and thereby mask men's specificities, interests, and perspectives. This means that the question of becoming itself becomes a broadly human, and indeed an even more general, phenomenon, a defining characteristic of life itself, a maneuver that desexualizes and obfuscates one of the major features of phallocentric thought—its subsumption of two sexual symmetries under a single norm. It is not clear that a "feminine" becoming woman would be the same as the one Deleuze and Guattari describe. It remains a block both to women's explorations and interrogations of their own specific, nongeneralizable modes of becoming and desiring production and to men's acceptance of the corporeal specificity of their own positions of becoming and desiring production.

Third, in both *Anti-Oedipus* and *A Thousand Plateaus*, Deleuze and Guattari invest in a romantic elevation of psychoses, schizophrenia, becoming, which on one hand ignores the very real torment of suffering individuals and, on the other hand, positions it as an unlivable ideal for others. Moreover, in making becoming woman the privileged site of all becomings, Deleuze and Guattari confirm a long historical association between femininity and madness which ignores the sexually specific forms that madness takes.

Fourth, in invoking metaphors of machinic functioning, in utilizing the terminology of the technocratic order, Deleuze and Guattari, like other masculinist philosophers, utilize tropes and terms made possible only through women's exclusion and denigration; while not inherently and irremediably masculinist, technocracies are in fact masculinist insofar as technological developments have thus far been historically predicated on women's exclusion.

These are of course very serious objections or reservations, ones which cannot be simply cast aside. They will be returned to. But they are the kinds of objections that can with equal validity be directed to virtually any male philosopher—and a good many female philosophers as well. Instead of either accepting Deleuze and Guattari's theoretical perspectives uncritically or feminist criticisms wholeheartedly, I want to explore how these writers may be of use for some feminist purposes, the points of their intersection or overlap, even if their works are phallocentric. No text, not even a "feminist" text, can be immune to this charge, insofar as the very categories, concepts, and methodologies for both phallocentrism and its critique are derived from our received history of texts and knowledges. It is significant that the "reversal of Platonism" Deleuze and Guattari seek shares the concern of many feminists to overcome the binary polarizations so pervasive in Western thought. Not only do they seek alternatives to contest or bypass the metaphysical bases of Western philosophy; they seek to position traditional metaphysical identities in a context which renders them effects or surface phenomena in an ontology conceived quite otherwise. In a sense, Deleuze and Guattari must be regarded as the contemporary heirs of Spinozism: in challenging theoretical paradigms that presume the centrality of the subject and the coherence and effectivity of signification, they problematize our most common assumptions regarding identity, relations between subject and object, substance, matter, corporeality. Even if their procedures and methods do not actively affirm or support feminist struggles around women's autonomy and self-determination, their work may help to clear the ground of metaphysical oppositions and concepts so that women may be able to devise their own knowledges, accounts of themselves and the world.

Also aligned with feminist struggles against prevailing forms of masculinism in philosophy is Deleuze and Guattari's interest in the question of difference, a difference capable of being understood outside the dominance or regime of the one, the self-same, the imaginary play of mirrors and doubles, the structure of duplication presumed by the notions of signification and subjectification. Deleuze claims to conceptualize difference beyond the four great "illusions" of representation: identity, opposition, analogy, and resemblance. In conceptualizing a difference in and of itself, a difference which is not subordinated to identity, Deleuze and Guattari invoke notions of becoming and of multiplicity beyond the mere doubling or proliferation of singular, unified subjectivities.[3]

Their notion of the body as a discontinuous, nontotalizable series of processes, organs, flows, energies, corporeal substances and incorporeal events, speeds and durations, may be of great value to feminists attempting to reconceive bodies outside the binary oppositions imposed on the body by the mind/body, nature/culture, subject/object and interior/exterior oppositions. They provide an altogether different way of understanding the body in its connections with other bodies, both human and nonhuman, animate and inanimate, linking organs and biological processes to material objects and social practices while refusing to subordinate the body to a unity or a homogeneity of the kind provided by the body's subordination to consciousness or to biological organization. Following Spinoza, the body is regarded as neither a locus for a consciousness nor an organically determined entity; it is understood more in terms of what it can do, the things it can perform, the linkages it establishes, the transformations and becomings it undergoes, and the machinic connections it forms with other bodies, what it can link with, how it can proliferate its capacities—a rare, affirmative understanding of the body (Deleuze and Guattari 1987: 74).

Not only do they develop alternative notions of corporeality and materiality; they also propose quite different, active, affirmative conceptions of desire. It has been argued[4] that while psychoanalysis relies on a notion of desire as a lack, an absence that strives to be filled through the attainment of an impossible object, desire can instead be seen as what produces, what connects, what makes machinic alliances. Instead of aligning desire with fantasy and opposing it to the real, instead of seeing it as a yearning, desire is an actualization, a series of practices, bringing things together or separating them, making machines, making reality. Desire does not take for itself a particular object whose attainment it requires; rather, it aims at nothing above its own proliferation or self-expansion. It assembles things out of singularities and breaks things, assemblages, down into their singularities. It moves; it does. Such a notion of desire cannot but be of interest to feminist theory insofar as women have been the traditional repositories and guardians of the lack constitutive of desire, and insofar as the opposition between presence and absence, reality and fantasy, has traditionally defined and constrained woman to inhabit the place of man's other. Lack only makes sense insofar as some other, woman, personifies and embodies it for man. Any model of desire that dispenses with the primacy of lack in conceiving desire seems to be a positive step forward and, for that reason alone, worthy of careful investigation. But the surpassing of the model of lack does not, should not, return us to the affirmation of pure plenitude or presence. Presence and absence are coupled in and to the same framework. In place of plenitude, being, fullness or self-identity is not lack, absence, rupture, but rather becoming.

Deleuze's writings may provide unexpectedly powerful weapons of analysis, critique, transgression, and transformation. They may demonstrate that other kinds of theoretical approaches, other intellectual paradigms, new ways of conceptualizing knowledge, power, bodies, representations, other than the kind of Freudo-Marxism that dominated and perhaps still dominates much of feminist theory in spite of Freudo-Marxism's well-recognized problems (the centrality of the phallus for psychoanalysis; the centrality of relations of production; monolithic, cohesive forms for Marxism).

It may be the case that feminists and theorists of the body have had good reason to be suspicious of the apparently joyous ease of Deleuze and Guattari's pronouncements, the hermeticism of their writings, the systematicity and elaborate complexity of their ontology or ontologies (for clearly their work has undergone considerable development and variation in the time between *Anti-Oedipus* and *A Thousand Plateaus*), in the differential and classificatory schemas on which their frameworks, insights, and methodology (if one can use these rather conventional designations of their work) are based. Their works—especially Deleuze's *(The Logic of Sense* is exemplary in this context)—make minute distinctions, operate with terminology and goals that seem, at first glance at least, to be alien, abstract, counter intuitive. Moreover, in order to persist in the reading/comprehension/use of their texts, one must suspend all critical attitudes, at least until some broad patterns of relevance emerge—which may not occur for considerable periods. Entry into their frameworks or conceptual space requires a kind of trust rarely required in philosophical texts, for it involves the provisional suspension of criticism one normally brings to the evaluation of texts. This trust is required in order to grasp, to be moved by, and to be able to utilize their works.[5] Such a trust is of course required of every reader—indeed, some degree of this trust is required to gain access to any new theoretical position. But in the case of Deleuze and Guattari, this is made even more difficult for the feminist reader insofar as the "rewards" for a patient reading are even less tangible. But in spite of these sometimes considerable reservations and difficulties, it seems to me well worthwhile to experiment with their writings, to take the risk of abandoning one's previous frameworks and terminology, of getting lost, of unsettling what was previously secure and clear, for they represent one of the more innovative and thoroughgoing upheavals of thought-politics-desire as we approach the end of the millennium. As Foucault has suggested, Deleuze may well be the philosopher of the next century, just as Nietzsche's writings of the later nineteenth century anticipate and chart out much of the terrain of twentieth-century thought. This, then, is a risky undertaking, one in which there is a danger that one may lose one's way, be pulled astray from the path one has chosen; but the risks and rewards may be worth taking insofar as new paths of exploration, new goals, new theoretical paradigms and frameworks, may be made possible which could bypass the dilemmas posed for feminists by binary or dichotomous thought.

Bodies, Bodies without Organs, Becomings

My goal here is not to be in any way "faithful" to the Deleuzian oeuvre but, on the contrary, and more in keeping with its spirit, to use it, to make it work, to develop and experiment with it in order to further develop theories and concepts that Deleuze and Guattari do not. In particular, I intend to develop only those elements of their work, only those plateaus, that are useful for feminist reconceptions of the body, for rethinking materiality, and for retranscribing the mind/body opposition—clearly a highly selective reading. Given that Deleuze and Guattari do not have a systematic account of the body, this will involve not only a selective reading of their elusive and immensely complex text *A Thousand Plateaus* but also a reconstruction which is inevitably more cohesive, more "arboreal" (systematic, centralized, ordered, and organized), than their own nomadic or rhizomatic understanding.[6] I will concentrate on a small number of concepts that I believe overlap with the concerns of feminist theories of the body: the rhizome, assemblage, machine, desire, multiplicity, becoming, and the Body without Organs (BwO). These concepts seem loosely linked together in an attempt to reject or displace prevailing centrisms, unities, and rigid strata.

In Deleuze and Guattari's work, subject and object can no longer be understood as discrete entities or binary opposites. Things, material or psychical, can no longer be seen in terms of rigid boundaries, clear demarcations; nor, on an opposite track, can they be seen as inherently united, singular or holistic. Subject and object are series of flows, energies, movements, strata, segments, organs, intensities—fragments capable of being linked together or severed in potentially infinite ways other than those which congeal them into identities. Production consists of those processes which create linkages between fragments, fragments of bodies and fragments of objects. Assemblages or machines are heterogeneous, disparate, discontinuous alignments or linkages brought together in conjunctions (x plus y plus z) or severed through disjunctions and breaks. But significantly, an assemblage follows no central or hierarchical order, organization, or distribution; rather, it is, like the contraption or gadget, a conjunction of different elements on the same level:

> An assemblage has neither base nor superstructure, neither deep structure nor superficial structure; it flattens all of its dimensions onto a single place of consistency upon which reciprocal presuppositions and mutual insertions play themselves out. (Deleuze and Guattari 1987: 90)[7]

Assemblages are the provisional linkages of elements, fragments, flows, of disparate status and substance: ideas, things—human, animate, and inanimate—all have the same ontological status. There is no hierarchy of being, no preordained order to the collection and conjunction of these various fragments, no central organization or plan to which they must conform. Their "law" is rather the imperative of endless experimentation, metamorphosis, or transmutation, alignment and realignment. It is not that the world is without strata, totally flattened; rather, the hierarchies are not the result of substances and their nature and value but of modes of organization of disparate substances. They are composed of lines, of movements, speeds, and intensities, rather than of things and their relations. Assemblages or multiplicities, then, because they are essentially in movement, in action, are always made, not found. They are the consequences of a practice, whether it be that of the bee in relation to the flower and the hive or of a subject making something using tools or implements. They are necessarily finite in space and time, provisional and temporary in status; they always have an outside; they do not, or need not, belong to a higher-order machine. Machines, for Deleuze and Guattari, are not simply mechanical replacements or corporeal prosthetics (as Freud suggests). They are not standardized, conforming to a plan or blueprint, the "application" of principles. Machines are opposed to mechanism. They are the condition as well as the effect of any making, any producing.

A "desiring machine" opposes the notion of unity or oneness: the elements or discontinuities that compose it do not belong to either an original totality that has been lost or one which finalizes or completes it, a telos. They do not re-present the real, for their function is not a signifying one: they produce and they themselves are real. They constitute, without distinction, individual, collective, and social reality. Desire does not create permanent multiplicities; it experiments, producing ever-new alignments, linkages, and connections, making things. It is fundamentally nomadic not teleological, meandering, creative, nonrepetitive, proliferative, unpredictable.

Insofar as the body can no longer be seen as a unified and unifying organism, an organism centered either biologically or psychically, organized in terms of an overarching consciousness or unconscious, cohesive through its intentionality or its capacity for reflection and self-reflection, Deleuze and Guattari see the body as elements or fragments of a desiring machine and themselves as composed of a series of desiring machines. When the body is freely amenable to the flows and intensities of the desiring machines that compose it, Deleuze and Guattari, following Antonin Artaud, call it "the Body without Organs," the BwO. The BwO is the body in abundance of its (biological, psychical, and signifying) organization and organs:

> The body without organs is not a dead body but a living body all the more alive and teeming once it has blown apart the organism and its organization. . . . The full body without organs is a body populated by multiplicities. (Deleuze and Guattari 1987: 30)

Their notion of the BwO is Deleuze and Guattari's attempt to denaturalize human bodies and to place them in direct relations with the flows or particles of other bodies or things. In presuming a Spinozist conception of the univocity of being ("Spinozist's ethics is a *physics*," Deleuze and Parnet write [1987:30]), in which all things, regardless of their type, have the same ontological status, the BwO refers indistinguishably to human, animal, textual, sociocultural, and physical bodies. That is why they seem less interested in the general question of embodiment than in the question of the capacities and unknown potential of the body to do things, to engage in practices:

> ... Spinoza's question: *what is a body capable of*? What affects is it capable of? Affects are becomings: somewhere they awaken us to the extent they diminish our strength of action and decompose our relations (sadness), sometimes they make us stronger through augmenting our force, and make us enter into a faster and higher individual (joy). Spinoza never ceases to be astonished at the body: not of having a body, but at what the body is capable of. Bodies are defined not by their genus and species, nor by their origins and functions, but by what they can do, the affects they are capable of, in passion as in action. (Deleuze and Parnet 1987: 74)[8]

Unlike psychoanalysis, which regards the body as a developmental union or aggregate of partial objects, organs, drives, orifices, each with their own significance, their own modalities of pleasure which, through the processes of Oedipal reorganization, bring these partial objects and erotogenic bodily zones into alignment in the service of a higher goal than their immediate, local gratification (the ultimate goal being reproduction), the BwO invokes a conception of the body that is disinvested of fantasy, images, projections, representations, a body without a psychical or secret interior, without internal cohesion and latent significance. Deleuze and Guattari speak of it as a surface of speeds and intensities before it is stratified, unified, organized, and hierarchized.

As they describe it, the BwO is not a body evacuated of all psychical interiority, a kind of blanket rewriting or remapping of the body. The BwO is a tendency to which all bodies, whatever their organization, aspire. Deleuze and Guattari speak of it as an egg, which instead of being composed of three kinds of substances is fluid throughout (neither Lacan's scrambled egg of a subject, the "hommelette," nor the egg in its differential properties, hard shell, clear white and yellow yolk), an unimpeded flow:

> The BwO is made in such a way that it can be occupied, populated, only by intensities. Only intensities pass and circulate. Still, the BwO is a scene, a place, or even a support upon which something comes to pass. It has nothing to do with phantasy, there is nothing to interpret. The BwO causes intensities to pass: it produces and distributes them in a *spatium* that is itself intensive, lacking extension. It is not a space nor is it in space; it is matter that occupies space to a given degree—to the degree corresponding to the intensities produced. It is non-stratified, unformed, intense matter. The matrix of intensity, intensity = 0. ... That is why we treat the BwO as the full egg before the extension of the organism and the organization of the organs, before the formation of the strata. ... Is not Spinoza's *Ethics* the great book of the BwO? (Deleuze and Guattari 1987: 153)

The BwO does not oppose or reject organs but is opposed to the structure or organization of bodies, the body as it is stratified, regulated, ordered, and functional, as it is subordinated to the exigencies of property and propriety. The BwO is the body before and in excess of the coalescence of its intensities and their sedimentation into meaningful, organized, transcendent totalities constituting the unity of the subject and of signification. The BwO is "the *field of immanence* of desire, the *plane of consistency* specific to desire (with desire defined as a process of production without reference to any exterior agency, whether it be a lack that hollows it out or a pleasure that fills it)" (154). It resists transcendence; it refuses the sedimentation and hierarchization required for the movement of transcendence, resists the stratifications and layerings and overcodings that produce the three great strata or identities: the union constituting the organism, the unification that constitutes the subject, and the structure of significance. It refuses all propriety: "The BwO is never yours or mine. It is always *a* body" (164).

> We come to the gradual realization that the BwO is not at all the opposite of the organs. The organs are not its enemies. The enemy is the organism. The BwO is opposed not to the organs but to that organization of the organs called the organism. It is true that Artaud wages a struggle against the organs, but at the same time what he is going after, what he has it in for, is the organism: the *body is the body. Alone it stands. And in no need of organs. Organism it never is. Organisms are the enemy of the body.* The BwO is not opposed to organs; rather, the BwO and its "true organs," which must be composed and positioned, are opposed to the organism, the organic organization of the organ. (Deleuze and Guattari 1987: 158)

The BwO is not uniform, a singular, definable "type" or structure. Rather, for Deleuze and Guattari one BwO can be differentiated from another in terms of the types or modalities of circulation, the movement and flow of intensities that it allows or produces on its surface. It is thus not a question of what the BwO is, what composes it, but what it does, how it functions, what it affects, what it produces. For example, they distinguish between two kinds of BwO: the emptied BwO of the drug addict, the masochist, and the hypochondriac and the full BwO in and through which intensities flow and circulate, where productions are engendered:

> What is certain is that the masochist has made himself a BwO under such conditions that the BwO can no longer be populated by anything but the intensities of pain, *pain waves*. It is false to say that the masochist is looking for pain but just as false to say that he is looking for pleasure in a particularly suspensive or roundabout way. The masochist is looking for a type of BwO that only pain can fill, or travel over, due to the very conditions under which that BwO was constituted. (Deleuze and Guattari 1987: 152)

In the case of the empty BwO, the body is evacuated not only of organs and organization but also of its intensities and forces. This body does not lack; its problem is the opposite: it fills itself to the point where nothing further can circulate. It is empty only in the sense that if a body is made up of proliferations, connections, and linkages, the empty BwO has ceased to flow. The hypochondriac destroys both organs and the circulation of matter and intensities, vitrifying the body, rendering it fragile, amenable to invasion, inducing certain flows— flows of pain and pleasure—while at the same time disconnecting it from others. In destabilizing the correlation of desire with pleasure and substituting pain for pleasure, the masochist creates new flows and movements, but only at the cost of self-enclosure, only by all other forms of openness being smothered or counteracted by what Deleuze and Guattari call pain waves. This is not a moral attitude or judgment regarding masochism but a description of its "microphysics," of its sub-subjective components in their relations among themselves and with objects or implements and even sadistic subjects or sources of torture.[9] Where the masochist emits "pain waves" to enliven and numb the body, the junkie is filled with "refrigerator-waves," with the numbing-enlivening Cold:

> [A junkie] wants The Cold like he wants his Junk—Not OUTSIDE where it does him no good but INSIDE so he can sit around with a spine like a frozen hydraulic jack . . . his metabolism approaching Absolute Zero. (William Burroughs, *The Naked Lunch*, quoted in Deleuze and Guattari, 1987: 153–54)

The empty BwO seems to have emptied itself too fast, too definitively. Instead of disconnecting some of its organization and putting it to work in other reconnections, the empty BwO empties itself too quickly, disarrays itself too much, so that it closes in on itself, unable to transmit its intensities differently, stuck in repetition. It does not deny becoming; rather, it establishes a line of flight that is unable to free the circulation of intensities, making other, further connections with other BwOs impossible. It is a line of flight that ends in its own annihilation:

> Instead of making a body without organs sufficiently rich or full for the passage of intensities, drug addicts erect a vitrified and emptied body, or a cancerous one: the causal line, creative line or, line of flight immediately turns into a line of death and abolition. (1987: 285)

While being neither a place nor a plane nor a scene nor a fantasy, the BwO is a field for the production, circulation, and intensification of desire, the locus of the immanence of desire. Although it is the field for the circulation of intensities and although it induces deterritorializations at its lines of flight, movements of becoming, the ability to sustain itself is the condition that seems to be missing in the empty BwO. There must, it seems, be a minimal level of cohesion and integration in the BwO in order to prevent its obliteration; there must be small pockets of subjectivity and signification left in order for the BwOs to survive in the face of the onslaughts of power and reality. A complete destratification renders even the BwO disconnected:

You have to keep enough of the organism for it to reform each dawn; and you have to keep small supplies of signifiance and subjectification, if only to turn them against their own systems when the circumstances demand it, when things, persons, even situations, force you to; and you have to keep small rations of subjectivity in sufficient quantity to enable you to respond to the dominant reality. Mimic the strata. You don't reach the BwO, and its plane of consistency, by wildly destratifying. That is why we encountered the paradox of those emptied and dreary bodies at the very beginning: *they had emptied themselves of their organs* instead of looking for the point at which they could patiently and momentarily dismantle the organization of the organs we call the organism. There are, in fact, several ways of botching the BwO: either one fails to produce it, or one produces it more or less, but nothing is produced on it, intensities do not pass or are blocked. This is because the BwO is always swinging between the surfaces that stratify it and the plane that sets it free. If you free it with too violent an action, if you blow apart the strata without taking precautions, then instead of drawing a plane you will be plunged into a black hole, or even dragged toward catastrophe. (1987: 160–61)

Destratification, freeing lines of flight, the production of connections, the movements of intensities and flows through and beyond the BwO, is thus a direction or movement rather than a fixed state or final position. Deleuze and Guattari do not advocate a dissolution of identity, a complete destabilization and defamiliarization of identity; rather, micro-destratifications, intensifications of some but clearly not all interactions, are necessary:

Staying stratified—organized, signified, subjected—is not the worst that can happen; the worst that can happen is that you throw the strata into demented or suicidal collapse, which brings them back down on us heavier than ever. (1987: 161)

Deleuze and Guattari distinguish the BwO from the singular, organized, self-contained organic body; they also distinguish between molar and molecular arrangements of flows and minoritarian and majoritarian organizational modes. Becomings are always molecular, traversing and realigning molar unities:

If we consider the great binary aggregates, such as the sexes or classes, it is evident that they also cross over into molecular assemblages of a different nature, and that there is a double reciprocal dependency between them. For the two sexes imply a multiplicity of molecular combinations bringing into play not only the man in the woman and the woman in the man, but the relation of each to the animal, the plant etc. (1987: 213)

If molar unities, like the divisions of classes, races, and sexes, attempt to form and stabilize an identity, a fixity, a system that functions homeostatically, sealing in its energies and intensities, molecular becomings traverse, create a path, destabilize, energize instabilities, vulnerabilities of the molar unities. It is clear that this de-massification of the great divisions of social power in culture must at first sight appear to undermine the power and justification of various oppressed groups—women, the working class, people of color, gays and lesbians, religious or cultural minorities and their struggles: it is not that Deleuze and Guattari are trying to explain away the great divisions and global categories that have thus far helped categorize and provide political positions for various social groups. Instead, as I read them, they seem to be rendering more complex the nature and forms that these oppressions take. I must admit that it makes me feel uncomfortable that Deleuze and Guattari choose to refer to the "man in the woman and the woman in the man," which tends to obliterate the very real bodily differences and experiences of the two sexes. Once again it is crucial to note that the man "in the woman" is not the same man as the man "in the man"! But in their defense, it is also crucial to recognize the micro-segmentarities we seize from or connect with in others which give us traits of "masculinity" and "femininity" whether we "are" men or women. In my opinion, this is politically dangerous ground to walk on, but if we do not walk in dangerous places and different types of terrain, nothing new will be found, no explorations are possible, and things remain the same. The risks seem to me worth taking: risking rethinking global oppositions and macroscopic hierarchies in order to have more optimistic propects for effecting transformations and realignments of these global relations, and moreover, seeing their capacity to infiltrate microscopic recesses which may appear immune to or outside of their influence. Thus, if the division or the binary opposition of sexes or, for that matter, the global system constituting patriarchy can be considered as molar lines, then traversing and interrupting them and transforming, breaking them down is what Deleuze and Guattari describe as the processes of "becoming woman."

Becoming Woman, Becoming Incorporeal

If the BwO never "belongs" to a subject or is the property of an object, if it is never "yours" or "mine" but simply a BwO in its particular configurations and connections, in what Deleuze and Guattari call "singularities," then by contrast, becomings are never indeterminate or generic; they are always becoming something. Becomings are always specific movements, specific forms of motion and rest, speed and slowness, points and flows of intensity; they are always a multiplicity, the movement or transformation from one "thing" to another that in no way resembles it. Captain Ahab becomes-whale, Willard becomes-rat, Hans becomes-horse. These becomings are not based on mimesis of or resemblance to the animal or, conversely, on the animal's ability to symbolically represent and act as a vehicle for the subject's fantasies and psychical investments (this of course is precisely Freud's analysis of the case of Little Hans: Hans projects his desire of the mother and subsequent Oedipal fear onto the falling horse). It is not a question of symbolization or of metaphoric representation but of the relation set up between a psychical subject, an object, and an animal.

Deleuze and Guattari suggest that becomings, and especially becoming-animal, involve a mediating third term, a relation to something else, neither animal nor human, through which the subject enters into connections with the animal. They even provide something like a recipe.

> An example: Do not imitate a dog, but make sure your organism enters into composition with *something else* in such a way, that the particles emitted from the aggregate thus composed will be canine as a function of the relations of movement and rest, or of molecular proximity, into which they enter. Clearly, this something else can be quite varied, and be more or less directly related to the animal in question: it can be the animal's natural food (dirt and worm), or its exterior relations with other animals (you can become-dog with cats, or become-monkey with a horse), or an apparatus or prosthesis to which a person subjects the animal (muzzle or reindeer, etc.), or something that does not have a localizable relation to the animal in question. . . . we have seen how Slepian bases his attempt to become dog on the idea of tying shoes to his hands using his mouth-muzzle. (1987: 274)

An intriguing idea, which once again lurches perilously close to an advocacy of a kind of theoretical and political self-making that marks the worst of liberal humanism but saved, always ambiguously, from the charges of self-indulgence and the aura of an advertising slogan ("Become whatever you want to be") through the insistence that these becomings are not simply a matter of choice, not simply a decision, but always involve a substantial remaking of the subject, a major risk to the subject's integration and social functioning. One cannot become-animal at will and then cease and function normally. It is not something that can be put on or taken off like a cloak or an activity. Nonetheless, what Deleuze and Guattari make clear is that there is a kind of wildness, pivots of unpredictability, elements whose trajectories, connections, and future relations remain unpredictable.[10]

While becoming-animal is a major line of flight from identity, undoubtedly the most privileged mode of becoming in their writings is becoming-woman, through which all other becomings are made possible: "Although all becomings are already molecular, including becoming-woman, it must be said that all becomings begin with and pass through becoming-woman. It is the law to all other becomings" (277).

The BwO and all becomings necessarily pass through and are part of the processes of becoming-woman. It is significant, though, that Deleuze and Guattari do not take as an example of becoming-woman the figure of woman herself; instead, the privileged personage, the figure of resistance they advocate, is the little girl. Not the little girl as vehicle for (pederastic) fantasy or the little girl as pure innocence, or indeed the girl as a romantic or representative figure, but rather the girl as the site of a culture's most intensified disinvestments and re-castings of the body. This is true not only in the crucial "plateau" on becoming in *A Thousand Plateaus*, "1730: Becoming-Intense, Becoming-Animal," but is prefigured considerably earlier in Deleuze's writings in his fascination with Lewis Carroll's Alice.[11]

> The question is fundamentally that of the body—the body they steal from us in order to fabricate opposable organisms. The body is stolen first from the girl: Stop behaving like that, you're not a little girl anymore, you're not a tom-boy etc. The girl's becoming is stolen first, in order to impose a history, or prehistory, upon her. The boy's turn comes next, but it is by using the girl as an example, by pointing to the girl as the object of his desire, that an opposed organism, a dominant history is fabricated for him too. The girl is the first victim, but she must also serve as an example and a trap. That is why, con-versely, the reconstruction of the body as a Body without Organs, the anorgan-ism of the body, is inseparable from a becoming-woman, or the production of a molecular woman. (276)

So far, their claims are hardly contentious: Freud and psychoanalytic theory have made very similar claims—the boy's Oedipalization is dependent on the stripping away of the female body, rendering it a lack for him, a lack that he wishes to avoid for himself. There is clearly no incompatibility thus far between rhizomatics and psychoanalysis for feminism. However, problems appear very shortly after, when they again seem to decorporealize the figure of the girl by generalizing "her" becoming into a universal movement:

> The girl is certainly not defined by virginity; she is defined by a relation of movement and rest, speed and slowness, by a combination of atoms, an emis-sion of particles: haecceity. She never ceases to roam upon a body without organs. She is an abstract line, or a line of flight. Thus girls do not belong to an age, group, sex, order or kingdom: they slip in everywhere, between orders, acts, ages, sexes: they produce *n* molecular sexes on the line of flight in relation to the dualism machines they cross right through. The only way to get outside the dualisms is to be-between, to pass between, the intermezzo. . . . The girl is like the block of becoming that remains contemporaneous to each opposable term, man, woman, child, adult. It is not the girl who becomes woman; it is becoming-woman that produces the universal girl. (276–77)

The girl's specificity, her body, is once again robbed, this time not by the anonymous "they" of the earlier passage but by Deleuze and Guattari, who ren-der it equivalent to a generalized and indeterminate in-betweenness, a transgres-sive movement in itself. This departicularization, the primary positioning not of the girl or her bodily specificity but the abstraction of becoming-woman, the placement of the girl's corporeality as its product or effect, is part of this dis-turbing and unsettling tendency many feminists have found in approaching or attempting to utilize Deleuze and Guattari's works from a feminist perspective.

Alice, for example, is perpetually changing, not simply in terms of growth, development, or maturation but in terms of orientations, directions, and trajectories. Deleuze and Guattari duplicate and reverse the concreteness of the girl. Still, there is something appealing and of great insight, I believe, regarding the potential volatility and impetus of a multiplicity of micro-struggles, micro-particularities, operating not simply at the level of the subject but also within and as the subject:

> It is certain the molecular politics proceeds via the girl and the child. But it is also certain that girls and children [they must mean boys] draw their strength . . . from the becoming-molecular they cause to pass between sexes and ages, the becoming-child of the adult as well as the child, the becoming-woman of the man as well as the woman. The girl and the child do not become; it is becoming itself that is a child or a girl. The child does not become an adult any more than the girl becomes a woman; the girl is the becoming-woman of each sex, just as the child is the becoming young of every age. Knowing how to age does not mean remaining young; it means extracting from one's age the particles, the speeds and slownesses, the flows that constitutes the young of *that* age. Knowing how to love does not mean remaining a man or a woman; it means extracting from one's sex the particles, the speeds and slowness, the flows, the *n* sexes that constitute the girl of *that* sexuality. It is Age itself that is a becoming-child, just as Sexuality, any sexuality, is a becoming woman, in other words, a girl. (277)

Not only must men become-woman (which in feminist terms may make political sense) but so too must women. For women as much as for men, the processes of becoming-woman involve the destabilization of molar, or feminine, identity. If one *is* a woman, it remains necessary to become-woman as a way of putting into question the coagulations, rigidifications, and impositions required by patriarchal (although this may well be a term they do not use) power relations. "Woman" is precisely the projection of (men's) fantasies, and rhizomatics, or the problematic of becoming-woman, may be a way of dismantling its fantasmatic form:

> What we term a molar entity is, for example, the woman as defined by her form, endowed with organs and functions, and assigned as a subject. Becoming-woman is not imitating this entity or even transforming oneself into it . . . not imitating or assuming the female form, but emitting particles that enter the relation of movement and rest, or the zone of proximity, of a micro-femininity, in other words, that produce in us a molecular woman, create the molecular woman. (275)

They explain that they are not advocating the cultivation of "bisexuality," which is simply the internalization of binarized sexuality, the miniaturization of the great molar polarities of the sexes without actually stretching or transforming them. Becoming-woman disengages the segments and constraints of the molar entity in order to reinvest and be able to use other particles and flows, speeds and intensities, of the BwO. Becoming-woman represents the dismantling of molar sexualities, molar identities, definite sexual positions as the prevailing social order defines them. Becoming-woman is the movement necessary not in its abstraction, outside of history; rather, becoming-woman is precisely what needs to be evoked as the fallout term, the term that scatters aggregations most effectively against the binarized models that position woman as the other, opposite of man.

Deleuze and Guattari describe all becomings as minoritarian, as molecular, rather than as majoritarian and molar. But the minority (as they well recognize) is not a quantitative or statistical concept; it refers only to molecular or subordinated process, while the majority refers to the great divisions of groups in terms of prevailing power relations. It is women's subordinated or minoritarian status in patriarchal power relations that dictates the significance of the movements of becoming-woman, nothing else—not inherent qualities of women per se or their metaphoric resonances:

> Majority implies a state of domination, not the reverse. . . . It is perhaps the special situation of women in relation to the man-standard that accounts for the fact that becomings, being minoritarian, always pass through a becoming-woman. It is important not to confuse "minoritarian" as becoming or process, with a "minority" as an aggregate or state. . . . There is no becoming-man because man is the molar entity par excellence, whereas becomings are molecular. (291–92)

Becoming-woman involves a series of processes and movements beyond the fixity of subjectivity and the structure of stable unities. It is an escape from the systems of binary polarization of unities that privilege men at the expense of women. It gradually becomes clear that what becoming-woman means or entails for men is different than for women. For men, it implies a de- and restructuring of male sexuality, of the forms of genital domination, bringing into play the microfemininities of behaviors, the particles of another sexuality, or many sexualities, *n* sexes, or as Deleuze and Guattari elsewhere describe it, "a thousand tiny sexes." [12] Men, as privileged adult and male subjects, must, then, invoke a becoming-woman, a becoming-child, and even a becoming-animal as ways of bringing into play the multiplicity of forces hitherto suppressed under the forms of the great dominations. But exactly what this means for women remains disturbingly unclear. Deleuze and Guattari state that for women to become-woman does not mean renouncing feminist struggles for the attainment of an identity or subject-position—the charges levelled at them by the feminists I mentioned earlier. But it does entail abandoning the very struggles by which feminists have sought to provide new social places and values for women. It is not that Deleuze and Guattari are demanding that women abandon the identities and struggles that have thus far helped define feminism as a struggle for women's rights, power and place in cultural life. They are not demanding that we become instead of that we *be:* but rather, that feminism, or indeed any political struggle must not content itself with a final goal, a resting point, a point of stability or identity. Political struggles are by their nature endless and ever-changing.

> It is, of course, indispensable for women to conduct a molar politics, with a view to winning back their own organism, their own history, their own subjectivity. . . . But it is dangerous to confine oneself to such a subject, which does not function without drying up a spring or stopping a flow. (276)

Becoming-woman means going beyond identity and subjectivity, fragmenting and freeing up lines of flight, "liberating" multiplicities, corporeal and otherwise, that identity subsumes under the one. Woman's becoming-woman is a movement for and of all subjects insofar as it is the putting into play of a series of microfemininities, impulses, wills, in all subjects: her becoming-woman carries all humanity's, in a striking reversal (but exact replication) of phallocentrism:

> A woman has to become-woman, but in a becoming-woman of all men. . . . A becoming-minoritarian exists only by virtue of a deterritorialized medium and subject that are like its elements. There is no subject of the becoming except as a deterritorialized variable of a majority; there is no medium of becoming except as a deterritorialized variable of a minority. We can be thrown into a becoming by anything at all, by the most unexpected, most insignificant of things. You don't deviate from the majority unless there is a little detail that starts to swell and carries you off. (292)

If becoming-woman is the medium through which all becomings must pass, it is however only a provisional becoming or stage, a trajectory or movement that in fact has an (asymptotic) "end," the most microscopic and fragmenting of becomings, which they describe as "becoming-imperceptible." This line of flight, this particular desiring-machine is the breakdown or shrinkage of all identities, molar and molecular, majoritarian and minoritarian, the freeing of infinitely microscopic lines, a process whose end is achieved only with complete dissolution, the production of the incredible ever-shrinking "man."

> If becoming-woman is the first quantum, or molecular segment with the becomings-animal that link up with it coming next, what are they all rushing towards? Without a doubt, toward becoming-imperceptible. The imperceptible is the immanent end of becoming, its cosmic formula. For example, Matheson's *Shrinking Man* passes through the kingdoms of nature, slips between molecules, to become an unfindable particle in infinite meditation on the infinite. (279)

Implicit here is the claim that there is a kind of direction to the quantum leap required by becomings, a labyrinthine but nonetheless goal-oriented movement in which becoming-woman is, for all subjects, a first trajectory. Becoming-woman desediments the masculinity of identity; becoming-child, the modes of cohesion and control of the adult; becoming-animal, the anthropocentrism of philosophical thought; and becoming-imperceptible replaces, dismantles, problematizes the most elementary notions of entity, thingness. Indiscernibility, imperceptibility, and impersonality remain the end points of becoming, their immanent orientation or internal impetus, the freeing of absolutely minuscule micro-intensities to the nth degree. Feminist struggles around the question of "women's identities," "women's rights," are thus only part of a stage setting for the processes of becoming woman; and becoming-woman is in turn the condition of human-becomings, which in their turn must deterritorialize and become-animal. This is a path toward "being like everybody else" (279), an absolute, indiscernible anonymity. Not the obliteration of all characteristics—which, of course, is annihilation—but the resonance of all kinds of machines with each other, the imperceptibility of traits, characteristics, identities, positions. It need no longer be woman who functions as the figure of radical otherness for identity. Deleuze and Guattari produce a radical antihumanism that renders animals, nature, atoms, even quasars as modes of radical alterity.

There are worrisome implications here. The ordering of these becomings is unmistakable in the language ("first," "coming next," etc.) and in its tone ("without a doubt"). Deleuze and Guattari describe here a process of the blowing apart of the fragments, elements, intensities at work in an entity, then the explosion of the fragments into smaller fragments and so on ad infinitum. How this occurs is nomadic, random, or contingent; but Deleuze and Guattari imply a clear movement toward imperceptibility that is in many ways similar to the quest of physics for the microscopic structures of matter, the smallest component, the most elementary particle. If it remains materialist at this level, it is a materialism that is far beyond or different from the body, or bodies: their work is like an acidic dissolution of the body, and the subject along with it.

Moreover, the presumption that women's molar struggles for identity are merely a stage or stepping stone in a broader struggle must be viewed with great suspicion, for Deleuze and Guattari begin to sound alarmingly similar to a number of (male) political groups that have supported feminism on condition that it be regarded as a stage, phase, element, or subdivision of a broader cause. These are very common claims, claims which have been used to tie women to struggles that in fact have little to do with them, or rather, to which women have been tied through a generalized "humanity" which in no way represents their interests, which is a projection or representation of men's specific fantasies about what it is to be human. The Marxist subordination of women's struggles to the class struggle or struggles for cultural identity, the subsumption of women's call for identities as women under a general call for the dissolution of all identities (Kristeva), the positing of women's pleasures and desires as the means of access to the

Other (Lacan and Levinas), all serve as relatively current examples of such phal-locentrism. But perhaps Deleuze and Guattari fit less easily into this category than it seems on a first reading.

Deleuzian Feminism?

Do the reservations and objections of the feminists I mentioned earlier in this chapter imply that Deleuze and Guattari's work is too problematic, too in-vested in phallocentrism, to be of value to feminist reconceptions of the body and subjectivity? What, in light of these objections, does their work with its focus on surfaces, networks, connections, and intensities have to offer feminist theory? What are the costs and benefits of an adoption of a Deleuzian perspective? It is important to tread warily on grounds where one knows there are risks involved. A selective reading and use of their work may, however, manage to capture and put to work valuable methodologies, questions, insights that may lead in direc-tions Deleuze and Guattari may not go or even may not accept.

The shift from psychoanalytic and semiotic perspective to a Deleuzian prob-lematics of surfaces brings with it a series of transformations in focus in concep-tions of corporeality, sexual specificity, and sexed subjectivity. Some of the major differences between them can be listed.

First, a Deleuzian framework insists on the flattening out of relations be-tween the social and the psychical so that there is neither a relation of causation (one- or two-way) nor hierarchies, levels, grounds, or foundations. The social is not privileged over the psychical (as crude Marxism entails); nor is the psychical privileged at the expense of the social (common charges directed against psycho-analytic theory). They are not parallel dimensions or orders; rather, they run into, as, and through each other. This means that individuals, subjects, microintensi-ties, blend with, connect to, neighborhood, local, regional, social, cultural, aes-thetic, and economic relations directly, not through mediation of systems of ide-ology or representation, not through the central organization of an apparatus like the state or the economic order, but directly, in the formation of desiring-ma-chines, war-machines, art-machines, etc. Questions related to subjectivity, inte-riority, female sexual specificity, are thus not symptoms of a patriarchal culture, not simply products or effects of it, but are forces, intensities, requiring codifica-tions or territorializations and in turn exerting their own deterritorializing and decodifying force, systems of compliance and resistance.

Second, eschewing psychical depth, the necessity of interpretation, the order of signification based on the latency of the signified in the signifier, a Deleuzian framework refuses to duplicate the world, to create a world and its reflection, whether that reflection appears on the psychical interior in the form of ideas, wishes, and hopes or on the social and signifying exterior as meanings, latencies, representations. This duplication of the world into the real and its representation, a necessary feature of psychoanalytic and semiotic frameworks, is problematized, and indeed seems an irrelevant and unnecessary assumption. This duplication is required to mediate between usually incompatible terms (the real and the ideal, the social and the individual, symptom and cause), but if their relation is construed as a direct and unmediated one, this double world is unnecessary.

Third, as a critique of binarism, along with deconstruction and other post-structuralisms, a Deleuzian framework poses a striking alternative: rather than the either-or choice imposed by binarisms, they posit a both-and relation. Deleuze and Guattari will readily acknowledge that one must pass by way of or through binaries, not in order to reproduce them but to find terms and modes that befuddle their operations, connections that demonstrate the impossibility of their binarization, terms, relations, and practices that link the binarily opposed terms.

Fourth, Deleuzian framework de-massifies the entities that binary thought counterposes against each other: the subject, the social order, even the natural world are theorized in terms of the microprocesses, a myriad of intensities and flows, with unaligned or unalignable components which refuse to conform to the requirements of order and organization. In this sense, their understanding of the body and subjectivity as excessive to hierarchical control implies that the body, as the realm of affectivity, is the site or sites of multiple struggles, ambiguously positioned in the reproduction of social habits, requirements, and regulations and in all sorts of production of unexpected and unpredictable linkages. Through Deleuze and Guattari's perspectives, the body, bodies, flows in bodies rather than "subjects," psychic beings, are what produce. Admittedly, this implies the de-massifications of the categories of sex, class, race, and sexual preference, so that even within these categories a whole range of forces is always in play. Identities and stabilities are not fixed.

Fifth, Deleuzian framework refuses to seek, as psychoanalysis tends to, a single explanatory paradigm, a single regime of explanation: the reduction of current adult factors to infantile precedents, the reduction of the relations between the sexes to those regulated by a respect for the phallus, the reduction of sexuality to genitality, the reduction of the body to erotogenic sites, the need to end-lessly read symptomatically, to read events and impulses as being about something else. Things and relations are not read in terms of something else or in terms of where they originate or their history but rather, pragmatically, in terms of their effects, what they do, what they make.

And sixth, given that psychoanalytic theory in particular, but also other accounts of femininity, cannot explain female subjectivity and female corporeality—in the case of psychoanalysis, Freud readily confesses his puzzlement regarding the nature, forms, and prehistory of femininity, and he makes manifest his inability to deal with or adequately explain female psychology and sexuality in the case of either heterosexual women or lesbians, as is evidenced from his rather crude and highly unsatisfactory accounts of female development in the case of Dora and in his study of the young homosexual woman—and particularly given Freud's necessary attribution of the status of lack to female sexual organs and of passivity to feminine desire, it seems to me that it is a clear requirement of feminist theory to seek alternatives, to provide explanatory frameworks and models which enable femininity, female subjectivity and corporeality, to be understood as a positivity.

These, it seems to me, are some of the advantages of a Deleuzian framework over a psychoanalytic one. There are of course a number of drawbacks which may be worth reiterating.

First, Deleuze and Guattari seem no more attentive to questions of the specificity and particularity of women than psychoanalytic frameworks. They seem to have little if any awareness of the masculinity of their pronouncements, of the sexual particularity of their own theoretical positions.

Second, the recoding of desire as a positivity, as a productive force, as what makes things and forges alliances, seems to offer women, feminists, the promise of at last a position other than the passive objects of desire, castrated in themselves, requiring the fulfilment provided by men and the phallus. But this may be simply another male ruse: for while women are cast into the position of objects and never subjects of desire in psychoanalytic theory, thereby occupying a secondary, dependent position, in rendering desire a positivity, women are still the vehicles, the receptacles of men's becomings, their machinic conditions. This may be simply the substitution of one inadequate account for another, equally problematic, which resolves or overcomes some problems but creates others. Women's specificity and particularity still remains obscured.

Third, Deleuze and Guattari's frameworks inevitably fall prey to their own criticisms (this of course is not a claim made only with reference to rhizomatics, but is probably emblematic of "the postmodern condition" insofar as all critiques succumb to what it is that they criticize), insofar as they deterritorialize women's bodies and subjectivities only to reterritorialize them as part of a more universalist movement of becoming. In short, the relation between "being" (in all its ambiguities and impossibilities) and becoming is obscured; until it becomes clearer what becoming-woman means for those beings who are women, as well as for those beings who are men, the value of their work for women and for feminism remains unclear.

These are serious problems, problems that cannot simply be ignored. But they are not problems of the order that would make this work of no value to feminists. There are problems, but Deleuze and Guattari also have a lot to offer if feminists are to seek ways beyond the confines of phallocentric and binarized thought. Their work is in no sense a "solution" to the dilemmas posed by Cartesianism and its dualist heritage, the separation of the psychical from the social, the surface from its latencies, presumed by psychoanalysis: there is no "singular" solution, a once-and-for-all time settlement with dichotomous thought, for even the idea of going beyond dichotomies creates and relies on a dichotomy (in this case, the dichotomy between dichotomous and nondichotomous thought!).[13] But it is the start of a series of explorations of possible alternatives, possible modes of entry into and exit from knowledges that enable knowledges to be used productively in day-to-day life, in political struggles of various kinds, and in cultural creation. Deleuze and Guattari, like a number of other theorists, are exploring some of the many possible avenues of investigation and interrogation at the limits of what is thinkable in the twentieth century; this they share in common with that broad spectrum of texts labeled feminist. Whether they share more than a common enemy and a common goal of moving beyond the terms of that enemy, whether there are further common concerns, further points of overlap—points feminists may find of value in their projects—remains an open question, dependent on the kinds of work on Deleuze and Guattari's texts that feminists are prepared to undertake.

PART IV

Sexual Difference

8 | Sexed Bodies

> The future must no longer be determined by the past. I do not deny that the effects of the past are still with us. But I refuse to strengthen them by repeating them, to confer upon them an irremovability the equivalent of destiny, to confuse the biological and the cultural. Anticipation is imperative.
>
> Hélène Cixous, "The Laugh of the Medusa" (1980: 245)

THUS FAR I have concentrated on apparently "neutral" or indeterminate accounts of human bodies considered in their generality. I have focused on a number of key male theorists and what they have had to say about "the" body: Freud, Lacan, Merleau-Ponty, the theorists of body image, Nietzsche, Foucault, Lingis, Deleuze and Guattari. All have contributed, in their various ways, to the broad terms by which we can understand human bodies and how we can wrest notions of corporeality away from the constraints which have polarized and opposed it to mind, the mental or the conceptual, not to mention away from the confines of a biology that is considered universal, innate, fundamentally nonhistorical, and capable of change only through the violent intervention of surgical, chemical, or physiological means, means which may alter details of the body but which leave its ontological status as inert and passive, as cultural "raw materials," intact. The various theorists discussed and sometimes criticized here have helped make explicit the claim that the body, as much as the psyche or the subject, can be regarded as a cultural and historical product. They testify to the permeability or incompleteness of the notion of nature. Individually and collectively, they have affirmed that the body is a pliable entity whose determinate form is provided not simply by biology but through the interaction of modes of psychical and physical inscription and the provision of a set of limiting biological codes. The body is constrained by its biological limits—limits, incidentally, whose framework or "stretchability" we cannot yet know, we cannot presume, even if we must presume some *limits*. The body is not open to *all* the whims, wishes, and hopes of the subject: the human body, for example, cannot fly in the air, it cannot breathe underwater unaided by prostheses, it requires a broad range of temperatures and environmental supports, without which it risks collapse and death. On the other hand, while there must be some kinds of biological limit or constraint, these constraints are perpetually capable of being superseded, overcome, through the human body's capacity to open itself up to prosthetic synthesis, to transform or rewrite its environment, to continually augment its powers and capacities through the incorporation into the body's own spaces and modalities of objects that, while external, are internalized, added to, supplementing and supplemented by the "organic body" (or what culturally passes for it), surpassing the body, not "beyond" nature but in collusion with a "nature" that never really lived up to its name, that represents always the most blatant cultural anxieties and projections.

I have concentrated on these apparently "neutral" presentations of the "human" body and have generally avoided many if not most feminist texts that have recently appeared on the question of the female body because up to this point I have been concerned with the ways in which a corporeal "universal" has in fact functioned as a veiled representation and projection of a masculine which takes itself as the unquestioned norm, the ideal representative without any idea of the violence that this representational positioning does to its others—women, the "disabled," cultural and racial minorities, different classes, homosexuals—who are reduced to the role of modifications or variations of the (implicity white, male, youthful, heterosexual, middle-class) human body.

I have attempted to read the male discourses dealt with here as discourses for and about men, discourses which have ignored or misunderstood the radical implications of insisting on a recognition of sexual specificity, discourses which have presented their claims—radical as these might be—without any understanding of their relevance to or usefulness for women's self-representations. I have not attempted to give an alternative account, one which provides materials directly useful for women's self-representation. To do so would involve knowing in advance, preempting, the developments in women's self-understandings which are now in the process of being formulated regarding what the best terms are for representing women as intellectual, social, moral, and sexual agents. It would involve producing new discourses and knowledges, new modes of art and new forms of representational practice outside of the patriarchal frameworks which have thus far ensured the impossibility of women's autonomous self-representations, thus being temporally outside or beyond itself. No one yet knows what the conditions are for developing knowledges, representations, models, programs, which provide women with nonpatriarchal terms for representing themselves and the world from women's interests and points of view. This book has been a preliminary exploration of some of the (patriarchal) texts which feminists may find useful in extricating the body from the mire of biologism in which it has been entrenched. But the terms by which feminists can move on from there, can supersede their patriarchal forebears, are not clear to me. But perhaps the framework I have been trying to use in this book—a framework which acknowledges both the psychical or interior dimensions of subjectivity and the surface corporeal exposures of the subject to social inscription and training; a model which resists, as much as possible, both dualism and monism; a model which insists on (at least) two surfaces which cannot be collapsed into one and which do not always harmoniously blend with and support each other; a model where the join, the interaction of the two surfaces, is always a question of power; a model that *may* be represented by the geometrical form of the Möbius strip's two-dimensional torsion in three-dimensional space—will nevertheless be of some use if feminists wish to avoid the impasses of traditional theorizing about the body.

In this chapter, I hope to present at least some of the elements of a more positive and detailed investigation of the question of the sexual specificity of bodies. In repeating the framework of the earlier chapters, the rotations of the Möbius strip from the inside out and from the outside in, the inversion from psychoanalytic and phenomenological investigations of sexual specificity to the inscriptive and productive functioning of social bodies marked in their sexual difference, I hope not only to provide a framework with which to begin asking questions of male and female bodies in their irreducible specificities but also to provide a series of displacements and criticisms of the very (male) models that helped make these investigations possible, a kind of feedback of the Möbius rotations on itself, a doubling that makes it problematize and extend its own boundaries. I am not suggesting that what is to follow represents a new nonpatriarchal or feminist framework; it clearly does not. But with the help of certain phallocentric discourses and through the establishment of some sort of theoretical distance from these frameworks (alongside of a recognition of their formative relations to their feminist transgressions), perhaps the project can at last begin.

This chapter seeks to elucidate and negotiate a certain aporia. It seeks to question the ontological status of the sexed body—an issue which has generally remained submerged up to now in this book but which underlies many of its speculations. What, ontologically speaking, is the body? What is its "stuff," its matter? What of its form? Is that given or produced? Or is there some relation between givenness and the cultural order? Are sexually neutral, indeterminate, or hermaphroditic bodies inscribed to produce the sexually specific forms with which we are familiar? Or do bodies, all bodies (even nonhuman bodies, it must be presumed), have a specifically sexual dimension (whether it be male or female or hermaphroditic) which is psychically and culturally inscribed according to its morphology? In other words, is sexual difference primary and sexual inscription a cultural overlay or rewriting of an ontologically prior differentiation? Or is sexual differentiation a product of the various forms of inscription of culturally specific bodies? Do inscriptions produce sexual differentiation? Or does sexual difference imply a differential mode of inscription?[1] Answering this series of questions involves examining the complex intertwining relations of mutual production and feedback of materially different bodies, substances, forms of matter, and materially different inscriptions, tracings, transformations, the interchanging between writing and bodies, bodies as the blank or already encoded surfaces of inscription.

I am reluctant to claim that sexual difference is purely a matter of the inscription and codification of somehow uncoded, absolutely raw material, as if these materials exert no resistance or recalcitrance to the processes of cultural inscription. This is to deny a materiality or a material specificity and determinateness to bodies. It is to deny the postulate of a pure, that is, material difference. It is to make them infinitely pliable, malleable. On the other hand, the opposite extreme also seems untenable. Bodies are not fixed, inert, purely genetically or biologically programmed entities that function in their particular ways and in their determinate forms independent of their cultural milieu and value. Differences between bodies, not only at the level of experience and subjectivity but also at the level of practical and physical capacities, enjoy considerable social and historical variation. Processes and activities that seem impossible for a body to undertake at some times and in some cultures are readily possible in others. What are regarded as purely fixed and unchangeable elements of facticity, biologically given factors, are amenable to wide historical vicissitudes and transformations.

Two brief illustrations. The formation of stigmata, perforations, cuts, bleeding, even the production of a quite literal alphabetic script across the body can be induced or produced through the adherence to certain beliefs (about religious piety, worship, a sense of worthlessness or supreme value, the notion of the body as a vessel for divine intervention or satanic interference, etc.). These indicate that biological and physiological processes can be induced in subjects through the inculcation into certain beliefs about the body and its place in social and religious life.[2] Or conversely, there is the transformation of apparently bedrock biological features through the disturbance of certain psychical functions, perhaps best illustrated in the case of multiple personality syndrome, in which one of the many personalities inhabiting an individual body has different abilities and defects than another. One personality may require glasses to correct faults in the optical apparatus while another personality has perfect vision; one personality is left-handed, the other right, one personality has certain allergies or disorders missing in the other. These are not simply transformations at the level of our ideas of or representations of the body. Our ideas and attitudes seep into the functioning of the body itself, making up the realm of its possibilities or impossibilities.

The scope and limit of the body's pliability is not yet adequately understood; nor is the biologically constitutive role played by the significances and meanings attributed to bodies, the codes and practices that tattoo it in various ways. Any model that links genetics and environment externally, bringing together two domains which are considered logically separable from each other, cannot explain the active interventions and limits each poses for the other. This cannot be understood on the kind of subtractive models that have hitherto informed many biological and psychological accounts: subtract the environment, culture, history, and what you are left with is nature or biology; compare identical twins brought up in different environments as if this somehow ensures a neutralization of the effects of the environment, and as if the twins' sameness can be assumed to be the consequence of their shared biologies.[3] Biology is somehow regarded as the subject minus culture, as if this could result in anything but an abstraction or bare universal category. The sexual difference I explore here cannot be understood in terms of a fixed or ahistorical biology, although it must clearly contain a biological dimension. But biology cannot be regarded as a form whose contents are historically provided, nor as a base on which cultural constructs are founded, nor indeed as a container for a mixture of culturally or individually specific ingredients. It is an open materiality, a set of (possibly infinite) tendencies and potentialities which may be developed, yet whose development will necessarily hinder or induce other developments and other trajectories. These are not individually or consciously chosen, nor are they amenable to will or intentionality: they are more like bodily styles, habits, practices, whose logic entails that one preference, one modality excludes or makes difficult other possibilities. The kind of model I have in mind here is not simply then a model of an imposition of inscription on a blank slate, a page with no "texture" and no resistance of its own. As any calligrapher knows, the kind of texts produced depends not only on the message to be inscribed, not only on the inscriptive tools—stylus, ink— used, but also on the quality and distinctiveness of the paper written upon. Perhaps, then, a more appropriate model for this kind of body writing is not the writing of the blank page—a model which minimizes the impact and effects of the paper itself—but a model of etching, a model which needs to take into account the specificities of the materials being thus inscribed and their concrete effects in the kind of text produced.[4]

Here I will explore the corporeal styles, the ontological structure, and the lived realities of sexually different bodies. This raises a further problem. The question of sexual difference admits of no outside position. The proclamation of a position outside, beyond, sexual difference is a luxury that only male arrogance allows. It is only men who can afford the belief that their perspective is an outside, disinterested, or objective position. The enigma that Woman has posed for men is an enigma only because the male subject has construed itself as the subject par excellence. The way (he fantasizes) that Woman differs from him makes her containable within his imagination (reduced to his size) but also produces her as a mystery for him to master and decipher within safe or unthreatening borders (the fantasy of the inscrutable that man attributes to women and the West attributes to its others as well). But if one takes seriously the problematic of sexual difference, then as mysterious as Woman must be for men, so too must men be for women (and indeed so too must Woman be for women, and Man for men). There is no Tiresian position, no position outside of or midway between the two sexes, from which to objectively analyze them. A midway position (if it makes any sense at all) would simply be another sexually specific position, but by no means a more encompassing position. The task, then, is not to establish a neutral or objective perspective on the question of sexual difference but to find a position encompassing enough for a sexually specific perspective to be able to open itself up to, meet with, and be surprised at the (reciprocal) otherness of the other sex(es). Sexual difference entails the existence of a sexual ethics, an ethics of the ongoing negotiations between beings whose differences, whose alterities, are left intact but with whom some kind of exchange is nonetheless possible. My exploration of the lived and social dimensions of sexual difference will therefore openly acknowledge that the perspectives, peculiarities, and enigmas encountered are those of a woman raising issues about men's, as well women's, sexual specificities.

Powers and Dangers: Body Fluids

In *Powers of Horror*, Julia Kristeva outlines a typology of personalized horror that marks the significance for the subject and for culture of the various orifices and boundaries of the body. Relying heavily on Mary Douglas's innovative text *Purity and Danger*, Kristeva asks about the conditions under which the clean and proper body, the obedient, law-abiding, social body, emerges, the cost of its emergence, which she designates by the term *abjection*, and the functions that demarcating a clean and proper body for the social subject have in the transmission and production of specific body types. The abject is what of the body falls away from it while remaining irreducible to the subject/object and inside/outside oppositions. The abject necessarily partakes of both polarized terms but cannot be clearly identified with either. What interests me here about Kristeva's work is the way in which this notion of abjection links the lived experience of the body, the social and culturally specific meanings of the body, the cultural investment in selectively marking the body, the privileging of some parts and functions while resolutely minimizing or leaving un- or underrepresented other parts and functions. It is the consequence of a culture effectively intervening into the constitution of the value of the body.

The abject is not that which is dirty or impure about the body: nothing in itself, as Douglas has argued, is dirty. Dirt, for her, is that which is not in its proper place, that which upsets or befuddles order. Nothing has the intrinsic property of disrupting or disturbing but can only be regarded as such in a specific context and system where order is imposed at the cost of the elements being thus ordered.[5] Dirt signals a site of possible danger to social and individual systems, a site of vulnerability insofar as the status of dirt as marginal and unincorporable always locates sites of potential threat to the system and to the order it both makes possible and problematizes.[6]

It is significant that from the outset of her analysis Douglas locates the question of purity and danger firmly in the relations between the two sexes, which function as her paradigm and sustained example.

> I believe that some pollutants are used as analogies for expressing a general view of the social order. For example, there are beliefs that each sex is a danger to the other through contact with sexual fluids. According to other beliefs only one sex is endangered by contact with the other, usually males from females, but sometimes the reverse. Such patterns of sexual danger can be seen to express symmetry or hierarchy which apply in the larger social system. What goes for sex pollution also goes for bodily pollution. The two sexes can serve as a model for the collaboration and distinctiveness for social units. So also can the processes of ingestion portray political absorption. Sometimes bodily orifices seem to represent points of entry or exit to social units, or bodily perfection can symbolise an ideal theocracy. (Douglas 1980: 3)

Douglas makes explicit here the notion that the body can and does function to represent, to symbolize, social and collective fantasies and obsessions: its orifices and surfaces can represent the sites of cultural marginality, places of social entry and exit, regions of confrontation or compromise. Rituals and practices designed to cleanse or purify the body may serve as metaphors for processes of cultural homogeneity. Although Douglas herself seems less interested in the psychical and individual significance of these rituals, concentrating instead on their religious and cultural importance, she does provide us with some relevant data in discussing the question of sexual difference. Perhaps most interesting for our purposes is her claim that in certain cultures each of the sexes can pose a threat to the other, a threat that is located in the polluting powers of the other's body fluids. This may prove a particularly significant site for an analysis of sexual difference in the era where sexuality has become reinvested with notions of contagion and death, of danger and purity, as a consequence of the AIDS crisis.

Kristeva's use of Douglas's work on pollution and defilement shifts it from a sociological and anthropological into a psychological and subjective register. While she indicates the social significance of the abject, its necessary implication in broader cultural values, she begins her analysis within a phenomenological framework. In discussing three broad categories of abjection—abjection toward food and thus toward bodily incorporation; abjection toward bodily waste, which reaches its extreme in the horror of the corpse; and abjection toward the signs of sexual difference—Kristeva is each time discussing the constitution of a proper social body, the processes of sorting, segregating, and demarcating the body so as to conform to but not exceed cultural expectations (excessiveness in itself pushes the question of the limit for the order which it exceeds).

Body fluids attest to the permeability of the body, its necessary dependence on an outside, its liability to collapse into this outside (this is what death implies), to the perilous divisions between the body's inside and its outside. They affront a subject's aspiration toward autonomy and self-identity. They attest to a certain irreducible "dirt" or disgust, a horror of the unknown or the unspecifiable that permeates, lurks, lingers, and at times leaks out of the body, a testimony of the fraudulence or impossibility of the "clean" and "proper." They resist the determination that marks solids, for they are without any shape or form of their own. They are engulfing, difficult to be rid of; any separation from them is not a matter of certainty, as it may be in the case of solids. Body fluids flow, they seep, they infiltrate; their control is a matter of vigilance, never guaranteed. In this sense, they betray a certain irreducible materiality; they assert the priority of the body over subjectivity; they demonstrate the limits of subjectivity in the body, the irreducible specificity of particular bodies. They force megalomaniacal aspirations to earth, refusing consciousness its supremacy; they level differences while also specifying them. In our culture, they are enduring; they are necessary but embarrassing. They are undignified, nonpoetic, daily attributes of existence, rich or poor, black or white, man or woman, that all must, in different ways, face, live with, reconcile themselves to.

> These body fluids, this defilement, this shit are what life withstands, hardly, and with difficulty, on the part of death. There, I am at the border of my condition as a living being. My body extricates itself, as being alive, from that border. Such waste drops so that I might live, until from loss to loss, nothing remains in me and my entire body falls beyond the limit—*cadere*, cadaver. (Kristeva 1982: 3)

Douglas herself refers to Sartre's analysis of the viscous in *Being and Nothingness* as some kind of explanation of our horror of the fluid. For both Douglas and Sartre, the viscous, the fluid, the flows which infiltrate and seep, are horrifying in themselves: there is something inherently disgusting about the incorporative, immersing properties of fluid:

> Viscosity repels in its own right, as a primary experience. An infant, plunging its hands into a jar of honey, is instantly involved in contemplating the formal properties of solids or liquids and the essential relation between the subjective experiencing self and the experienced world. The viscous is a state half-way between solid and liquid. It is like a cross-section in a process of change. It is unstable, but it does not flow. It is soft, yielding and compressible. There is no gliding on its surface. Its stickiness is a trap, it clings like a leech; it attacks the boundary between myself and it. Long columns falling off my fingers suggest my own substance flowing into the pool of stickiness . . . to touch stickiness is to risk diluting myself into viscosity. Stickiness is clinging, like a too possessive dog or mistress. (Douglas 1980: 38)

Like Sartre, Douglas associates this clinging viscosity with the horror of femininity, the voraciousness and indeterminacy of the *vagina dentata*. It is clear, to me at least, that this horror of submersion, the fear of being absorbed into something which has no boundaries of its own, is not a property of the viscous itself;

in keeping with Douglas's claims about dirt, what is disturbing about the viscous or the fluid is its refusal to conform to the laws governing the clean and proper, the solid and the self-identical, its otherness to the notion of an entity—the very notion that governs our self-representations and understanding of the body. It is not that female sexuality is like, resembles, an inherently horrifying viscosity. Rather, it is the production of an order that renders female sexuality and corporeality marginal, indeterminate, and viscous that constitutes the sticky and the viscous with their disgusting, horrifying connotations. Irigaray claims that this disquiet about the fluid, the viscous, the half-formed, or the indeterminate has to do with the cultural unrepresentability of fluids within prevailing philosophical models of ontology, their implicit association with femininity, with maternity, with the corporeal, all elements subordinated to the privilege of the self-identical, the one, the unified, the solid.[7]

Douglas refers to all borderline states, functions, and positions as dangers, sites of possible pollution or contamination. That which is marginal is always located as a site of danger and vulnerability. She, like Kristeva, conceives of the fluid as a borderline state, disruptive of the solidity of things, entities, and objects. Blood, vomit, saliva, phlegm, pus, sweat, tears, menstrual blood, seminal fluids, seep, flow, pass with different degrees of control, tracing the paths of entry or exit, the routes of interchange or traffic with the world, which must nevertheless be clear of these bodily "products" for an interchange to be possible.

These body fluids have different indices of control, disgust, and revulsion. There is a kind of hierarchy of propriety governing these fluids themselves. Those which function with clarity, unclouded by the specter of infection, can be represented as cleansing and purifying: tears carry with them none of the disgust associated with the cloudiness of pus, the chunkiness of vomit, the stickiness of menstrual blood. Acquiring a social representation as a clean fluid, as waterlike, transparent, purifying, tears take on a different psychological and sociological status than the polluting fluids that dirty the body. Douglas distinguishes between one kind of body fluid and another on the basis of their intrinsic properties, on the model of her (and Sartre's) analysis of the viscous:

Why [are] saliva and genital excretions . . . more pollution-worthy than tears? If I can fervently drink his tears, wrote Jean Genet, why not so the limpid drop on the end of his nose? To this we can reply: first, that nasal secretions are not so limpid as tears. They are more like treacle than water. When a thick rheum oozes from the eye, it is no more apt for poetry than nasal rheum. But admittedly clear, fast-running tears are the stuff of romantic poetry: they do not defile. This is partly because tears are naturally preempted by the symbolism of washing. Tears are like rivers of moving water. They purify, cleanse, bathe the eyes so how can they pollute? But more significantly tears are not related to the bodily functions of digestion and procreation. Therefore their scope for symbolising social relations and social processes. (Douglas 1980: 125)

Douglas suggests that it is the excessiveness of tears, their superfluity to the species and cultural requirements of biological preservation and reproduction, that leaves them free to represent elements of the social order. Perhaps this is true. But by the logic of her own argument, those bodily processes construed or constituted as marginal—most particularly, the sites of sexuality and jouissance— are readily able to function as loci for the representation of social and collective anxieties and fantasies. Douglas relies on a thinly veiled understanding of analogies, in which functions sharing broad similarities are able to act as metaphors for each other: tears, like a river, wash and flow, therefore tears are lived and function as cleansing and purifying. But if there is nothing inherently polluting, inherently disordered, then this does not explain why body fluids are constituted as polluting, as entrapping. She makes a similar presumption regarding cultural investments in the representation of sexual organs. She bases her claims once again on the apparently similarities between sexual processes and functions and cultural artifacts, with no recognition of implicit models she relies on for her very conception of human physiology:

> Both male and female physiology lend themselves to the analogy with the vessel which must not pour away or dilute its vital bodily fluids. Females are correctly seen as, literally, the entry by which the pure content may be adulterated. Males are treated as pores through which the precious stuff may ooze out and be lost, with the whole system being thereby enfeebled. (Douglas 1980: 126)

By her own arguments, though, male and female physiology, whatever their forms, lend themselves to all sorts of models and representations. None seem more "natural" and inevitable than any others. Douglas here merely carries on a long tradition of rationalizing the models she finds useful in terms of some kind of natural resemblance, this time positing the body in a synecdochical relation to the fluids it contains. But hydraulic models, models of absorption, of incorporation, are all culturally validated representations that may make sense in our culture but are by no means inevitable. They all share the characteristic of establishing male sexuality and corporeality as the singular form, which is inadequate in establishing a symmetrical female sexuality and body morphology. The "precious stuff" circulating in sexual relations is not the movement of desire, the exchange of pleasures, but the transmission of seminal fluids, oozing through the male body into its resting place, the female body. This is seen as the only fluid exchanged, the one for which the female flows are merely preparatory, the media or conduits for male sexual flow. Douglas's view is by no means alien to or even very far from the dominant biological models today.

Douglas is, however, right in claiming that we live our sexual bodies, our body fluids and their particular forms of jouissance or tension, never as it were "in the raw," unmediated by cultural representations. Our pleasures and anxieties are always lived and experienced through models, images, representations,

and expectations. Those regulating and contextualizing the body and its pleasures have thus far in our cultural history established models which do not regard
the polluting contamination of sexual bodies as a two-way process, in which each
affects or infiltrates the other. Such a model involves a dual sexual symmetry that
is missing in patriarchal structures. It is not the case that men's bodily fluids are
regarded as polluting and contaminating for women in the same way or to the
same extent as women's are for men. It is women and what men consider to be
their inherent capacity for contagion, their draining, demanding bodily processes
that have figured so strongly in cultural representations, and that have emerged
so clearly as a problem for social control.

This has become alarmingly clear in contemporary AIDS discourse, where
programs to halt the spread of the disease into the heterosexual community are
aimed at women: women are, ironically, the ones urged to function as the guardians of the purity of sexual exchange. It is they who have been targeted by medical groups and community health centers as the site for the insistence on condom
use. This targeting is not explicitly aimed at self-protection but rather at arresting
the circulation of contaminants throughout the community. This remains particularly ironic insofar as the transmission of the disease, in the West at least, has
moved from a largely gay male community through the sexual activities of bisexual men into the heterosexual community. Women are of course far more at
risk from men than men are from women: it seems statistically likely that men
will catch the HIV virus from other men, even if the virus's transmission is heterosexual. Making women responsible for the use of condoms and safe sex practices not only presumes a model of sexual conduct represented as a contract or
a form of consent, in which women are "equal consenting partners," a model
powerfully problematized in Carole Pateman's incisive analysis of liberal representations of sexual exchange in *The Sexual Contract*; it makes women, in line
with the conventions and practices associated with contraceptive procedures, the
guardians of the sexual fluids of both men and women. Men seem to refuse to
believe that *their* body fluids are the "contaminants." It must be women who are
the contaminants. Yet, paradoxically, the distinction between a "clean" woman
and an "unclean" one does not come from any presumption about the inherent
polluting properties of the self-enclosure of female sexuality, as one might presume, but is a function of the quantity, and to a lesser extent the quality, of the
men she has already been with. So she is in fact regarded as a kind of sponge or
conduit of *other men's* "dirt." [8]

While it is clear that one cannot provide universal or general claims about
the ways in which either men as a group or women as a group live and experience
their sexualities and corporealities or about the ways in which their bodies are
culturally codified and constituted, this does not mean that these issues are ille-
gitimate and undiscussable; nor does it absolve us of the responsibility to discuss
at least those forms with which we are concerned. What follows thus makes no

claim to universal relevance, but it does aspire to capture at least some key features that mark the ways in which men and women in contemporary Western cultures signify, live, and practice their sexualities and desires.

Seminal Fluids

Perhaps the great mystery, the great unknown, of the body comes not from the peculiarities and enigmas of female sexuality, from the cyclically regulated flows that emanate from women's bodies, but from the unspoken and generally unrepresented particularities of the male body. I have claimed in earlier chapters that the specificities of the masculine have always been hidden under the generality of the universal, the human. Men have functioned as if they represented masculinity only incidentally or only in moments of passion and sexual encounter, while the rest of the time they are representatives of the human, the generic "person." Thus what remains unanalyzed, what men can have no distance on, is the mystery, the enigma, the unspoken of the male body.[9]

In researching this chapter I was at first puzzled and shocked that where there seems to a huge volume of literature—medical, experiential, cultural—on the specificities of the female body (the growth of literature on menstruation and menopause since the feminist awakenings of the 1960s and 1970s is truly astonishing), there is virtually nothing—beyond the discourses of medicine and biology[10]—on men's body fluids. This has changed to some extent with the AIDS crisis, but it still remains true that the vast bulk of literature emerging from AIDS discourses on seminal fluids and male body fluids remains medicalized. Even pornography, the most explicit discourse of (men's representations of) female pleasure, remains focused on the body of woman. There are virtually no phenomenological accounts of men's body fluids, except in the borderline literatures of homosexuality and voyeurism (the writings of de Sade, Genet, and others are as close as we get to a philosophical or reflective account of the lived experiences of male flow).

In an important analysis of pornography in *Hard Core* (1990), Linda Williams presents a significant confirmation of this claim when she argues that even in the most explicit visual representations of male sexual fluids, what in the industry is known as the "money shot," the come shot, functions primarily as a mode of metaphorization of the invisible and graphically unrepresentable mysteries of the vagina and woman's interior. I don't want to suggest that female sexuality or anatomy is graphically unrepresentable. On the contrary, with the development of newer and more complex imaging techniques, no part of the body is graphically unrepresentable. The point is that the graphic representation necessarily transforms the parameters and terms of the body thus represented. The tactile exploration of the vagina and female sexual organs establishes a difference space, different points of registration, different forms, shapes, intensities than visual representation.

The ejaculation shot is an externalization of (the presumption) of her pleasure, not his:

> The stag film, seeking to learn more about the wonders of the "unseen world," encounters its limits of visibility.[11] . . . for the male performer to penetrate the wonders is to make it nearly impossible for the viewer to see what is penetrated.
>
> The money shot, however, succeeds in extending visibility to the next stage of representation of the heterosexual sex act: to the point of seeing climax. But this new visibility extends only to a knowledge of the hydraulics of male ejaculation, which, though certainly of interest, is a poor substitute for the knowledge of female wonders that the genre as a whole still seeks. The gynecological sense of the speculum that penetrates the female interior here really does give way to that of a self-reflecting mirror. While undoubtedly spectacular, the money shot is also hopelessly specular; it can only reflect back to the male gaze that purports to want knowledge of the woman's pleasure the man's own climax. (Williams 1990: 94)

This argument has a certain plausibility insofar as pornography, at least in part, offers itself to the (male) spectator as a form of knowledge and conceptual/perceptual mastery of the enigmas of female sexuality but is in fact his own projection of sexual pleasure. The come shot is thus no longer an unmediated representation and demonstration of his pleasure (as one would expect); it becomes an index of his prowess to generate her pleasure. His sexual specificity is not the object of the gaze but remains a mirror or rather a displacement of her pleasure (or at least his fantasy of her pleasure).

Phenomenology is generally displaced in favor of externalization, medicalization, solidification. Seminal fluid is understood primarily as what it makes, what it achieves, a causal agent and thus a thing, a solid: its fluidity, its potential seepage, the element in it that is uncontrollable, its spread, its formlessness, is perpetually displaced in discourse onto its properties, its capacity to fertilize, to father, to produce an object. Man sees that his "function" is to create, and own, at a (temporal and spatial) distance, and thus to extend bodily interests beyond the male body's skin through its proprietorial role, its "extended corporeality" in the mother whom he has impregnated and the child thereby produced, making them *his* products, possessions, responsibilities.

Irigaray sees in this maneuver a reduction of the fluid to the solid, the establishment of a boundary that congeals, phallicizes, male flows, flows which link male bodies to the modes of representation they commonly attribute to female bodies. This lies behind her question: why does Lacan, or psychoanalytic theory, censor the fluid, the seminal? Why does not sperm qualify as the *objet a*?

> . . . we might ask (ourselves) why sperm is never treated as an object *a*? Isn't the subjection of sperm to the imperatives of reproduction alone symptomatic

of a permanence historically allocated to the solid (product)? And if, in the dynamics of desire, the problem of castration intervenes—fantasy/reality of an amputation, of a "crumbling" of that solid that the penis represents—a reckoning with *sperm-fluid* as an obstacle to the generalization of an economy restricted to solids remains in suspension. (Irigaray 1985b: 113)

Could the reduction of men's body fluids to the by-products of pleasure and the raw materials of reproduction, along with men's refusal to acknowledge the effects of flows that move through various parts of the body[12] and from the inside out, have to do with men's attempt to distance themselves from the very kind of corporeality—uncontrollable, excessive, expansive, disruptive, irrational—they have attributed to women? Could the ways in which men's body fluids are lived coalesce with the demands of a heterosexualized opposition between men and women in which women are attributed the very powers and capacities that men fear in themselves? The ways in which men disavow their dependence on what they construe as femininity (in themselves) may account for the contempt (or reverence; they may amount to the same thing) in which many of them hold women. It may help explain the alienness to many women of men's capacity to distance themselves, their subjectivities, from their sexualities in such a way that men (both gay and straight) regard their sexual desires as overwhelming or uncontrollable impulses and find themselves to be "different persons" when comparing daily life with sexual encounters, regarding their sexual organs on the model of the homunculus, a little man within the man, with a quasi-autonomy of its own. It may help explain the alienness of men's capacity to reify bodily organs, to be interested in organs rather than the subjects to whom they belong, to seek sexuality without intimacy, to strive for anonymity amid promiscuity, to detach themselves from sexual engagement in order to establish voyeuristic distance, to enjoy witnessing and enacting violence and associate it with sexual pleasure, to enjoy the idea or actuality of sex with children, as an act of conscious cruelty, to use their sexual organs as weapons (and indeed to produce weapons modeled on the image of their sexual organs).

I am struck by the very different attitudes and relations at least some gay men take to their own bodies, body parts, and body fluids compared with heterosexuals, although of course there are also major similarities between them not shared by women which should not be ignored. I am not making claims for *all* gay men here and certainly not for gay men in all cultures or times: there are many ways in which gay men's bodies can be lived and invested, which are largely a function of the practices they undertake, the desires that feed them, and the meanings attributed to these desires and practices (or desires as practices). But perhaps many gay men are allowing a sort of "latent femininity" to appear which heterosexual men need to repress. I am suggesting that a different type of body is produced in and through the different sexual and cultural practices that men undertake. Part of the process of phallicizing the male body, of subordinat-

ing the rest of the body to the valorized functioning of the penis, with the culmination of sexual activities occurring, ideally at least, in sexual penetration and
male orgasm, involves the constitution of the sealed-up, impermeable body. Perhaps it is not after all flow in itself that a certain phallicized masculinity abhors
but the idea that flow moves or can move in two-way or indeterminable directions that elicits horror, the possibility of being not only an active agent in the
transmission of flow but also a passive receptacle. It may be this, among other
things, that distinguishes heterosexual men from many gay men who are prepared not only to send out but also to receive flow and in this process to assert
other bodily regions than those singled out by the phallic function. A body that
is permeable, that transmits in a circuit, that opens itself up rather than seals itself
off, that is prepared to respond as well as to initiate, that does not revile its masculinity (as the transsexual commonly does) or virilize it (as a number of gay
men, as well as heterosexuals, tend to do) would involve a quite radical rethinking of male sexual morphology. This rethinking is, I hope, partly being undertaken, whether consciously or not, in the rethinking of sexual encounters and
sexual pleasure demanded by the AIDS crisis, with its possibilities of a nonphal-
licized male sexual pleasure. I do not want to suggest that this is impossible for
heterosexual men, but it must involve a radical transformation in the kinds of
sexual practices they engage in and an even more difficult transformation in the
structure of desire whereby they are not weakened as men, do not see themselves
as "feminized," in their willingness of take on passive positions, to explore the
rest of their bodies (as well as women's), taking on pleasure of a different order,
but are able to reclaim, reuse, reintensify, body parts, zones, and functions that
have been phallically disinvested.

Earlier in this chapter I suggested, in agreement with Douglas, that what is
considered disruptive or transgressive of borders or boundaries is represented as
dirt and may be experienced, in keeping with Kristeva's terminology, as abject.
Dirt is what disrupts order, and order is conceived of as an arbitrary arrangement
of elements in relative stability or harmony. It is only through the attempted ex-
pulsion of the improper, the disarranging, the unclean (an attempt, as Kristeva
observes, that is always provisional and ultimately impossible), that the representation of order can continue. By excluding men's body fluids from their self-representation, or rather, by exerting a quasi- or apparent control over them (not
the control implied by abstinence, which is an attempt to control the flow by
preventing it from occurring, a fear of the disarray implied by the flow), by either
separating them from the body as soon as possible (the familiar gesture of washing, or even ritual cleansing, after sexual intercourse) or, more commonly, representing the flow as a mark of appropriation, as the production of a solid, with
all its attendant rights and occasional responsibilities, men demarcate their own
bodies as clean and proper. Moreover, through this dispossession or transmission
of possession men take on the right of the proprietors of women's bodies too

insofar as women's bodies are conceived as the receptacles of men's body fluids and the nesting place of their product—the fetus. This may explain the anger of many men directed not so much against the principle of abortion on demand—which, if recent surveys are correct, most men and women support—as against "their" women's use of this principle, described in some of the literature of "male feminism" as "lost fatherhood"; men mourn not the loss of their body fluids but its wastage.[13] It seems clear that it is only when men take responsibility for and pleasure in the forms of seepage that are their own, when they cease to reduce it to its products, when they accept the sexual specificity, particularity, and limit that is their own, that they will respect women's bodily autonomy and sexual specificity as well.

Thus far in the history of recent feminist theory, men have operated reactively, often with confusion and anger, to the changes and upheavals women have effected in their lives. They have been forced to disrupt their expectations and sometimes their practices, especially in the sphere of sexual encounters, but they have commonly done so unwillingly and with a sense of nostalgia at what they believe they have lost. It is only when these kinds of changes and transformations are also actively sought and affirmed, only when men themselves are willing and desire to make positive and expansive changes to their own sexual horizons, that they are able to meet women half way in the transformation of the sexually binarized body. This is a rewriting of the Oedipalized body (note that I am not suggesting a voluntaristic willful changing of the deepest structure of the unconscious: such a change is not readily possible, in psychoanalytic terms, or if it is, it is the result of a very detailed psychotherapy that may accompany but is not necessary for the kinds of changes that I have in mind here), both from the point of view of establishing an experimental desire, a desire for experiment, change, transformation, and of developing procedures for rewriting of the kind involved in transforming one's practices and activities.

Women's Corporeal Flows

Women's bodies and sexualities have been structured and lived in terms that not only differentiate them from men's but also attempt, not always or even usually entirely successfully, to position them in a relation of passive dependence and secondariness to men's. This is not to say that women necessarily experience their sexualities and desires in this way but rather that the only socially recognized and validated representations of women's sexuality are those which conform to and accord with the expectations and desires of a certain heterosexual structuring of male desire. This, I believe, is part of the explanation of why feminists have found that psychoanalytic discourse, in spite of its well-recognized problems, has been useful in explaining the sexual structuring and positioning of the two sexes relative to each other. Psychoanalysis has provided a series of insights regarding the ways in which a desire for passivity is constructed and reproduced for women. But, as already discussed, psychoanalysis does not provide a way of transforming the structure of power relations between the sexes, although it has been strategically used by a number of feminists to demonstrate the inherent paradoxes, ironies, and tensions associated with the passages to masculinity and femininity expected for men and women respectively.

Rather than add to the plethora of feminist texts on psychoanalysis and tread the well-worn pathway from the polymorphous infantile to the Oedipalized, castrated feminine or the phallic masculine positions, a different kind of approach, one not incompatible with psychoanalysis, one perhaps closer to the kinds of phenomenological approach already discussed, might be worth pursuing. Here I am interested not so much in the genesis and structure of libidinal zones according a model of infantile development outlined by psychoanalysis as in a tracing of the kinds of libidinal pathway across women's bodies that various corporeal flows make possible and in turn respond to.

Can it be that in the West, in our time, the female body has been constructed not only as a lack or absence but with more complexity, as a leaking, uncontrollable, seeping liquid; as formless flow; as viscosity, entrapping, secreting; as lacking not so much or simply the phallus but self-containment[14]—not a cracked or porous vessel, like a leaking ship, but a formlessness that engulfs all form, a disorder that threatens all order? I am not suggesting that this is how women *are*, that it is their ontological status. Instead, my hypothesis is that women's corporeality is inscribed as a mode of seepage. My claim is not that women have been somehow desolidified but the more limited one which sees that women, insofar as they are human, have the same degree of solidity, occupy the same genus, as men, yet insofar as they are women, they are represented and live themselves as seepage, liquidity. The metaphorics of uncontrollability, the ambivalence between desperate, fatal attraction and strong revulsion, the deep-seated fear of absorption, the association of femininity with contagion and disorder, the undecidability of the limits of the female body (particularly, but not only, with the onset of puberty and in the case of pregnancy),[15] its powers of cynical seduction and allure are all common themes in literary and cultural representations of women. But these may well be a function of the projection outward of their corporealities, the liquidities that men seem to want to cast out of their own self-representations.

If women have been defined on the side of the body and men on the side of the mind, then there are particular bodily zones that serve to emphasize both women's difference from and otherness to men. There is nothing inherent in these regions and zones that makes them more suitable for culturally representing sexual difference—many others would have served this function just as well; what culturally marks sexual difference is biologically arbitrary, conventional. With the developments of puberty, what becomes visible and tangible as a measure of womanhood is the development of the so-called secondary sexual characteristics, the filling out of breasts and hips, the growth of pubic hair, and perhaps most strikingly, the onset of menses. While clearly the development of these characteristics leads to many different attitudes and responses—some girls relish their new-found maturation, while others approach it with dread and shame—nonetheless there remains a broadly common coding of the female body as a body which leaks, which bleeds, which is at the mercy of hormonal and reproductive functions. Boys' bodies too mature at this time, but what their biological developments entail is a preparedness not simply for reproduction and fatherhood but also for "mature" sexual activity (primarily intercourse).

It is significant that Iris Young, in her definitive phenomenological study of the experience of being/having breasts, also has recourse to the kind of metaphorics of fluidity proposed by Irigaray. From Young's point of view, Irigaray is not posing a new ontological truth about women's inherent fluidity as opposed to men's solidity and self-identity. Rather, her gesture is openly acknowledged as strategic. A "mechanics of solids," which works in fundamental complicity with Cartesian dualism and the metaphysics of realism and self-identity that it supports, entails a thing (including a subject) that is identical to itself. This metaphysics is dualist not simply in terms of presuming and establishing an opposition between mind and body but in binarizing existence with the distinction between subject and object, thus implicitly (and at times explicit) coding women on the side of body and object. Young resorts to the Irigarayan metaphorics of fluids insofar as it befuddles and complicates this Cartesian ontology and is as capable of rewriting male corporeality as female. Moreover, as Young validates, Irigaray's refusal to subordinate the tactile and the morphological under the domination of the visual is consistent with this strategy of problematizing the self-identical, problematizing the ready separation between subject and object (which is most readily confirmed, as I have already argued in chapter 4, through the distance separating the seer from the seen). This is not a new "fact" of female or human existence but a different way of looking at subjectivity and corporeality, highlighting quite different facets and features. Here is Young's suggestion for displacing the alienating objectification and sometimes self-objectification undergone by women when breasts become an object of the male gaze and male "possession":

My conceptualization of a woman-centered experience of breasts is a construction, an imagining, that I will locate in the theme of desubstantialization. If we move from the male gaze in which woman is the Other, the object, the solid and definite, to imagine the woman's point of view, the breasted body becomes blurry, mushy, indefinite, multiple and without clear identity. . . . A metaphysics generated from feminine desire, Luce Irigaray suggests, might conceptualize being as fluid rather than as solid substances, of things. Fluids, unlike objects, have no definite borders; they are unstable, which does not mean that they are without pattern. Fluids surge and move, and a metaphysic that thinks being as fluid would tend to privilege the living, moving, pulsing over the inert dead matter of the Cartesian world view. . . .

As far as I am concerned, it is not at all a matter of making a claim about women's biology or bodies, for conceptualized in a radically different way, men's bodies are at least as fluid as women's. The point is that a metaphysics of self-identical objects has clear ties to the domination of nature in which the domination of women has been implicated because culture has projected onto us identification with the abject body. (Young 1990: 192–93)

The fluidity and indeterminacy of female body parts, most notably the breasts but no less the female sexual organs, are confined, constrained, solidified, through more or less temporary or permanent means of solidification by clothing or, at the limit, by surgery. This indeterminacy is again not a fact of nature but a function of the modes of representation that privilege the solid and the determinate over the fluid. This process too may account for the valorization of the erect over the flaccid penis and the humiliation, the feminization, presumed in men's sexual impotence.

Women's bodies do not develop their adult forms with reference to their newly awakened sexual capacities, for these are dramatically overcoded with the resonances of motherhood. Puberty for girls marks the development of the breasts and the beginning of menstruation as an entry into the reproductive reality that is presumed to be women's prime domain. Puberty is not figured as the coming of a self-chosen sexual maturity but as the signal of immanent reproductive capacities. The first issuing forth of sperm, the onset of nocturnal emissions, signals coming manhood for the boy, the sexual pleasures and encounters fantasized and yet to come; but the onset of menstruation is not an indication at all for the girl of her developing sexuality, only her coming womanhood. And moreover, whereas the boy is able to psychically solidify the flow of sperm, connecting it metonymically to a corporeal pleasure and metaphorically with a desired object (or at least a place), for the girl, menstruation, associated as it is with blood, with injury and the wound, with a mess that does not dry invisibly, that leaks, uncontrollable, not in sleep, in dreams, but whenever it occurs, indicates the beginning of an out-of-control status that she was led to believe ends with childhood. The idea of soiling oneself, of dirt, of the very dirt produced by the body itself, staining the subject, is a "normal" condition of infancy, but in the case of the maturing woman it is a mark or stain of her future status, the impulsion into a future of a past that she thought she had left behind. This necessarily marks womanhood, whatever else it may mean for particular women, as outside itself, outside its time (the time of a self-contained adulthood) and place (the place definitively within its own skin, as a self-identical being), and thus a paradoxical entity, on the very border between infancy and adulthood, nature and culture, subject and object, rational being and irrational animal.

Kristeva too seems to think there is a link between menstruation and dirt. She creates a dual set of pairings: on one hand there are nonpolluting body fluids and on the other, polluting body fluids. The two nonpolluting but still marginal fluids she mentions are, in keeping with Douglas, tears (as earlier quoted) and, significantly, semen.[16] Douglas has adequately, even if not entirely plausibly, explained why tears are regarded as purifying rather than polluting (for her it has to do with the resemblance between clear tears and water, the cleansing element par excellence); but it is less plausible to argue that semen inherently, as a consequence of its own natural "properties" or "qualities"—its translucence, its clarity, its purity—is nonpolluting. Tears and semen are in any case not structurally symmetrical. While tears are commonly culturally associated with femininity, they are of course a capacity of both men's and women's bodies. Semen, by contrast, is a specifically male sexual flow, indeed, in the light of current medical knowledge, it is the only specifically male sexual flow. Its nonpolluting status cannot be simply a function of its role in the fertilization of the ovum and the reproduction of the species, for this is a relatively recent medical discovery and does not, for example, explain the sacred status of semen in many non-Western cultures, not to mention in our own cultural history. Nor does it explain the differential status of menstruation, which also has its role in the reproduction of the species.

Kristeva distinguishes these nonpolluting body fluids from those which defile. The latter she divides into two classes or types, each of which elicits the reaction of abjection: excrement and menstrual blood. This coupling is itself significant insofar as menstrual blood, as I have been arguing, becomes associated with the characteristics of excrement. The representation of female sexuality as an uncontainable flow, as seepage associated with what is unclean, coupled with the idea of female sexuality as a vessel, a container, a home empty or lacking in itself but fillable from the outside, has enabled men to associate women with infection, with disease, with the idea of festering putrefaction, no longer contained simply in female genitals but at any or all points of the female body. Bodily differences, marked and given psychical and cultural significance, are of course not restricted to the particular bodily regions in which they originate: they seep not only outside of and beyond the body, forming a kind of zone of contamination, but also into all other regions of the body, passing on a kind of aura or mode of operation that is no longer localized or localizable.

The development of shame, disgust, and other moral functions is, as Freud has argued, a consequence of the child's learning to control its bowels. The clean and proper body's development is directly linked to the child's negotiations with the demands of toilet training and the regulation of body fluids. Within this cultural constellation it is not surprising, then, that women's menstrual flow is regarded not only with shame and embarrassment but with disgust and the powers of contaminating. Kristeva distinguishes these two classes of abject in terms of the kinds and location of the danger each poses:

> Excrement and its equivalents (decay, infection, disease, corpse, etc.) stand for
> the danger to identity that comes from without: the ego threatened by the non-

ego, society threatened by its outside, life by death. Menstrual blood, on the contrary, stands for the danger issuing from within the identity (social or sexual); it threatens the relationship between the sexes within a social aggregate, and through internalization, the identity of each sex in the face of sexual difference. (Kristeva 1982: 71)

Excrement poses a threat to the center—to life, to the proper, the clean—not from within but from its outermost margin. While there is no escape from excrementality, from mortality, from the corpse, these do not or need not impinge on the everyday operations of the subject or body. The (social and psychical) goal is to establish as great a separation as possible from the excremental, to get rid of it quickly, to clean up after the mess. What Kristeva suggests about menstrual flow seems more complicated and problematic: for her, it is a danger, internal to identity, and threatens the relations between the sexes. It cannot be escaped or fled from, for it is the condition, *qua* maternity, of life and sexual difference.

I cannot understand how Kristeva can claim that menstrual blood represents a danger to both sexes in a way that semen does not. She links excrement and menstrual blood through the figure of the (phallic) mother, so presumably sperm is attributed to the father. Is it that paternity is less threatening, less dangerous, less vulnerable, than maternity? Or rather, is it less dangerous and threatening for men? The grounds of Kristeva's analysis remain obscure and not entirely convincing.

The specific, particular developments surrounding women's coming to maturity are thus linked with and may be represented in terms of various cycles of bodily flow: women's genitals and breasts are the loci of (potential) flows, red and white, blood and milk, flows that are difficult to appropriate while under constant threats of personal and legal appropriation, flows that signal both a self-contained autoerotic pleasure and a site of potential social danger insofar as they are resistant to various cultural overlays (being unamenable to coercion and pressure, though in a sense absolutely open to cultural inscription), and insofar as they insist on the irreducible specificity of women's bodies, the bodies of *all* women, independent of class, race, and history.[17] This irreducible specificity in no way universalizes the particular ways in which women experience their bodies and bodily flows. But given the social significance of these bodily processes that are invested in and by the processes of reproduction, all women's bodies are marked as different from men's (and inferior to them) particularly at those bodily regions where women's differences are most visibly manifest.

There will always remain a kind of outsideness or alienness of the experiences and lived reality of each sex for the other. Men, contrary to the fantasy of the transsexual, can never, even with surgical intervention, feel or experience what it is like to be, to live, as women. At best the transsexual can live out his fantasy of femininity—a fantasy that in itself is usually disappointed with the rather crude transformations effected by surgical and chemical intervention. The transsexual may look like a woman but can never feel like or be a woman. The one sex, whether male or female or some other term, can only experience, live, according to (and hopefully in excess of) the cultural significations of the sexually specific body. The problematic of sexual difference entails a certain failure of knowledge to bridge the gap, the interval, between the sexes. There remains something ungraspable, something outside, unpredictable, and uncontainable, about the other sex for each sex. This irreducible difference under the best conditions evokes awe and surprise; under less favorable conditions it evinces horror, fear, struggle, resistance. When respected, this difference implies distance, division, an interval: it involves each relating to the other without being engulfed or overwhelmed. In other words, it involves a remainder, an indigestible residue, which remains unconsumed in any relation between them. More commonly, though, this gulf, this irremediable distance, is what remains intolerable to masculinist regimes bent on the disavowal of difference and the insistence on sameness and identity: these regimes make the other over into a (lesser) version of the same. While sexual difference entails its own forms of violence (the violence of differentiation), the insistence on sameness, identity, equivalence, formalized exchange, exerts a different kind of violence, a violence that occurs to a group (in this case women) whose difference is effaced. The former is a constitutive, formative, ineliminable violence, the violence of existence and becoming; the latter is a wanton, gratuitous violence, a violence that undergoes historical and cultural transformation, a violence capable of being transformed, rewritten, even reversed, through the counterviolence of resistance. This book has been an attempt to promote this counterviolence while at the same time recognizing the constitutive violence of the operations of difference itself.

I have been concerned with establishing models, concepts, categories, and methodologies that tie subjectivity irreducibly to the specificities of sexed bodies. But in doing so, instead of seeking sexual identities, the notion of two absolutely separate types of entity, men and women, I have attempted to seek out traces and residues of sexual difference, a difference impossible to unify, impossible to separate from its various others and impossible to identify or seal off in clear-cut terms. Once the subject is no longer seen as an entity—whether psychical or corporeal—but fundamentally an effect of the pure difference that constitutes all modes of materiality, new terms need to be sought by which to think this alterity within and outside the subject.

In using the notion of the sexed body as the frame for my analysis of (sexual) difference, I risk that ready slippage from a focus on difference to one on identity. It is clear that there must be a relation between sexual difference and sexual identity; sexual difference, though, cannot be understood, as is commonly the case in much feminist literature, in terms of a comparison and contrast between two types of sexual identity independently formed and formulated. Instead it must be seen as the very ground on which sexual identities and their external relations are made possible. Sexual difference is related to sexual identity in the same way that Saussure's notion of pure difference provides the grounds or conditions of existence of linguistic value. But just as, for Saussure and Derrida, pure difference can never appear as such because it must consistently erase its contribution to signification and linguistic value, because for it to appear as such is for it to transform itself, to render itself present, so too sexual difference is a framework or horizon that must disappear as such in the codings that constitute sexual identity and the relations between the sexes. Sexual difference is the horizon that cannot appear in its own terms but is implied in the very possibility of an entity, an identity, a subject, an other and their relations.

This notion of sexual difference, a difference that is originary and constitutive, is not, strictly speaking, ontological; if anything it occupies a preontological—certainly a preepistemological—terrain insofar as it makes possible what things or entities, what beings, exist (the ontological question) and insofar as it must preexist and condition what we can know (the epistemological question). The framework or terrain of sexual difference entails not the concept of a continuum, a wholeness, a predivisional world as plenum, but the simultaneous recognition and effacement of the spacings, the intervals, the irreducible if unspecifiable positioning, the fissures and ruptures, that bind each "thing" to every other and to the whole of existence without, however, linking them into an organic or metaphysical wholeness or unity.

These are no longer either independent units each with their own internal cohesion; nor are they unbounded relations with no specificity or location. Bodies themselves, in their materialities, are never self-present, given things, immediate, certain self-evidences because embodiment, corporeality, insist on alterity, both that alterity they carry within themselves (the heart of the psyche lies in the body; the body's principles of functioning are psychological and cultural) and that alterity that gives them their own concreteness and specificity (the alterities constituting race, sex, sexualities, ethnic and cultural specificities). Alterity is the very possibility and process of embodiment: it conditions but is also a product of the pliability or plasticity of bodies which makes them other than themselves, other than their "nature," their functions and identities.

My goal, though, was not to provide a definitive model by which bodies and their sexual differences are to be understood. For one thing, that seems to misunderstand what a model entails. A model is a heuristic device which facilitates a certain understanding, highlighting certain features while diminishing the significance of others; it is a selective rewriting of a situation whose complexity entails the possibility of other, alternative models, models which highlight different features, presenting different emphases. The Möbius strip model has the advantage of showing that there can be a relation between two "things"—mind and body—which presumes neither their identity nor their radical disjunction, a model which shows that while there are disparate "things" being related, they have the capacity to twist one into the other. This enables the mind/body relation to avoid the impasses of reductionism, of a narrow causal relation or the retention of the binary divide. It enables subjectivity to be understood not as the combination of a psychical depth and a corporeal superficiality but as a surface whose inscriptions and rotations in three-dimensional space produce all the effects of depth. It enables subjectivity to be understood as fully material and for materiality to be extended and to include and explain the operations of language, desire, and significance. It stretches and represents the conceptual possibilities that this book has attempted to explore. But the Möbius strip is only one possible representation; it neither precludes other possibilities nor is necessarily the best or most enabling representation. Nor is it without its own problems or limits (any model has them). For one thing, utilizing the Möbius model limits our understanding of the subject in terms of dualism but links it to a kind of monism, autonomy, or self-presence that precludes understanding the body, bodies, as the terrain and effect of difference. Moreover, it is a model not well suited for representing modes of becoming, modes of transformation. But in a sense the field of differences, the trajectories of becoming, do not lend themselves readily to representation, to handy models. The infinite pliability of the body that I have suggested throughout implies that a host of other models may, for other purposes and in other contexts, prove just as useful. The task ahead involves exploring and experimenting with as many of these models as we may need and find useful for the various infinite contexts in which the question of bodies, their powers and differences, arises. It involves taking theoretical risks in the hope that new methods and models, new techniques and contexts, may one day develop which will readily acknowledge the centrality of the problematic of sexual difference to the ways in which we conceive of and act in the world. It involves not a death of man or of God but the generation of a new productivity between and of the two sexes.

Notes

1. Refiguring Bodies

1. The problem of dichotomous thought is not the dominance of the pair (some sort of inherent problem with the number two); rather, it is the *one* which makes it problematic, the fact that the one can allow itself no independent, autonomous other. All otherness is cast in the mold of sameness, with the primary term acting as the only autonomous or pseudo-autonomous term. The one allows no twos, threes, fours. It cannot tolerate any *other*. The one, in order to be a one, must draw a barrier or boundary around itself, in which case it is necessarily implicated in the establishment of a binary—inside/outside, presence/absence.

On the question of the inherent violence of binary polarization, see Nancy Jay (1981), Jacques Derrida (1972, 1976, 1981a, and 1981b), and Elizabeth Gross (1986b). Derrida's position differs markedly from Jay's, insofar as Jay posits the possibility of a third term or a middle ground between binary pairs, a point that is somehow outside the polarizing structure, a point or term that can resolve or clarify the tensions that compose the dyadic structure, a kind of Hegelian synthesis of the opposed terms. Derrida is explicit in his denial of this reconstitution of the binary through its supersession. The sublation or relief of the binary pair obliterates the interval between them, which both Derrida and Irigaray insist on being recognized:

> Henceforth, in order better to mark this interval . . . it has been necessary to analyze, to set to work, *within* the text of the history of philosophy . . . certain marks, shall we say . . . , that *by analogy* . . . I have called undecidables, that is, unities of simulacrum, "false" verbal properties (nominal and semantic) that can no longer be included within philosophical (binary) opposition, resisting and disorganizing it, *without ever* constituting a third term, without ever leaving room for a solution in the form of speculative dialectics. . . . In fact, I attempt to bring the critical operation to bear against the unceasing reappropriation of this work of the simulacrum by a dialectics of the Hegelian type . . . , for Hegelian idealism consists precisely of a *relève* of a binary opposition of classical idealism, a resolution of contradiction into a third term that comes in order to *aufheben*, to deny while raising up, while idealizing, while sublimating into an anamnesic interiority (*Errinnerung*), while *interning* difference in a self-presence. (Derrida 1972: 42–43)

I am grateful to Vicki Kirby for pointing out this difference between Jay and Derrida.

2. See Genevieve Lloyd (1984).

3. It is significant that according to at least one philosopher—Michèle Le Doeuff—women have gained access to the discipline of philosophy, at least until the middle of this century, largely through a theoretico-amorous relationship to a "great" male philosopher rather than to the discipline of philosophy itself, with all its various positions, agreements, and disagreements. Eloise and Abelard, Wollstonecraft and Mill, Beauvoir and Sartre serve as examples of such philosophical couples; here the female "partner" may be presumed to take on the

role of body to the male philosopher's position as mind. See Le Doeuff (1989), Gatens (1986b and 1991b), and Grosz (1989, esp. chap. 6).

4. *Disavowal* is the term Freud uses to describe the split attitude of the fetishist and the pre-Oedipal child. It involves a simultaneous recognition and refusal to recognize (in the case of the fetishist, a recognition and refusal of the mother's castration). It results in the process of the "splitting of the ego." See Freud, "Negation" (1925a), "Fetishism" (1927), and "The Splitting of the Ego in the Process of Defence" (1938).

5. "Woman" is represented as an impossible and unattainable truth, for example, in the work of Nietzsche, one of the few philosophers exploring the body's positivity; "Woman's" pleasure is represented as unknowable and unspeakable by Lacan, esp. in "God and the Jouissance of the Woman" in J. Mitchell and J. Rose 1982.

6. See Dodds (1973) and Adkins (1970).

7. For further details, see Elizabeth V. Spelman (1982: 111–19).

8. This is outlined in considerable detail in a book devoted to medieval accounts of and explanation for leprosy. See Brody (1974, esp. 11).

9. See *The Meditations* in R. Descartes (1931–34). Erwin Straus's analysis is particularly astute and relevant; see Straus (1962: 141–50).

10. See D. M. Armstrong (1968) or the works of Paul Churchland (1989) and Patricia Churchland (1986), which have ingeniously if condescendingly written off the notion of mind or psychical interiority as "folk psychology."

11. A number of neurophysiologists and neuropsychologists, whose work will be examined in more detail in later chapters, argue that it is impossible to give exact localization for the neurological correlates of psychical and behavioral phenomena, particularly because neurological processes can shift their localizations as a result of lesions or other forms of neurological damage. See Kurt Goldstein (1963, 1971), A. S. Luria (1973), and Oliver Sacks (1985).

12. Indeed, it is only on such an assumption that medical experimentation using animals in place of human subjects makes any sense.

13. For a feminist evaluation of the relevance of Spinoza, see Moira Gatens (1988, esp. 66–70).

14. For further examples of the Cartesian and mechanistic account of the body, see Hobbes, *The Leviathan*; La Mettrie, *Man a Machine* (1988), and Descartes, *The Meditations*.

15. Essentialism is best understood as the postulation of a fixed essence, unchanged historically or culturally. Very often, essentialism resorts to naturalism or biologism, but it may also plausibly appeal to cultural or theological factors. Biologism is the postulation of a biological universality, which is used to explain cultural and behavioral characteristics; and naturalism, which may or may not (but usually does) appeal to biologism, invokes some kind of nature—whether God-given, cultural, or biological—to justify its universalist assertions. For further differentiations in these usually elided terms, see Grosz (1990c).

16. Among those involved in this broadly conceived feminist project are Alison Caddick (1986), Philipa Rothfield (1986, 1988), Susan Bordo (1988, 1989a, and 1989b), Judith Butler (1990), Moira Gatens (1988, 1990, and 1991a), Diana Fuss (1989), Vicki Kirby (1987, 1989a and b), and Elspeth Probyn (1987).

17. This is, incidentally, very similar to the first category suggested by Kristeva in her description of three "generations" of feminists in her paper "Women's Time" (Kristeva 1986): it coincides with her first generation, in which she is clearly referring to Beauvoir.

18. Anorexics seem to take to extremes the egalitarian disdain for female corporeality in their attempts to think the subject as a pure transcendence, a pure will unbounded by bodily needs and limitations. They exhibit a kind of wishful megalomania, the fantasy of the self-made and completely self-controlled subject, the subject who needs nothing and no one.

19. Even in the case of racist oppression, it is men's color or ethnic background, not their masculinity, which restrains men to immanence. In this sense, it seems to me that Elizabeth V. Spelman's claims (1988) that the specificities of class and race oppression are internally tied to sexual oppression (a claim with which I agree) nevertheless misses its mark: the point is that men as men are not oppressed; insofar as men are oppressed, and it is clear that a good many— possibly even a majority of men—are oppressed, it is not as men, but as "colored" or as members of class alignments, in terms of sexual preferences or religious affiliations that men are oppressed.

20. The opposition between essentialism and constructionism seems to me a false one: constructionism is inherently reliant on essentialism, for it needs to make explicit what are the raw materials of its processes of construction and these cannot themselves be constructed without the assumption of an infinite regress. The building blocks or raw materials must in some sense be essentialist. In short, constructionism ultimately implies and relies on essentialism.

21. See Spelman (1982).

22. See Gatens (1990) and the ensuing debates around Gatens's work, including Val Plumwood (1989) and Gatens's response in *Radical Philosophy* 52 (1990). See also Gatens (1989), Denise Thompson (1989), Genevieve Lloyd (1989), and Anne Edwards (1989).

23. There is no reason, in spite of the popularized and aestheticized cult of health, to presume that the most fit or exercised body is the most beautiful. On the construction of the norm of the "healthy" body, see Jill Matthews (1987).

2. Psychoanalysis and Psychical Topographies

1. See Freud, "On Narcissism: An Introduction" (1914), for his comparison of the ego to an amoeba and the libido to its pseudopodia and *The Ego and the Id* (1923) for his notion of the psyche as a "living vesicle," as well as his representation of the psyche on the model of a brain.

2. For a more detailed discussion of the differences between Freud's two accounts of the ego, see Grosz (1990a), esp. 24–31.

3. An exception is Didier Anzieu, who has devoted considerable research to the notion of the "skin ego," the ego as a sensorimotor projection of the body's surface. See Anzieu (1989 and 1990). See also John O'Neill (1989).

4. Freud reverts to this kind of explanation in his 1923 model.

5. Warren Gorman (1969: 19–23) provides a brief history of this concept.

6. Gorman (1969) points out that the brain is peculiarly insensitive to sensory stimulation. Only the membranes, blood vessels, and nerves surrounding the brain—on the surface of the brain—are sensitive to stimulation, and even when the largest blood vessels on the brain's surface are stimulated, this does not result in a "brain-ache" but in a headache, located through experience at certain points on or in the head but not the brain. This is confirmed in brain surgery, which can be readily performed without anaesthetic.

7. It is significant that whereas Freud places special emphasis on the surface of the body in his account of the genesis and functioning of the ego, he gives a privileged role to the acoustical register in the establishment of the superego, the "voice" of conscience. The superego in Freud's other writings ("The Dissolution of the Oedipus Complex" [1924], "Some Psychical Consequences of the Anatomical Distinction between the Sexes" [1925]) is a part of the identificatory ego that has been separated off from the rest through the introjection of the father's authority. It becomes a separate psychical agency which judges the ego's accomplishments by measuring the ego against its ego ideal. The larger the disparity, the more forceful and harsh are the superego's judgments. Freud claims that the superego is the congealed residue of orders,

injunctions, and threats that the child has heard. In other words, the child's acoustical registration of parental voices forms the basis of the superego in its function as judgmental censor.
Freud's model in *The Ego and the Id* has a privileged position for the acoustical register:

> . . . the ego wears the "cap of hearing" (auditory lobe) on the one side only, as we learn from
> cerebral anatomy. It might be said to wear it awry. (Freud 1923: 25)

8. Among them Head, Hughlings Jackson—from whom Freud also derived much regarding the body image—Wallon (in Voyat 1984), Spitz (1965), Schilder (1978), and Kurt
Goldstein (1948, 1963, 1971).

9. The official medical and psychiatric statistics seem to massively underestimate the
range and scope of eating disorders. Official statistics rank the ratio of eating disorders among
women at about one in forty, but recent surveys of primary and secondary school girls recently
undertaken indicated that four out of five school girls are worried about their weight.

10. Particularly anosognosia, in which the patient is unaware of or denies a paralyzed
limb. In the phantom limb, there is a refusal to accept the loss of a limb; in anosognosia, there
is a refusal to accept its (nonfunctional) presence. In hemiasomatognosia, in which the patient
behaves as if half of the body were nonexistent, there is a refusal to recognize half the body.
When asked to perform various tasks, the patient feels as if these were successfully accomplished although the limb does not move. Even where the patient can apparently observe no
movement of the limb, there seems to be the belief that the limb has performed the desired
actions. See Head (1920), Schilder (1931, 1953, 1978), Sacks (1981), Goldstein (1971), and
Luria (1973).

11. See Tiemersma (1989: 25–27) and Gorman (1969: 97). There are some cases of the
phantom limb appearing before the age of seven; and in the case of malformed limbs or limbs
incapable of independent motion, even in children over seven, there is usually no phantom. This
tends to indicate that both movement and the perception of movement are necessary for the
registration of a body phantom. On the other hand, in cases of paralysis, there are rare occa-
sions in which the object will develop a supernumerary phantom of the paralysed limb, thus
experiencing the existence of three limbs.

12. There is strong confirmation of the rapid assimilation of and fascination with images
of the human form in the writings of Wallon, Spitz, and Guillaume:

> Many animals react when they see themselves in a mirror. None, however, react to their like-
> nesses in a drawing, in a piece of sculpture, or in a photograph. In the fifth month it [the
> child] seemed to be interested in a photographic reproduction of Franz Hals's *Head of a
> Child.* . . . From seven to eight months, it definitely reacted to snapshots. . . . During the last
> three months of the first year, indications of interest in pictures increased. The child contem-
> plated photographs at length and tried to comb the hair of a woman in a portrait. . . . (Guil-
> laume 1971: 126–27)

13. Cf. Schilder's analysis in *Medical Psychology*:

> The patients complain that they no longer have an ego, but are mechanisms, automatons,
> puppets, that what they do seems not to be done by them but happens mechanically; that
> they no longer feel joy or sorrow, hatred or love; that they are as though dead, not alive, not
> real, that they cannot imagine their body, it is feelingless, and they experience neither hunger,
> thirst, nor any other bodily needs; that they cannot imagine or remember. (Quoted in Mellor
> 1988: 15)

14. Perhaps the most frightening of all representations—and often capitalized on in hor-

ror films—is that of the ghostly double, or *Doppelgänger*, the subject's own body phantom, which threatens to steal away the subject's very identity and position and by which the subject may be deranged with the possibility of finding itself, its space and place, taken over or displaced by an indiscernible double. Films such as Cronenberg's *Dead Ringers* and *The Kray Brothers* and Altman's *Three Women* hauntingly represent the murderous danger posed by the double and the narcissistic, psychotic identification it prompts.

15. See M. R. Trimble (1988: 12–14).

16. Lacan's account of psychosis explains it as a foreclosure of the symbolic and the return of what has been foreclosed—usually castration—from the real itself, in hallucinatory form. See Roustang (1982).

17. See Lacan (1977a), "On the Question Preliminary to Any Possible Treatment of Psychosis," esp. 196–99.

18. See Grosz (1990a), chap. 2, and Grosz (1988a).

19. Caillois claims that mimicry cannot be explained in terms of adaptation or natural survival for there seems to be no survival value in the insect's ability to camouflage itself:

> Generally speaking, one finds many remains of mimetic insects in the stomachs of predators. So it should come as no surprise that such insects sometimes have other and more effective ways to protect themselves. And conversely, some species that are inedible and would thus have nothing to fear, are also mimetic. It therefore seems that one ought to conclude with Cunot that this is an "epiphenomenon" whose "defensive utility appears to be nul." (Caillois 1984: 24–25)

20. Schilder, Guillaume, and Spitz confirm Caillois's assertions about the function of mimicry in insects by examining not psychosis but the "normal," that is, developmental processes operating in the child's earliest acts of imitation, which is clearly a central activity in its acquisition of a social and sexual identity. Imitation in children is an act of enormous intellectual complexity, for it involves both the confusion and separation of the imitated acts of others and one's own imitative actions. It is so complex because in judging whether one's own actions are the same as or similar to those being imitated, the subject locates itself from the point of view of another. In assuming that it is like others, the child's identity is captured and assimilated by the gaze and visual field of the other. Imitation is conditioned on the child's acquisition of an image of itself, its image or perception of another, and a categorical assimilation of both to broadly similar general types. Guillaume makes explicit the connections between the child's imitative behavior and its conceptions of space:

> One may conclude that the infant gradually constructs a visual image of his body and movements, even if he has never happened to contemplate them in a mirror. As the image becomes more specific, it will become assimilated with the objective perception of the human body of others. Imitation therefore will be founded on assimilation that will be only a specific instance of the development of the idea of space. (Guillaume 1971: 84)

21. Spitz and, following him, Wilden, maintain that at least eight models are represented in Freud's texts. For details, see Spitz (1965: 6–11) and Wilden (1972: 40).

22. Laplanche describes "The Project for a Scientific Psychology" as "the great Freudian text on the ego, a far more focussed consideration of the question than any of Freud's subsequent writings" (1976: 54). The ego is a constantly cathected nucleus of neurones in the memory systems, in which a permanent component can be distinguished from changing neuronal cathexes. Psychical defenses consist in the creation of different kinds of "side cathexes" through which part or all of the neuronal charge is deviated from a facilitated pathway between neu-

rones to surrounding neurones, securing a deflection of intensity which Freud elsewhere identifies with the mechanisms of condensation and displacement (1895: 325).

23. Freud writes: "The physiological events do not cease as soon as the psychical ones begin; on the contrary, the physiological chain continues. What happens is simply that, after a certain point in time, each (or some) of its links has a psychical phenomenon corresponding to it. Accordingly, the psychical is a process parallel to the physiological—a 'dependent concomitant' " (appendix to 1915a: 207).

24. Although even here there are problems. See Goldstein (1948) on the isolationism involved in the notion of a uniform and predictable reflex action. The effectivity of the reflex depends entirely on the context of the stimulation and the state and position of the body.

25. Freud refers to two types of loving in his account of object love in "On Narcissism" (1914), anaclisis and (secondary) narcissism. He describes a masculine, or anaclitic, mode of loving, in which the lover chooses a love object modeled on those figures who supported him during his own stage of primary narcissism—modeled on the woman who nursed him (in the case of heterosexuality) and the man who protected him (in the case of homosexuality).

26. See Freud (1905) for the range of possible sexual zones marked on the body.

27. See, for example, Louis Malston, *The Wild Child*, where the "savage of Aveyron," Victor, is analyzed in considerable detail. It is significant that although the boy was "lost" in the forest at around the age of two—well into the anal stage—he is incapable of understanding sexual processes. It is clear that the boy, "found" sometime after puberty, experiences various physiological and hormonal processes, including erections, but these have no value or meaning for him and are experienced by him as strange and unpleasurable.

28. Laplanche and Leclaire (1972) argue that the most elementary of signifiers to become psychically significant are those which are anchored in a primitive movement of the body. In the case of Philippe, analyzed by Leclaire, the shape of cupped hands—out of which one can drink water and which is the action of the infant's hand on the breast—is precisely such a primitive signifier, foundational in the establishment of his unconscious.

29. Laplanche writes:

> The very term *genesis* evokes the notion of an emergence, the possibility of a linear understanding of what is later by what precedes it. But this perspective should be corrected by a reversal; on the one hand, the proposed genesis implies in fact that what comes first—say, the vital order—contains what might be called a fundamental imperfection in the human being: a dehiscence. What is "perverted" by sexuality is indeed the function, but a function which is somehow feeble or premature. Therein lies the whole problem of the "vital order" in man and of the possibility, or rather, the impossibility of grasping it "beneath" what has come to "cover" it over. . . . On the one hand, to that extent, it is the latter which is perhaps more important, and alone allows us to understand and to interpret what we persist in calling the *prior*. (Laplanche 1976: 25)

30. See Lacan (1970).

31. See Jane Gallop (1982), Luce Irigaray (1985a and 1985b), and Grosz (1989 and 1990).

32. Medical studies of hermaphroditism, which indicate a strikingly high percentage of hermaphroditic bodily features in the general population—one in two thousand—have indicated that the visible or manifest primary and secondary sexual characteristics cannot be so easily binarized into male and female categories. The morphology of external genitalia does not provide a clear-cut delineation of the differences between the sexes, even if it does provide the primary criterion used for determining the sex of the neonate. Sex is a multilayered psychobiological function in which a number of levels coalesce. These include organic, genetic, somatic,

behavioral, and psychological factors. I have examined the various medical and popular notions of hermaphroditism elsewhere (Grosz 1991).

33. See Freud (1909) and M. Campioni and E. Gross (1979).

34. In the case of clitoridectomy; see Kirby (1987).

35. This is what I understand Irigaray's broad project to entail. See, in particular, Grosz (1989) and Whitford (1991).

3. Body Images: Neurophysiology and Corporeal Mappings

1. Paré postulated three major categories of monstrosity: anomalies of excess, anomalies of default, and anomalies of duplicity. For details, see Grosz (1991).

2. Kurt Goldstein makes clear his own intellectual debt to the study of war injuries:

> A great part of my own material has come from brain injuries incurred during the first World War. These injuries were very well suited for study because they occurred in young people in good general physical condition. Furthermore, we have the unusual opportunity of being able to observe our patients for a very long period of time, some for more than eight years, in a relatively favorable environment. (Goldstein 1963: 36–37)

3. See Weisenberg and McBride (1935) for a detailed historical survey of the clinical, neurological, and psychological researches on aphasia.

4. I am grateful to Elizabeth Wilson for pointing out this strikingly sexist assumption underlying localizationism.

5. Schilder devotes one-third of his *Image and Appearance of the Human Body* to neurological considerations, one-third to psychological factors, and one-third to sociological influences.

6. Schilder lays considerable emphasis on the psychical meaning of anatomical symmetry and the lateral divisibility of the body into mirror images. He cites a number of theorists who attempt to explain this ability to transfer sensations from the functional side of the body to a corresponding point on the symmetrically opposite side of the body in terms of the specificity of sensations located in particular parts of the body:

> According to them, all touches of one point must have a particular individuality, which the pain and temperature sensations of the same point have in common. (1978: 19)

But Schilder claims that this is not simply the result of the similarity of sensations in symmetrical bodily regions, for these sensations need to be registered, not simply in terms of their quality but also in terms of their location. Moreover, the middle line of the body, the line which divides the body into symmetrical halves, is also significant in other neurological disorders. Head, for example, devised as a test for aphasia where the patient had to point, using either the left or right hand, to the right or left eye. It is significant that patients who show difficulty or inability can nevertheless readily point to their right or left knee. Schilder claims that

> the middle line of the head is different from that of other parts of the body. Patients who are unable to cross the middle line region of the head, are quite well able to show their left knee with their right hand and *vice-versa*. The psychological middle line and the geometrical middle line are certainly not identical with one another. (1978: 48)

7. For example, Gerstmann's syndrome and finger aphasia, in which the patient is unable to name or recognize the different fingers of the hand or to indicate specific fingers. These patients suffer agnosia not only regarding their own hand; they also have difficulty in distinguishing the fingers of others. Related to finger agnosia is agraphia (difficulties in writing) and

acalculia (difficulties in calculations). Surprisingly, these patients do not show any disturbances in their relations to other body parts.

8. As Schilder states,

When such a patient tries to light a match, he may take the matchbox in his fingers and press them with his thumb and index finger in spite of the fact that he has full knowledge of the object. Even if helped by having the matchbox opened for him, he will not profit by this. He now touches the wrong side of the box. When he finally succeeds in taking a match, he cannot bring it to the broad side of the box, putting it flatly on the box. When given a lighted match, he cannot bring it near a candlestick. Given an unlighted match, he may try to light the candle in spite of the fact that he knows the match is not lit. (Schilder 1978: 46)

9. Any marking of or intervention into the body is psychically as well as physically inscribed. For example, part of the "pleasure" of the tattoo is not simply, as Schilder suggests, a visual transformation of the surface of the body. The tattoo or, similarly, the surgical scar libidinally invests the incised region in tactile and sensory terms, marking it as a special, significant bodily site, eroticizing the region.

10. Mellor notes that

although depersonalization had been described by earlier writers, it was Schilder who not only provided a comprehensive description, but set it in the context of the concept of self and of body-image. . . . depersonalization appears to lie close to fundamental issues such as the mind-body problem, the relationship between physiological and mental events, the question of self-perception. (Mellor 1988: 18)

11. "I have observed a singer who showed depersonalization concerning speech and concerning the mouth, an organ to which she paid special attention, in herself as well as in others" (Schilder 1978: 139).

12. Here I am not suggesting that there is a determinism at work in the privileging of certain bodily zones over others or that there may be some basis for prediction using psychoanalytic discourse. On the contrary, determinism and predictability are not presumed by psychoanalytic theory—and neither does neurophysiology claim this status (although no doubt some of its practitioners aspire to such theoretical qualities). Rather, it is only in a retrospective mode that one can describe what must have happened in the past in order to account for a present (or past) state of affairs.

13. Dora's hysterical coughing, which signals an identification with the genital catarrh with which her mother was infected by her father's syphilis, utilizes for its own purposes the organic connections between oral and genital tracts.

14. "There are . . . many organic diseases in which the psychogenic factor can apparently play a greater part. . . . We often wonder why organic diseases occur at times when the life situation of the individual has come to a crisis, and why they so often occur when the individual seems to need them out of his innermost strivings" (Schilder 1978: 188).

15. Schilder describes the interchange between the subject and the world in the ways in which the body image shrinks or expands, incorporates objects into itself, or expels impulses from within. He says of his own reactions to an automobile accident:

. . . the body is certainly not only where the borderline of the body and its clothes are. In an automobile accident I sustained a rather severe injury to my hand (that resulted in a deformity) which was for some time connected with painful sensations. In the early days after the accident, every approaching car seemed to involve a particular dangerous element which encroached into the sphere of the body, even when it was still a considerable distance away. In other words, around the body there was a zone closely interrelated with the body-image which was in some way an extension of the body. Later on this general zone diminished in size until finally there remained only a zone around the hand. These experiences induced in me the conviction that the body is surrounded by a sphere of particular sensitiveness. This is true even in the physiological sense, since the smell of the body goes further than the body itself. (Quoted in Gorman 1969: 52–53)

16. The child only gradually comes to acquire the adult's notion of spatiality. It has not yet learned to distinguish virtual or specular space from real space. It does not understand perspectives or the relations between figure and ground, which require oppositions that the child has not yet acquired. For the infant, space is not yet conceived as a regular grid into which objects are placed or from which they can be removed. In other words, space is never "empty," subsisting simply without objects. This requires an abstraction from its experiences and an ability to position *itself* as an object available for inspection by others. Instead, the child perceives within a pre-Oedipal space which is orally or kinesthetically rather than visually constituted. The child perceives a "space of adherence" (Merleau-Ponty), a space that clings to objects and images without being able to distinguish them.

17. Indeed, this may explain the superstitious and religious rituals surrounding various body parts in some cultures. That these body residues still contain metonymic connections to the subject is the condition of their ability to substitute for the subject in various incantations and magic rites. Roman Jakobson discusses what he calls homeopathic magic in terms of metonymy in Jakobson and Halle 1956.

18. Irigaray characterizes female sexuality as uncontainable within the terms of identity governing male sexuality; it is irreducible to a single organ, a single sexual zone, or a single orgasm and cannot be regarded simply as the addition of a number of singular processes. It is incapable of the kind of hierarchical regulation to which the Oedipus complex subjects the boy's sexual impulses. See Irigaray 1985a and 1985b.

19. See Woodward, 1988–89 and 1991.

4. Lived Bodies: Phenomenology and the Flesh

1. "Merleau-Ponty inherited the soul as Being and as Nothingness and set out alone to do what none before him—or since him—could think to do; first, he made the soul a thing, a body, and then, he incarnated all things into the Flesh. His successors have yet to appear. Those who follow him in time are still resisting incarnation; they are still trying to make the Flesh become word; they are still seeking to obtain release from the world by transforming it and themselves into a text" (M. C. Dillon, *Merleau-Ponty's Ontology* 1988: 100). While I believe that Dillon has misunderstood the force of the inscriptive model, the model of pure difference or the trace as the condition of corporeality, nonetheless I believe that he has singled out Merleau-Ponty's unique contribution to contemporary philosophy and feminist theory, his focus on corporeality. I do not, however, share his lament for the loss of immediacy implied by the intervention of representation.

2. Goldstein explains the various aphasic disorders in terms of the patient's inability to undertake abstract behavior. The patient is stuck in the concrete, unable to gain any distance from or perspective on it. Reflection, imagination, judgment—alternatives which involve the abstract attitude—are impossible. The patient may be able to use an implement, even describe what it can be used for, but is unable to name it. On being shown a pen, Goldstein's patient could say "this is for writing" (Goldstein 1963: 70). The aphasic seems to live in the immediacy of animal existence. That seems to be why, despite the often overwhelming and debilitating sets of disorders from which aphasics suffer, they rarely if ever commit suicide: "Suicide is a phe-

nomenon we observe only in man. No animal commits suicide. . . . Suicide is a voluntary act, and with that, a phenomenon belonging to abstract behavior and thus characteristic of human nature alone" (116–17).

3. Clearly perception is not the only such term hovering between mind and body and requiring both apparently mutually exclusive terms for its explanation. Another strategically significant term is, as I have argued in the previous chapter, the notion of the drive.

4. In many ways, Merleau-Ponty's writings in this last text anticipate many of the methodological and epistemological strategies Derrida uses in his deconstruction of philosophical oppositions and key terms. I am unaware of any secondary literature linking Derrida to Merleau-Ponty. Although there are undoubtedly many ways in which their theoretical allegiances and orientations are different, it is clear that they share a number of theoretical sources, including Spinoza, Heidegger, Freud, and Saussure.

5. The problem is not vision per se but the ways in which vision has been used in patriarchal frameworks to define the notion of lack—a notion that, incidentally, makes no sense in reference to the tactile. I have no objection to the perceptual and metaphoric primacy accorded to the visual, except that vision, like the phallus, has tended to function as a master or organizing term, a term or process which hierarchically subordinates the other senses (or bodily zones) under its direction and control. While it is not clear that this is the case in Merleau-Ponty's use, it does nevertheless indicate a possible problem, one that must be carefully evaluated in feminist terms.

6. From the time of the Greeks, visual metaphors, metaphors utilizing the notion of the image, where the object is construed as exhibitionistic and the knowing subject as voyeuristic, have dominated conceptions of knowledge. Thought is regarded as speculative, imagistic: the visible coincides with the intelligible. Knowledge is "depicted" as revelation, manifestation, or aletheia: the proposition is pictorial. This sustained series of metaphors confirms the singularity and self-identity of both subject and object. These metaphors provide a series of usually unexamined presumptions governing the ways in which knowledge is construed; they are deeply implicated in the history of epistemology.

7. Morris Bender performed a series of experiments to demonstrate that if two areas of the body are simultaneously touched, only one stimulus will be perceived. The part which is more sensitive to stimulation he described as dominant. Of all the body parts, he argued that the face was the most dominant, in the sense that when it and any other part of the body are touched, the stimulation to the face is most easily perceived; the hand is the least dominant, being the region least likely to provide a conscious registration of the stimulus. Bender devised a hierarchical chain of body parts from the most to the least dominant: face-genitals-shoulder-foot-buttocks-breast-back-thigh-abdomen-hand. (See Gorman 1969: 73–74.)

8. *Invagination* is a notoriously ambiguous and slippery term in the hands of philosophers, although it has relatively precise anatomical and physiological references. Its ambiguity arises when the philosopher plays with the undecidability between the literal and the metaphoric, between the anatomical vagina and its formation, and a kind of philosophical or ontological self-enfolding. The problem is not that there is not and cannot be a clear-cut separation between the literal and the metaphoric; the problem is what is at stake in covering the literal in the metaphoric. Anzieu signals at least some of the anatomical resonances thus:

"Invagination," the term used in anatomy and physiology . . . is a useful reminder that the vagina *is* not an organ of particular contexture but fold of the skin, just like the lips, the anus, the nose or the eyelids. It has no hardened layer or cornea to act as a protective shield; its mucous membrane is exposed, its sensitivity and erogeneity right on the surface . . . (Anzieu 1989: 10)

9. Merleau-Ponty's notion of the reversibility of vision is strikingly similar to Lacan's "double dihedral of vision" (see Lacan 1977b: 106–8). Lacan refers to *The Phenomenology of Perception* and to Gelb and Goldstein's study of Schneider in his discussion. Like Merleau-Ponty, he claims that what is missing for Schneider is the frame (he calls it "the screen") which gives meaning to what is seen. He agrees with Merleau-Ponty that to see entails the possibility of being seen:

> . . . in the scopic field, the gaze is outside. I am looked at, that is to say, I am a picture. This is the function that is found at the heart of the institution of the subject in the visible. What determines me, at the most profound level, in the visible, is the gaze that is outside. It is through the gaze that I enter light and it is from the gaze that I receive its effects. Hence it comes about that the gaze is the instrument through which light is embodied and through which . . . I am *photo-graphed*. (Lacan 1977b: 106)

However, Lacan disagrees with Merleau-Ponty insofar as he introduces a rift into the subject of the gaze which does not exist for the subject of vision. He distinguishes between the gaze at work in the picture and the functioning of vision in perception, a distinction that Merleau-Ponty ignores in accounting for the painter's vision in the same terms as everyday perception:

> Indeed, there is something whose absence can always be observed in a picture—which is not the case in perception. This is the central field, where the separating power of the eye is exercised to the maximum in vision. In every picture, this central field cannot but be absent, and replaced by a hole—a reflection, in short, of the pupil behind which is situated the gaze. Consequently, and in as much as the picture enters into a relation to desire, the place of a central screen is always marked, which is precisely that by which in front of the picture I am elided as subject of the geometral plane. (Lacan 1977b: 108)

10. As M. C. Dillon states,

> There is no reason to attribute seeing to mountains and trees or to introduce an ontological bifurcation within the flesh of the world. There is flesh which is sensitive to light, flesh which is not, and degrees of sensitivity linking the extremes. We need not convert the animals, vegetables, and minerals of the world to humanity to overcome ontological dualism. Trees and mountains do not see; they are blind witnesses to my own visibility. . . . The human body is that particular kind of flesh that allows the flesh of the world to double back on itself and be seen. The fact remains that there would not be human vision without human bodies. (Dillon 1988: 168–69)

11. As chance would have it, Irigaray finds striking confirmation of her claims regarding how women are rendered invisible in a typographical error which has Merleau-Ponty's translator, Alphonso Lingis, mistranslating *levres* as "laps" rather than "lips" (Merleau-Ponty 1968: 146).

12. From her other writings, most notably *This Sex Which Is Not One*, Irigaray makes clear some of these dangers, most notably that the mirror only reveals a picture of the subject—the other remains at best an imperfect double, always defined by the parameters of the subject's self-attributions. The mirror identifications also must remain blind to the plane that constitutes the mirror—a kind of "invisible," quite different from Merleau-Ponty's conception, which conditions the visible, in this case, the specular.

13. Butler seems to develop a most convincing case against the apparent sexual neutrality of Merleau-Ponty's claims. For example, she argues that "indeed it is difficult to understand how Merleau-Ponty . . . makes general claims about bodies, unless by "the body" he means the

male body, just as . . . the "normal subject" turned out to be male. . . . If the female body denotes an essence, while bodies in general denote existence, then it appears that bodies in general must be male" (1990: 94).

14. According to Lingis,

> To see someone sprawled on the bed as seductive is to feel, forming within oneself, the movements of taking him or her. The other is structured perceptibly as the surface destined for kisses and embraces, the exterior relief of one's inward lines of feeling. . . . In sexual experience, what exposes itself outside of oneself afflicts and captivates; and, conversely, the more active one becomes, the more one becomes surface and substance supinely demanding the hold and palpations of the other. (Lingis 1985: 51)

However insightful Lingis is regarding his critical reading of Merleau-Ponty, his description is almost transparently masculinist. It is not at all clear that women "see someone sprawled on the bed as seductive" (although this is a stereotypical description of male sexual response), and it is certainly not clear that women see it as seductive in the same way that men do.

15. I am grateful to Pheng Cheah for his insightful comments on the whole of this book, but particularly for his insistence on the irreducibility of otherness, whether sexual, racial, or cultural, and the necessary gap or interval always and ineliminably dividing (while producing) self and other.

5. Nietzsche and the Choreography of Knowledge

1. It is significant that the history of the concept of desire is itself a chart of the history and vicissitudes undergone by notions of corporeality. Although the correlation is not exact, there are, broadly speaking, two conceptions of desire—negative and positive—as there are (at least) two broad understandings of the body. The negative notion of desire, like the subordination of body to mind, can be traced to Plato. In *The Symposium*, for example, Socrates claims, in a speech to Agathon, that "one desires what one lacks" (199e). Hegel, along with Freud and Lacan, continue this long tradition insofar as each sees desire as a yearning for what is lost, absent, or impossible. Desire is posited in an economy of scarcity, where reality itself is missing something (the object whose attainment would yield completion), and linked to death (the struggle for mutual recognition) and annihilation (which the object of desire threatens). In opposition to this broad, Platonic tradition is a second, less pervasive and privileged notion of desire, which may be located in Spinoza, in which desire is seen as a positivity or mode of fullness which produces, transforms, and engages directly with reality. Instead of seeing desire as a lack, Spinoza sees it as a form of production, including self-production, a process of making or becoming (see the *Ethics*, III, ix). As part of this second tradition, Nietzsche, Foucault, and particularly Deleuze and Guattari are contemporary examples: "If desire produces, its product is real. If desire is productive, it can only be so in reality and of reality" (Deleuze and Guattari 1983: 26). Where desire is construed as negative, a lack or incompletion, it is a function and effect of the mind, psyche, or idea: its phenomenal form dictates its key characteristics. Where desire is understood as positive production, it is viewed "behaviorally," in terms of its manifest connections and allegiances, its artifice, its bodily impetus. The psychoanalytic and phenomenological accounts of the body thus presume and entail the notion of desire and the ontology of lack, while the Spinozist, productivist notion entails an externalized perspective of the kind I explore in this chapter.

2. See Scott Lash (1984: 3–5), who makes this claim even more strongly.

3. Consciousness is present only to the extent that consciousness is useful. It cannot be doubted that all sense perceptions are permeated with value judgements. (Nietzsche, 1968: 274)

4. See Lingis (1985b: 42–43).

5. Lingis states:

> The artist is the first figure of powerful life. What is powerful in the artist is the compulsion to dream and the compulsion to orgiastic state. The noble is the second figure of powerful life. What is powerful in the noble is the power to forget. The third figure of powerful life is the sovereign individual. What is powerful in the sovereign individual is the memory of his will, his power to keep his word. (Lingis 1985b: 58)

6. See "What Is a Minor Literature?" in Deleuze (1986).

6. The Body as Inscriptive Surface

1. See Homi Bhabha (1990) and Vicki Kirby (1987).

2. Leni Riefenstahl, *The People of Kau* (1976).

3. In her moving book *The Body in Pain: The Making and Unmaking of the World* (1985), Elaine Scarry presents a graphic account of the psychology and practice of the subjection of the body to the pain of torture and interrogation, a worthy companion piece to Nietzsche's writings on punishment and Foucault's analysis of the prison. Scarry analyzes the ways in which corporeal pain itself is manipulated and controlled during the sanctioned and underground forms of torture still perpetrated in much of the world today. This torture is clearly one of the more permanent modes of scarification and inscription of the body (although these terms may be too weak to convey the relative intensity of torture procedures when compared with the more benign forms of social inscription). For Scarry, three features characterize torture and serve to distinguish it from other forms of pain or interrogation:

> First, pain is inflicted on a person in ever-intensifying ways. Second, the pain, continually amplified within the person's body, is also amplified in the sense that it is objectified, made visible to those outside the person's body (thus rendering pain communicable in a way that is highly atypical). Third, the objectified pain is denied as pain and read as power, a translation made possible by the obsessive mediation of agency. (28)

4. See Grosz (1992), where I try to outline some of the ways in which urban geography inscribes the body.

5. Nietzsche writes:

> A naked human being is generally a shameful sight. I am speaking of US Europeans (and not even of female Europeans!). Suppose that, owing to some magician's malice, the most cheerful company at table suddenly saw itself disrobed and undressed; I believe that not only their cheerfulness would vanish and that the strongest appetite would be discouraged—it seems that we Europeans simply cannot dispense with that masquerade which one calls clothes. (1974: 295)

6. Nietzsche has this to say about gait:

> By certain manners of the spirit even great spirits betray that they come from the mob or semi-mob; it is above all the gait and stride of their thoughts that betrays them; they cannot walk. Thus Napoleon, too, was unable, to his profound chagrin, to walk like a prince, "legitimately," on occasions when that is really required, such as great coronation processions. Even then he was always only the leader of a column—proud and hasty at the same time, and very conscious of this. There is something laughable about the sight of authors who enjoy

the rustling folds of long and involved sentences: they are trying to cover up their feet. (1974: 227)

7. Where for men (at least for many men) body building can be seen as the fulfillment of a certain notion of masculinity or even virility—in this sense, body building can be seen as an attempt to render the whole of the male body into the phallus, creating the male body as hard, impenetrable, pure muscle—it is considerably more difficult to read female body building in this way. While it may be difficult to claim a single meaning or strategy to women's body building (or, for that matter, men's), it may be possible to represent it in two ways. On one hand, it may, depending on the woman's goals, be part of an attempt to conform to stereotyped images of femininity, a form of narcissistic investment in maintaining her attractiveness to others and herself. On the other hand, it can be seen as an attempt on the part of the woman to take on for herself many of the attributes usually granted only to men—strength, stamina, muscularity—in a mode of defiance of patriarchal attempts to render women physically weak and incapable. Paradoxically, using elements of psychoanalytic theory, it could be argued that underlying the display of virility and hypermasculinity evinced by many male body builders, the attempt to render the whole body into a phallus, and the narcissistic reinvestment in the whole of the male body, body building (in men) is a "feminine" activity and that, moreover, in spite of the attempt of body-building journals and magazines to represent the female body builder as simply a healthy but nevertheless feminine and heterosexual woman, for many women, possibly even a majority (for body building, unlike aerobics, jazzercise, or other exercise programs, tends to attract more lesbians than heterosexual women), body building can be seen as a mode of resistance to the requirements of femininity.

8. For more on the logic of supplementarity, see Derrida (1981a), esp. the first essay, and "That Dangerous Supplement . . . " in Derrida (1976).

9. The genealogical texts of Foucault can be dated from "The Discourse on Language," its earliest anticipation in Foucault's writings, and includes *Discipline and Punish*; *I, Pierre Riviere*; *The History of Sexuality*, vol. 1, *An Introduction*; and *Herculine Barbin*. The second and third volumes of *The History of Sexuality*, at least for my purposes here, can be understood as postgenealogical (for want of a better term).

10. Foucault discusses the threat imposed by the ponderous, awesome materiality of texts in "The Discourse on Language" (in 1972). One may presume that this threat of unpredictability is even greater in the case of the materiality of bodies than it is in the case of the materiality of texts.

11. " . . . perhaps the entire evolution of the spirit is a question of the body. . . . Our lust for knowledge of nature is a means through which the body desires to perfect itself" (Nietzsche 1968: 358).

12. Just as Foucault seems uniquely uninterested in the question of the meaning, reference, or internality of texts—one of the major innovations of "The Discourse on Language"—he is not interested in the question of the subject's psychological interior, and similarly, he is not interested in the composition, constitution, or internal functioning of the body.

13. See "What Is an Author?" in Foucault (1977b) and "The Discourse on Language."

14. The distinction between the true and the false is one of the three major modes for the internal regulation of discourses which Foucault suggests in "The Discourse on Language" (1972).

15. On the relations between Foucault's earlier "archaeological" writings and his later "genealogical" texts, see my chapter, "Contemporary Theories of Power and Subjectivity," in S. Gunew, 1990.

16. "The Life of Infamous Men" is in Morris and Patton 1979; see also Foucault (1975 and 1980).

17. Linda Alcoff has presented a convincing argument that renders Foucault's claims more complicated: for, while a politics of representation, a politics in which one speaks on behalf of others not so able to speak for themselves, has its major power investments, so too does the opposite claim, that one speaks only for oneself. It is not possible to speak only for oneself, and even if it were possible it would remain of extremely limited relevance. See Alcoff (1992), esp. 11.

7. Intensities and Flows

1. Of those feminists with whom I am familiar, there are certainly a number who have written on Deleuze and Guattari's work—but this is very far from the capturing of feminist imagination that has occurred with the writings of other French theorists, such as Lacan, Foucault, and Derrida. I have in mind here such diverse feminist writers as Rosi Braidotti, Judith Butler, Dianne Chisholm, Marie Curnick, Karin Emerton, Anna Gibbs, Alice Jardine, Meaghan Morris, and Dorothea Olkowski.

2. This is, more broadly, Kroker's claim (1991: 113–17).

3. A multiplicity is not a pluralized identity, an identity multiplied by n locations, but is a nontotalizable collectivity of partial components which never make up a whole. An assemblage or multiplicity is defined not by its abiding identity over time or by any principle of sameness but through its capacities to undergo permutations, transformations, and realignments: "Multiplicities are defined by the outside: by the abstract line, the line of flight or deterritorialization according to which they change in nature and connections with other multiplicities" (Deleuze and Guattari 1987: 9).

4. E.g., Grisoni (1982).

5. In the relatively rare secondary literature on their work in English, one "introduction" stands out by virtue of its aversion to jargonized, sloganized readings of Deleuze and Guattari's work: Brian Massumi's *Reader's Guide to Capitalism and Schizophrenia* (1992).

6. Deleuze and Guattari point out that

unlike the tree, the rhizome is not the object of reproduction: neither external reproduction as image-root nor internal reproduction as tree-structure. The rhizome is an antigenealogy. It is short-term memory or antimemory. The rhizome operates by variation, expansion, conquest, capture, offshoots . . . the rhizome is an acentered, nonhierarchical, nonsignifying system without a General and without an organizing memory or central automaton, defined solely by a circulation of states. (1987: 21)

7. Colin Gordon provides a plausible explanation of the notion of multiplicity which relates it closely to the concept of assemblage and machine; the notion of a multiplicity is based on developments in non-Euclidian geometry: "Multiplicities. . . . This concept, due originally to Reimann's non-Euclidean geometries description of certain kinds of 'assemblages' as 'flat'. . . . By 'flatness' Deleuze and Guattari mean a situation . . . where condition and conditioned inhabit the same space, with no extra dimension for an overview 'in depth'. The fact that there is no resemblance or analogy of condition and conditioned is what gives its point to their concept of 'assemblage' " (Gordon 1981: 35–36).

8. Spinoza and Spinozism clearly remain an abiding interest for Deleuze throughout his intellectual career; see Deleuze (1990a and 1988).

9. Deleuze's understanding of masochism seems to have developed considerably in the period between *Masochism: Coldness and Cruelty* and *A Thousand Plateaus*. In the latter, he discusses masochism not as a devious detour of pleasure through or around pain (the psychoanalytic view, which reduces masochism to the counterpart of sadism through the restructuring

provided by Oedipalization), but as the production of intricate machinic connections which distribute intensities across bodies and objects, experimenting with the plane of consistency of desire itself:

> Take the [psychoanalytic] interpretation of masochism: when the ridiculous death instinct is not invoked, it is claimed that the masochist, like everybody else, is after pleasure but can only get it through pain and phantasied humiliations whose function is to allay or ward off deep anxiety. This is inaccurate; the masochist suffering is the price he must pay, not to achieve pleasure but to untie some pseudobond between desire and pleasure as an extrinsic measure. Pleasure is in no way something that can be attained only by a detour though suffering; it is something that must be delayed as long as possible because it interrupts the continuous process of positive desire. . . . In short, the masochist uses suffering as a way of constituting a body without organs and bringing forth a plane of consistency of desire. That there are other ways, other procedures, and certainly better ones is beside the point. It is enough that some find this procedure suitable for them. (Deleuze and Guattari 1987: 155)

The masochist engages in the conversion of body parts, partial objects, libidinal investments, pleasures, and desires into machinic components, the transformation of organs into sites and rituals, the becoming or partial becoming of a BwO.

10. "The actor Robert De Niro walks 'like' a crab in a certain film sequence; but, he says, it is not a question of his imitating a crab; it is a question of making something that has to do with the crab enter into composition with the image, with the speed of the image" (Deleuze and Guattari 1987: 274).

11. See in particular Deleuze (1990), esp. the first series. I am grateful to Karin Emerton, and particularly her unpublished 1987 paper "Figures of the Feminine," for her discussion of the link between Deleuze's use of the image of Alice and Irigaray's use of Alice in *This Sex Which Is Not One* (1985b).

12. "Sexuality is the production of a thousand sexes, which are so many uncontrollable becomings" (278).

13. I am indebted here to Vicki Kirby's critical understanding of deconstruction, and particularly our discussions of the concept of "beyond" (logocentrism, patriarchy, dichotomies, metaphysics).

8. Sexed Bodies

1. Derrida's notion of inscription or the trace in a way preempts this question, insofar as, for him, the trace precedes both nature and culture:

> Thus, . . . the trace whereof I speak is not more natural than cultural, not more physical than psychical, biological than spiritual. It is that starting from which a becoming unmotivated of the sign, and with it all the ulterior oppositions between *physis* and its other, is possible. (Derrida, 1976: 47–48)

My question to Derrida, then, is whether the trace itself is marked by or the mark of sexual difference. What is the relation between the trace and sexual difference?

2. See Didi-Huberman (1987) and Kirby (1987 and 1989a).

3. Recent studies on monozygotic twins reared apart indicate that such twins are likely to have more in common with each other than siblings reared in the same environment. Data such as these have commonly been used by sociobiologists and others to indicate the dominance of genetic over environmental factors. But it is significant that even the researchers undertaking

these studies are unwilling to accept that genetics has an unmediated effect on the particularities of the subject. See Bouchard, Lykken, et al. (1990: 227).

4. Of course, even the model of etching has its problems: it assumes the independent preexistence of its raw materials, whereas what I want to suggest is that these very elements themselves are produced in the inscriptive process.

5. Hence Douglas's claim: "Dirt is essentially disorder. There is no such thing as absolute dirt: it exists in the eye of the beholder. If we shun dirt, it is not because of craven fear, still less dread or holy terror. Nor do our ideas about disease account for the range of our behaviour in cleaning or avoiding dirt. Dirt offends against order" (Douglas 1980: 2).

6. Douglas again makes clear the complex relation of reciprocal involvement and the necessary repulsion between the ordering system and that which it must expel in order to retain its systematicity. She clearly recognizes that as much as the system of order and organization must expel what Kristeva calls the abject, at the same time it must rely upon and harness this dangerous raw material for its contents, for its resources:

> Granted that disorder spoils pattern; it also provides the materials of pattern. Order implies restriction; from all possible materials, a limited selection has been made from all possible relations a limited set has been used. So disorder by implication is unlimited, no pattern has been realised in it, but its potential for patterning is indefinite. (Douglas 1980: 94)

7. Irigaray states:

> *The object of desire itself,* and for psychoanalysts, *would be the transformation of fluid to solid?* Which seals—this is well worth repeating—*the triumph of rationality.* Solid mechanics and rationality have maintained a relationship of very long standing, one against which fluids have never stopped arguing. (Irigaray 1985b: 113)

8. See the work of Cathy Waldby on AIDS discourses and practices and Judith Allen on contraceptive and abortion practices. I am particularly grateful to Cathy Waldby for a number of discussions we have had about the dissymmetry between the meanings of sexual fluids in the two sexes.

9. Cixous's analysis of masculinity, relegated to a footnote in "The Laugh of the Medusa" (1981), is particularly astute:

> Men still have everything to say about their sexuality, and everything to write. For what they have said so far, for the most part, stems from the opposition activity/passivity from the power relation between a fantasized obligatory virility meant to invade, to colonize, and the consequential phantasm of woman as a "dark continent" to penetrate and "pacify." (We know here what "pacify" means in terms of scotomizing the other and misrecognizing the self.) Conquering her, they've made haste to depart from her borders, to get out of sight, out of body. The way man has of getting out of himself, and into her whom he takes not for the other but for his own, deprives him, he knows, of his own bodily territory. One can understand how man, confusing himself with his penis and rushing in for the attack, might feel resentment and fear of being "taken" by the woman, of being lost in her, absorbed or alone. (247)

10. Medicine and biology have always served as significant indices of broad cultural attitudes, which is why a history of the discourses of sexual reproduction from the earliest records would be well worth undertaking, not as a model of the progress toward truth witnessed by the passage of time—as traditional models of the history of science presume—but as an

analysis of the historically specific projection of fantasies of the body, a projection which is as strong today as it ever was but which today, more than ever, refuses to see itself.

11. There is not in fact any technical reason for this invisibility. The invention of the endoscope, of the CT scan, and other imaging techniques means that no part of the body is inherently unseeable. The point is that rendering various body parts visible destroys the aura of their enigma; it reduces the sexual mystery of the body to the organic functioning of medicalized body parts. There is no future for medical imaging in the realm of pornography. This may be because *any* visualization of the tactile mysteries of female sexuality provides knowledge, perhaps, but reduces pleasure.

12. Aristotle was at least partly responsible for the localization of semen and for restricting its operations and representational powers to the (male) reproductive system. In opposition to many of the atomists, he argued that in spite of the resemblance between the whole of an offspring's body to the whole of the parents' bodies, semen is not drawn from all the body parts. See *On the Generation of Animals*.

13. I am indebted to Judith Allen for pointing this significant factor in men's attitudes to abortion out to me in conversation.

14. For Aristotle, semen provides form not only for the growing fetus and eventually the child but also to the very formlessness of menstrual fluid itself. As he describes it, semen is a kind of "setting gel" for congealing menstrual fluids into a form:

> The action of the semen in the male in "setting" the female's secretions in the uterus is similar to that of rennet upon milk. Rennet is milk which contains vital heat, as semen does, and this integrates the homogeneous substance and makes it "set." As the nature of milk and the menstrual fluid is one and the same, the action of the semen upon the substance of the menstrual fluid is the same as that of rennet upon milk. Thus when the "setting" is effected, that is, when the bulky portion "sets," the fluid portion comes off; and as the earthy portion solidifies membranes form all round its outer surface. . . . Once the fetation has "set," it behaves like seeds sown in the ground. (*On the Generation of Animals*, book II.IV)

15. See particularly Iris Marion Young's discussion of the phenomenology of the breasted body and the ways it may confound the basic terms of the very phenomenological program from which it was derived (1990, chap. 11).

16. Douglas never explicitly discusses the polluting function of sperm as a genus of "dangerous" body fluid. Her only reference to sperm occurs in the context not of the polluting qualities associated with bodily waste but of sacredness.

17. I am not suggesting that menstruation and lactation are without their historical and cultural inflections. Quite the contrary: particularly in the case of menstruation, the ways these are experienced, the frequency and duration of periods, their regularity, the effects they have on the woman's nutritional status and her social status vary quite broadly, not only from culture to culture but, within a particular culture, from individual to individual. The same can be said about lactation, although there may be a tendency to regard it as a question of choice or decision, at least in contemporary Western cultures and those Third World cultures which are now the dumping grounds for international conglomerates for powdered formula milk. Lactation and menstruation, as is well documented, are immensely sensitive to emotional upsets and psychical belief systems. So I am not advocating a naturalist or even a universalist attribute. Nonetheless, it is also true that all women, whatever the details of their physiology and fertility, are culturally understood in terms of these bodily flows.

Bibliography

Adams, Parveen. (1978). "Representation and Sexuality." *m/f* 1: 65–82.
———. (1986). "Versions of the Body." *m/f* 11/12: 27–34.
Adkins, A. W. H. (1970). *From the Many to the One*. London: Constable.
Alcoff, Linda. (1992). "The Problem of Speaking for Others." *Cultural Critique* 20: 5–32.
Allison, David B., ed. (1985). *The New Nietzsche: Contemporary Styles of Interpretation*. Cambridge: MIT Press.
Alonso, Ana Maria, and Maria Teresa Koreck. (1989). "Silences: 'Hispanics,' AIDS, and Sexual Practices." *differences* 1, no. 1: 101–24.
Altizier, Thomas J. J. (1985). "Eternal Recurrence and the Kingdom of God." In David B. Allison, ed., *The New Nietzsche: Contemporary Styles of Interpretation*. Cambridge: MIT Press.
Anzieu, Didier. (1989). *The Skin Ego*. London: Karnac.
———. (1990). *A Skin for Thought: Interviews with Gilbert Tarrab*. London: Karnac.
Apter, Emily. (1991). *Feminizing the Fetish: Psychoanalysis and Narrative Obsession in Turn-of-the-Century France*. Ithaca: Cornell University Press.
Ardener, Shirley, ed. (1981). *Women and Space: Ground Rules and Social Maps*. New York: Croom Helm.
Aristotle. (1953). *On the Generation of Animals*. Translated by Al Peck. London: Heinemann.
Armstrong, D. M. (1968). *A Materialist Theory of Mind*. London: Routledge and Kegan Paul.
Armstrong, Timothy J., ed. (1992). *Michel Foucault Philosopher: Essays Translated from the French and German*. New York: Routledge.
Barral, Mary Rose. (1965). *Merleau-Ponty: The Role of the Body-Subject in Interpersonal Relations*. Pittsburgh: Duquesne University Press.
Barrett, Michele. (1980). *Women's Oppression Today*. London: Verso.
Bartky, Sandra Lee. (1988). "Foucault, Femininity and the Modernization of Patriarchal Power." In Irene Diamond and Lee Quinby, eds., *Feminism and Foucault: Reflections on Resistance*. Boston: Northeastern University Press.
Bender, Lauretta. (1952). *Child Psychiatric Techniques*. Springfield, Ill.: Thomas.
Benhabib, Seyla, and Drucilla Cornell, eds. (1987). *Feminism as Critique: Essays on the Politics of Gender in Late-Capitalist Societies*. Cambridge: Polity Press.
Benjamin, Andrew, ed. (1989). *The Lyotard Reader*. Oxford: Blackwell.
Bernauer, James W. (1990). *Michel Foucault's Force of Flight: Toward an Ethics of Thought*. Newark, N.J.: Humanities Press.
———, and David Rasmussen, eds. (1988). *The Final Foucault*. Cambridge: MIT Press.
Bersani, Leo. (1986). *The Freudian Body: Psychoanalysis and Art*. New York: Columbia University Press.

———. (1987). "Is the Rectum a Grave?" *October* 43 (Winter): 198–222.

Bhabha, Homi K., ed. (1990). *Nation and Narration*. New York: Routledge.

Binswanger, Ludwig. (1962). "The Case of Ellen West." In Rollo May et al., eds., *Existence: A New Dimension in Psychiatry and Psychology*. New York: Basic Books.

Birault, Henri. (1985). "Beatitude in Nietzsche." In David B. Allison, ed., *The New Nietzsche: Contemporary Styles of Interpretation*, 219–31. Cambridge: MIT Press.

Blanchot, Maurice. (1985). "The Limits of Experience: Nihilism." In David B. Allison, ed., *The New Nietzsche: Contemporary Styles of Interpretation*, 121–28. Cambridge: MIT Press.

Blondel, Eric. (1985). "Nietzsche: Life as Metaphor." In David B. Allison, ed., *The New Nietzsche: Contemporary Styles of Interpretation*, 150–75. Cambridge: MIT Press.

———. (1991). *Nietzsche: The Body and Culture. Philosophy as a Philological Genealogy*. Translated by Seàn Hand. Stanford: Stanford University Press.

Bordo, Susan. (1988). "Anorexia Nervosa: Psychopathology as the Crystallization of Culture." In Irene Diamond and Lee Quinby, eds., *Feminism and Foucault: Reflections on Resistance*. Boston: Northeastern University Press.

———. (1989a). "The Body and Reproduction of Femininity: A Feminist Appropriation of Foucault." In Alison M. Jaggar and Susan R. Bordo, eds., *Gender/Body/Knowledge: Feminist Reconstructions of Being and Knowing*. New Brunswick: Rutgers University Press.

———. (1989b). "Reading the Slender Body." In Mary Jacobus et al., eds., *Women, Science, and the Body-Politic: Discourses and Representations*. New York: Methuen.

Bouchard, Thomas J., et al. (1990). "Sources of Human Psychological Differences: The Minnesota Study of Twins Reared Apart." *Science* 250: 223–28.

Bottomley, Frank. (1979). *Attitudes to the Body in Western Christendom*. London: Lepus Books.

Boyne, Roy. (1990). *Foucault and Derrida: The Other Side of Reason*. London: Unwin Hyman.

Braidotti, Rosi. (1986). "The Ethics of Sexual Difference: The Case of Foucault and Irigaray." *Australian Feminist Studies* 3.

———. (1986). "Ethics Revisited: Women in/and Philosophy." In Carole Pateman and Elizabeth Gross, eds., *Feminist Challenges: Social and Political Theory*, 44–60. Sydney: Allen and Unwin.

———. (1989). "Organs without Bodies." *differences* 1, no. 1: 147–61.

———. (1989). "The Politics of Ontological Difference." In Teresa Brennan, ed., *Between Feminism and Psychoanalysis*, 89–105. London: Routledge.

———. (1991). *Patterns of Dissonance*. Oxford: Polity Press.

Brain, Robert. (1979). *The Decorated Body*. London: Hutchinson.

Brennan, Teresa. (1992). *The Interpretation of the Flesh: Freud and Femininity*. London: Routledge.

———, ed. (1989). *Between Feminism and Psychoanalysis*. London: Routledge.

Brody, Saul Nathaniel. (1974). *The Disease of the Soul: Leprosy in Medieval Literature*. Ithaca: Cornell University Press.

Brown, Beverley, and Parveen Adams. (1979). "The Feminine Body and Feminist Politics." *m/f* 3: 33–50.

Bruch, Hilda. (1973). *Eating Disorders*. New York: Basic Books.

Bühler, Charlotte, H. Hexler, and B. Tudor-Hart. (1927). *Sociological and Psychological Studies on the First Year of Life*. Jena: Mansdorf.

Butler, Judith. (1987). *Subjects of Desire: Hegelian Reflections in Twentieth Century France*. New York: Columbia University Press.

———. (1989a). "Sexual Ideology and Phenomenological Description: A Feminist Critique of Merleau-Ponty's *Phenomenology of Perception*." In Jeffner Allen and Iris Marion Young, eds., *The Thinking Muse: Feminism and Modern French Philosophy*. Bloomington: Indiana University Press.

———. (1989b). "Gendering the Body: Beauvoir's Philosophical Contributions." In Ann Garry and Marilyn Pearsall, eds., *Women, Knowing and Reality: Explorations in Feminist Philosophy*, 253–62. Boston: Unwin Hyman.

———. (1990). *Gender Trouble: Feminism and the Subversion of Identity*. New York: Routledge.

Caddick, Alison. (1986). "Feminism and the Body." *Arena* 74: 60–88.

Caillois, Roger. (1984). "Mimicry and Legendary Psychasthenia." *October* 31 (Winter): 17–32.

Caine, Barbara, E. A. Grosz, and Marie de Lepervanche, eds. (1988). *Crossing Boundaries: Feminisms and the Critique of Knowledges*. Sydney: Allen and Unwin.

Campioni, Mia, and Elizabeth Gross. (1979). "Little Hans: The Production of Oedipus." In Paul Foss and Meaghan Morris, eds., *Language, Sexuality and Subversion*. Sydney: Feral.

Canguilhem, Georges. (1962). "Monstrosity and the Monstrous." *Diogenes* 40: 27–42.

———. (1980). "What Is Psychology?" *Ideology and Consciousness* 7: 37–50.

Canning, Peter M. (1984). "Fluidentity." *Sub-Stance* 44/45: 35–45.

Carcenac de Tourné, Brigitte. (1986). "On the Male Sex in Luce Irigaray's Theorising." *Art and Text* 20: 100–106.

Celermajer, Danielle. (1987). "Submission and Rebellion: Anorexia and a Feminism of the Body." *Australian Feminist Studies* 5: 57–70.

Chisholm, Dianne. (1992). "Feminist Deleuzians: James Joyce and the Politics of 'Becoming-Woman.' " *Canadian Review of Comparative Literature* (March–June): 201–24.

Churchland, Patricia. (1986). *Neurophilosophy: Toward a Unified Understanding of the Mind-Brain*. Cambridge: MIT Press.

Churchland, Paul. (1989). *A Neurocomputational Perspective*. Cambridge: MIT Press.

Cixous, Hélène. (1980). "The Laugh of the Medusa." In Elaine Marks and Isabelle de Courtivron, eds., *New French Feminisms*, 245–64. Amherst: University of Massachusetts Press.

———. (1981). "Castration or Decapitation?" *Signs* 7, no. 1: 41–55.

Code, Chris. (1987). *Language Aphasia and the Right Hemisphere*. Chichester: Wiley.

Cohen, Richard A. (1984). "Merleau-Ponty, the Flesh and Foucault." *Philosophy Today* (Winter): 329–38.

Cole, F. J. (1930). *Early Theories of Sexual Generation*. Oxford: Oxford University Press.

Collins, Margery, and Christine Pierce. (1976). "Holes and Slime: Sexism in Sartre's Psychoanalysis." In Carol C. Gould and Mary W. Wartofsky, eds., *Woman and Philosophy: Toward a Theory of Liberation*, 112–28. New York: Putnam.

Colombat, André Pierre. (1991). "A Thousand Trails to Work with Deleuze." *Sub-Stance* 66: 10–23.

Cumming, W. J. K. (1988). "The Neurobiology of the Body Schema." *British Journal of Psychiatry* 153, supplement 2: 7–11.

de Beauvoir, Simone. (1953). *The Second Sex*. Translated by H. M. Parshley. Harmondsworth: Penguin.

de Certeau, Michel. (1979). "Des outils pour écrire le corps." *Traverses* 14/15.

———. (1986). *Heterologies: Discourse of the Other*. Translated by Brian Massumi. Minneapolis: University of Minnesota Press.

———. (1988). *The Practice of Everyday Life*. Translated by Steven Rendall. Berkeley: University of California Press.

de la Mettrie, Julien Offray. (1988). *Man a Machine*. La Salle, Ill.: Open Court Classics.

de Lauretis, Teresa. (1989). "The Essence of the Triangle or, Taking the Risk of Essentialism Seriously: Feminist Theory in Italy, the U.S., and Britain." *differences* 1, no. 2: 3–37.

Deleuze, Gilles. (1973). *Proust and Signs*. Translated by Richard Howard. London: Allen Lane.

———. (1983). *Nietzsche and Philosophy*. Translated by Hugh Tomlinson. London: Athlone.

———. (1986a). *Foucault*. Translated by Seàn Hand. Minneapolis: University of Minnesota Press.

———. (1986b). *Kafka: Towards a Minor Literature*. Translated by Dana Polan. Minneapolis: University of Minnesota Press.

———. (1988). *Spinoza: Practical Philosophy*. Translated by Robert Hurley. San Francisco: City Lights Books.

———. (1989). *Masochism: Coldness and Cruelty*. Translated by Jean McNeil. New York: Zone Books.

———. (1990a). *Expressionism in Philosophy: Spinoza*. Translated by Martin Joughin. New York: Zone Books.

———. (1990b). *The Logic of Sense*. Translated by Mark Lester with Charles Stivale. New York: Columbia University Press.

———, and Felix Guattari. (1983). *Anti-Oedipus: Capitalism and Schizophrenia*. Translated by Robert Hurley, Mark Seem, and H. R. Lane. Minneapolis: University of Minnesota Press.

———, and Felix Guattari. (1987). *A Thousand Plateaus: Capitalism and Schizophrenia*. Translated by Brian Massumi. Minneapolis: University of Minnesota Press.

———, and Claire Parnet. (1987). *Dialogues*. Translated by Hugh Tomlinson and Barbara Habberjam. London: Athlone.

Derrida, Jacques. (1972). *Positions*. Translated by Alan Bass. London: Athlone.

———. (1973). *Speech and Phenomena and Other Essays on Husserl's Theory of Signs*. Translated by Alan Bass. Evanston: Northwestern University Press.

———. (1976). *Of Grammatology*. Translated by Gayatri Chakravorty Spivak. Baltimore: Johns Hopkins University Press.

———. (1978). *Writing and Difference*. Translated by Alan Bass. London: Routledge and Kegan Paul.

———. (1979). *Spurs: Nietzsche's Styles*. Translated by Barbara Harlow. Chicago: University of Chicago Press.

———. (1981a). *Dissemination*. Translated by Barbara Johnson. London: Athlone.

———. (1981b). "Economimesis." *Diacritics* 11: 3–25.

————. (1982). *Margins of Philosophy*. Translated by Alan Bass. Chicago: University of Chicago Press.

————. (1985). *The Ear of the Other: Otobiography, Transference, Translation*. Translated by Avital Ronell. New York: Schocken Books.

————. (1987a). *The Post-Card: From Socrates to Freud and Beyond*. Translated by Alan Bass. Chicago: University of Chicago Press.

————. (1987b). *The Truth in Painting*. Translated by Geoff Bennington and Ian McLeod. Chicago: University of Chicago Press.

————. (1988). "Signature, Event, Context." In *Limited Inc.*, 1–23. Evanston: Northwestern University Press.

————. (1989). "Right of Inspection." *Art and Text* 32.

Descartes, René. (1931–34). *The Philosophical Works of Descartes*. 2 vols. Translated by E. S. Haldane and G. T. R. Ross. Cambridge: Cambridge University Press.

Dewhurst, Christopher, and Ronald R. Gordon. (1969). *The Intersexual Disorders*. London: Baillere, Tindall and Cassell.

Diamond, Irene, and Lee Quinby, eds. (1988). *Feminism and Foucault: Reflections on Resistance*. Boston: Northeastern University Press.

Diamond, Nicky. (1985). "Thin Is a Feminist Issue." *Feminist Review* (19 March): 45–64.

Didi-Huberman, Georges. (1987). "The Figurative Incarnation of the Sentence (Notes on the Autographic Skin)." *Journal: A Contemporary Art Magazine* (Spring): 67–70.

Dillon, M. C. (1974). "Sartre on the Phenomenal Body and Merleau-Ponty's Critique." *Journal of the British Society for Phenomenology* 5, no. 2: 144–58.

————. (1988). *Merleau-Ponty's Ontology*. Bloomington: Indiana University Press.

Diprose, Rosalyn. (1989). "Nietzsche, Ethics and Sexual Difference." *Radical Philosophy* 52: 27–33.

————. (1990). "In Excess: The Body and the Habit of Sexual Difference." *Hypatia* 6, no. 3: 156–71.

Dodds, E. R. (1973). *The Greeks and the Irrational*. Berkeley: University of California Press.

Douglas, Mary. (1980). *Purity and Danger: An Analysis of the Concepts of Pollution and Taboo*. London: Routledge and Kegan Paul.

————. (1982). *Natural Symbols: Explorations in Cosmology*. New York: Pantheon.

Drummer, Frederick. (1973). *Very Special People*. New York: Amjon.

Duden, Barbara. (1991). *The Woman beneath the Skin: A Doctor's Patients in Eighteenth Century Germany*. Cambridge: Harvard University Press.

Edwards, Anne. (1989). "The Sex/Gender Distinction: Has It Outlived Its Usefulness?" *Australian Feminist Studies* 10: 1–12.

Eisenstein, Zilla. (1988). *The Female Body and the Law*. Berkeley: University of California Press.

Eribon, Didier. (1991). *Michel Foucault*. Translated by Betsy Wing. Cambridge: Harvard University Press.

Export, Valie. (1988–89). "The Real and Its Double: The Body." *Discourse* 11, no. 1: 3–27.

Falk, Pasi. (1985). "Corporeality and Its Fates in History." *Acta Sociologica* 28: 115–36.

Feher, Michel, with Ramona Nadoff and Nadia Tazi, eds. (1989). *Fragments for a History of the Human Body*. Vols. 1–3. New York: Zone Books.

Fiedler, Leslie. (1978). *Freaks: Myths and Images of the Secret Self*. New York: Simon and Schuster.

Fisher, Seymour. (1970). *Body Experience in Fantasy and Behavior*. New York: Appleton-Century-Crofts.

———. (1973). *Body Consciousness: You Are What You Feel*. Englewood Cliffs, N.J.: Prentice-Hall.

———. (1986). *Development and Structure of the Body Image*. Hillsdale, N.J.: Lawrence Erlbaum.

Flax, Jane. (1987). "Postmodernism and Gender Relations in Feminist Theory." *Signs* 12, no. 4: 621–43.

Flynn, Bernhard Charles. (1984). "Textuality and the Flesh: Derrida and Merleau-Ponty." *Journal for the British Society for Phenomenology* 15, no. 2: 164–77.

Forrester, John. (1991). *The Seductions of Psychoanalysis: Freud, Lacan and Derrida*. Cambridge: Cambridge University Press.

Foss, Paul. (1986). "Eyes, Fetishism and the Gaze." *Art and Text* 20: 24–36.

Foucault, Michel. (1972). "The Discourse on Language." *The Archaeology of Knowledge*. Translated by A. M. Sheridan. New York: Harper Colophon.

———. (1977a). *Discipline and Punish: The Birth of the Prison*. Translated by Alan Sheridan. London: Allen Lane.

———. (1977b). *Language, Counter-Memory, Practice: Selected Essays and Interviews*. Edited by Donald Bouchard. Oxford: Blackwell.

———. (1978). *The History of Sexuality*. Vol. 1, *An Introduction*. Translated by Robert Hurley. London: Allen Lane.

———. (1979). "The Life of Infamous Men." In Meaghan Morris and Paul Patton, eds., *Michel Foucault: Power, Truth, Strategy*. Sydney: Feral.

———. (1985). *The Use of Pleasure*. Vol. 2 of *The History of Sexuality*. Translated by Robert Hurley. New York: Pantheon.

———. (1986). *The Care of the Self*. Vol. 3 of *The History of Sexuality*. Translated by Robert Hurley. New York: Pantheon.

———, ed. (1975). *I, Pierre Riviere, Having Slaughtered My Mother, My Sister, and My Brother....* Translated by Frank Jellinek Harmondsworth: Penguin.

———, ed. (1980). *Herculine Barbin: Being the Recently Discovered Memoirs of a Nineteenth-Century Hermaphrodite*. Trans. R. McDougall. New York: Pantheon.

Freud, Sigmund. (1895). "Project for a Scientific Psychology." In James Strachey, ed., *The Standard Edition of the Complete Psychological Works of Sigmund Freud*. Vol. 1. London: Hogarth Press.

———. (1905a). "Fragments of an Analysis of a Case of Hysteria." In *Standard Edition*. Vol. 10.

———. (1905b). "Psychical (or Mental) Treatment." In *Standard Edition*. Vol. 7.

———. (1905c). "The Three Essays on the Theory of Sexuality." In *Standard Edition*. Vol. 7.

———. (1909). "Analysis of a Phobia in a Five Year Old Boy." In *Standard Edition*. Vol. 10.

———. (1914). "On Narcissism: An Introduction." In *Standard Edition*. Vol. 14.

———. (1915a). "The Unconscious." In *Standard Edition*. Vol. 14.

———. (1915b). "Instincts and Their Vicissitudes." In *Standard Edition*. Vol. 14.

———. (1915c). "Repression." In *Standard Edition*. Vol. 14.

———. (1920). "Beyond the Pleasure Principle." In *Standard Edition*. Vol. 18.

———. (1923). "The Ego and the Id." In *Standard Edition*. Vol. 19.

———. (1924). "The Dissolution of the Oedipus Complex." In *Standard Edition*. Vol. 19.

———. (1925a). "Negation." In *Standard Edition*. Vol. 19.

———. (1925b). "Some Psychical Consequences of the Anatomical Distinction between the Sexes." In *Standard Edition*. Vol. 19.

———. (1927). "Fetishism." In *Standard Edition*. Vol. 19.

———. (1929). "Civilization and Its Discontents." In *Standard Edition*. Vol. 21.

———. (1938). "The Splitting of the Ego in the Process of Defence." In *Standard Edition*. Vol. 23.

Freund, Peter E. S. (1982). *The Civilized Body: Social Domination, Control and Health*. Philadelphia: Temple University Press.

Frueh, Joanna. (1988). "Has the Body Lost Its Mind?" *High Performance* (Summer): 44–47.

Fuss, Diana. (1989a). *Essentially Speaking: Feminism, Nature and Difference*. New York: Routledge.

———. (1989b). "Reading Like a Feminist." *differences* 1, no. 2: 77–92.

Gallop, Jane. (1982). *Feminism and Psychoanalysis: The Daughter's Seduction*. London: MacMillan.

———. (1985). *Reading Lacan*. Ithaca: Cornell University Press.

———. (1988). *Thinking Through the Body*. New York: Columbia.

———. (1992). *Around 1981: Academic Feminist Literary Theory*. New York: Routledge.

Gasché, Rodolphe. (1985). "*Ecce Homo* or the Written Body." *Oxford Literary Review* 7: 1–2.

Gatens, Moira. (1986a). *Dualisms and Difference: Constructions of Subjectivity in Modern Philosophy*. Ph.D. diss., University of Sydney.

———. (1986b). "Feminism, Philosophy and Riddles without Answers." In Carole Pateman and Elizabeth Gross, eds., *Feminist Challenges: Social and Political Theory*, 13–29. Sydney: Allen and Unwin.

———. (1988). "Towards a Feminist Philosophy of the Body." In Barbara Caine, E. A. Grosz, and Marie de Lepervanche, eds., *Crossing Boundaries: Feminism and the Critique of Knowledges*, 59–70. Sydney: Allen and Unwin.

———. (1989). "Woman and Her Double(s): Sex, Gender and Ethics." *Australian Feminist Studies* 10.

———. (1990). "A Critique of the Sex/Gender Distinction." In Sneja Gunew, ed., *A Reader in Feminist Knowledge*. London: Routledge.

———. (1991a). "Corporeal Representation in/and the Body Politic." In Rosalyn Diprose and Robyn Ferrell, eds., *Cartographies: Poststructuralism and the Mapping of Bodies and Spaces*, 79–87. Sydney: Allen and Unwin.

———. (1991b). *Feminism and Philosophy: Perspectives on Difference and Equality*. Cambridge: Polity Press.

Gillan, Garth. (1973). *The Horizons of the Flesh: Critical Perspectives on the Thoughts of Merleau-Ponty*. Carbondale: Southern Illinois University Press.

Gillespie, Michael Allen, and Tracy B. Strong, eds. (1988). *Nietzsche's New Seas: Explorations in Philosophy, Aesthetics and Politics*. Chicago: University of Chicago Press.

Gilman, Sander. (1991). *The Jew's Body*. New York: Routledge.

Goldstein, Kurt. (1948). *Language and Language Disturbances: Aphasic Symptom Complexes and Their Significance for Medicine and the Theory of Language*. New York: Grune and Stratton.

———. (1963). *Human Nature in the Light of Psychotherapy*. New York: Schocken Books.

———. (1971). *Selected Papers*. The Hague: Martinus Nijoff.

Goldstein, Laurence, ed. (1991). *The Female Body: Figures, Styles, Speculations*. Ann Arbor: University of Michigan Press.

Gordon, Colin. (1981). "The Subtracting Machine." *IC*, no. 8 (Spring).

———, ed., (1980). *Power/Knowledge: Selected Interviews and Other Writings by Michel Foucault 1972–1977* . New York: Pantheon.

Gorman, Warren. (1969). *Body Image and the Image of the Brain*. St. Louis: Warren H. Green.

Gould, George M., and Walter L. Pyle. (1897). *Anomalies and Curiosities of Medicine*. Philadelphia: Saunders.

Granier, Jean. (1985). "Nietzsche's Conception of Chaos." In David B. Allison, ed., *The New Nietzsche: Contemporary Styles of Interpretation*, 135–41. Cambridge: MIT Press.

Griffith, Richard. (1970). "Anthropodology: Man A-Foot." In Stuart Spicker, ed., *Philosophy of the Body*, 273–92. Chicago: Quadrangle Books.

Grisoni, Dominique. (1982). "The Onomatopoeia of Desire." In Peter Botsman, ed., *Theoretical Strategies*, 162–89. Sydney: Local Consumption.

Gross, Elizabeth. (1986a). "Philosophy, Subjectivity and the Body." In Carole Pateman and Elizabeth Gross, eds., *Feminist Challenges: Social and Political Theory*, 125–44. Sydney: Allen and Unwin.

———. (1986b). "Derrida and the Limits of Philosophy." *Thesis Eleven* 14: 26–42.

Grosz, Elizabeth. (1987). "Notes towards a Corporeal Feminism." *Australian Feminist Studies* 5: 1–17.

———. (1988a). "Space, Time and Bodies." *On The Beach* (April): 13–22.

———. (1988b). "Desire and the Body in Recent French Feminisms." *Intervention* 21/22: 28–34.

———. (1989). *Sexual Subversions: Three French Feminists*. Sydney: Allen and Unwin.

———. (1990a). *Jacques Lacan: A Feminist Introduction*. London: Routledge.

———. (1990b). "Inscriptions and Body-Maps: Representation and the Corporeal." In Terry Threadgold and Anne Cranny-Francis, eds., *Feminine/Masculine/Representation*.

———. (1990c). "A Note on Essentialism and Difference." In Sneja Gunew, ed., *Feminist Knowledge: Critique and Construct*, 332–44. London: Routledge.

———. (1990d). "The Body of Signification." In John Fletcher and Andrew Benjamin, eds., *Abjection, Melancholia and Love: The Work of Julia Kristeva*, 80–104. London: Routledge.

———. (1991). "Freaks." *Social Semiotics* 1, no. 2: 22–38.

———. (1992). "Bodies/Cities." In Beatriz Colomina, ed., *Sexuality and Space*, 241–54. Princeton: Princeton Architectural Press.

Grosz, E. A., et al., eds. (1987a). *Futur*Fall: Excursions into Postmodernity*. Sydney: Power Institute.

Guillaume, Paul. (1971). *Imitation in Children*. Translated by Elaine P. Halperin. Chicago: University of Chicago Press.

Gunew, Sneja, ed. (1990). *Feminist Knowledge: Critique and Construct.* London: Routledge.

Haar, Michael. (1985). "Nietzsche and Metaphysical Language." In David B. Allison, ed., *The New Nietzsche: Contemporary Styles of Interpretation.* Cambridge: MIT Press.

Handelman, Susan A. (1982). *The Slayers of Moses: The Emergence of Rabbinic Interpretation in Modern Literary Theory.* Albany: State University of New York Press.

Haraway, Donna. (1988). "Situated Knowledges: The Science Question in Feminism and the Privilege of Partial Perspective." *Feminist Studies* 14, no. 3: 575–99.

———. (1989). "The Biopolitics of Postmodern Bodies: Determinations of Self in Immune System Discourse." *differences* 1, no. 1: 3–43.

Harding, Sandra. (1986). "From the Woman Question in Science to the Science Question in Feminism." *The Science Question in Feminism*, 15–29. Ithaca: Cornell University Press.

———. (1987). "The Instability of the Analytical Categories of Feminist Theory." In S. Harding and J. O'Barr, eds., *Sex and Scientific Inquiry*, 283–302. Chicago: University of Chicago Press.

Head, Henry. (1920a). "Aphasia and Kindred Disorders." *Brain* 43.

———. (1920b). *Studies in Neurology.* Oxford: Oxford University Press.

———, and G. Holmes. (1911). "Sensory Disturbances from Cerebral Lesions." *Brain* 34: 102–254.

Heath, Stephen. (1982). *The Sexual Fix.* London: Macmillan.

Hirst, B.C., and G. A. Piersol. (1893). *Human Monstrosities.* Philadelphia: Lea.

Hollier, Denis. (1984). "Mimesis and Castration 1937." *October* 31 (Winter): 3–16.

Hopwood, P., and G. P. MacGuire. (1988). "Body Image Problems in Cancer Patients." *British Journal of Psychiatry* 153, supplement 2: 47–51.

Hoy, David Couzens, ed. (1986). *Foucault: A Critical Reader.* Oxford: Blackwell.

Irigaray, Luce. (1977). "Women's Exile." *Ideology and Consciousness* 1: 62–76.

———. (1983). "An Interview with Luce Irigaray." *Hecate* 9, no. 1/2: 192–202.

———. (1984). *Ethique de la différence sexuelle.* Paris: Minuit.

———. (1985a). *Speculum of the Other Woman.* Translated by Gillian Gill. Ithaca: Cornell University Press.

———. (1985b). *This Sex Which Is Not One.* Translated by Catherine Porter with Carolyn Burke. Ithaca: Cornell University Press.

———. (1986). *Divine Women.* Translated by Stephen Muecke. Sydney: Local Consumption Press.

———. (1987). "Is the Subject of Science Sexed?" *Hypatia* 2 (Fall): 65–87.

———. (1989). "Equal to Whom?" *differences* 1, no. 2: 59–76.

———. (1991). *Marine Lover: Of Friedrich Nietzsche.* Translated by Gillian Gill. New York: Columbia University Press.

Jaggar, Alison M., and Susan R. Bordo, eds. (1989). *Gender/Body/Knowledge: Feminist Reconstructions of Being and Knowing.* New Brunswick: Rutgers University Press.

Jakobson, Roman, and Morris Halle. (1956). *The Fundamentals of Language.* The Hague: Mouton.

Jardine, Alice. (1984). "Woman in Limbo: Deleuze and His (Br)others." *Sub-Stance* 44/45: 46–60.

———. (1985). *Gynesis: Configurations of Woman and Modernity.* Ithaca: Cornell University Press.

——, and Paul Smith, eds. (1987). *Men in Feminism.* New York: Methuen.

Jay, Martin. (1986). "In the Empire of the Gaze: Foucault and the Denigration of Vision in Twentieth Century French Thought." In David Couzens Hoy, ed., *Foucault: A Critical Reader.* Oxford: Blackwell.

Jay, Nancy. (1981). "Gender and Dichotomy." *Feminist Studies* 1: 38–56.

Johnson, Mark. (1987). *The Body in the Mind: The Bodily Basis of Meaning, Imagination and Reason.* Chicago: University of Chicago Press.

Jonas, Hans. (1970a). "Spinoza and the Theory of Organism." In Stuart Spicker, ed., *Philosophy of the Body,* 50–69. Chicago: Quadrangle Books.

——. (1970b). "The Nobility of Sight." In Stuart Spicker, ed., *Philosophy of the Body.* Chicago: Quadrangle Books.

Jones, Ann Rosalind. (1986). "Writing the Body: Toward an Understanding of *L'Ecriture féminine.*" In Elaine Showalter, ed., *The New Feminist Criticism: Essays on Women, Literature and Theory,* 361–77. London: Virago.

Jones, Howard J. W., and William W. Scott. (1971). *Hermaphroditism, Genital Anomalies and Related Endocrine Disorders.* Baltimore: Williams and Wilkins.

Josso, Nathalie, ed. (1979). *The Intersex Child.* Basle: Kanger.

Kafka, Franz. (1969). "The Penal Settlement." In *Metamorphosis and Other Short Stories.* Harmondsworth: Penguin.

Kirby, Vicki. (1987). "On the Cutting Edge: Feminism and Clitoridectomy." *Australian Feminist Studies* 5: 35–56.

——. (1989a). "Corporeographies." *Inscriptions: Journal for the Critique of Colonial Discourse* 5: 103–19.

——. (1989b). "Habeas Corpus." *AfterImage* 17, no. 3: 8–9.

——. (1991). "*Corpus Delecti*: The Body at the Scene of Writing." In Rosalyn Diprose and Robyn Ferrell, eds., *Cartographies: Poststructuralism and the Mappings of Bodies and Spaces,* 88–102. Sydney: Allen and Unwin.

Klossowski, Pierre. (1985). "The Phantasms of Perversion: Sade and Fourier." *Art and Text* 18.

Kofman, Sarah. (1985). "Metaphor, Symbol, Metamorphosis." In David B. Allison, ed., *The New Nietzsche: Contemporary Styles of Interpretation.* Cambridge: MIT Press.

Köhler, Wolfgang. (1951). *The Mentality of Apes.* London: Routledge and Kegan Paul.

Kovacs, George. (1982–83). "The Personalistic Understanding of the Body and Sexuality in Merleau-Ponty." *Review of Existential Psychology and Psychiatry* 18, nos. 1, 2, and 3: 207–18.

Krell, David Farrell. (1986). *Postponements: Woman, Sensuality and Death in Nietzsche.* Bloomington: Indiana University Press.

——. (1990). *Of Memory, Reminiscence, and Writing: On the Verge.* Bloomington: Indiana University Press.

Kristeva, Julia. (1980). *Desire in Language.* Translated by Leon Roudiez. New York: Columbia University Press.

——. (1982). *Powers of Horror: An Essay on Abjection.* Translated by Leon Roudiez. New York: Columbia University Press.

——. (1984). "Histoires d'amour." *ICA Documents,* 1: *Desire,* 18–21.

——. (1986). "Women's Time." In Toril Moi, ed., *The Kristeva Reader,* 187–213. Oxford: Blackwell.

Kroker, Arthur. (1991). *The Possessed Individual.* New York: St. Martin's Press.

Kroker, Arthur and Marilouise, eds. (1988). *Body Invaders: Sexuality and the Postmodern Condition*. London: Macmillan.

Lacan, Jacques. (1953). "Some Reflections on the Ego." *International Journal of Psychoanalysis* 34.

———. (1970). "Of Structure as an Inmixing of Otherness Prerequisite to any Subject Whatever." In Richard Mackesay and Eugenio Donato, eds., *The Languages of Criticism and the Sciences of Man: The Structuralist Controversy*. New York: Doubleday Anchor.

———. (1977a). *Ecrits: A Selection*. Translated by Alan Sheridan. London: Tavistock.

———. (1977b). *The Four Fundamental Concepts of Psychoanalysis*. Translated by Alan Sheridan. London: Tavistock.

Laplanche, Jean. (1976). *Life and Death in Psychoanalysis*. Translated by Jeffrey Mehlman. Baltimore: Johns Hopkins University Press.

———. (1989). *New Foundations for Psychoanalysis*. Translated by David Macey. Oxford: Blackwell.

———, and Serge Leclaire. (1972). "The Unconscious: A Psychoanalytic Study." *Yale French Studies* 48.

———, and J-B. Pontalis. (1968). "Fantasy and the Origins of Sexuality." *International Journal of Psychoanalysis* 149.

———, and J-B. Pontalis. (1973). *The Language of Psychoanalysis*. Translated by David Nicholson-Smith. London: Hogarth Press.

Lash, Scott. (1984). "Genealogy of the Body: Foucault/Deleuze/Nietzsche." *Theory, Culture and Society* 2, no. 2: 1–8.

Le Doeuff, Michèle. (1987). "Women and Philosophy." In Toril Moi, ed., *French Feminist Thought: A Reader*, 181–209. Oxford: Blackwell.

———. (1989). *The Philosophical Imaginary*. Translated by Colin Gordon. London: Athlone.

———. (1991). *Hipparchia's Choice: An Essay Concerning Women, Philosophy Etc.* Translated by Trista Selous. Oxford: Blackwell.

Lee, Jonathon Scott. (1990). *Jacques Lacan*. Amherst: University of Massachusetts Press.

Lemert, Charles C., and Garth Gillan. (1982). *Michel Foucault: Social Theory and Transgression*. New York: Columbia University Press.

Levin, David Michael. (1985). *The Body's Recollection of Being: Phenomenological Psychology and the Deconstruction of Nihilism*. London: Routledge and Kegan Paul.

Lingis, Alphonso. (1968). Translator's Preface. In Maurice Merleau-Ponty, ed., *The Visible and the Invisible*. Evanston: Northwestern University Press.

———. (1984). *Excesses: Eros and Culture*. New York: State University of New York.

———. (1985a). *Libido: The French Existential Theories*. Bloomington: Indiana University Press.

———. (1985b). "The Will to Power." In David B. Allison, ed., *The New Nietzsche: Contemporary Styles of Interpretation*. Cambridge: MIT Press.

———. (1989). *Deathbound Subjectivity*. Albany: State University of New York Press.

Lloyd, Genevieve. (1984). *The Man of Reason: "Male" and "Female" in Western Philosophy*. London: Methuen.

———. (1989). "Woman as Other: Sex, Gender and Subjectivity." *Australian Feminist Studies* 10: 13–22.

Luria, A. R. (1968). *The Mind of a Mnemonist*. Translated by Lynn Solataroff. Chicago: University of Chicago Press.

———. (1970). *Traumatic Aphasia: Its Syndromes, Psychology and Treatment*. Translated by MacDonald Critcheley. The Hague: Mouton.

———. (1972). *The Man with a Shattered World*. New York: Schocken.

———. (1973). *The Working Brain: An Introduction to Neuropsychology*. Translated by Basil Haigh. Harmondsworth: Penguin.

Lyotard, Jean-François. (1984). *The Postmodern Condition: A Report on Knowledge*. Translated by Geoff Bennington and Brian Massumi. Minneapolis: University of Minnesota Press.

———. (1988–89). "Can Thought Go without a Body?" *Discourse* 11.1 (Fall/Winter): 74–87.

———. (March 22, 1990). *Seminar on the Penal Colony*. Humanities Institute at SUNY Stony Brook.

———. (1991). *Phenomenology*. Translated by Brian Beakley. Albany: State University of New York Press.

McCurdy, John Derrickson. (1978). *Visionary Appropriation*. New York: Philosophical Library.

McMillan, Elizabeth. (1987). "Female Difference in the Texts of Merleau-Ponty." *Philosophy Today* 31: 359–66.

Martin, Luthor H., Huck Gutman, and Patrick H. Hutton, eds. (1988). *Technologies of the Self: A Seminar with Michel Foucault*. Amherst: University of Massachusetts Press.

Massumi, Brian. (1992). *A Reader's Guide to Capitalism and Schizophrenia*. Minneapolis: University of Minnesota Press.

Matthews, Jill Julius. (1987). "Building the Body Beautiful: The Femininity of Modernity." *Australian Feminist Studies* 5: 17–34.

May, Rollo, E. Angel, and H. F. Ellenberger, eds. (1962). *Existence: A New Dimension in Psychiatry and Psychology*. New York: Basic Books.

May, Todd G. (1991). "The Politics of Life in the Thought of Gilles Deleuze." *Sub-Stance* 66: 24–35.

Mellor, Clive S. (1988). "Depersonalization and Self-Perception." *British Journal of Psychiatry* 152, supplement 2: 15–19.

Merleau-Ponty, Maurice. (1962). *The Phenomenology of Perception*. Translated by Colin Smith. London: Routledge and Kegan Paul.

———. (1963). *The Primacy of Perception*. Evanston: Northwestern University Press.

———. (1964). *Signs*. Evanston: Northwestern University Press.

———. (1968). *The Visible and the Invisible*. Translated by Alphonso Lingis. Evanston: Northwestern University Press.

———. (1970). *Themes from the Lectures at the Collège de France*. Translated by John O'Neill. Evanston: Northwestern University Press.

———. (1983). *The Structure of Behavior*. Translated by Alden L. Fisher. Pittsburgh: Duquesne University Press.

Millot, Catherine. (1990). *Horsexe: Essays on Transsexuality*. Translated by Kenneth Hylton. New York: Autonomedia.

Milner, Andrew. (1991). *Contemporary Cultural Theory: An Introduction*. Sydney: Allen and Unwin.

Mitchell, Juliet, and Jacqueline Rose, eds. (1982). *Feminine Sexuality: Jacques Lacan and the École Freudienne*. London: MacMillan.

Mitchell, S. Weir. (1965). *Injuries of Nerves*. New York: Humanities Press.

Mittwoch, Ursula. (1973). *Genetics of Sexual Differentiation*. London: Academic Press.

Moi, Toril. (1985). *Sexual/Textual Politics: Feminist Literary Theory*. London: Methuen.

———, ed. (1986). *The Kristeva Reader*. Oxford: Blackwell.

———, ed. (1987). *French Feminist Thought*. Oxford: Blackwell.

Money, John. (1968). *Sex Errors of the Body: Dilemmas, Education and Counselling*. Baltimore: Johns Hopkins University Press.

Money, John, and Patricia Tucker. (1975). *Sexual Signatures: On Being a Man or a Woman*. Boston: Little, Brown.

Morris, Meaghan. (1988). *The Pirate's Fiancée: Feminism, Reading, Postmodernism*. London: Verso.

———, and Patton, Paul, eds. (1979). *Michel Foucault: Power, Truth, Strategy*. Sydney: Feral.

Mortley, Raoul, ed. (1991). *French Philosophers in Conversation*. London: Routledge.

Nehamas, Alexander. (1985). *Nietzsche: Life as Literature*. Cambridge: Harvard University Press.

Nicholson, Linda J., ed. (1990). *Feminism/Postmodernism*. New York: Routledge.

Nietzsche, Friedrich. (1966). *Beyond Good and Evil: Prelude to a Philosophy of the Future*. Translated by Walter Kaufmann. New York: Vintage Books.

———. (1967). *The Birth of Tragedy/The Case of Wagner*. Translated by Walter Kaufmann. New York: Vintage Books.

———. (1968). *The Will to Power*. Translated by Walter Kaufmann. New York: Vintage Books.

———. (1969). *On the Genealogy of Morals/Ecce Homo*. Translated by Walter Kaufmann. New York: Vintage Books.

———. (1972). *Twilight of the Idols/The Anti-Christ*. Translated by R. J. Hollingdale. Harmondsworth: Penguin.

———. (1974). *The Gay Science*. Translated by Walter Kaufmann. New York: Vintage Books.

———. (1979). *Philosophy and Truth: Selections from Nietzsche's Notebooks of the Early 1870s*. Translated by Daniel Breazeale. Atlantic Highlands, N.J.: Humanities International Press.

———. (1982a). *Daybreak: Thoughts on the Prejudices of Morality*. Translated by R. J. Hollingdale. Cambridge: Cambridge University Press.

———. (1982b). "On Truth and Lie in an Extra-Moral Sense." *The Portable Nietzsche*. Edited by W. Kaufman. New York: Viking.

———. (1983). *Untimely Meditations*. Translated by R. J. Hollingdale. Cambridge: Cambridge University Press.

———. (1985). *Thus Spoke Zarathustra: A Book for All and None*. Translated by Walter Kaufmann. Harmondsworth: Penguin.

———. (1986). *Human, All Too Human: A Book for Free Spirits*. Translated by R. J. Hollingdale. Cambridge: Cambridge University Press.

Nishimura, Hideo, and James R. Miller. (1969). *Methods for Teratological Studies in Experimental Animals and Man*. London: Pitman.

Norris, Christopher. (1991). *Spinoza and the Origins of Modern Critical Theory*. Oxford: Blackwell.

Olkowski, Dorothea. (1982–83). "Merleau-Ponty's Freudianism: From the Body of Consciousness to the Body of the Flesh." *Review of Existential Psychology and Psychiatry* 18, nos. 1, 2, and 3: 97–118.

O'Neill, John. (1985). *Five Bodies: The Human Shape of Modern Society.* Ithaca: Cornell University Press.

———. (1989). *The Communicative Body: Studies in Communicative Philosophy, Politics and Sociology.* Evanston: Northwestern University Press.

Onians, R. B. (1951). *Origins of European Thought about the Body, the Mind, etc.* Cambridge: Cambridge University Press.

Ormiston, Gayle L. (1984). "Traces of Derrida: Nietzsche's Image of Women." *Philosophy Today* (Summer): 178–87.

Paglia, Camille. (1990). *Sexual Personae: Art and Decadence from Nefertiti to Emily Dickinson.* New Haven: Yale University Press.

Pateman, Carole. (1988). *The Sexual Contract.* Oxford: Polity Press.

———, and Elizabeth Gross, eds. (1986). *Feminist Challenges: Social and Political Theory.* Sydney: Allen and Unwin.

Patton, Paul. (1984). "Conceptual Politics and the War-Machine in *Mille Plateaus.*" *SubStance* 44/45: 61–80.

———. (1991). "Nietzsche and the Body of the Philosopher." In Rosalyn Diprose and Robyn Ferrell, eds., *Cartographies: Poststructuralism and the Mappings of Bodies and Spaces,* 43–54. Sydney: Allen and Unwin.

Plato. (1951). *The Symposium.* Harmondsworth: Penguin.

Plügge, Herbert. (1970). "Man and His Body." In Stuart Spicker, ed., *Philosophy of the Body,* 293–311. Chicago: Quadrangle Books.

Plumwood, Val. (1989). "Do We Need a Sex/Gender Distinction?" *Radical Philosophy* 51 (Spring): 1–11.

Probyn, Elspeth. (1987). "Bodies and Anti-Bodies: Feminism and the Postmodern." *Cultural Studies* 1, no. 3: 349–61.

Readings, Bill. (1991). *Introducing Lyotard: Art and Politics.* London: Routledge.

Reichenbach, Hans. (1958). *The Philosophy of Space and Time.* Translated by Maria Reichenbach and John Freund. New York: Dover.

Reilly, T. M. (1988). "Delusional Infestation." *British Journal of Psychiatry* 153, supplement 2: 44–47.

Reiser, Morton F. (1984). *Mind, Brain, Body: Towards a Convergence of Psychoanalysis and Neurobiology.* New York: Basic Books.

Rickels, Laurence A., ed. (1990). *Looking after Nietzsche.* Albany: State University of New York Press.

Riefenstahl, Leni. (1976). *The People of Kau.* Translated by J. Maxwell Brownjohn. London: Collins.

Ronell, Avital. (1989). "The Worst Neighborhoods of the Real: Philosophy—Telephone—Contamination." *differences* 1 no. 1: 125–45.

———. (1990). *The Telephone Book: Technology, Schizophrenia and Electric Speech.* Lincoln: University of Nebraska Press.

———. (1992). *Crack Wars: Literature, Addiction, Mania.* Lincoln: University of Nebraska Press.

Rose, Jacqueline. (1986). *Sexuality in the Field of Vision.* London: Verso.

Rose, Steven. (1976). *The Conscious Brain.* Harmondsworth: Penguin.

Rothfield, Philipa. (1986). "Subjectivity and the Language of the Body." *Arena* 75: 157–65.

———. (1988). "Habeus Corpus: Discourse and the Body." *Writings on Dance* 3: 6–12.

Roustang, François. (1982). *Dire Mastery: Discipleship from Freud to Lacan*. Baltimore: Johns Hopkins University Press.

Rubin, Alan. (1967). *Handbook of Congenital Malformations*. Philadelphia: Saunders.

Sacks, Oliver. *A Leg to Stand On*. London: Picador.

———. (1983). *Awakenings*. New York: Dutton.

———. (1985). *The Man Who Mistook His Wife for a Hat*. London: Picador.

———. (1989). *Seeing Voices*. Berkeley: University of California Press.

Safouan, Moustafa. (1983). *Pleasure and Being: Hedonism from a Psychoanalytic Point of View*. London: Macmillan.

Sartre, Jean-Paul. (1956). *Being and Nothingness*. Translated by Hazel E. Barnes. New York: Philosophical Library.

Scarry, Elaine. (1985). *The Body in Pain: The Making and Unmaking of the World*. Oxford: Oxford University Press.

Schilder, Paul. (1931). *Brain and Personality*. New York: International Universities Press.

———. (1953). *Medical Psychology*. Translated by D. Rapaport. New York: International Universities Press.

———. (1978). *The Image and Appearance of the Human Body: Studies in the Constructive Energies of the Psyche*. New York: International Universities Press.

Schmidt, James. (1985). *Maurice Merleau-Ponty: Between Phenomenology and Structuralism*. London: MacMillan.

Schor, Naomi. (1989). "This Essentialism Which Is Not One: Coming to Grips with Irigaray." *differences* 1, no. 2: 38–58.

Shapiro, Gary. (1991). *Alcyone: Nietzsche on Gifts, Noise and Women*. Albany: State University of New York Press.

Shapiro, Kenneth Joel. (1985). *Bodily Reflective Modes: A Phenomenological Method for Psychology*. Durham: Duke University Press.

Shiach, Morag. (1991). *Hélène Cixous: A Politics of Writing*. London: Routledge.

Simel, Marianne L., ed. (1968). *The Reach of Mind: Essays in Memory of Kurt Goldstein*. New York: Springer.

Singer, Linda. (1989). "Bodies—Pleasures—Powers." *differences* 1, no. 1: 45–65.

Slade, P. D. (1988). "Body Image in Anorexia Nervosa." *British Journal of Psychiatry* 153, supplement 2: 20–23.

Smart, Barry. (1985). *Michel Foucault*. London: Tavistock.

Smith, David. (1976). *Recognizable Patterns of Human Malformation*. Philadelphia: Saunders.

Solomon, Robert, ed. (1973). *Nietzsche: A Collection of Critical Essays*. New York: Anchor Books.

Solomon, Robert C., and Higgins, Kathleen M., eds. (1988). *Reading Nietzsche*. Oxford: Oxford University Press.

Spelman, Elizabeth V. (1982). "Woman as Body: Ancient and Contemporary Views." *Feminist Studies* 8, no. 1: 109–31.

———. (1988). *Inessential Woman: Problems of Exclusion in Feminist Thought*. Boston: Beacon Press.

Spicker, Stuart, ed. (1970). *Philosophy of the Body: Rejections of Cartesian Dualism*. Chicago: Quadrangle Books.

Spinoza, Baruch. (1986). *The Ethics and On the Correction of the Understanding.* Translated by Andrew Boyle. London: Dent.

Spitz, René A. (1965). *The First Year of Life: A Psychoanalytic Study of Normal and Deviant Development of Object Relations.* New York: International Universities Press.

Spivak, Gayatri Chakravorty. (1984). "Love Me, Love My Ombre, Elle." *Diacritics* (Winter): 19–36.

———. (1989). "In a Word: Interview." *differences* 1, no. 2: 124–56.

———. (1988). *In Other Worlds.* New York: Routledge.

Stern, Richard. (1986). *The Position of the Body.* Evanston: Northwestern University Press.

Stoller, Robert. (1968). *Sex and Gender: On the Development of Masculinity and Femininity.* New York: Jason Aronson.

Straus, Erwin W. (1962). "Aesthesiology and Hallucinations." In Rollo May, E. Angel, and H. F. Ellenberger, eds., *Existence: A New Dimension in Psychiatry and Psychology,* 139–69. New York: Basic Books.

Straus, Erwin W., Maurice Natanson, and Henri Ey. (1969). *Psychiatry and Philosophy.* New York: Springer.

Studlar, Gaylyn. (1988). *In the Realm of Pleasure: von Sternberg, Dietrich and the Masochistic Aesthetic.* Urbana: University of Illinois Press.

Thompson, Denise. (1989). "The "Sex/Gender" Distinction: A Reconsideration." *Australian Feminist Studies* 10: 23–32.

Thompson, William Irwin. (n. d.). *The Time Falling Bodies Take to Light: Mythology, Sexuality and the Origins of Culture.* New York: St. Martin's Press.

Tiemersma, Douwe. (1989). *Body Schema and Body Image: An Interdisciplinary and Philosophical Study.* Amsterdam: Swets and Zeitlinger.

Trimble, M. R. (1988). "Body Image and the Temporal Lobes." *British Journal of Psychiatry* 153, supplement 2: 112–15.

Turner, Bryan S. (1984). *The Body and Society: Explorations in Social Theory.* Oxford: Blackwell.

van Fraasen, Bastiaan. (1970). *An Introduction to the Philosophy of Space and Time.* New York: Columbia University Press.

Vasseleu, Cathryn. (1991). "Life Itself." In Rosalyn Diprose and Robyn Ferrell, eds., *Cartographies: Poststructuralism and the Mappings of Bodies and Spaces,* 55–64. Sydney: Allen and Unwin.

Voyat, Gilbert. (1984). *The Work of Henri Wallon.* New York: Jason Aronson.

Waldby, Cathy, Suzanne Kippax, and June Crawford. (1990). "Theory in the Bedroom: A Report from the Macquarie University AIDS and Heterosexuality Project." *Australian Journal of Social Issues* 25, no. 3: 177–85.

Wallace, Irving, and Amy Wallace. (1978). *The Two.* London: Cassell.

Wallon, Henri. (1934). *Les Origines du caractère chez l'enfant.* Paris: Presses Universitaires de France.

———. (1945). *Les Origines de la pensée chez l'enfant.* 2 vols. Paris: Presses Universitaires de France.

Warner, Marina. (1985). *Monuments and Maidens: The Allegory of the Female Form.* London: Weidenfeld and Nicolson.

Watney, Simon. (1989). "Missionary Positions: AIDS, "Africa," and Race." *differences* 1, no. 1: 83–100.

Weisenberg, Theodore, and Katharine McBride. (1935). *Aphasia*. New York: Commonwealth.

Weiss, Allan S. (1985). "The Logic of the Simulacrum of the Anti-Roberte." *Art and Text* 18: 115–25.

———. (1989a). *The Aesthetics of Excess*. New York: State University of New York Press.

———. (1989b). *Iconology and Perversion*. Melbourne: Art and Text.

Whitford, Margaret. (1982). *Merleau-Ponty's Critique of Sartre's Philosophy*. Lexington, Ky.: French Forum.

———. (1991). *Luce Irigaray: Philosophy in the Feminine*. London: Routledge.

Whitford, Margaret, ed. (1991). *The Irigaray Reader*. Oxford: Blackwell.

Wilden, Anthony. (1972). *System and Structure: Essays in Communication and Exchange*. London: Tavistock.

———. (1981). *Speech and Language in Psychoanalysis*. Baltimore: Johns Hopkins University Press.

Williams, Linda. (1990). *Hard Core: Power, Pleasure and the "Frenzy of the Visible."* London: Pandora Press.

Wilson, James G. (1973). *Environment and Birth Defects*. New York: Academic Press.

Woodward, Kathleen. (1988–89). "Youthfulness as a Masquerade." *Discourse* 11, no. 1: 119–42.

———. (1991). *Aging and Its Discontents: Freud and Other Fictions*. Bloomington: Indiana University Press.

———, and Murray M. Schwartz, eds. (1986). *Memory and Desire: Aging-Literature-Psychoanalysis*. Bloomington: Indiana University Press.

Young, Iris Marion. (1990). *Throwing Like a Girl and Other Essays in Feminist Philosophy and Social Theory*. Bloomington: Indiana University Press.

Zaner, Richard M. (1985). *The Problem of Embodiment: Some Contributions to a Phenomenology of the Body*. The Hague: Nijhoff.

Index

ELIZABETH GROSZ is Director of the Institute for Critical and Cultural Studies, Monash University. She is the author of *Sexual Subversions: Three French Feminists* and *Jacques Lacan: A Feminist Introduction*.